Their Own Frontier

Women in the West

Series Editors

SARAH J. DEUTSCH
Duke University

MARGARET D. JACOBS
New Mexico State University

CHARLENE L. PORSILD
University of New Mexico

VICKI L. RUIZ
University of California, Irvine

ELLIOTT WEST
University of Arkansas

THEIR OWN FRONTIER

Women Intellectuals Re-Visioning the American West

Edited and with an introduction by

Shirley A. Leckie and Nancy J. Parezo

UNIVERSITY OF NEBRASKA PRESS
LINCOLN AND LONDON

Portions of chapter 2, "Angie Debo: From the Old to the
New Western History," by Shirley A. Leckie, previously
appeared in *Angie Debo, Pioneering Historian* (University
of Oklahoma Press, 2002); used by permission. Chapter
6, "Alice Marriott: Recording the Lives of American
Indian Women," by Patricia Loughlin, previously
appeared in *Hidden Treasures of the American West*
(University of New Mexico Press, 2005);
used by permission.

Library of Congress Cataloging-in-Publication Data
Their own frontier : women intellectuals re-visioning
the American West / edited and with an introduction by
Shirley A. Leckie and Nancy J. Parezo.
p. cm. — (Women in the West)
Includes bibliographical references.
ISBN 978-0-8032-2958-7 (pbk. : alk. paper)
1. Women anthropologists—West (U.S.)—Biography. 2.
Women folklorists—West (U.S.)—Biography. 3. Women
authors—West (U.S.)—Biography. 4. Women scholars—
West (U.S.)—Biography. 5. Indians in literature. 6.
Indians of North America—West (U.S.)—Research.
7. Indians of North America—West (U.S.)—Study and
teaching. I. Leckie, Shirley A., 1937– II. Parezo, Nancy J.
GN20.T44 2008   301.092′273—dc22
2008001839

Set in Scala by Bob Reitz.
Designed by Ashley Muehlbauer.

To Bill — SAL

*For my mother, Georgia,
whose strength and wisdom
guided me on my life's
journey* — NJP

Contents

Illustrations

Acknowledgments

A multifaceted undertaking such as this volume is indebted to more individuals than we can possibly ever thank. First and foremost, our profound appreciation must go to the women whom we celebrate in this volume for their dedication and scholarship, their activism and insight. It is because of them that we are here today, assessing their contribution to our understanding of the American West and their quests to ensure that Native peoples were not forgotten by the academy or America in general. These committed, intelligent, and determined women have been overlooked or taken for granted, a situation which, we feel, should not continue. Each deserves to be recognized and honored by critical assessments of their scholarship contextualized by their lives and their times. But this volume is also intended to fill larger disciplinary needs. With each essay we have sought to show how two disciplines, history and anthropology, went their own way in 1900 but increasingly with time worked together, learning from the perspectives of the other, experiencing the same growing pains and prejudices as they professionalized. This volume should be seen as an example of the interdisciplinary collaboration that we believe should be the foundation of future scholarship.

Our thanks to Gary Dunham, Director of the University of Nebraska Press, for introducing us and encouraging us to coedit a volume on women intellectuals in the twentieth century and their contribution to the re-visioning of the American West and its Native peoples. For an undertaking of this magnitude we needed imaginative and insightful colleagues to help us. We extend our heartfelt thanks to the nine scholars who answered our call and submitted the essays that have made this volume a reality. Each has added immensely to our own understandings of the women portrayed in this volume, the contexts out of which their work grew, the issues with which they struggled, and the contributions they made to history, anthropology, and the story of indigenous peoples in the American West. We would also like to extend our thanks to the many individuals who helped each contributor complete his or her chapter.

We would also like to thank the editorial, production, and publicity staff of the University of Nebraska Press—Ann Baker, Bridget Barry, Wendi Foster, and Heather Lundine—and our copyeditor, Jonathan Lawrence.

As all who write scholarly books and articles know, no scholar completes any work without substantial help and feedback from numerous others or without assistance when such is needed. As always, my colleagues in the Department of History at the University of Central Florida listened to my ideas, encouraged me to keep on researching and writing, and proved good friends over the past years. I want to especially thank Richard and Patricia Crepeau, José and Mimi Fernández, Rose Beiler, Carole Gonzalez, Nancy Rauscher, Edith MacDonald, Patricia Farless, and Jonathan Scott Perry. I wish also to thank fellow historian Charles Robinson. As always, I am immeasurably grateful to the interlibrary loan staff at the University of Central Florida, who always managed to locate the books and articles, often long out of print or only available in small and obscure publications, for my research. Special thanks should also go to an individual who passed away. As director of Special Collections at Oklahoma State University, Heather Lloyd provided unfailing and invaluable help in researching my biography of Angie Debo, a work that spawned my interest in the larger question of women historians and the American West and its Native peoples. Finally, in 2006 and 2007 I had the opportunity to teach at Benedictine College in Atchison, Kansas, and appreciated the support of history colleagues Everett Dague and Susan Snyder there.

It has been an honor to work with Professor Nancy Parezo, whose work I have long admired. As we have coedited this volume, she has added greatly to my understanding of the development and the history of the discipline of anthropology, and she has deepened my understanding of the issues that have confronted Native peoples in the United States. Most of all, she has added more than anyone else to my understanding of the issues and stereotypes women professionals confronted in academic life. I also wish to thank the scholars who contributed to this volume and have taught me so very much more than they will ever know.

As always, my children and grandchildren have been a source of support and pleasure and, above all, laughter and good times. Finally, I am grateful to my husband, Bill Leckie, who is with me now in spirit and who, as a fierce supporter of women intellectuals, wanted me and my coeditor to complete this volume and make certain that the story of these ten women intellectuals and their contribution to new developments in both western history and American Indian history could be recognized at long last.

Shirley A. Leckie

I have long been interested in the professionalization of anthropology, including honoring the men and women whose lives of scholarship have made my own studies possible. In particular, this work is part of my long-term quest to provide a comprehensive survey and critical assessment of the men and women who have contributed to our understanding of the American Southwest and to comprehending the nature of disciplinary professionalization and how its processes have affected the theories and methodologies of the discipline. In this sense, my contributions to this volume are an extension of my previous work with a wealth of other fine scholars that resulted in the books *Daughters of the Desert* and *Hidden Scholars*. In fact, many of the anthropologists honored in this volume were women who I felt had not been honored enough in my earlier work.

I would like to thank again, therefore, the many hundreds of people who have helped with my work, including Sydel Silverman and the late Lita Osmundsen of the Wenner-Gren Foundation for Anthropological Research for funding the interviews and archival retrieval project, the women who were interviewed, the fine scholars who contributed to our joint projects, and the numerous archival and library personnel who helped us amass data over a twenty-five-year period. In addition, I would like to thank new friends and colleagues who have helped me with my tasks for the current volume, such as Karen Underhill, head of Special Collections, Cline Library, Northern Arizona University; Sara Heitshu, reference librarian at the University of Arizona; and old friends like Don and Kay Fowler, Richard and Nathalie Woodbury, Raymond Thompson, and a host of others who have been adding to my knowledge for a quarter of a century. In addition, I would like to thank the fine men and women who have begun to write their own assessments of the women who have worked in the American Southwest and who have shared their insights and new readings of their work. I look forward to many more.

I would also like to give my thanks to the people who have expanded my horizons in recent years. First my gratitude must be extended to my colleagues in American Indian studies who have instilled in me a more multidisciplinary perspective and have nurtured me though a series of illnesses, making sure that I always landed on my feet, always made it to class, and always made it home again safely: K. Tsianina Lomawaima, Tom Holm, Joseph Stauss, Franci Washburn, Luci Tapahonso, Robert Martin, Jennie Joe, Manley Begay, Roger Nichols, Steven Cornell, Robert Hershey, Robert Williams, Mary Willie, Barbara Babcock, Ofelia Zepeda, and Eileen Luna-Firebaugh. Without their care and nurturing I would not have been able to work on this volume. In addition, being part of an interdisciplinary program has made me more aware of disciplinary insularity and the need to view scholarly endeavors in the light of knowledge production in fields besides anthropology and working always outward from the perspective and needs of indigenous peoples.

Second, I would like to thank my coeditor, Shirley Leckie, from whom I have learned a great deal about the production of history over time and who keeps introducing me to new women scholars. It has been a delight to work with her. And, of course, I want to thank my husband, Richard Ahlstrom, for always being there and supporting me on my multi-year projects and making my life meaningful.

Nancy J. Parezo

Their Own Frontier

Introduction

Shirley A. Leckie and Nancy J. Parezo

Master Narratives of the American West

The writings of the American West have long dealt with masculine ideals. In narratives of the Euro-American westward movement, Brigitte Georgi-Findlay observes, "Women were assigned to the margins of a cultural plot in which gender played a significant role." This occurred, she adds, because "westward expansion has been encoded as a male activity, and the American West has served as a generating force and a proving ground for the definition of American manhood."[1]

Susan Armitage noted in 1987, in "Through Women's Eyes: A New View of the West," that the American West has long been a veritable "Hisland," and recent scholars have not disagreed. Until the 1970s, when historians began retrieving neglected works by female authors to reinsert women into the historical record of the West, Euro-American women, when they drew notice, played stereotyped roles such as the "genteel civilizer" or "oppressed drudge."[2] Indian women were portrayed as beasts of burden, downtrodden "squaws," or princesses, and Hispanas or Mexicanas as "fiery senoritas."[3]

If this bipolar portrayal prevailed for women as subjects in studies of the West, one finds that the works of early women scholars also received less attention than those of men. Two major historiographical studies published in 1991—*Writing Western History: Essays on Major Western Historians*, edited by Richard W. Etulain, and Gerald D. Nash's *Creating the West: Historical Interpretations, 1890–1990*—gave women historians before the 1970s little more than passing attention. Neither Annie Heloise Abel nor Angie Debo, important figures in this work, was examined in either volume. Nash mentioned Nebraska historian Mari Sandoz as one who "uncovered the native lore of the Great Plains," but the trivializing word "lore" downgraded her contribution; she needed to be mentioned, but she was not doing "real" history.[4]

From these two historiographical works one readily concludes that in the first seven decades of the twentieth century no female historian contributed important ideas to the historical debates concerning the American West.

R. David Edmunds's 1995 bibliographic essay on American Indian history for the centennial of the *American Historical Review* treated women scholars more fairly and presents quite an extensive list of prolific and influential contemporary women scholars. Edmunds referred to Angie Debo, Mari Sandoz, and Mary Young as contributors to the field before 1960 but failed to note Annie Heloise Abel.[5] Again, one is left believing that women added little to historical understanding and interpretation in the early decades of the twentieth century. Or, if women were writing, which they were, male scholars were ignoring their work, as frivolous, quaint, or unimportant.

This marginalization of women as both subjects and scholars continued well into the twentieth century. Historians of the West, following in Frederick Jackson Turner's footsteps, chose topics and themes that celebrated a male saga of conquest, expansion, and extraction of the region's resources.[6] Popular textbooks by Frederic Paxson, Ray Allen Billington, and Thomas D. Clark narrated the progression of male traders, trappers, soldiers, miners, cowboys, and farmers moving into "open uninhabited wilderness" or "free land" beyond Euro-American settlement. Here, according to Turner's 1893 essay, "The Significance of the Frontier in American History," older institutions, originating in Europe, broke down and were rebuilt in a uniquely American fashion on every new frontier.

The existence of an expanse of "free land" set the United States apart from other nations, Turner and his followers maintained, and provided the context within which democracy and individualism emerged as predominant American traits and cultural values.[7] As for the Native peoples who lived on the "free land," the Turnerians saw them as expendable, evolutionarily backward barriers to settlement. By 1900 these historians considered American Indians properly corralled and isolated on reservations where they were being taught "to walk the white's man's road," that is, were in the process of being assimilated into the larger society.[8] Either way, Turnerians viewed American Indians as "disappearing" people, historically unimportant except as a foil to glorify American militaristic and technological supremacy.

Nineteenth-century anthropologists who were unilinear evolutionists reinforced Turnerian historians. These anthropologists also assumed that American Indians would disappear in the onslaught of an invincible, advancing, and "enlightened American civilization." Indians, by definition "savages" and "barbarians" or people living in "lower stages of civilization," would automatically advance once they met enlightened civilization.[9] However, these anthropologists differed from historians in an important way. They saw American Indians not as obstinate barriers to civilization's expansion but as groups of people who deserved study in their own right.

Anthropology departed from history in another sense. The discipline's founders—that is, first-generation anthropologists intent on professionalizing their discipline—inverted history's invisibility of women as both subjects and researchers. This occurred because a few prominent individuals understood that if anthropology was to gain a complete understanding of Indian cultures, it needed women to gain access to "women's spheres." American Indian women were not meekly answering male researchers' questions; most women actively ignored the field-workers. Unfortunately, most early male anthropologists (generally self-trained army officers and physicians, naturalists, and geologists) felt uncomfortable questioning women and avoided them. Many perceived them as unimportant background figures who cooked the food. Others saw them as individuals who knew nothing about the topics scholars were interested in—that is, religion, politics, and warfare. Many Native peoples, moreover, thought it inappropriate for Euro-American men to question women, or believed that men should not talk about matters belonging to the realm of women, or their responsibilities involving female powers and spiritual knowledge.

If foundational anthropologists had continued to base their choice of field respondents on Victorian assumptions about women and their cultural roles, ignoring what they saw with their own eyes, anthropological studies of the American West would have quickly become a sterile undertaking with no real cross-cultural understanding. But, as the foremost British anthropologist of his day, Edward B. Tylor of

Oxford University, remarked in addressing the Anthropological Society of Washington in 1884 after having visited the Bureau of Ethnology–sponsored research team of James and Matilda Coxe Stevenson at Zuni, "One thing I particularly noticed was this, that to get at the confidence of a tribe, the man of the house, though he can do a great deal, cannot do it all. If his wife sympathizes with his work, and is able to do it," he added, "really half the work of investigation seems to me to fall to her, so much is to be learned through the women of the tribe, which the men will not readily disclose." Tylor further warned the new profession not to exclude women, nor to "warn the ladies off from their proceedings, but rather to avail themselves thankfully of their help."[10]

Anthropology needed women, but their help was still seen as ancillary. The men shaping the new discipline in the late nineteenth and early twentieth centuries, like those in other budding sciences, commonly viewed women as poor material for conducting scientific research. Hence men, with their purportedly more "objective," "rational" natures, would control theory and grand syntheses, while women, with their supposedly "subjective," "irrational," and "emotional" natures, would conduct interviews and collect the necessary observational and material culture data for them. In other words, women would serve as men's helpmates and research assistants.[11]

But scholars like Alice Fletcher, Matilda Stevenson, Sara Yorke Stevenson, Zelia Nuttall, Lucy Wilson, Anita McGee, and a host of others would not be ignored, erased, or marginalized. When these strong women realized that they would be excluded from public forums that would validate their scholarly status—publishing outlets, professional association memberships, and presentation venues—they quickly fought back. On June 8, 1885, ten women founded the Women's Anthropological Society of America (WASA) to provide a place for all women "clear in thought, logical in mental processes, exact in expression, and earnest in the search for truth" who would contribute to anthropology and raise the status of women in science.[12]

In November 1898 the WASA members, now forty-nine strong, were invited to join the Anthropological Society of Washington, which became the American Anthropological Association in 1903. The association's flagship journal, the *American Anthropologist*, welcomed their manuscripts, and immediately after the merger it published Matilda Stevenson's "Zuñi Ancestral Gods and Masks," followed the next year by Alice Fletcher's "A Pawnee Ritual."[13]

Women, however, were not completely successful. As extensively documented in *Hidden Scholars: Women Anthropologists and the Native American Southwest* and a wealth of fine biographies on individual female scholars written over the last twenty years, many women fell by the wayside. Others turned to popularizing rather than trying to penetrate the world of academia, while still others dropped out and moved to the gendered professions of education or librarianship. But many fought for and gained a foothold in anthropology and expanded significantly the existing knowledge about the American West. Unfortunately, most standard histories of anthropology, instead of giving them centrality of place in the main text, have ignored them or condemned them to footnote status as data collectors rather than analysts or synthesizers or theoreticians, or have treated them as anomalies. The women who had to be mentioned (Margaret Mead and Ruth Benedict) became exceptional mavericks who could be explained away or treated as charismatic rebels.

Unlike history, there were many studies by women and an unofficial recognition of women's disciplinary spaces and roles. From their places in the discipline's center and on its margins, women experimented with narrative style and humanistic perspectives to gain recognition, even though some forms of tenacious editorial demands, such as the use of the default pronoun "he" before 1980, were battles yet to be won. Still, it was a difficult road to disciplinary acknowledgment. Whatever their achievements, women had to demonstrate time and again that they were as objective and scientific as men. The stereotypes were simply too entrenched.[14]

While American Indian women had gained a firm if circumscribed place in anthropological narratives before the 1960s, they, like all women, were largely ignored as subjects for historical inquiry unless they occupied positions of power when men were unavailable or were related or married to noted men. Since most women were consigned to domestic roles, seen as unworthy of historical examination, they were outside the purview of history, often defined as involving the "important" events—those having to do with statecraft, diplomacy, and warfare. Although Turner was among those who broadened the cast of historical characters by including common people as subjects, those he selected were men. As T. A. Larson noted in a 1974 essay and John R. Wunder reiterates in this volume, the only woman Turner mentioned in his famous 1893 essay was "Kit Carson's mother." Noteworthy only because of her relationship to her son, she was naturally bounded and labeled by kinship relations and required no individualizing first name.[15]

In this context, the writings of female Euro-American or African American participants in the westward movement received little attention until scholars, influenced by the second-wave feminism beginning in the 1960s, started resurrecting the diaries, journals, and publications pioneer women had written largely from a Euro-American, middle-class, and often agrarian perspective. Annette Kolodny argues in *The Land Before Her: Fantasy and Experience on the American Frontier* (1984) that Euro-American women saw western lands as gardens or future homes rather than a "virginal paradise" for development, as was true of male writers.[16] Brigitte Georgi-Findlay suggests a more complicated legacy. Her 1996 survey of nineteenth-and early-twentieth-century writings of women migrating to or working in the West discovered that most women seldom challenged the prevailing stereotypes of themselves as helpmates who brought "civilization" to the West or of Indians as barbarians.[17]

Most nineteenth-century women writers, Georgi-Findlay continues, wrote not as authorities on the West, as did male explorers, traders, or soldiers, but rather as onlookers sharing their travel, domestic, or familial experiences. Many left behind overland trail diaries never intended for publication. A few sought a paying readership, but middle-class women, whom the established ideology of domesticity relegated to the private sphere of the home, had to justify assuming the public role of author. They did so by convincing themselves and their readers that their works were not intended for self-aggrandizement.[18] Rather, they offered a service for other women, especially those interested in family life in regions newly opened to settlement. Often they emphasized their endurance in surviving in less developed areas, where common goods, services, and a female culture were lacking or minimal. By chronicling their growing self-mastery as they faced difficulties and deprivations, these women conveyed the message that their sacrifices in opening the West were paving the way for future settlement.[19]

Even while sympathizing with the struggles Native peoples waged to retain their homeland, and despite the friendships they sometimes formed with Indian women who occasionally visited their homes, nineteenth-century Euro-American women writers usually considered them "savages."[20] Elizabeth Bacon Custer justified her publications about her life at frontier forts with her husband, George Armstrong Custer, as a way of honoring the sacrifices of soldiers and their families on lonely army posts. Subtly but unmistakably, she emphasized the "superiority" of Euro-American family life and presented army officers as unfailingly chivalrous toward women because of their roles as wives and mothers.

In her works, Custer invariably depicted Indian family life as demeaning to female members, identified as "squaws" and beasts of burden. This was a propagandistic perspective established through tenacious stereotypical images designed to assuage potential American guilt. Since Victorian Americans judged the level of civilization by the public honor accorded womanhood (whatever the private realities in an Anglo-American system of law that stripped wives of property and voting rights, leaving them vulnerable to domestic violence), Custer's writings both rationalized and justified Indian removal to isolated and confining reservations. American Indians could escape their fate only if they relinquished their cultures, ceased being Indians, and assimilated into the larger American society, but only on the margins as rural, semi-skilled vocational workers or farmers.[21]

In the nineteenth-century Victorian climate that extended into the next century, some remarkable women saw that the convergence of American Indian and non-Indian populations required justice for Native peoples. These intrepid individuals placed themselves, figuratively speaking, on the other side of advancing settlement and viewed the westward movement as conquest—the subjugation of Native peoples and the taking of their land by force. Moreover, they expressed fear that the act of conquest and colonialism exacted a toll not only on American

Indians but also on the purported ideals of their own country. See-ing value in American Indian societies and culture, especially holis-tic worldviews that respected environmental stewardship rather than raw exploitation and resource extraction, women scholars struggled to comprehend events from Native points of view.

To varying degrees, these early female rebels (like their male coun-terparts) anticipated ideas that have since become a part of the New Western history, the New Indian history, ethnohistory, and modern an-thropological studies of the West. These women, who included strong Native women activist-orators like Sara Winnemucca Hopkins and reformers such as abolitionist and Indian rights activist Lydia Maria Child and Indian rights activist Helen Hunt Jackson, were not aca-demically trained historians or ethnologists.[22]

But at the time no one was academically trained in anthropology, neither men nor women. One learned by doing, and women made their own opportunities by defying Victorian conventions and becom-ing tenacious peripatetic travelers and close observers. Their obser-vational fieldwork and documentary research, their writings and ac-tivities, cannot be denied. It just takes a close reading and the will to re-acknowledge their accomplishments, to see them in the contexts of their time. As has proven the case when reassessing the work of many scholarly pioneers, the process of remembering and critically as-sessing knowledge production as a corpus of works produced over a lifetime shows that women scholars were actually the individuals who made many theoretical, methodological, and informational advances for which men later received credit.

Toward Alternative Narratives of the American West

Before we turn to the pioneering women historians and anthropolo-gists honored in this volume, a discussion of more recent scholarly developments they foreshadowed will contextualize our analyses.[23] The practitioners of the New Western history take issue with Turner and his followers. They see the West primarily as place and view the movement of Euro-Americans into the region as conquest rather than settlement.[24] Equally important, Turner saw the trans-Mississippi West as experiencing a dichotomized past arising from the disappearance of America's "free land." The break came and was institutionally authenticated when the federal government, in the form of the U.S. Census Bureau, declared in 1890 that "isolated settlements" had moved into all counties in the United States—a statement that conveniently ignored the Native peoples living in their homelands. The New Western historians disagree with this declaration and its consequences. They argue instead that the problems persisting in the region today stem from the conquest of the land and the commandeering of its resources.

Furthermore, these historians make new assumptions about the injustices that arose when Euro-Americans converged with Native and Hispanic peoples. The latter were conquerors who had inadvertently decimated the Native population by spreading their diseases among peoples who had no resistance to them and also by harshly attempting to impose on them their religious and cultural perspectives. These encounters left behind unresolved issues that defy easy solutions for all Americans generations later. Both Native peoples (classified as barbarians) and Hispanic peoples (classified as peasants) came to be seen as barriers to capitalistic Euro-American advancement and endured numerous assaults on their laws, traditions, religious practices, economies, lands, and water rights.

In the field of American Indian history, New Indian historians now strive to write their narratives and analyses from indigenous points of view. They also seek to show that Native people were and are agents or active players in events, not simply passive victims or powerless subalterns, and that historical interpretation is frequently based on perspective.[25] Their approaches stand in contrast to an older history of Indian-white relations that sees Native peoples simply as mute foils in a Euro-American epic of masculine prowess, expansion, and progress.

New Indian historians, such as R. David Edmunds, Loretta Fowler, Tom Holm, K. Tsianina Lomawaima, Devon A. Mihesuah, and Richard White, also try to rectify two additional past historiographical errors: first, to place American Indians as fully as possible in the context of their cultures, which often proves a difficult and problematic exercise due to biases in the extant documentary record; and second, to remind readers that Native peoples had long histories before their first contacts with Europeans, that they are still present, and that they have futures. To accomplish this task they use an interdisciplinary and, at times, multidisciplinary approach, made possible through established anthropological and historical perspectives and methodologies as signified by the development of rigorous ethnohistory. No single voice predominates; scholars consult indigenous men and women about their perspectives of the past, thereby revaluing and challenging the notion of a primary document. Originally a melding of history and cultural anthropology in the 1940s, ethnohistory now includes other anthropological subdisciplines (archaeology and linguistics), sociology (demography and the sociology of culture), political science, women's studies, and, most recently, American Indian and indigenous and Native studies.[26]

Ethnohistory, the common view holds, arose out of the need for historians and anthropologists to collaborate on Indian issues brought before the Indian Claims Commission, formed in 1946 to settle remaining disputes between Native peoples and the federal government.[27] This was followed by the work of anthropologists such as Erminie Wheeler-Voegelin, Anthony F. C. Wallace, and John C. Ewers, who studied changes in Indian cultures due to European contact and colonialism. This volume discloses, however, that historians Angie Debo and Mari Sandoz and anthropologists Ruth Underhill, Alice Marriott, Marjorie Lambert, Isabel Kelly, and Ella Deloria were already incorporating many of the methods and concepts associated with ethnohistory into their works long before the formation of the Claims Commission.

Finally, practitioners of the New Indian history depart from the once-predominant view that American Indians are "disappearing." Instead, they maintain that the most important fact of Native peoples' existence is, as Robert F. Berkhofer put it, "the remarkable persistence of cultural and personality traits and ethnic identity . . . in the face of white conquests and efforts at elimination or assimilation."[28] This idea, new to many historians, was hardly news for anthropologists. They were already acknowledging this fact en masse by the 1920s, and most had tacitly recognized it by 1900, especially those who did not hold with the tenets of social Darwinism, which few cultural anthropologists who worked in the American West actually did.[29] Thus, although the anthropologists in this volume entered the field when the general public thought they were involved in "salvage" ethnography—that is, capturing or documenting information about peoples who were disappearing—these women were willing and generally eager to learn from Native peoples. They understood that the cultures of Native peoples were not dying but instead were changing. These women anthropologists found the American Indians' ways of life attractive and relevant to their own lives, especially in matrilineal societies, where women were accorded great respect. Moreover, the women who studied under Boas and Benedict especially adopted the stance that they were to respect the boundaries their informants established, while simultaneously giving them as full a voice as possible within the 1920–40s tenets of anonymity.[30]

Today, after a great deal of soul-searching, due to World War II associations, research subjects' demands for more equal status, and debates over scientific objectivity versus interpretive frameworks, the word *informant* has gone out of style. In its place anthropologists are trying out a number of terms—such as *respondent* for survey work and *consultant*, *elder*, and *collaborator* for qualitative interviews—that more accurately reflect ownership of knowledge, recognition that anthropological work is a collaborative endeavor, and awareness that ethnographic writing primarily entails cross-culturally translating the words and knowledge of Native peoples for readers. Because of these ethical concerns, we and our contributors use the word *collaborator*.

The New Indian historians became prominent in the 1970s, and the New Western historians arrived as a distinct school with the publication of Patricia N. Limerick's *The Legacy of Conquest: The Unbroken Past of the American West* in 1987. The historian foremothers of these scholarly developments—Angie Debo, for example, influenced Patricia Limerick—not only placed themselves on the other side of Turner's line of settlement but also questioned the justice meted out to Native peoples and the assumptions about their "savagery."[31] Scholars did so by documenting the savagery of their own people and calling for its redress.[32]

The latter was a process that anthropologists had been documenting since the earliest days of the discipline. With the discipline's strong activist bent and from their common backgrounds in social work, education, and health, women anthropologists have long tried to make their field socially relevant. One of the hallmarks of women's anthropological endeavors is that, while advancing the anthropological perspective, their work must benefit the people they study as well as their own society. At first many women adapted the tenets of Victorian society to their anthropology. This meant that they identified as women's work bringing "civilization" to unknown places and helping the poor and downtrodden, such as European immigrants, African Americans, and American Indians. Over time, however, women anthropologists became more involved in studying Native peoples for the sheer delight of discovering not only the variation within individual societies but also how different—and in their view, how constructive—their approaches could be to addressing the common problems of being human.

Whether their motivation was to uplift the downtrodden or to expand knowledge of the variety of human experiences, women attempted to utilize anthropology for the betterment of all people, not only other anthropologists or themselves as professionals. This theme will be especially evident in the lives of the women who worked during the Great Depression and World Wars I and II. At times their work took on the patina of missions and quests, but the missions and quests helped sustain women like Dorothea Leighton, Ruth Underhill, Alice Marriott, and Angie Debo when they met barriers in obtaining employment due to sexism, ageism, and nepotism laws that prevented wives from working for the same institution or agency their husband worked for.[33]

In addition, all the women interviewed for the Daughters of the Desert Project in 1985 and 1986 stated that women anthropologists who worked between 1900 and 1970, including the women in this volume, had a broader agenda than simply speaking to members of academia. They intentionally took their writings beyond the ivory tower, successfully reaching the general public. There is a reason why Margaret Mead is the best-known anthropologist, followed closely by Ruth Benedict: both intentionally made their writings accessible. Ruth Underhill and Alice Marriott followed suit, and their books, like Mead's and Benedict's, are still in print and rightly so. Among the historians of this volume, Angie Debo and Mari Sandoz sought and attracted a wide popular readership. Their writings have never gone out of style, nor has the information they conveyed been seriously challenged.

This commitment to making information about American Indians accessible often found expression in activism. Because of Americans' conceptual models that women were cultured and refined in contrast to wild, uncouth, and rough men, activism was a successful strategy for politically astute women.[34] Gender assumptions also stressed the ideals of cooperation and social concern perceived as congenial to the female temperament. Women manipulated these preconceptions to benefit Native peoples. For example, ethnomusicologist and folklorist Natalie Curtis Burlin, who had a gift for conveying complicated information clearly and for seeing its policy implications, convinced Washington politicians that Native Americans should have religious determinacy, which resulted in lifting the assimilationist ban against the singing and playing of Native American religious music.

As this volume stresses, other women encouraged and promoted American Indian arts and crafts and the protection of homelands and water rights for indigenous peoples. All the anthropologists interviewed for the Daughters of the Desert Project mentioned that many of their research and writing activities sought to give back to the Native peoples whatever could be useful to them and to enable them to serve as cultural brokers and mediators between asymmetrically powerful cultures. Accomplishing this generally required alternative texts that showed strong peoples who had survived conquest, colonization, and attempts to erase them but who were marginalized within the larger society.

Non-Native scholars who wrote sympathetically about American Indians in the early decades of the twentieth century often found themselves at odds with their own society. Frequently they perceived qualities in Indian life that they viewed as lacking in their own worlds. A number of scholars and writers in the 1920s, such as Mary Austin, Ruth Benedict, Elsie Clews Parsons, Amelia White, and Oliver LaFarge, saw in the Pueblo peoples of the Southwest a sense of community and a reverence for tradition that were besieged in modern life.[35] Perhaps the most powerful and famous of these was John Collier, who in 1933 became commissioner of Indian Affairs. His studies of Indian life convinced him that Native peoples lived in communal societies that flowed reverentially from the natural world and produced integrated individuals at home spiritually as well as physically in their own world.[36]

Women writers such as Mary Shepardson, Ruth Underhill, Elsie Clews Parsons, Amelia White, and Mabel Luhan Dodge often saw their own society, purportedly a republic, tolerating racial and social injustice and acting unfairly toward women. Indians, by contrast, frequently organized their lives around complementary rather than hierarchical gender roles.[37] This was especially true of the matrilineal societies in which many early anthropologists, such as Gladys Reichard, Erna Gunther, Matilda Coxe Stevenson, Erminnie Smith, Cora Du Bois, Carobeth Laird, Viola Garfield, Ruth Bunzel, and Esther Goldfrank worked. Others, such as Phoebe Apperson Hearst and Muriel Hemenway, used their wealth to finance anthropological research to provide societal models to improve industrializing America.[38] Still others, like the wealthy expatriate and historical anthropologist/documentary archaeologist Zelia Nuttall, foreshadowed the career of the less wealthy but equally dedicated Isabel Kelly.

Professionalization and Its Impact on Women Historians and Anthropologists

In the late nineteenth century, Alice Fletcher became an anthropologist through self-directed study and fieldwork. No universities were offering degrees in her chosen field at the time. Most anthropologists learned their trade through firsthand observation and, in some cases, incipient participant observation. The best-known case is the charismatic Frank Hamilton Cushing, who spent two years at Zuni learning the language and immersing himself in their daily activities, even when he was unwelcome. Matilda Coxe Stevenson did the same, as did other foundational anthropologists.

Experiential learning was a common practice for scholarly disciplines in the nineteenth century. Other professionals, in law and medicine especially, entered their fields through apprenticeships, while some clergy received the call and ministered to congregations without formal study. Most college teachers in the antebellum era had only a master's degree if that. Americans who wanted to earn a doctorate in history, for example, had to attend European universities, such as Leipzig and Heidelberg, until 1882. That year John Franklin Jameson and Clarence Bowen received doctorates in history from Johns Hopkins and Yale University, respectively. Both schools, having adopted the German model, specialized in archival research presented in graduate seminars. From this time forward, growing numbers of American universities began turning out professional historians, dedicated to advancing knowledge rather than simply transmitting it in the classroom.[39]

With this transition in the nature and conceptualization of work, professions began to seek more stringent ways to train and credential recruits. In the process they ensured that individuals who did not match their social criteria—that is, could not become white, middle- to upper-class gentlemen—were routed out. As Samuel Haber has shown, men seeking increased social authority and status drew on predemocratic and preindustrial techniques to embed values of authority and honor in certain occupations they were engaged in. They fused these with duties and responsibilities that reflected the prescriptions of eighteenth-century gentlemen—in other words, the landed gentry unsullied by commerce.[40]

More and more ascribed criteria were attached to "professionals" to distinguish them from tradesmen or laborers, and more barriers and hurdles were erected to make obtaining the status more difficult. Increasingly, this meant higher degrees and the following of agreed-upon, rigorous, standardized, replicable methodologies. Also necessary was the passing of licensing tests, which for academic disciplines meant years of amassing esoteric information and learning value-laden jargon, increasingly difficult to acquire on one's own. Often it also meant unquestioning adherence to the theories of professionals with the highest national status and prestige. Men like Turner in history and Boas in anthropology had the power to control access to education, degrees, jobs, and publication outlets.

As older avenues for gaining professional status began to close, individuals seeking entry into law, medicine, established religion, and the professoriat found it necessary to be admitted to law, medical, divinity, and graduate schools offering terminal or highest degrees. As this occurred, leading scholars established national associations that set standards for the professional and academic disciplines that the credentialing schools and academic programs had to abide by—all with the aim of eradicating "irregulars."

By 1905 anthropologists like Daniel Brinton, Frank Russell, Franz Boas, Alice Fletcher, and Frederic Putnam—the men and women who formed the new American Anthropological Association and served as the leadership for Section H of the American Association for the advancement of Science—wanted to ensure that anthropology became a science. To do so, the discipline would require special training in both theory and methodology. There would be lab work and field schools as well as training in the field and mentorship.[41]

Overall, advocates of professionalization sought to raise the prestige and remuneration of credentialed practitioners by forcing them to meet increasingly rigorous standards and pass more difficult tests. In theory, the tests were administered impartially and objectively and the determination of who met them took no notice of color, class, age, or sex. In reality, however, those setting the standards, administering the tests, and determining whether individuals met their criteria held the common prejudices against women, people of color, and, as Ruth M. Underhill discovered when she applied for graduate school, people who were older. Since society not only saw women as physically, mentally, and emotionally inferior to men but also viewed their gendered roles and responsibilities as requiring less skill and preparation than those that men performed, advocates of professionalization resisted admitting women into educational programs requiring credentialing. They feared that once women gained a foothold, men would leave and their fields would become feminized. Their own compensation and prestige would decline. Obviously, the credentialed gatekeepers had tremendous power to eliminate women from educational programs. More important, rejected women could not complain about any assessment they received, since the tests and standards were, everyone agreed, impartial and objective. To challenge that fact was to act unprofessionally, thereby verifying the judgment rendered.

Some women passed the tests and met the standards, despite formidable obstacles and male hostility. Once one was admitted to a profession, however, one's fate depended on the ability to rise within the ranks, and that often required strong mentoring from a respected older professional. Despite the "objective" credentialing devices of attending classes, writing term papers, engaging in original research, passing doctoral exams, and publishing a dissertation, an apprenticeship based on a fictive father-son dyad was an imperative if informal requirement. This mentoring often occurred in locations where women were not welcome—smokers where pipes and cigars could be lit, faculty (i.e., men's) clubs, and, for anthropology, field schools or research trips with the mentor. Women were less likely to receive such support, either because of prejudice against them or because men were often uncomfortable about initiating and maintaining a personal relationship with a woman. At the same time, the few women in the professions were often too concerned about their own standing to provide the needed guidance or were employed in positions where they could not open doors, such as in libraries or as research associates in museums and historical societies. Women were rarely employed at elite research universities, the hubs of intellectual social networks.

Even when a woman did receive the prerequisite gatekeeping mentoring, she encountered yet another problem. The attributes that society expected of women ran counter to those that professionals were expected to display. As Robyn Muncy explains, the proper characteristics for women were based on "lingering nineteenth-century feminine ideals [that] urged women toward passivity, humility, and self-sacrifice while professionalism demanded activity, confidence, and self-assertion. By validating behaviors traditionally associated with men," she continues, "professionalization put aspiring women into perpetual conflict. If they donned the behavioral garb appropriate to professional life, they invited criticism for being unfeminine. If they refused to wear the suit, they lost the aura of professional authority." In that light, women "endured unique conflicts in the professionalization process, devised unique strategies for coping with those conflicts, and often followed unique career paths as a result."[42] Even then, female scholars had to fight extra battles that men did not. These included nepotism rules, which precluded wives from working where their husbands were employed; the idea that women needed less money to live on than men and, therefore, deserved lower salaries; and the belief that women's true and proper calling was to marriage and raising children. Hence, for them, wedlock and a professional career were incompatible.

The first profession that had become feminized for women in the United States had been schoolteaching, largely because women worked for less and their responsibilities were seen as an extension of maternal duties within the home. College teaching, carrying more prestige than teaching in primary and secondary schools, initially offered women opportunities in the women's colleges, newly formed after the Civil War. When it came to positions in the coeducational institutions, however, women often found their homes primarily in newly formed departments such as domestic science (later home economics) or "motherly" administrative positions, such as dean of women students.[43]

Although the master's degree had once sufficed for college teaching, by the early twentieth century the more prestigious colleges and universities were increasingly expanding graduate offerings and demanding doctorates of their faculty. Over time liberal arts and teaching colleges followed their example and increasingly emphasized research. With each passing decade, the doctoral degree became more and more the proverbial "license to practice."[44] Women thus faced another barrier, since many graduate schools were reluctant to admit them to doctoral programs, fearing that they would be incapable of mastering the material because of their "delicate" natures.[45]

When women succeeded, professors and administrators predicted that their education would be wasted when they married and bore children. Thus women who pursued professions were almost forced (or not-too-subtly encouraged) to remain single, a restriction that was relaxed slightly in the 1920s, only to resurge later. Even in the 1920s, unless a woman carved out a profession in a field related to rearing children, as Clara Savage Littledale did when she became editor of *Parents' Magazine*, or was a person of substantial wealth, capable of employing maids and nannies, such as anthropologist Elsie Clews Parsons, raising children was perceived as incompatible with maintaining a professional life. The small family sizes and the interrupted career paths of the women in this volume testify to the choices they had to make.[46] The questions concerning the compatibility of engaging in a profession and being married and rearing a family haunted women well into the twentieth century and still persist today.[47]

Although women had comprised 36 percent of all professors in the 1880s, due largely to the growing number of women's colleges and some openings at coeducational institutions, that situation did not last.[48] By 1890, as the number of colleges expanded and men increasingly became the preferred teachers, bringing more prestige to departments and institutions, the overall percentage of women faculty members declined to 20 percent.[49] Two decades later women still comprised 20 percent of the faculty, overwhelmingly congregated in the lower-level and adjunct positions. According to one study, women held 73 percent of instructorships but only 10 percent of full professorships. Moreover, those women who rose to professorial rank took longer, often because they were burdened with large undergraduate classes that left less time for publishing. And women were disproportionately concentrated in home economics, English, music, and modern language departments.[50]

Until the implementation of affirmative action programs in the 1970s, women encountered difficulties entering the most prestigious graduate programs. Johns Hopkins University, the first American school to offer graduate seminars based on the German model, refused to award the doctorate in psychology to Christine Ladd-Franklin, who as a special student (one denied official admittance, in this instance because of her sex) had successfully completed all of the requirements in 1882. Not until 1926—when she was seventy-nine—and after a life of scientific inquiry and publication did the university finally award her the credential she had earned forty-four years earlier.[51]

History, as a professionalized field in Europe and the United States, was dismissive of women from its inception. As Bonnie Smith notes, although amateur men and women were writing popular history on a wide range of topics, in academia history was seen as a male activity that focused almost exclusively on "great" men and public affairs. Scholars trained in European and American graduate schools adopted a methodology based on rigorous immersion in primary documents and archival sources that they sought to analyze as objectively as possible while striving to remain impartial, irrespective of their personal background, nationality, or religion. These university-trained scholars researched "important" subjects (the nation-state, international affairs, and wars), all topics for which they found ready publication outlets. After all, male professors generally controlled access to prestigious journals and presses through editorial control and the peer review process, which has always been harder on women than men.[52]

Because professionalization occurred when Western societies were still wedded to an ideology of separate spheres, which allocated the public sphere of remunerative labor and politics to men and the private sphere of home and family to women, women were largely excluded from professionalized history. As Smith reminds us, the rationalization for this situation held that given their home responsibilities, how could women possibly travel to archives to do the necessary research? In the light of prevailing ideas about gender differences between the sexes, moreover, women were seen as too emotional to be capable of writing dispassionate and hence professional history. Deemed poor material for making scientific historians, those women who sought graduate training were often denied entry into programs or faced intense prejudice and scrutiny once admitted.[53]

As for women as subjects in history, Judith P. Zinsser finds evidence of continuing misogyny toward them in the works of professional historians well into the late decades of the twentieth century. In describing women as queens, regents, or the mistresses of kings, male historians often painted them as weak-willed, uncontrollably emotional, and subject to male domination, and, thus, dangerous interlopers in public affairs.[54] Little wonder, then, that Edward Everett Dale, Angie Debo's mentor in graduate school at the University of Oklahoma, wrote a paper at Harvard University when he was in his thirties while attending Frederick Jackson Turner's seminar that argued that the influence of women on the French Revolution was confined to the actions of men who adopted what he termed "feminine" traits. These included engaging in senseless and emotional debates and demonstrating their inability to accomplish the business before them.[55]

The experience of one woman scholar who overcame such attitudes and won admittance to the graduate program in history at the University of Wisconsin is worth examining as a case study of what often happened to promising women. Louise Phelps Kellogg (1862–1942) was one of Turner's most gifted students. As the winner of a fellowship that enabled her to spend her second year of graduate study at the London School of History and Economics and the Sorbonne in Paris, she became a teaching scholar at Wisconsin, one of the few women to gain that position. After writing a Winsor Prize–winning dissertation, "The American Colonial Charter: A Study of English Administration in Relation Thereto, Chiefly after 1688," she sought a teaching position at a college or university. Instead she could gain professional employment only in a subordinate research position at the State Historical Society of Wisconsin; she worked there until her death, carving out a secure niche. Turner never used his network to find her a more appropriate position. He accepted a few brilliant women as graduate students but thought that when male and female scholars were equal in ability and intellect, males deserved preference when teaching positions opened. Thus, he was a dismal mentor for women.[56]

At the Wisconsin Historical Society, Kellogg, whose increasing deafness made it ever more difficult for her to obtain a teaching position despite her prodigious output, worked with Rueben Thwaites editing the multivolume *Early Western Travels, 1748–1846*.[57] Invariably she was listed as second rather than senior editor on their coedited works. Perhaps this listing was fair, but she may have bowed to the convention that when the coauthor or coeditor was female, her name appeared second. After Thwaites's death in 1913, Kellogg edited the Lyman C. Draper collection, better known as the Draper Series, meticulously translating nearly indecipherable documents on which future historical research would depend. Kellogg used these new sources in *The French Regime in Wisconsin and the Northwest*, a reinterpretation of the history of New France that shed new light not only on Indian-white relations but also on the relationships among various Indian peoples. Ten years later she performed a similar feat with *The British Regime in Wisconsin and the Northwest*. Her extraordinary output won her the first female presidency of the Mississippi Valley Historical Society, the forerunner of the Organization of American Historians.[58] Today her translated documents and monographs and her edited and coedited works remain classic sources valuable to contemporary scholars.[59]

The strategy of working as research assistants to dominant men and then, after their deaths or departures from a museum, library, or archive, moving slowly through the ranks of the organization to positions of authority gained women historians regional if not national recognition for their years of hard work. As will be seen, this is a common strategy that will appear throughout this volume for both historians and anthropologists. Nonprofit institutions valued individuals who could perform a wealth of jobs, who were willing to take on any task when needed (including the most tedious ones), and who were extremely loyal to the institutions and the information they contained in objects, books, and documents. Finally, these institutions appreciated individuals who continued to produce a massive amount of work for a small salary. Archaeologist Marjorie Lambert is the archetype of this type of female professional. Similarly, Kellogg, once she became director of research, made herself a vital part of the Wisconsin Historical Society, as did other women such as Annie Nunns, who worked with Kellogg as assistant superintendent (assistant director today). Significantly, almost no woman who used this strategy rose to the position of director. In one sense, however, all were fortunate. They were likely to keep their jobs throughout the Great Depression and after World War II when returning veterans reclaimed well-paid and more prestigious positions.

In the 1930s, women in every profession, including feminized and lower-paying jobs (schoolteaching, social work, and librarianship), lost ground. Governments at all levels cut budgets and staff, and when openings did arise, many schools, agencies, and libraries hired men, arguing that with families to support, men needed the jobs more. Ironically, however, the percentage of married women in the workforce actually increased 25 percent, in part because many husbands lost their jobs and the expansion of government agencies created new clerical opportunities specifically classified for women. For archaeology this meant lab work for women and excavation for men. But the reigning ideology held that given the high level of unemployment, men should be hired whenever possible and that women with employed husbands should resign any jobs they held. In that spirit, Congress passed the 1932 Economy Act, with Section 213 decreeing that in the event of government layoffs of civil service employees, those with spouses also in government service would be laid off first. States, counties, and municipalities did likewise. The person who lost the job was almost invariably the woman.[60]

Most relief programs during Franklin Delano Roosevelt's New Deal targeted men for the jobs they created. Thankfully, the Works Progress Administration had a separate directorate, the Women's and Professional Division, whose director, Ellen Woodward, chose women as her state directors whenever possible.[61] Angie Debo served in this position when she was appointed director of the Federal Writers' Program in Oklahoma in 1941. Mari Sandoz also benefited from an earlier federal humanities program that enabled the Nebraska State Historical Society to rehire her in 1933, at one of the most desperate moments in her life, financially and emotionally.

Anthropologists followed the same socioeconomic pattern. Depression recovery programs opened a wealth of opportunities for women like Dorothea Leighton, Alice Marriott, Laura Thompson, Marjorie Lambert, and many others who were documented in *Hidden Scholars*, especially in programs sponsored by the Bureau of Indian Affairs and the Indian Arts and Crafts Board. Museums as well were considered ideal places for women to work, especially those with master's degrees. Margaret Mead recalled that, according to Clark Wissler, "museum work fitted women because it was like housekeeping." Archaeologist Bertha Dutton noted that, like libraries, historical societies, and archives where female historians found work, in museums "men are in the top jobs and women are doing the work."[62] But they had jobs and professional status at a time when there was over 80 percent unemployment in anthropology.

Following the entry of the United States into World War II in December 1941, some sixteen million Americans joined the military. Since the United States had functioned as "the arsenal of democracy," even before declaring war on Japan after its attack on Pearl Harbor the resulting labor shortage throughout the nation brought new employment opportunities. The single-fastest-growing female segment of the workplace became women over thirty-five.[63] Angie Debo, offered no jobs in academia, taught high school in her hometown of Marshall, Oklahoma.[64] Some professional women found employment as replacements for male college and university teachers. As Margaret Rossiter notes, from 1943 until 1945 the extensive shortage of university professors meant that women were welcome in the classroom, and between 1942 and 1946 their numbers in higher education tripled. By war's end they held positions even in all-male schools. Most understood, however, that their jobs existed only for the war's duration; afterwards men would replace them.[65]

World War II also created new opportunities outside higher education for women anthropologists. At the instigation of Gladys Reichard, the federal government turned to anthropologists to explain "strange people and languages." The Office of Wartime Information employed Ruth Benedict to write an interpretation of Japan and the Japanese mind. The result was the 1946 best-seller *The Chrysanthemum and the Sword*, which categorized the Japanese mind as a blend of "aestheticism and militarism." Cora Du Bois, a scholar who had unsuccessfully sought employment in the 1930s, became chief of the Indonesia section of the Office of Strategic Services from 1942 to 1944 and then chief of its Ceylon research branch from 1944 to 1945.[66]

By 1946 the ideological tide had again turned against women as workers. Americans, fearing that a new depression loomed, believed that good jobs were owed to returning veterans. Women wartime workers usually lost their high-paying positions, and a new cult of domesticity proclaimed the home their proper place.[67] A best-seller of 1947, Marynia Farnham and Ferdinand Lundberg's *Modern Woman, the Lost Sex*, pronounced feminism a form of neurosis and urged women to recognize that they would find their largest satisfaction in cultivating the traits of traditional femininity.[68] Women began to be excluded from undergraduate and graduate schools as universities and colleges took advantage of the government subsidies from the GI Bill and the rise of government-sponsored research. Beneath the surface, nonetheless, older, middle-class married women joined or rejoined the paid labor force in rising numbers. Most of their jobs were now the sex-segregated and lower-paying jobs women had held before World War II.

Professional women of this era found their strongest opportunities in teaching in elementary and secondary schools and as nurses, the latter an occupation that had opened to them as a result of the Civil War but was still not accorded respect as a bona fide profession. Previously expanding professions for women witnessed a decline; women now entered medicine in diminishing numbers, and their percentage, formerly as high as 10 percent of medical school graduates, fell to 5 percent. This change arose largely from quotas limiting women to a percentage of students accepted, while 70 percent of hospitals barred them from internships altogether.[69] In colleges and universities by the mid-1950s, the percentage of women teachers, having risen to 25 percent in 1940, had fallen to 23 percent and a decade later stagnated at 22 percent.[70] Again women held positions in the lower ranks and found jobs at institutions that concentrated on undergraduate education rather than in the more prestigious and scholarship-oriented new Research 1 universities.

Women in history departments fared poorly. Perhaps the best evidence of attitudes toward professional women historians comes from a report written in 1942 by two noted historians, William Hesseltine and Louis Kaplan, and published in the 1943 *Journal of Higher Education*. They observed that women earned 18 percent of the doctorates in history between 1891 and 1935 but had not achieved academic prominence. Seventy-four percent of men earning the doctorate found employment in history departments, but only 49 percent of women were that fortunate. The jobs women held, moreover, were largely in smaller and poorer colleges where they had higher teaching loads and lesser salaries; few held senior positions or endowed chairs.

Despite these inferior work conditions, Hesseltine and Kaplan identified women's lack of productivity in research as the reason for their lagging status. They noted that women published "but 13 per cent of the books and 7 per cent of the articles." They concluded: "Whatever discrimination might exist against women as teachers or administrators"—overlooking entirely such issues as the fact that editors and peer reviewers often devalued the academic work women produced—"there were none against them as productive scholars." Moreover, in their view, granting agencies were not "misogynists," which meant that if women wanted to publish despite their higher teaching loads and lower salaries, they could do so by getting grants and working harder. In summarizing, the authors concluded that, after half a century, "the record of the average woman who persevered in academic study until she attained the doctorate is not impressive. She has seldom held high or responsible positions in the teaching profession, and she has not proved a productive scholar." Expanding or improving her opportunities or working conditions would not, they concluded, change her professional status.[71]

Given the persistence of such "blame the victim" attitudes, it is not surprising that, with the rise of second-wave feminism in the 1960s, the American Historical Association agreed to examine the status of women as professional historians, whose percentage in the discipline now stood at only 12 percent. Willie Lee Rose, a prominent scholar in the study of the Reconstruction era, chaired the investigating committee. The Rose Committee, drawing partly on surveys the American Council on Education ACE had recently conducted, found the situation for women deplorable. In examining the ten leading graduate departments of history in 1966, the ACE had discovered that between 98 and 99 percent of history professors were men. Women on those campuses served in the lowest ranks. Five of these departments had no women whatsoever at even an assistant professor's level, and none had a woman serving as full professor.[72]

The situation was little better at ten coeducational liberal arts colleges, where women represented about 10 percent of the members of undergraduate history departments but only 2 percent in the graduate departments. The "most startling" finding was the "progressive deterioration in the status of women in the departments of coeducational colleges." A study in 1959–60 had found women representing 16 percent of the professors in these institutions, but as of 1968–69 "only one woman full professor remained and she retired the following year." The Rose Committee Report concluded that this decline arose from the retirement of women professors "trained in the twenties" and "the tendency to hire men in the post-war years" as their replacements. The Rose Committee also discovered that although women's colleges had once hired many women as professors, the last decade had seen "a decline" in female representation there as well.

In accounting for its findings, the Rose Committee Report identified first the view that women preferred domestic life to a professional career, and second that those most likely to discriminate against women saw them as inferior to men, an especially strong belief among men who had been in their careers five to thirty years, that is, departmental decision makers. In a departure from the earlier Hesseltine and Kaplan report, the Rose Committee Report saw such attitudes as counterproductive. Recent studies by Rita Simon, Shirley Merritt Clark, and Kathleen Galway indicated that married women PhDs with full-time jobs published at a rate that actually exceeded that of unmarried women PhDs or male PhDs. Finally, women PhDs were so eager to teach that they were easily exploited as part-time or adjunct faculty. In conclusion, the Rose Committee Report noted that, as an association, the American Historical Association "has no better record than the colleges and universities" it had been studying when it came to "engaging the participation of women in its central activities."[73]

While the Rose Committee Report uncovered a pattern of egregious discrimination against women, the fact that the oldest American historical society was confronting such issues was the first step toward rectifying the situation. Although sexism would remain firmly entrenched for years to come, conditions began improving slowly for women intellectuals, and their voices, as historians, began receiving a more serious hearing. Still, decades later, much remains to be done.

By the 1970s and into the 1980s and beyond, historians of women who were also experts in the American West laid the foundation for a new history of the American West that is less male-centered and increasingly multicultural. At the same time, they began following in the footsteps of the historians discussed in this volume by incorporating into their accounts the perspectives of people of color, especially American Indians, minorities, and those from lower classes, especially the poor and dispossessed.[74] In many instances, since the works of earlier women scholars had not received due recognition and, more importantly, because women had been excluded from producing and mentoring graduate students, these new developments would not proceed as smoothly or as quickly as they might have otherwise. It is time consuming and difficult to be constantly reinventing academic wheels. Had these earlier women scholars been acknowledged and integrated into the discipline at the time they were making their contributions, they would have moved the intellectual conversation that is history along faster.

To be fair, some, such as Angie Debo, had witnessed the incorpora-
tion of their ideas into the literature of the field, but their provenance
often went unacknowledged. These oversights and intentional slights
meant that women intellectuals entering the study of the American
West after 1970 were frequently unaware of their intellectual foremothers. Lacking that understanding, many new women scholars had only a
truncated sense of their own scholarly potential.

Anthropology experienced a similar situation, but for different reasons. The expanded opportunities of the second women's movement
in the United States came when anthropology had turned away from
studying American Indians as it internationalized its agenda. Those
anthropologists who worked with Native communities were concentrated in applied anthropology, ethnohistory, medical anthropology,
and interdisciplinary endeavors. They began to pull away from the
American Anthropological Association and work through the dozens
of new associations now flourishing and setting agendas of their own.

Thus the rise in feminist scholarship began occurring when cultural anthropology and archaeology were changing through topical
specialization and regional shifts. That fact made it easier to forget the
contributions that the women honored in this volume made to the re-
visioning of the American West and its Native peoples.

In their practice and theory, nonetheless, these women intellectuals
left behind works that have provided essential materials for building
bridges from older, more ethnocentric scholarship to research that today incorporates diverse peoples, perspectives, and methods. Finally,
their works have bequeathed intellectual tools that have proved invaluable to the study of indigenous peoples everywhere, not only the Native
peoples of the West. Even in a postcolonial world, all indigenous people still struggle to exist as separate peoples with the right to recover,
maintain, and transmit their traditions, histories, and cultures as they
continue to fight for self-determination.

The women historians chosen for this volume—Annie Abel, Angie Debo, and Mari Sandoz—produced works that helped to lay the
foundation for the New Indian history and ethnohistory. That is the
primary reason for their selection. Abel played a vital role in establishing American Indian history as a field separate from the history of the

American West. By choosing to write a trilogy about the Five Tribes of Indian Territory—usually called the Five Civilized Tribes, but referred to in this volume as the Five Southern Tribes, since they were forcibly removed from the southeastern part of the United States—and by focusing on their experiences during the Civil War and Reconstruction, Abel acknowledged their interests as separate and diverse people and their ability to wield historical agency, even in the face of immensely difficult conditions.[75] Building on Abel's works, Debo and her contemporary Sandoz pioneered in writing history that incorporated the Native point of view and used the tools of anthropologists. In the process they played important and often overlooked roles in the establishment of ethnohistory.

Others whom we chose were anthropologists, including some who were archaeologists and others who pioneered in anthropology's new subfields, such as medical and community anthropology. We have purposefully not included women whose lives were documented in *Hidden Scholars*, important scholars such as Ruth Benedict, Ruth Bunzel, and Laura Thompson; instead, we have chosen those women who were not adequately honored in that work and who made tremendous contributions. We selected individuals who represent the range of anthropological responses to evolutionary paradigms and to the Turnerian thesis, which justified Manifest Destiny and the idea that Indians would either assimilate or perish. The women we chose all consciously rejected these ideas and instead spent their lives publishing about a wealth of strong tribal cultures and societies and demonstrating that the Native peoples of the West—especially of the Southwest, to which most of the anthropologists were drawn—were strong and dynamic. Rather than being disappearing peoples, they were peoples who had been hurt by their loss of Native lands in exchange for reservations and the inequitable political and economic system, which the U.S. government imposed on them through Indian Service policies. Knowledge of these facts, these women believed, could assist American Indians, who, despite the ongoing assaults on their lands, their resources, and their cultures, still struggled to retain their Native identities and to achieve greater self-determination.

We have also chosen women who consciously worked at disciplinary intersections as well as those who promoted more holistic studies of American Indian nations by combining multiple perspectives. This was especially true among those whose lives paralleled those of the historians in this volume. As a result, these women helped found new disciplines and new subfields. Marjorie Lambert assisted in establishing public archaeology, historic archaeology, and ethnohistory. Dorothea Leighton contributed to medical anthropology, public health, and public policy. Ruth Underhill played an important role in the creation of ethnohistory. Isabel Kelly helped to establish ethnographic archaeology and contributed to medical anthropology, community anthropology, public health, and applied anthropology. Among these women, some also utilized new forms of writing for multiple audiences. Alice Marriott and Ruth Underhill, especially, sought to reach the general public, and their success marginalized them from academia but ensured that they are still better known by a popular audience than by more "successful" male academicians. By reaching and educating the general public about who American Indians were and why they wished to retain elements of their Native cultures even as they adapted to the changes wrought by modern life, these women helped Americans understand the Native quest for greater self-determination.

All the women of this volume were dedicated to improving the lives of the peoples with whom they worked. Many developed new research methodologies and ethical standards that today are models for contemporary scholars who work with all indigenous peoples in multicultural and multisocietial/multiethnic complex societies.

Two of our choices were American Indian women and thus deserve special attention. As a cultural anthropologist and linguist working with her own people, Dakota Ella Cara Deloria developed skills that Native scholars utilize today and which have overcome many of the distancing assumptions and methods that "objective" outsiders often brought to their ethnography earlier in the twentieth century. The other is Yankton Dakota Gertrude Simmons Bonnin, known by her assumed name, Zitkala-Ša. Bonnin's writings cross the disciplines and include autobiography, American Indian folklore and legends, political and social tracts and essays, short stories, and historical investigations with groups such as the General Federation of Women's Clubs. What makes her especially important in the context of this volume is that she lived through the shifting and often abhorrent changes in attitudes and policies toward American Indians in the first four decades of the twentieth century. Thus her work represents a constant attempt to retain for her people those traditions and values that would benefit them the most. Simultaneously, she strove to identify those elements of white society that would prove most useful for American Indian advancement. Above all, she called on the U.S. government to grant American Indians justice and citizenship.

In our own ongoing effort to give these intellectual foremothers the credit they so fully deserve, we asked nine other scholars to contribute to this volume. Suzanne Julin's special interest in Annie Abel grew out of her undergraduate studies at the University of South Dakota and her later graduate studies at Washington State University, where Abel's papers are archived. John R. Wunder, as past president of the Mari Sandoz Heritage Society, brought his deep understanding of this important historian to this volume. Catherine S. Fowler and Robert Van Kemper have long followed Isabel T. Kelly's career and knew her personally. Fowler published with Kelly, and Kemper oversees the Isabel T. Kelly Ethnographic Archive at the DeGolyer Library, Southern Methodist University.[76] Shelby Tisdale has long researched Marjorie F. Lambert and is working on her biography of this pioneer, who died shortly before this volume went to press. Patricia Loughlin provided the chapter on Alice Marriott, one of the three figures whom she covered recently in her acclaimed work on women intellectuals from Oklahoma.[77] Maria Eugenia Cotera, whom we first encountered after discovering her masterful dissertation dealing with Ella Deloria and Jovita González and who has published important essays on these women, agreed to provide her keenly insightful essay on Ella Deloria.[78] Franci Washburn, herself a Native scholar, took on the challenge of examining Zitkala-Ša in the context of her time, thereby bringing to bear new insights on this important activist and writer. Catherine J. Lavender, coauthor of the essay on Ruth M. Underhill, studied Columbia University–trained women anthropologists of the American Southwest, including Underhill, and this research led to her most recent publication, *Scientists and Storytellers: Feminist Anthropologists and the Construction of the American*

Southwest, another strong contribution to efforts to recover the intellectual history of women who wrote on the American West.[79] Shirley A. Leckie, author of the chapter on Angie Debo, wrote a biography of the Oklahoma historian.[80] Nancy J. Parezo, author of the chapter on Dorothea Leighton and coauthor of the chapter on Underhill, has pioneered in recovering the intellectual history of women anthropologists.[81] In this volume she manages the intricate task of placing two women anthropologists in the context of their achievements—Leighton, who introduced a new sense of ethics in applied anthropology, one that is emic, meaning that it answers the needs of the Native peoples studied based on their own value system and worldview; and Underhill, who did so much to establish ethnohistory and who remains important to many peoples of the American Southwest, but most especially to the Tohono O'odham people of that region.

We asked all of the contributors to assess their subjects' methods and insights so that the heritage of these women can become more fully a part of the provenance of their respective disciplines. In that light, let us now introduce you to these pioneering scholars in history and anthropology who helped to pave the way for ethnohistory.

Notes

1. Brigitte Georgi-Findlay, *The Frontiers of Women's Writing: Women's Narratives and the Rhetoric of Westward Expansion* (Tucson: University of Arizona Press, 1996), ix. In this essay we examine the experience of historians more than anthropologists, since much of the contextualizing information for anthropology appears in Nancy J. Parezo, ed., *Hidden Scholars: Women Anthropologists and the Native American Southwest* (Albuquerque: University of New Mexico Press, 1993).

2. Susan Armitage, "Through Women's Eyes: A New View of the West," in *The Women's West*, ed. and introd. Susan Armitage and Elizabeth Jameson (Norman: University of Oklahoma Press, 1987), 3, 13. Dee Brown in 1958 published *The Gentle Tamers: Women of the Old Wild West* (New York: Putnam, 1958), a study that focused on famous western women such as army wife Elizabeth Custer and Martha Cannary, known as Calamity Jane.

3. See Nancy J. Parezo, "Stereotypes: Persistent Cultural Blindness," *Red*

Ink 9–10, nos. 1–2 (2001): 41–55; Philip J. Deloria, *Playing Indians* (New Haven: Yale University Press, 1998); Robert F. Berkhofer Jr., *The White Man's Indian: Images of the American Indian from Columbus to the Present* (New York: Knopf, 1978); Reyna Green, "The Pocahontas Perplex: The Image of Indian Women in American Culture," *Massachusetts Review* 16 (1975): 698–714; Reyna Green, "Review Essay: Native American Women," *SIGNS* 6 (1980): 248.

4. Richard W. Etulain, ed., *Writing Western History: Essays on Major Western Historians* (1991; reprinted with an introduction by Glenda Riley, Reno: University of Nevada Press, 2002); Gerald D. Nash, *Creating the West: Historical Interpretations, 1890–1990* (Albuquerque: University of New Mexico Press, 1991), 112.

5. R. David Edmunds, "Native Americas, New Voices: American Indian History, 1895–1995," *American Historical Review* 100, no. 3 (1995): 717–40, here referring to 721–23. Edmunds characterizes Debo's studies on the Choctaws and Creeks and *And Still the Waters Run* as "the standard works" on these topics. He praises Sandoz's inclusion of Native voices and testimony and the "literary" quality of *Crazy Horse: The Strange Man of the Oglalas* and *Cheyenne Autumn*. He lauds Young for "Indian Removal and Land Allotment: Land Allotment and Jacksonian Justice," *American Historical Review* 64 (October 1958): 31–45. Edmunds's list of post-1960s writers contains mention of few women compared to men. In footnotes and main text Edmunds lists twenty-four female historians and seven female anthropologist-ethnohistorians; many wrote about women and education, i.e., women's topics, and much of their work is cited for the 1990s. In contrast, the work of over 135 men is cited.

6. Henry Nash Smith, *The Virgin Land: The American West as Symbol and Myth* (New York: Vintage Books, 1950). Female writers are analyzed briefly in the chapter on the agricultural frontier.

7. Frederick Jackson Turner, "The Significance of the Frontier in American History," in *Frontier and Section: Selected Essays of Frederick Jackson Turner*, introduction and notes by Ray Allen Billington (Englewood Cliffs NJ: Prentice-Hall, 1961), 37–62. For textbooks, see Frederick Paxson, *History of the American Frontier, 1763–1893* (1924); Ray Allen Billington, *Westward Expansion: A History of the American Frontier* (1949); Thomas D. Clark, *Frontier America: The Story of Westward Movement* (1959). Turner never lacked critics. Walter Prescott Webb, in *The Great Plains* (1931), emphasized the West as a place west of the ninety-eighth parallel where Euro-Americans had to invent new tools and revise laws

and practices to live in a semiarid environment. New Western historian Donald Worster continues that tradition today in *Dust Bowl: The Southern Plains in the 1930s* (New York: Oxford University Press, 1979) and, more recently, *A River Running West: The Life of John Wesley Powell* (New York: Oxford University Press, 2001). Turner moved beyond his famous thesis and in 1935 published his Pulitzer Prize–winning *The United States, 1830–1850: The Nation and Its Sections* (New York: Henry Holt, 1935). However, as William Cronon, George Miles, and Jay Gitlin note, Turner bequeathed historians a powerful narrative in his account of "the colonization of the Great West," which the three authors see as "the pivotal event in American history." "Becoming West: Toward a New Meaning for Western History," in *Under an Open Sky: Rethinking America's Western Past*, ed. William Cronon, George Miles, and Jay Gitlin (New York: Norton, 1992), 6–7. Today the term "colonization" denotes imperialism, but Turner in his frontier thesis saw the process of Euro-American entry into new lands as progress. In 1890 settlements had broken into the "free land" in all counties, and Turner saw the frontier as gone and the United States now lacking its former safety valve. Finally, the Turner narrative of various frontiers remains so compelling that many teachers, although critical of his thesis, still use his frontier thesis narrative to structure courses.

8. For Turner's views on American Indians see David Nichols, "'Civilization over Savage': Frederick Jackson Turner and the Indian," *South Dakota History* 2 (Fall 1972): 383–405. The late Martin Ridge collaborated with Ray Billington to update *Westward Expansion* (see note 7 above). Ridge edited and abridged the sixth edition, published by the University of New Mexico Press in 2001. Despite his scholarly updating, Ridge retained the chapter on the Indian Wars as "The Indian Barrier." One noted male historian—the exception that proves the rule—did see American Indians as more than foils in a story of Euro-American expansion. Herbert Bolton, dedicated to studying the Spanish borderlands to turn attention to the impact of the Spanish Empire and its aftermath on the formation of the United States, in pioneering fashion collaborated with the Bureau of Indian Affairs anthropologists Frederick Hodges and John Swanton and incorporated American Indian views and voices into his works. See Edmunds, "Native Americas, New Voices," 720.

9. For examples of this paradigm see W J McGee, "Piratical Acculturation," *American Anthropologist* (o.s.), 11, no. 2 (1898): 243–60; W J McGee, "The Trend of Human Progress," *American Anthropologist* 1, no. 4 (1899): 401–47; Lewis

Henry Morgan, *Ancient Society, or Researches in the Lines of Human Progress from Savagery through Barbarism to Civilization* (New York: Henry Holt, 1877); and for an analysis see Curtis M. Hinsley Jr., *Savages and Scientists: The Smithsonian Institution and the Development of American Anthropology, 1846–1906* (Washington DC: Smithsonian Institution Press, 1981); George W. Stocking Jr., *Race, Culture, and Evolution: Essays in the History of Anthropology* (New York: Free Press, 1968); and Don D. Fowler, *A Laboratory of Anthropology: Science and Romanticism in the American Southwest, 1846–1930* (Albuquerque: University of New Mexico Press, 2000).

10. Edward B. Tylor, "How the Problems of American Anthropology Present Themselves to the English Mind," *Science* 4 (1884): 545–51, quote on 550.

11. See Parezo, *Hidden Scholars*, 5–7; Evelyn Fox Keller, *Reflections on Gender and Science* (New Haven: Yale University Press, 1985); Sally Kohlstedt, *The Formation of the American Scientific Community: The American Association for the Advancement of Science, 1848–1860* (Champagne: University of Illinois Press, 1976); Rosalind Rosenberg, *Beyond Separate Spheres: Intellectual Roots of Modern Feminism* (New Haven: Yale University Press, 1982); Margaret W. Rossiter, *Women Scientists in America*, vol. 1, *Struggle and Strategies to 1940* (Baltimore: Johns Hopkins University Press, 1982); H. Silverberg, *Gender and American Social Science: The Formative Years* (Princeton: Princeton University Press, 1998).

12. "The Organization and the Constitution of the Women's Anthropological Society, Washington DC, 1885," Matilda Coxe Stevenson Papers, Series 21, National Anthropological Archives, Smithsonian Institution. See also Nancy J. Parezo, "Anthropology: The Welcoming Science," in Parezo, *Hidden Scholars*, 3–37; Nancy J. Parezo, "Matilda Coxe Stevenson: Pioneer Ethnologist," in Parezo, *Hidden Scholars*, 38–62; Joy Elizabeth Rhode, "It Was No 'Pink Tea': Gender and American Anthropology, 1885–1903," in *Significant Others: Interpersonal and Professional Commitments in Anthropology*, ed. Richard Handler (Madison: University of Wisconsin Press, 2004), 261–90.

13. Matilda Coxe Stevenson, "Zuñi Ancestral Gods and Masks," *American Anthropologist* (o.s.), 11, no. 2 (1898): 33–40; Alice Fletcher, "A Pawnee Ritual Used When Changing a Man's Name," *American Anthropologist*, n.s., 1, no. 1 (1899): 82–97. Another change noted at this time was that women's books began to be reviewed. Earlier their activities had been described in the journal's notes section, even though women were not allowed to be members of the association. While

women's contributions were never as numerous as men's, many of their papers were published, especially in ethnography, linguistics, and folklore, less often in archaeology and physical anthropology. Unfortunately but not unexpectedly, the studies on the history of anthropology have ignored this fact. See A. Irving Hallowell, "The Beginnings of Anthropology in America," in *Selected Papers from the American Anthropologist, 1888–1920*, ed. Frederica de Laguna (Washington DC: American Anthropological Association, 1960), 1–90.

14. Parezo, "Anthropology the Welcoming Science."

15. T. A. Larson, "Women's Role in the American West," *Montana: The Magazine of Western History* 24 (Summer 1974): 4–5. Ironically, this designation by kin relation without using someone's special name is very common among American Indians for both men and women.

16. Annette Kolodny, *The Land Before Her: Fantasy and Experience on the American Frontier* (Chapel Hill: University of North Carolina Press, 1984). Army officers' wives on western posts often appraised lands newly opened to Euro-American settlement in terms of their economic potential. Sandra L. Myres, "Romance and Reality on the American Frontier: Views of Army Wives," *Western Historical Quarterly* 13 (October 1982): 407–27.

17. Georgi-Findlay, *Frontiers of Women's Writing*, 11–12.

18. See Mary Kelley, *Private Woman, Public Stage: Literary Domesticity in Nineteenth-Century America* (New York: Oxford University Press, 1984).

19. See, for example, Eliza Woodson Farnham, *Life in Prairie Land* (1846; reprint, New York: Arno Press, 1972), especially her comments on 237, 345; Teresa Vielé, *"Following the Drum": A Glimpse of Frontier Life* (1857; reprint, Lincoln: University of Nebraska Press, 1984); Elizabeth B. Custer, *"Boots and Saddles": or, Life in Dakota with General Custer* (New York: Harper and Brothers, 1885); Mary Clavers [Caroline M. Kirkland], *A New Home—Who'll Follow, or Glimpses of Western Life*, 5th ed. (Boston: J. H. Francis, 1855). See also JoAnn Levy, *Unsettling the West: Eliza Farnham and Georgiana Bruce Kirby in Frontier California* (Santa Clara CA: Santa Clara University, Heyday Books, 2004).

20. In *Women and Indians on the Frontier, 1825–1915* (Albuquerque: University of New Mexico Press, 1984), Glenda Riley demonstrates that when white women actually came in contact with American Indian women, initial fears often gave way to friendships based on their common maternal roles. Early female anthropologists quickly overcame these prejudices, although they still tended to use the tropes and scientific classificatory terminology of the day. In

their descriptive writings they used fewer negative classifiers and adjectives than male foundational anthropologists did.

21. See Elizabeth B. Custer, *Following the Guidon* (New York: Harper & Brothers, 1890), 58–62, in addition to her *"Boots and Saddles,"* 109, 196–97. See also Shirley A. Leckie, *Elizabeth Bacon Custer and the Making of a Myth* (Norman: University of Oklahoma Press, 1993), 236–55; and K. Tsianina Lomawaima, "American Indian Education: by Indians versus for Indians," in *A Companion to American Indian History*, ed. Philip J. Deloria and Neal Salisbury (Malden MA: Blackwell, 2002), 422–40.

22. Sara Winnemucca Hopkins, *Life among the Paiutes: Their Wrongs and Claims*, ed. Mrs. Horace Mann (1883; Reno: University of Nevada Press, 1994); Lydia Maria Child, *The First Settlers of New England* (Boston: Munroe and Francis, 1829); L. Maria Child, *An Appeal for the Indians* (New York: Wm. P. Tomlinson, 1868); Helen Hunt Jackson, *A Century of Dishonor: A Sketch of the Government's Dealing with Some of the Indian Tribes* (1881; Norman: University of Oklahoma Press, 1995).

23. Some of this remembering and contextualizing has already been done in *Hidden Scholars* for anthropologists who worked in the American Southwest. The same patterns hold for the rest of the American West, and we will not repeat them here.

24. Conversely, male and female anthropologists have always seen the American West as place and as the homelands of a diverse group of Native American peoples. Until after World War II they tried to pretend that Euro-Americans were not there in much of their ethnographic writing in their quest to gain understandings of uncontaminated—i.e., pure—cultures and societies. Anthropologists also made an early and lasting distinction between pure science and applied science, a distinction that affected whether one studied culture change. It was not until assimilation and acculturation became important topics in the 1930s that Americans became part of the research picture. History and anthropology had very different trajectories in this case.

25. Unfortunately, some New Indian historians think they are writing from *the* Indian point of view, overgeneralizing in their attempt to create a binary dichotomy of Indian versus European-based American society and ignoring critical cultural and historical diversity important to Native cultures.

26. American Indian studies departments grew out of anthropology departments and the frustration of 1960s Indian activists who felt that anthropolo-

gists only cared about a romanticized ethnographic present, not contemporary issues, and that they ignored political and legal aspects. See Duane Champagne and Joseph Stauss, *Native American Studies in Higher Education: Models for Collaboration between Universities and Indigenous Nations* (Walnut Creek CA: AltaMira, 2002).

27. Francis Jennings, "A Growing Partnership: Historians, Anthropologists, and American Indian History," *Ethnohistory* 29, no. 1 (1982): 21–34; James Axtell, "Ethnohistory: An Historian's Viewpoint," in *The European and the Indian: Essays in the Ethnohistory of Colonial North America*, ed. James Axtell (New York: Oxford University Press, 1981), 3–15; Edmunds, "Native America, New Voices," 725. It did take the efforts of the men and women who worked in this area to formalize the blended methods into a named interdisciplinary effort and to legitimize it in the academy. The American Society for Ethnohistory was founded from the efforts of Erminie Wheeler-Voegelin, who had worked on the Indian Claims Commission in 1954.

28. Robert Berkhofer, "The Political Context of a New Indian History," *Pacific Historical Review* 40, no. 2 (1971): 357–58.

29. Social Darwinism, developed by Herbert Spencer and others, consisted of common social theories held from the latter part of the nineteenth century until World War II. It applied Darwin's theory of evolution by natural selection of biological traits in a population to societies, races, ethnicities, and nation-states. Social Darwinists argued that because of "survival of the fittest," those who were dominant, such as Caucasians, WASPS (white, Anglo-Saxon Protestants), Teutonics, or "Aryans" (the latter actually a linguistic category), should rule as the strongest and fittest. For societies with inequities based on ethnicity or race, social Darwinism justified inequalities, racism, and imperialism. Eugenicists argued that "inferior" peoples should be discouraged from reproducing so that society could advance toward a higher civilization. Anthropological unilinear evolutionary models were diverse, and few American anthropologists even in the Victorian and Edwardian periods espoused eugenics or social Darwinism. Most anthropologists fought it, including the women highlighted in this book. Sadly, many recent scholars have misrepresented this fact in their quest to make anthropology into a megalithic and homogeneous discipline.

30. Boas began his career as a "salvage" anthropologist but around 1905 began realizing that Native peoples were not "disappearing." He had repudiated that stance entirely by 1920.

31. Patricia Nelson Limerick's second book was *The Legacy of Conquest: The Unbroken Past of the American West* (New York: Norton, 1987). In her third, *Something in the Soil: Legacies and Reckonings in the New West* (New York: Norton, 2001), she affirms her indebtedness to Angie Debo on pages 331–32.

32. See Richard White, *"It's Your Misfortune": A New History of the American West* (Norman: University of Oklahoma Press, 1991).

33. Parezo, "Conclusion: The Beginning of the Quest," in Parezo, *Hidden Scholars*, 344.

34. Sherry B. Ortner, "Is Female to Male as Nature Is to Culture?" in *Women, Culture and Society*, ed. Michelle Rosaldo and Louise Lamphere (Palo Alto: Stanford University Press, 1974), 67–87; Rosenberg, *Beyond Separate Spheres*; Natalie Curtis (Burlin), *The Indians' Book* (New York: Harper and Brothers, 1907).

35. Barbara A. Babcock, "'Not in the Absolute Singular': Rereading Ruth Benedict," in Parezo, *Hidden Scholars*, 107–29; Barbara A. Babcock and Nancy J. Parezo, *Daughters of the Desert: Women Anthropologists and the Native American Southwest, 1880–1980* (Tucson: University of Arizona Press, 1988).

36. John Collier, *Indians of the Americas: The Long Hope* (New York: New American Library, 1947), 7, 22–24.

37. Margaret D. Jacobs, in *Engendered Encounters: Feminism and Pueblo Culture, 1879–34* (Lincoln: University of Nebraska Press, 1999), sees both an earlier group of maternalistic or "uplift" feminists and a later group of "antimodern" feminists who idealized the Pueblo people as living in more authentic and egalitarian societies. Both had agendas. The first wanted to change the Pueblo people, and the second often wanted to keep them as they *wished* they were. More recently, Catherine S. Lavender, in *Scientists and Storytellers: Feminist Anthropologists and the Construction of the American Southwest* (Albuquerque: University of New Mexico Press, 2006), finds that the four feminists anthropologists she studies—Elsie Clews Parsons, Ruth Benedict, Gladys Reichard, and Ruth Underhill—published works that at times presented the Pueblo women they studied differently from the women who emerge in their field notes.

38. Theda Perdue sees complementary gender roles among the Cherokees until men's involvement in the fur trade and the market revolution changed the status of women and men. See *Cherokee Women: Gender and Culture Change, 1700 to 1835* (Lincoln: University of Nebraska Press, 1997). For women as anthropologists see T. Thorensen, "Paying the Piper and Calling the Tune: The

Beginnings of Academic Anthropology in California," *Journal of the History of the Behavioral Sciences* 11 (1975): 257–75; and Alfred Tozzer, "Zelia Nuttall," *American Anthropologist* 35 (1933): 475–82. For information on foundational women anthropologists see Ute Gacs, Aisha Khan, Jerrie McIntyre, and Ruth Weinberg, eds., *Women Anthropologists: A Biographical Dictionary* (New York: Greenwood Press, 1988).

39. William B. Hesseltine and Louis Kaplan, "Doctors of Philosophy of History: A Statistical Study," *American Historical Review* 47 (July 1942): 765–800.

40. Samuel Haber, *The Quest for Authority and Honor in American Professions, 1750–1900* (Chicago: University of Chicago Press, 1991).

41. See Daniel G. Brinton, "The Character and Aims of Scientific Investigation," *Science*, n.s., 1 (1895): 3–4; Daniel G. Brinton, "The Nomenclature and Teaching of Anthropology," *American Anthropologist* 5 (1892): 263–71; Regna Darnell, "The Emergence of Academic Anthropology at the University of Pennsylvania," *Journal of the History of the Behavioral Sciences* 6 (1970): 80–92; Regna Darnell, "The Professionalization of American Anthropology: A Case Study in the Sociology of Knowledge," *Social Science Information* 19, no. 2 (1971): 83–103; Frank Russell, "Know, Then, Thyself," *Journal of American Folklore* 15 (June 1902): 1–13.

42. Robyn Muncy, *Creating a Female Dominion in American Reform, 1890–1935* (New York: Oxford University Press, 1991), xiii.

43. Ellen Swallow Richards, teaching chemistry at the Massachusetts Institute of Technology, developed Sanitary Science, which combined chemistry, nutrition, sanitation, and sociology, to enable women to tackle the problems of family life in an increasingly urbanized and industrialized America. Eventually it became home economics, a less sociological and more family-oriented field. See Rossiter, *Women Scientists in America: Struggles and Strategies to 1940*, 68–70; and Ellen Fitzpatrick, *Endless Crusade: Women Social Scientists and Progressive Reform* (New York: Oxford University Press, 1990), 15, 31–32.

44. Patricia A. Graham, "Expansion and Exclusion: A History of Women in American Higher Education," *SIGNS* 3 (Summer 1978): 762–63; Rossiter, *Women Scientists in America: Struggles and Strategies to 1940*, 15–25; Barbara J. Harris, *Beyond Her Sphere: Women and the Professions in American History* (Westport CT: Greenwood Press, 1978), 115–21.

45. Martha Carey Thomas, *The Making of a Feminist: Early Journals and Letters of M. Carey Thomas* (Kent OH: Kent State University Press, 1980). Thomas

obtained an education, despite the disasters Edward H. Clarke had predicted in *Sex in Education: Or, a Fair Chance for Girls* (Boston: J. R. Osgood, 1874).

46. Nancy F. Cott, *The Grounding of Modern Feminism* (New Haven: Yale University Press, 1987), 179–211.

47. Cott, *The Grounding of Modern Feminism*, 179–211.

48. Barbara Miller Solomon, *In the Company of Educated Women: A History of Women and Higher Education in America* (New Haven: Yale University Press), 133; Rossiter, *Women Scientists in America: Struggles and Strategies to 1940*, 15–28.

49. Solomon, *In the Company of Educated Women*, 133. Rossiter notes that even when women constituted a third of the professors, at women's colleges they were busy planning curricula, but with minimally equipped laboratories and underdeveloped libraries, they had little time for research. Largely excluded from doctoral programs, many realized that without PhDs they could not go elsewhere. Rossiter, *Women Scientists in America: Struggles and Strategies to 1940*, 175–80.

50. C. H. Handschin, "The Percentage of Women Teachers in State Colleges and Universities," *Science*, January 12, 1912, 55–57.

51. Rossiter, *Women Scientists in America: Struggles and Strategies to 1940*, 45–46.

52. Bonnie Smith, *The Gender of History: Men, Women, and Historical Practice* (Cambridge: Harvard University Press, 1998), 59, 103–56. On the added scrutiny women's research received, see Joan Abramson, *The Invisible Woman: Discrimination in the Academic Profession* (San Francisco: Jossey-Bass, 1975); Jonathan R. Cole, *Fair Science: Women in the Scientific Community* (New York: Free Press, 1979); and "A Two-Tier Faculty System Reflects Old Social Rules That Restrict Women's Professional Development," *Chronicle of Higher Education*, October 26, 1988, A56. Women also get acknowledged less often. See Eyal Ben-Ari, "On Acknowledgements in Ethnographies," *Journal of Anthropological Research* 43, no. 1 (1987): 63–84; Marianne Ferber, "Citations: Are They an Objective Measure of Scholarly Merit?" *SIGNS* 11 (1986): 381–89; and Catherine Lutz, "The Erasure of Women's Writing in Sociocultural Anthropology," *American Ethnologist* 17, no. 4 (1990): 611–27. For the ideal of historical objectivity, see Peter Novick, *That Noble Dream: The "Objectivity Question" and the American Historical Profession* (Cambridge: Cambridge University Press, 1988).

53. B. Smith, *The Gender of History*, 2–3, 116–29; Elizabeth Seymour Esch-

bach, *The Higher Education of Women in England and America, 1865–1920* (New York: Garland, 1993), 189–90. Eschbach notes that one reason for creating the American Collegiate Association in 1882 (now the American Association of University Women) was to press for women's entry into graduate schools and raise money for their fellowships.

54. Judith P. Zinsser, *History and Feminism: A Glass Half Full* (New York: Twayne, 1993), 6–9.

55. E. E. Dale, "Woman's Influence on the French Revolution," unpublished paper from the seminar with Frederick Jackson Turner, "History of the West," fall 1913 through spring 1914, Edward Everett Dale Collection, Western History Collection, University of Oklahoma, Norman.

56. Alan G. Bogue, *Frederick Jackson Turner: Strange Roads Going Down* (Norman: University of Oklahoma Press, 1997), 237. Turner taught at Wisconsin before moving to Harvard.

57. Bogue, *Frederick Jackson Turner,* 123, 236.

58. The State Historical Society of Wisconsin published both *The French Regime* and *The British Regime.* An excellent overview of Kellogg's career and contributions is Dwight L. Smith, "Louise Phelps Kellogg," in *Historians of the American Frontier: A Bio-Bibliographical Sourcebook,* ed. John R. Wunder (New York: Greenwood Press, 1988), 351–73.

59. Although Kellogg understood the importance of Indian-Indian relations, her viewpoint remained centered on administrations in Europe and the colonies they governed. Julie Des Jardins observes that Kellogg was also among those historians who campaigned to advance women in academe, while strategically pursuing male topics exclusively. See *Women and the Historical Enterprise in America: Gender, Race, and the Politics of Memory, 1880–1945* (Chapel Hill: University of North Carolina Press, 2003), 58, 102.

60. In 1930 married women were 11.7 percent of the female labor force; by 1940 their total percentage had risen to 15.2 percent. William C. Chafe, *The Paradox of Change: American Women in the 20th Century* (New York: Oxford University Press, 1991), 68–69; Alice Kessler-Harris, *Out to Work: A History of Wage-Earning Women in the United States* (New York: Oxford University Press, 1982), 258–72, and *In Pursuit of Equity: Women, Men, and the Quest for Economic Citizenship in Twentieth-Century America* (New York: Oxford University Press, 2001), 59–61.

61. Martha H. Swain, *Ellen S. Woodward: New Deal Advocate for Women* (Jackson: University Press of Mississippi, 1995).

62. Margaret Mead quoted in Jane Howard, *Margaret Mead: A Life* (New York: Simon and Schuster, 1984); Bertha Dutton, interview for the Daughters of the Desert Project under the direction of Barbara A. Babcock and Nancy J. Parezo, papers archived at the Wenner-Gren Foundation for Anthropological Research, 1985. For an analysis of women working in museums see Nancy J. Parezo and Margaret A. Hardin, "In the Realm of the Muses," in Parezo, *Hidden Scholars*, 270–93.

63. Kessler-Harris, *Out to Work*, 278.

64. Shirley A. Leckie, *Angie Debo, Pioneering Historian* (Norman: University of Oklahoma Press, 2000), 93–94.

65. Margaret Rossiter, *Women Scientists in America: Before Affirmative Action, 1940–1972* (Baltimore: Johns Hopkins University Press, 1995), 9–10.

66. Rossiter, *Women Scientists in America: Before Affirmative Action*, 4.

67. Chafe, *Paradox of Change*, 154–62.

68. Marynia Farnham and Ferdinand Lundberg, *Modern Woman: The Lost Sex* (New York: Harper & Brothers, 1947).

69. Chafe, *Paradox of Change*, 163.

70. Association of American Colleges and Universities, "Diversifying the Faculty," Diversity Web: An Interactive Resource Hub for Higher Education, Association of American Colleges and Universities, http://www.diversityweb .org/ diversity_innovations/faculty_staff (accessed June 14, 2005).

71. William B. Hesseltine and Louis Kaplan, "Women Doctors of Philosophy in History," *Journal of Higher Education* 14 (May 1943): 254–59. These authors never noted that male historians usually had wives who performed all domestic labor, thus relieving them of such tasks.

72. American Historical Association, "Report of the American Historical Association Committee on the Status of Women, Part Three: Summary of Findings" (1970), commonly referred to as the Rose Committee Report, http:// www.historians.org/pubs/archives/Rosereport/ partthree.html (accessed June 11, 2005). The American Anthropological Association and the Society for American Archaeology conducted similar surveys for anthropology with similar result, although the percentage of female practitioners was higher.

73. Rose Committee Report.

74. Julie Roy Jeffrey's *Frontier Women: The Trans-Mississippi West, 1840–1880* (New York: Hill & Wang, 1979) marked the beginning of a prodigious outpouring of works away from the male-centered western history. Other important

early works include John Mack Faragher, *Women and Men on the Overland Trail* (New Haven: Yale University Press, 1980); and Joan Jensen and Darlis Miller, "Gentle Tamers Revisited: New Approaches to the History of Women in the American West," *Pacific Historical Review* 49, no. 2 (1980): 173–213. The last has inspired pathbreaking articles and books that examine gender in the American West. See *Women and Gender in the American West: Jensen-Miller Prize Essays from the Coalition for Western Women's History*, ed. Mary Ann Irwin and James F. Brooks (Albuquerque: University of New Mexico Press, 2004). See also the essays in *Writing the Range: Race, Class, and Culture in the Women's West*, ed. Elizabeth Jameson and Susan Armitage (Norman: University of Oklahoma Press, 1997).

75. The editors of this volume agree with R. David Edmunds, who "prefer[s] this term since all Native American People are civilized, within the parameters of their own cultures." "Native America, New Voices," 722 n. 8. For Abel's pathbreaking insights into the Five Southern Tribes as peoples who were acting as agents instead of foils on the stage of history, see Theda Perdue and Michael D. Green's introduction to Annie Heloise Abel, *The American Indian as Slaveholder and Secessionist* (Lincoln: University of Nebraska Press, 1992).

76. See Isabel T. Kelly and Catherine S. Fowler, "Southern Paiute," in *Handbook of North American Indians*, vol. 11, *Great Basin*, ed. Warren d'Azevedo (Washington DC: Smithsonian Institution, 1986), 368–97.

77. Patricia Loughlin, *Hidden Treasures of the American West: Muriel H. Wright, Angie Debo, and Alice Marriott* (Albuquerque: University of New Mexico Press, 2005).

78. See especially Maria Eugenia Cotera, "'All My Relatives Are Noble': Recovering the Feminine in *Waterlily*," *American Indian Quarterly* 28 (Fall 2004): 52–72.

79. Lavender, *Scientists and Storytellers*.

80. Leckie, *Angie Debo*.

81. See Babcock and Parezo, *Daughters of the Desert*; Parezo, *Hidden Scholars*.

I

ANNIE HELOISE ABEL

Groundbreaking Historian

Suzanne Julin

AFTER ANNIE HELOISE ABEL died in 1947, one of her sisters, Rose Abel Wright, wrote to one of Abel's colleagues that Annie "was in the truest sense of the word, a research student."[1] Indeed, Abel's career and publications are most often associated with her tenacious research methods and her nearly obsessive attention to detail and documentation; her work as a researcher overshadows her years in academia. Abel's publications about American Indians and Indian policy during the Civil War era and her edited editions of the journals of fur traders and explorers broke new ground in the topics they addressed and provided new primary sources to other scholars and the public. They continue to stand as important contributions to the history of the American West and its Native peoples.

Born in Fernhurst, Sussex, England, on February 18, 1873, Annie Heloise Abel spent her childhood in England and her adolescence and adult life in the United States. Her parents, George and Amelia Anne (Hogben) Abel, immigrated to Kansas in 1871 but became disillusioned and returned to England before the birth of Annie, their third child and first daughter. The couple had four more children before returning to Kansas in 1884, where George Abel began work as a gardener. Annie remained in England for a year after her parents' departure, then joined her family in the United States in 1885.[2]

After graduating from high school in 1893 and teaching at the high school level for two years, Abel attended the University of Kansas, receiving her bachelor's degree in 1898. Two years later she earned her master's, after defending her thesis, "Indian Reservations in Kansas and the Extinguishment of Their Title." Abel's interest in American Indians began as a child in England, when she read her brothers' books about adventures on the American frontier. That interest deepened when her thesis director, Frank Heywood Hodder, gave her an assignment that introduced her to the study of U.S. policy toward the country's Native peoples and stimulated the studies she would continue throughout her career. Deeply impressed by Abel's talents as a historian, Hodder encouraged her to pursue a doctorate at Cornell University, and Abel studied there for a year. Apparently constrained by a lack of funds, she returned to Kansas and taught high school in Lawrence for two years while taking additional history courses at the University of Kansas.[3]

Abel's fortunes changed when she won a Bulkley Fellowship in 1905. The prize made possible her full-time study at Yale University under Edward Gaylord Bourne. The attention she received as the first woman to receive this award, however, colored her attitude about publicity and about her position as a woman scholar. In particular, she was irritated by a newspaper article about her winning the Bulkley that referred to her as a "coed."[4] The thirty-year-old Abel, with a reputation as a gifted student and years of financial struggle behind her, hardly considered herself a coed. Further, she resented the implication that her achievement was some sort of aberration. Decades later, she wrote to a colleague, "I have had ever since an extreme aversion to the sight of my name in a newspaper."[5]

Abel's accomplishments as a doctoral student confirmed her abilities. She earned a doctorate in 1905. Her dissertation, "The History of Events Resulting in Indian Consolidation West of the Mississippi," based on research in the Indian Office and congressional records, won the American Historical Association's Justin Winsor Prize in 1906 and was published that year in the association's *Annual Report*.[6]

After accepting the award at the American Historical Association's 1906 meeting, Abel visited a seriously ill Edward Gaylord Bourne. Delighted that his student had won the Winsor Prize—it was the first time the award had come to a Yale student since its inception in 1896—Bourne urged her to continue her studies in Indian policy. In particular, he encouraged her to investigate the treatment of American Indians in California under the mission system. The pertinent records, held by the Indian Office, had never been perused by a researcher. For the next several months, while teaching at Wells College and then at Women's College of Baltimore (later Goucher College), Abel spent two days a week studying the Indian Office records. She took copious notes and sometimes copied entire documents in longhand. Under her supervision, her youngest sister typed and organized the notes.[7]

The project furthered Abel's experience in working with Indian Office documents but never resulted in publication. The distance between the East Coast and California interfered with further research that might have expanded upon her work in the records. In addition, she failed to interest a publisher in the topic, except on terms she could not accept. The Bureau of American Ethnology considered publishing her transcripts, but Abel refused permission because the bureau planned to omit all references to politics. "After all," she later noted, "my interest was historical rather than ethnological."[8] Abel's interest in the topic centered on the application of government policy, and it was that knowledge she wanted to present.

The academic career Abel launched while conducting this research continued almost uninterrupted for nearly two decades. She taught as an instructor at Wells College in 1905 and a year later accepted the position as instructor at Women's College of Baltimore. She was promoted to associate professor in 1908 and to professor and head of the history department in 1914. She also taught English history at Johns Hopkins University Teachers College from 1910 to 1915. In 1915 she became an associate professor at Smith College, reaching the rank of professor before leaving in 1922.[9]

While serving as chairman of the Honors Committee at Smith College, Abel corresponded at length with faculty in other institutions, inquiring in detail about their own programs. The letters attest to her dedication and also reveal glimpses of the personal and collegial relationships she maintained with her peers. She shared her concern over her grueling work schedule with one of her woman colleagues and made tentative Christmas vacation plans with another. She discussed with a professor at Yale her interest in studying Ireland and self-determination; he encouraged her and offered to read the manuscript she was planning. Another man with whom she consulted gave her news of a mutual friend who had been passed over for a temporary position at Wells.[10] The responses she received to her letters, both professional and personal, point to a circle of friendships upon which she could depend.

During this period, Abel established a substantial publishing record based on significant archival research. The first two volumes of her trilogy, *The Slaveholding Indians*, appeared during these years: *The American Indian as Slaveholder and Secessionist: An Omitted Chapter in the Diplomatic History of the Southern Confederacy* (1915) and *The American Indian as Participant in the Civil War* (1919). Under an appointment as the Indian bureau's historian, she edited *The Official Correspondence of James S. Calhoun while Indian Agent at Santa Fe and Superintendent of Indian Affairs in New Mexico* (1915) and *A Report from Natchitoches in 1807 by Dr. John Sibley* (1922). In addition, she published a number of articles in scholarly journals.[11] This body of work provides an overview of her early scholarship and the forms it took. Abel was inspired by the rich document sources she found at the Indian Office, and that agency would provide subjects for her work to the end of her career.

The trilogy, the final volume of which was published in 1925 as *The American Indian under Reconstruction*, was Abel's major contribution to the study of American Indians. Francis Paul Prucha judged it "the most complete and thoroughly documented study of these Indians" during the Civil War.[12] Drawing heavily on government records, Abel documented and analyzed the events of the period within the context of governmental actions. The work addresses Union and Confederate relations with the Five Southern Tribes (originally known as the Five Civilized Tribes)—the Creeks, Chickasaws, Choctaws, Cherokees, and Seminoles who had been relocated to west of the Mississippi from the Southeast under the Removal Act of 1830. The trilogy describes the development of diplomatic relations between the Confederacy and American Indians and the participation of the Indians in the conflict. In addition, it details the experiences of the Native peoples who remained loyal to the Union and became refugees as a result, and the negotiation of treaties with the tribes after the war. Abel brought to light this aspect of the Civil War and official policy toward the American Indians.

Abel also presented a new attitude toward Native Americans. In an era still dominated by the Turnerian school, which portrayed American Indians chiefly as temporary roadblocks to the inevitable progress of white society in America, her work sounds a different theme. She provides evidence that these groups made their own decisions about allying with the Confederacy or with the Union and about participating in the Civil War. In acknowledging and documenting the agency of Native peoples, as Theda Perdue and Michael P. Green point out in their introduction to reprints of the trilogy, and in her criticism of official policy toward American Indians, Abel broke new ground and presaged modern historians' treatments of marginalized populations.

Despite this independence of thought, however, Abel was a product of her time, as Perdue and Green also observe. Abel produced her work when the Dunning school predominated in its interpretation of post–Civil War studies. The works of William Dunning and his followers took for granted the inferiority of African Americans, and Abel's own language about American Indians is at times similarly ethnocentric.[13] For example, she states that "all Indians, no matter how high their type, have an aversion for work," and refers to "absence without leave" as the "chronic weakness of all Indian soldiers."[14] Yet her acknowledgment of the independent nature of their actions and her pointed criticism of U.S. policy toward them reveal a more balanced attitude.

Abel's other publications during this period—in particular, *The Official Correspondence of James S. Calhoun* (1915) and John A. Sibley's *A Report from Natchitoches* (1922)—reflect her penchant for archival research and predict the nature of her post-academic scholarship. A dogged researcher, Abel increasingly concentrated on single documents or collections of documents, which she annotated fully—sometimes obsessively. In this she was partially a product of her time. As Perdue and Green also note, historians of the early twentieth century saw their field as a social science, with successful research dependent on strong evidence.[15]

Even so, Abel's documentation and annotation often seem excessive; they provide readers with supporting and explanatory information but also overwhelm them by the sheer mass of data. In an unsigned review of *The American Indian as Slaveholder and Secessionist*, one writer stated, "letters and reports printed in foot-notes or appendices add little to the evidence before the reader and some appear absolutely trivial."[16] A reviewer of *Tabeau's Narrative*, an edited work published in 1939, told readers the volume contained more than five hundred footnotes and complained that "on occasions one becomes very impatient at having the smooth flow of a rather charming narrative impeded by so much editorial paraphernalia."[17]

For Abel that "paraphernalia" constituted an important element of her craft. In an undated draft of a book review, she expressed her philosophy about the "fundamental principles of historical criticism," illuminating her standards of scholarship. These she characterized as "the exhaustive use of original material, freedom from prejudice, clearness and precision of statement, accuracy, and, above all, honesty of citation."[18] Abel seemed to consider "honesty of citation" not only an issue of due credit but also a matter of comprehensive accounting of sources.

Some of Abel's peers saw her adherence to her "fundamental principles of historical criticism" as beyond excessive. In 1908, Francis F. Browne, editor of the *Dial*, responded to a book review Abel had submitted by pointing out that although she had concluded by saying the book was one of the most important to be published that year, her review was "too much a catalogue of defects" rather than a discussion of the book's significance.[19] On another occasion she wrote a fourteen-page critique of an article about the War of 1812 that appeared in *History Teacher's Magazine*.[20] After her death, one of her colleagues noted that as a book reviewer she habitually checked the footnotes "to trace to the original sources all statements of fact used by an author to form a conclusion."[21] Abel held others to the same extremely high standards she set for herself.

By the early 1920s her academic career was well under way and Abel had established an impressive publication record. When Smith College granted her a sabbatical in 1921 and 1922 she traveled to London, New Zealand, and Australia to conduct archival research related to her interest in comparing governmental policy toward aboriginal peoples. The sabbatical had far-reaching effects on her professional and personal life.[22]

At the University of Adelaide, Abel met George Cockburn Henderson. Born in 1870 in New South Wales to a coal miner and his wife, Henderson, one of nine children, had grown up in modest circumstances. Always intellectually curious, he—like Abel—obtained an education through dint of hard work and by earning scholarships and awards. Henderson graduated with a bachelor's from Oxford in 1898.[23] A friend characterized him as an emotional, unconventional man who was physically vigorous, intellectually engaged, and constitutionally cheerful. Henderson and the other Australians at Oxford, he remembered, "had sunshine in their veins."[24]

The sunshine in Henderson's veins soon receded into shadows. His final year at Oxford was marred by confusion about degree requirements; he believed he had been excused from a course, only to find that he was not eligible for the dispensation and had to complete the requirement after finishing his final exams. The issue caused him great anguish and affected his performance as a student. He graduated in 1898 and the next year married the daughter of a prominent Quaker family. They moved to Sydney, where Henderson taught temporarily at the university before returning to England as a lecturer for Oxford University's extension programs. In 1902 he took an appointment as professor at the University of Adelaide in English and modern history. His wife did not join him in Australia, and they divorced in 1911.[25]

A popular teacher, Henderson was devoted to his academic career, but that devotion took its toll. As the number of his students increased, so did the pressures upon him. By the early 1920s he was plagued with insomnia.[26] Then, as his biographer recalled, he faced "the second crisis of his personal life."[27] Late in 1921, a tall, brown-haired, energetic Annie Heloise Abel arrived in Adelaide with a letter of introduction from the principal librarian of New South Wales. Henderson assisted her in her research, and the two quickly formed a strong bond. In the summer of 1922, Abel returned briefly to the United States to resign her position at Smith. On October 27, a few months before her fiftieth birthday, she and Henderson married.[28]

The union was ill-fated. The couple established housekeeping in an isolated location that offered a beautiful view but few amenities, and visitors observed a serious scholar stirring laundry in a tub atop a wood stove. The acquisition of household help eased some of the pressures of domesticity but did not solve larger problems. Henderson's insomnia was by now chronic, and his moods became unstable; in June 1923 he was hospitalized for treatment. At his insistence, Abel returned to the United States. One of Henderson's brothers took him back to New

South Wales, and he submitted his resignation to the University of Adelaide.[29]

Abel apparently saw the separation as a temporary necessity rather than a break in their marriage bond. In 1925 the third volume of her trilogy, *The American Indian under Reconstruction*, was published, and the title page listed her as "Annie Heloise Abel, Ph.D." with "Mrs. George Cockburn Henderson" in parentheses underneath.[30] Abel took a post as acting professor of history at Sweet Briar College during the 1924–25 academic year, and then received the Alice Freeman Palmer Fellowship from the American Association for University Women for 1925–27. This award enabled her to study in England, where she continued to expand her research about British policies toward aborigines. The fellowship also allowed her to return to Australia, where she continued her studies and made a final attempt to reconcile with her husband.[31]

By the time she returned to the United States, Abel had accepted the end of her relationship with Henderson. In correspondence with an Australian friend, she wondered what to call herself now that her marriage had failed. The friend suggested she use Dr. (rather than Mrs.) followed by Abel-Henderson, suggesting that this title would help her maintain her position as a scholar. Wistfully, however, the friend commented, "of course it is as Mrs. Henderson that I learned to [know] and love you but you have bravely passed through the time and taken up life again." Reflecting on the confusion that Abel herself must have felt, she concluded, "I cannot understand it all but have the absolute confidence in you both doing all for the best."[32]

The end of the marriage closed a chapter for Abel; her professional life continued. In 1927, *A Side-light on Anglo-American Relations, 1839–1858*, edited by Abel and Frank J. Klingberg, was published. The volume was a collection of the correspondence of Lewis Tappan and other Americans with the British and Foreign Anti-Slavery Society. Abel had discovered some of the Tappan letters while researching British policy toward Native peoples. After she and Klingberg agreed to pursue the topic, she made a thorough search of the archives of the Anti-Slavery and Aborigines' Protection Society for other correspondence pertinent to their study. The letters, their editors concluded, illustrated common humanitarian interests between the two countries in the period before the Civil War.[33]

The publication illustrates Abel's talent for discovering and identifying documents and manuscript collections worthy of publication. It also represents her ability to forge relationships with male colleagues on her own terms. Abel had been encouraged in her career by Frank Heywood Hodder at Kansas, by Edward Gaylord Bourne at Yale, and by Howard Hamblin at the Indian Office, and she had received notable awards in a male-dominated field. One of the most prominent historians of the time recognized her abilities in a 1919 correspondence. In response to her apparent suggestion that he might review her forthcoming volume *The American Indian in the Civil War* Frederick Jackson Turner replied, "you do me too much honor in intimating that I have a proper competence to review it." Her work, Turner said, was "so thorough that a by-and-large historian of the West like myself can only admire it."[34] Her collaboration with Klingberg, who had received a research grant form the University of California for antislavery studies, confirms her strength of position. In the preface the editors refer to Klingberg twice as the "junior editor."[35] Abel's aversion to being publicized as a woman historian may have been countered by her success and by the assistance she had received from her male mentors, but the Klingberg collaboration indicates a determination to make her position clear.

Abel briefly continued her career in academia following her final trip to Australia. She took an appointment at the University of Kansas in the fall of 1928. After one semester, she left to pursue research in Canadian, northwestern, and midwestern archives, funded in part by a grant from the Social Science Research Council.[36]

Earlier, Abel had identified other areas of western history that led her eventually to two of her most important publications. Although her main interest remained official policy toward Native peoples, she had been intrigued when her contacts at the Indian Office led her to records of early-eighteenth-century fur traders and explorers. U.S. War Department records were moved to a new location in 1921, and in the process the collections of the department's Topographical Bureau yielded a wooden box containing papers of Joseph Nicollet, an early-nineteenth-century explorer and cartographer of the American Northwest. Howard Hamblin, with whom Abel had conducted research in the Indian Office, pointed her to manuscripts in Nicollet's papers that she found so fascinating and important that they consumed much of her time for nearly two decades.[37]

The first of these to see print, *Chardon's Journal at Fort Clark; Descriptive of Life on the Upper Missouri; of A Fur Trader's Experiences among the Mandans, Gros Ventres and Their Neighbors; of the Ravages of the Small-Pox Epidemic of 1837*, was both a fulfilling and a frustrating work for Abel. Uncertainty about how the document should be framed posed one problem; delays in publication became another. Abel saw a positive aspect to those delays, however: they created more time for her to conduct research, and that research enabled her to enrich the manuscript with her meticulous documentation. Finally published by the state of South Dakota's Department of History in 1932, the journal itself contains relatively short entries that, despite their brevity, present a defining picture of the upper Missouri during this pivotal period. Abel introduced the volume with thirty-two pages of historical background annotated by 260 footnotes and provided additional notes throughout the manuscript.[38]

Tabeau's Narrative of Loisel's Expedition to the Upper Missouri also began to emerge from the documents discovered in Nicollet's chest. Abel's sister, Rose Abel Wright, translated the manuscript from the French, and Abel took on the editing, completing the task in the early 1930s. The original manuscript was unsigned, and for a time its authorship remained a mystery. Rose Abel Wright believed the fur trader Pierre Antoine Tabeau was the writer, and Abel's investigations led her to agree. When a colleague identified a revised copy of the document carrying Tabeau's name on the title page, the sisters considered their judgment confirmed.[39] One of Abel's colleagues later noted, "in pursuit of this treasure, she revealed all of the patience, astuteness, and penetrating powers of deduction expected only of a Sherlock Holmes or G-man."[40] While Loisel's journal was essentially an accounting of day-to-day business, Tabeau's narrative discussed at much greater length the environments and societies he saw around him. In particular, he described the cultures of the tribes of the northern Great Plains as viewed through the lens of an outsider. Abel's annotations provide a comprehensive context, comparing Tabeau's observations with those of other explorers and traders.

Once again, the work faced delays in publication. Abel was determined that the edited narrative should be published together with the French text from which her sister had worked. Potential publishers did not agree, and the Great Depression further delayed publication. Finally, in 1939, the University of Oklahoma Press published *Tabeau's Narrative*, without the French version included, but with Abel's blessing. Several footnotes in the published work replicate the original French and compare the language of the original document with its revised version.[41]

By the time *Tabeau's Narrative* appeared, Abel was in her mid-sixties and considered herself retired. From about 1930 she made her home with Rose Abel Wright in Aberdeen, Washington. There she struggled through the problems with the publication of the Chardon and Tabeau journals and continued to study policies toward aboriginal peoples. She established a relationship with Washington State College in Pullman, located in eastern Washington, and began donating selected books and documents to the college's library system. Early in 1939 she sent the California transcripts she and her sister had produced three decades before and her own copies of the three volumes of *Slaveholding Indians*.[42]

Even as Abel reflected on a long career and began to divest herself of her papers and her library, she was asked to travel to New Zealand to evaluate a collection of private papers. She enthusiastically made plans to travel there in late summer of 1939 and remain for twelve months. The entreaties of friends and relatives concerned about the dangers of war convinced her to delay her departure until October, but the situation dismayed her.[43] "I am beginning to despair lest I never get across at all," she wrote to Eugene Holland, a colleague at Washington State.[44]

Indeed, the war ruined her plans to work in New Zealand, and when Holland suggested she conduct a seminar of her choosing for Washington State's history department, she responded with grateful enthusiasm. "What a wonderful surprise your letter contained!" she wrote. "Here I've been wondering and wondering how I can make this coming winter less of a disappointment than it at present promises to be." She urged that policy toward Native peoples be the seminar subject "if I am to be at my best," with emphasis upon either "treatment of aboriginal folk" or U.S. Indian policy "as a phase of the American Westward Movement."[45] Her ties to Washington State gave her an institutional affiliation she had not experienced since her days at Smith, two decades earlier.

During the war, Abel volunteered for British-American War Relief in Seattle, and in 1946 she was presented His Majesty's Medal for her service.[46] She also continued to give books and papers to Washington State. Late in 1946, her health failing, she wrote to Holland, by then president emeritus, "As soon as the weather permits I shall cross over to my wee study in a detached building and pack a few rare books for your Treasury." She added, "What wouldn't I give to be able to come to Pullman as in other days."[47] A few months later she notified Holland that she was leaving Washington State College the bulk of her manuscripts, notes, notebooks, and books, especially those pertaining to British Native policy and U.S. Indian affairs.[48]

The correspondence between Holland and Abel came to an end early in 1947. Rose Abel Wright read her sister the last letter she received from him, but Abel could not respond. After Abel died on March 14, 1947, Holland wrote that her colleagues at Washington State were "grieved that a beautiful spirit and superior mind should be lost to society."[49]

That spirit and mind had sustained Abel during a long career. Her pursuit of an advanced degree despite financial constraints reveals the determination that continued to drive her as teacher, researcher, and scholar. Her academic career lasted for nearly twenty years; perhaps she would have remained in academia had she not decided to marry. As Nancy Parezo points out in *Hidden Scholars: Women Anthropologists and the Native American Southwest*, the proportion of women teaching and serving as administrators in higher education grew dramatically during the 1920s, reaching 32 percent (although the vast majority were still congregated at the instructor ranks) at the end of the decade before beginning to decline.[50] Abel was well established at Smith in an era when opportunities for women were growing because of the continuing influence of the successful suffrage movement and before they began diminishing. Her personal choice to leave her position at Smith may have derailed a potentially lengthy career as a professor, since women held more senior positions at women's colleges.

Her turn to full-time research and writing, however, may have been as much a matter of interest as of expediency. Abel obviously was an independent and adventurous woman who enjoyed travel and traveled alone comfortably; she also relished the hunt for primary documents and supporting evidence. Neither her words nor her actions indicate she was disappointed with the turn her career had taken. As her sister said, Abel was at heart a "research student."

Abel left behind a legacy of groundbreaking scholarship, though it is sometimes hidden behind the minutiae of her documentation. Early in the twentieth century she discussed American Indians as human beings struggling to control their own destiny rather than as minor characters on a stage dominated by the march of white civilization. Abel was no apologist for national policy, nor did she see the spread of white settlement as a sign of progress. In a draft of a review of Angie Debo's *Rise and Fall of the Choctaw Republic*, Abel noted that by 1855 "and always thereafter" any plans for a permanent Native American state in the United States were secondary to the "needs either of Sectionalism or Capitalism. The vested interests of the white man[,] real or imaginary, were paramount first, last and always."[51] In a book review published shortly before her death, Abel wrote: "We should have less of local patriotism, less of hypocrisy and complacency and understand 'manifest destiny' for what it most certainly was, the American type of imperialism."[52] In these attitudes she anticipated a fresh perspective in western history.

In these attitudes Abel broke new ground. Although she saw herself primarily as a historian of governmental policy toward Native peoples; her works on the Five Southern Tribes during the Civil War highlighted the effects of policy decisions during the era. They also illuminated the American Indians as more than simply barriers to progress. Her blunt criticisms of the government's actions toward them anticipated a new history of the West that refuted the Turnerian mold. As her career turned more directly to archival research and editing of primary materials, Abel continued to employ her beliefs about the study of history. She uncovered these documents, clarified them, and put them in an objective context. The edited publications of the Chardon and Tabeau journals, in particular, provided scholars with a new body of historical and ethnological knowledge about the upper Missouri country in the early nineteenth century and advanced the study of that place and that time.

Annie Heloise Abel's contribution to western history remains significant and valuable; her stature as a woman scholar in a field dominated by men is inspiring. As student, teacher, writer, researcher, and editor, she proved herself capable of producing work that not only equaled but very often outshone that of her male colleagues; at the same time, she forged alliances with them that were important to her personally as well as professionally. Her aversion to publicity and her distaste for being identified as a "woman" historian notwithstanding, Abel became, and remains, an important figure in the study of the American West.

Notes

1. Wright to Eugene O. Holland, March 31, 1947, folder 1, box 1, Annie Abel-Henderson Papers, Manuscripts, Archives, and Special Collections, Washington State University, Pullman [hereafter AHP]. These papers are collected under Abel's post-marriage name, Annie Heloise Abel Henderson. Throughout this chapter she is referred to as Annie Heloise Abel, the name by which she is most commonly identified as a scholar.

2. Francis Paul Prucha, "Abel, Annie Heloise," in *Notable American Women, 1607–1950*, ed. Edward T. James, Janet Wilson James, and Paul S. Boyer, 3 vols. (Cambridge: Belknap Press of Harvard University Press, 1971), 1:4; John A. Garraty and Mark C. Carnes, eds., *American National Biography*, vol. 1 (New York: Oxford University Press, 1999), 35.

3. Harry Kelsey, "A Dedication to the Memory of Annie Heloise Abel-Henderson, 1873–1947," *Arizona and the West* 15 (Winter 1973): 1.

4. Kelsey, "A Dedication," 1.

5. Abel to Eugene O. Holland, April 12, 1939, folder 1, box 1, AHP.

6. Prucha, "Abel, Annie Heloise," 4; Kelsey, "A Dedication," 2; Garraty and Carnes, *American National Biography* 35.

7. Abel to Eugene O. Holland, January 31, 1939, folder 1, box 1, AHP; Kelsey, "A Dedication," 2.

8. Abel to Eugene O. Holland, January 31, 1939, folder 1, box 1, AHP.

9. Notebook, folder 1, box 1, AHP; Prucha, "Abel, Annie Heloise," 5.

10. Lucy E. [Trextor] to Abel, December 15, 1918, Frances Davenport to Abel, December 14, 1918, George B. Adams to Abel, February 8, 1919, and Robert W. Rogers to Abel, December 13, 1918, folder 3, box 1, AHP.

11. Prucha, "Abel, Annie Heloise," 5; Kelsey, "A Dedication," 2. Annie Heloise Abel, *The American Indian as Slaveholder and Secessionist: An Omitted Chapter in the Diplomatic History of the Southern Confederacy* (Cleveland: Arthur H. Clark, 1919), has been reprinted with an introduction by Theda Perdue and Michael D. Green as *The American Indian as Slaveholder and Secessionist* (Lincoln: University of Nebraska Press, 1992). Annie Heloise Abel, *The American Indian as Participant in the Civil War* (Cleveland: Arthur H. Clark, 1919), has been reprinted with an introduction by Perdue and Green as *The American Indian in the Civil War, 1862–1865* (Lincoln: University of Nebraska Press, 1992). Abel's edited works during this period were *The Official Correspondence of James S. Calhoun While Indian Agent at Santa Fe and Superintendent of Indian Affairs in New Mexico, Collected Mainly from the Files of the Indian Office and Edited Under Its Direction* (Washington DC: Government Printing Office, 1915) and *A Report from Natchitoches in 1807 by Dr. John Sibley*, Indian Notes and monographs, Miscellaneous no. 25 (New York: Museum of the American Indian, Heye Foundation, 1922). For a listing of her articles in scholarly journals, see Connie G. Armstrong, "Oklahoma Historians Hall of Fame: Annie Heloise Abel," *Chronicles of Oklahoma* 80 (Summer 2002): 217–19.

12. Francis Paul Prucha, *The Great White Father*, 2 vols. (Lincoln: University of Nebraska Press, 1984), 1:416 n. 1.

13. Perdue and Green, introduction to Abel, *The American Indian as Slaveholder and Secessionist*, 5–6. The same introduction appears in the other two volumes reprinted by the University of Nebraska Press.

14. Abel, *The American Indian as Slaveholder and Secessionist*, 49; Abel, *The American Indian in the Civil War*, 252.

15. Perdue and Green, introduction to Abel, *The American Indian as Slaveholder and Secessionist*, 7.

16. Review of *The American Indian as Slaveholder and Secessionist*, by Annie Heloise Abel, *American Historical Review* 21 (January 1916): 360.

17. Grace Lee Nute, review of *Tabeau's Narrative*, ed. Annie Heloise Abel, *Mississippi Valley Historical Review* 26 (December 1939): 414.

18. Annie Heloise Abel, "One of the Makers of Canada," typescript, n.d., folder 51, box 8, AHP.

19. Browne to Abel, January 4, 1908, folder 1, box 1, AHP.

20. Annie Heloise Abel, untitled typescript, folder 2, box 1, AHP.

21. [Herman J. Deutsch], typescript, n.d. [1947], folder 1, box 1, AHP (published in Friends of the Library, "The Record," State College of Washington, January 1948, 6–7).

22. Prucha, "Abel, Annie Heloise," 5.

23. Marjory R. Casson, "George Cockburn Henderson: A Memoir," *South Australiana*, March 1964, 6.

24. Sir Ernest Brubaker, quoted in Casson, "George Cockburn Henderson," 9.

25. Casson, "George Cockburn Henderson," 11–17.

26. Casson, "George Cockburn Henderson," 22–35.

27. Casson, "George Cockburn Henderson," 35.

28. Casson, "George Cockburn Henderson," 35–36.

29. Casson, "George Cockburn Henderson," 36–37.

30. Annie Heloise Abel, *The American Indian under Reconstruction* (Cleveland: Arthur H. Clark, 1925), title page. The volume has been reprinted with introduction by Theda Perdue and Michael D. Greene as *The American Indian and the End of the Confederacy, 1863–1866* (Lincoln: University of Nebraska Press, 1993).

31. Prucha, "Abel, Annie Heloise," 5; Kelsey, "A Dedication," 3.

32. Gertrude M. Farr to Abel, January 18, 1928, folder 16, box 4, AHP. In 1944, apparently plagued by a recurrence of the insomnia and depression that had affected his marriage, Henderson committed suicide. Casson, "George Cockburn Henderson," 48–49.

33. Annie Heloise Abel and Frank J. Klingberg, eds., *A Side-light on Anglo-American Relations, 1839–1858* (Lancaster PA: Association for the Study of Negro Life and History, 1927), v, 369.

34. Turner to Abel, February 12, 1919, folder 3, box 1, AHP.

35. Abel and Klingberg, *A Side-light on Anglo-American Relations*, v.

36. Kelsey, "A Dedication," 3. Correspondence from friends hints that Abel was in need of a position but may have been ambivalent about her post at

Kansas. Gertrude M. Farr to Abel, August 17, 1928, David Chamberlin to Abel, August 1, 1928, and M. E. Clark to Abel, September 21, 1928, folder 16, box 4, AHP.

37. Martha Coleman Bray, *Joseph Nicollet and His Map* (Philadelphia: American Philosophical Society, 1980), xv; Annie Heloise Abel, ed., *Chardon's Journal at Fort Clark: 1834–1839* (Pierre: Department of History, State of South Dakota, 1932), xi; Annie Heloise Abel, *Tabeau's Narrative of Loisel's Expedition to the Upper Missouri* (Norman: University of Oklahoma Press, 1939), vii.

38. Abel, *Chardon's Journal at Fort Clark*, especially ix.

39. Abel, *Tabeau's Narrative*, vi–ix, xi.

40. [Herman Deutsch], untitled manuscript, folder 1, box 1, AHP.

41. Abel, *Tabeau's Narrative*, ix–xi.

42. Prucha, "Abel, Annie Heloise," 5; Abel to Eugene O. Holland, January 31, 1939, folder 1, box 1, AHP.

43. Abel to Eugene O. Holland, December 29, 1938, and October 3, 1939, folder 1, box 1, AHP.

44. Abel to Holland, October 3, 1939, folder 1, box 1, AHP.

45. Abel to Holland, October 15, 1939, folder 1, box 1, AHP.

46. Kelsey, "A Dedication," 304; "Dr. Henderson, Author, Passes," unidentified clipping, March 14, 1947, folder 1, box 1, AHP.

47. Abel to Holland, November 2, 1946, folder 1, box 1, AHP.

48. Abel to Holland, January 13, 1947, folder 1, box 1, AHP. Abel also donated some research documents to the University of British Columbia, Vancouver, and the Library of Congress. Prucha, "Abel, Annie Heloise," 6.

49. Rose Abel Wright to Holland, March 19, 1947, and Holland to Wright, March 21, 1947, folder 1, box 1, AHP.

50. Nancy J. Parezo, ed., *Hidden Scholars: Woman Anthropologists and the Native American Southwest* (Albuquerque: University of New Mexico Press, 1993), 21.

51. Abel to Editor, *Oregonian*, n.d. [1934], folder 5, box 1, AHP.

52. Annie H. Abel Henderson, review of *The Last Trek of the Indians*, by Grant Foreman, *American Historical Review* 52 (January 1947): 337.

2

ANGIE DEBO

From the Old to the New Western History

Shirley A. Leckie

IN 1958, CITIZENS OF Marshall, Oklahoma, honored their most famous resident by setting aside March 28 as Angie Debo Recognition Day. Among those attending, in addition to Debo's neighbors and friends, was the noted Muscogee-Creek and Pawnee artist, Acee Blue Eagle. Oklahoma Supreme Court justice and past president of the National Congress of American Indians, Cherokee N. B. Johnson, was also present, as was John Joseph Mathews, an Osage writer whose 1932 best-selling *Wa'Kon-Tah* had brought national attention to the new University of Oklahoma Press.

C. T. Shades, superintendent of Marshall's local schools and master of ceremonies, read congratulatory letters from dignitaries, including President Dwight D. Eisenhower and Oliver La Farge, president of the Indian advocacy group the Association on American Indian Affairs. Afterward, Raymond Bryson, one of Angie's closest friends, announced an additional honor. Marshall High School's first graduating class (1913), which included Debo, had belatedly selected as its motto "Making through the trackless wilds a trail for others to follow." Since Debo was a pioneering scholar in Indian history, a plaque bearing that inscription was placed in her alma mater in her honor.[1]

Marshall residents correctly identified the significance of Debo's trailblazing career as a historian. Her work is significant for two reasons. First, Debo served as a bridge between the older school of west-

2. (*Opposite Top*) Angie Debo, 1930s. During this decade, as the first woman professor at West Texas State Teacher's College, Debo lost her job teaching and won the Dunning Prize from the American Historical Association for her published dissertation, *The Rise and Fall of the Choctaw Republic. Courtesy of Angie Debo Papers no. 1988-013.9, Special Collections and University Archives, Oklahoma State University Libraries, Stillwater OK. Photograph no. B63 F44.2.*

3. (*Opposite Bottom*) Charles Banks Wilson, well known for his paintings of Oklahoma Indians, painted the portrait of Angie Debo that hangs in the capitol rotunda in Oklahoma City. Debo is the only woman who has been so honored. *Courtesy of Angie Debo Papers no. 1988-013.9, Special Collections and University Archives, Oklahoma State University Libraries, Stillwater OK. Photograph no. B63 F58.1.*

ern historians, heavily influenced by Frederick Jackson Turner and his frontier thesis, and the more recent New Western historians. The latter group, which includes Patricia Limerick, Richard White, and Donald Worster, among others, views Euro-American movement into the trans-Mississippi West as the conquest of indigenous people rather than benign settlement of "free land."[2] Second, Debo's scholarship on American Indians, bringing to bear the insights of ethnologists and her own fieldwork, was a forerunner of ethnohistory. Although she chronicled Indian-white relations, Debo narrated her account from the Indian point of view, thereby bringing Native peoples rather than Euro-Americans to the foreground. In this way she anticipated the New Indian history, still the cutting edge of the field at the beginning of the twenty-first century.[3] Because of her impact on these two fields—western American history and American Indian history—an examination of her work illuminates the ways that a woman who never held a tenured position in a history department and never trained graduate students made her voice heard in the ongoing discourse of history.

Given her background and upbringing, Angie Debo was an unlikely person to play these roles. Born in 1890 in Beattie, Kansas, to tenant farmers Edward and Lina Debo, Angie and her family moved in 1899 to a one-room shack in "Old Oklahoma," the region opened to white settlement in the famous land run of April 22, 1889. Angie vividly recalled November 8, 1899, when, as a nine-year-old, she had sat beside her mother in a covered wagon. Peering out at the tall "green wheat stretching to the low horizon," in Marshall, Oklahoma Territory, she had wondered where the Indians of Oklahoma were. They lived in the territory, she knew, but so far in her family's travels from Kansas she had seen only farmers and ranchers along the way to their new home.[4]

As the Debo family settled in and added to their one-room shack, Edward and Lina bequeathed their children a sense of pride in their family's heritage. In their stories of forebears moving westward and persevering through "starving times" in areas such as Rooks County, western Kansas, they celebrated themselves as the latest in a long line of sturdy pioneers. Not surprisingly, Edward and Lina instilled in their children the "spirit of Oklahoma," or the acceptance of hardships and reverses with cheerful stoicism.[5]

For Debo, growing up in Oklahoma Territory proved both exhilarating and frustrating. On the one hand, she loved the new land and its summer expanses of wildflowers and winter fields of wheat.[6] On the other hand, she found that Oklahoma offered fewer educational opportunities than Kansas. Marshall did not open a four-year high school until 1910, three years after Oklahoma achieved statehood.[7]

In 1915, two years after graduating from high school, Debo entered the University of Oklahoma, where she "came under the influence" of Edward Everett Dale. In his late thirties, the tall, slim "unprofessorial" Dale, who had once been a cowboy, was a captivating figure. In his southwestern drawl, he illustrated his lectures with humorous tales drawn from his own experiences on the range.[8]

Fresh from Harvard University, Dale had recently obtained a master's degree under Frederick Jackson Turner, the historian whose famous essay "On the Significance of the Frontier in American History" had laid the foundation for studying the West as the source of America's democratic institutions. Dale, having lived through the period when ordinary people had helped formulate new laws and transform old institutions on the Texas and Oklahoma ranching frontier, credited his mentor with having "opened up a new heaven and a new earth in the field of American history."[9] The cowboy professor sought to inspire the same enthusiasm among the offspring of Oklahoma pioneers seated before him. Debo, as a descendant of a struggling farming family, concluded that if Dale could become a college professor despite his late entry into college, she could aspire to a similar career. Since childhood she had wanted to teach, even though she believed that, for a woman, a career meant forgoing marriage and children. It was a price she was willing to pay.[10]

After graduating in 1918, Debo served as principal and teacher in North Enid and Enid, Oklahoma. Saving as much of her salary as possible, she was determined to earn a master's degree, which in that era qualified one for teaching in smaller colleges and universities. Like many other rural women, she felt the magnetism of the large city and considered attending Columbia University in New York City or the University of Chicago. She chose the latter because in her disappointment over her country's failure to ratify the Treaty of Versailles, she wanted to study the history of international affairs. The University of Chicago, she thought, had the better program in this area.[11]

Another factor in her decision might have been the University of Chicago's improvement in its support services for female students, due largely to the efforts of Marion Talbot, the dean of women students. Off-campus women, including Angie, enjoyed their own reading room, a lounge at the Woman's Union, and gymnasium and swimming pool in Ida Noyes Hall. The university's graduate school, like others throughout the United States, welcomed women as replacements for male students, whose numbers had declined during World War I. Talbot, always seeking to advance female students, proudly informed her superiors that women won proportionately more of the highest academic honors than their male counterparts and that their attrition rates were lower. Regretfully, female graduate students still received fewer fellowships relative to their numbers than men.[12]

Debo completed her master's by the spring of 1924. With her thesis director, James Fred Rippy, listed as coauthor (and listed first, although the work was entirely hers), *Smith College, Studies in History* published "The Historical Background of the American Policy of Isolation."[13] Angie, with careful attention to primary sources, had discovered that isolationism had been a strong element in American thinking well before President George Washington had advocated strict avoidance of foreign alliances in his 1793 neutrality proclamation.

Despite her publication, when Angie sought a position in higher education she discovered that history departments wanted only men. Two colleges would accept a woman, but only if a man was unavailable. Debo was shocked. She knew that women faced discrimination, but she had hoped that hard work and exemplary research and writing could overcome prejudice. When she talked to Frances Ada Knox, the sole female member of the history faculty at the University of Chicago, she learned that the latter had won her appointment when the United States had entered World War I and many young men had been drafted into the armed services. Knox had retained her position as an extension teacher by working harder than the men in her department.[14]

Practical as always, Debo expanded her job hunt to include teachers' colleges, which were traditionally more open to hiring women. Eventually, she found a position at West Texas State Teachers College, a small college in the ranching community of Canyon. This appointment gave her hope that she could ignite the same love for history among the offspring of pioneering ranchers that Dale had inspired in her at the University of Oklahoma.[15]

At West Texas, Debo taught demonstration high school classes for the college's aspiring teachers. Frustrated when her chair, Lester Fields Sheffy, transferred newcomers with similar or lesser credentials into the history department and promoted them to associate professor above her, she took a leave in 1930 to return to Oklahoma.[16] Settling in Norman, the location of the university, she worked again under Dale. After completing his doctoral degree under Professor Turner at Harvard in 1921, Dale had become chair of the department in 1924.[17]

During her first year of doctoral work, Debo wrote an essay evaluating her mentor. Terming Dale "the historian of progress," she wrote that "imperialism, if he thinks of it at all, is the march of civilization across the waste places of the earth."[18] As a graduate student she was beginning to question the ideas advanced by Turner, Dale, and others. Increasingly aware that the movement of new populations into Indian lands had exacted a terrible toll on Native peoples, now her major focus of study, she no longer saw westward expansion as an unalloyed blessing to humanity but rather as a more complicated and, at times, sordid story.

In 1933, in the depths of the Great Depression, Debo obtained her doctorate. As she returned to Canyon, the state of Texas, after earlier cuts, slashed appropriations by another 50 percent for West Texas State Teachers College. Forced to dismiss someone, Sheffy fired Debo and kept Ima Barlow, her replacement during her leave. Quite likely, Debo's decision to become the first female faculty member at West Texas to earn a doctorate played a part in his action.[19] Debo later characterized him as having "an unfounded distrust of his own ability and a corresponding fear of people with advanced degrees."[20]

After Debo complained about her termination to college president Andrew Jackson Hill, she was given a position as curator of the newly opened Panhandle Plains Museum. When Sheffy pointedly excluded her from a speech that Warren K. Moorehead, a former member of the Board of Indian Commissioners, made at the museum, Debo succumbed to severe depression. Once, while traveling with colleagues, she and the group halted to fix a flat tire. As Angie stood in the way of oncoming traffic, her friends called her back. In a "flat voice," she responded, "Oh, it doesn't matter," meaning that, at that moment, she cared little whether she lived or died.[21] Since Debo was resilient, her optimism returned; realizing how much she wanted to research and write, she left the museum in the summer of 1934. By now the University of Oklahoma Press had published her doctoral dissertation, "History of the Choctaw Nation from the End of the Civil War to the Close of the Tribal Period," as *The Rise and Fall of the Choctaw Republic*.

This work, which received the 1934 John A. Dunning Award from the American Historical Association, marked a break with Dale. Debo had made use of anthropologist John Swanton's older ethnological studies in her dissertation. In transforming her work into a book, she expanded her first chapter into three to cover the pre–Civil War history of the Choctaws more fully. Here she relied heavily on Swanton's *Source Material for the Social and Ceremonial Life of the Choctaw Indians*, published in 1931. Thus, although her first chapter is entitled "The Primitive Choctaws," gone is the opening statement in the preface to her dissertation: "The history of the Choctaw Indians records the development of a primitive people with innate capacities for civilization."[22] Instead, her first chapter begins: "The Choctaw Indians constituted the most numerous branch of the great Muskogean linguistic stock."[23]

Written from the Indian viewpoint, *Choctaw Republic* approached its subject convinced that the Choctaws had established a society that, despite some governmental corruption and some crime, had provided its people with good health care and education. These were the two areas that a recent publication, the 1928 *The Problem of Indian Administration* (better known as the Meriam Report), had found lacking among American Indians in the aftermath of the 1887 Dawes Act.[24]

Under that act, the Office of Indian Affairs had divided tribal land into allotments, awarding 160 acres (expanded for ranching) to those Indians whom agents considered heads of households and awarding lesser amounts to others in their families. "Surplus" or "excess" land was sold to outsiders. The proceeds from these sales funded schools that sought to teach Indian children to "walk the white man's road."

The act assumed that ownership of private property would propel Indian families into prosperity and that the new schools would educate Indian children to forsake their tribal ways and traditions and assimilate into the larger society. Instead, Indians had fallen into abject poverty and, by 1933, had lost 60 percent of their land. As for the Indian schools, many graduates, denied opportunities because of continuing discrimination, returned to their families and communities, caught between two worlds and at home in neither one.[25]

Where the Choctaw republic lagged, Debo admitted, was not in the education offered Indian children but in those facilities available to non-Indian children living in their communities. Their families had moved into Choctaw country knowing they had no voting rights and could not acquire land in fee simple since the Choctaws held their land communally.[26] They also knew that the Choctaws never intended to build schools for uninvited newcomers.

Not surprisingly, these newcomers (often led by mixed-blood assimilated promoters) had begun campaigning for an end to the Indian republics of the Five Southern Tribes (these were, in addition to the Choctaws and the Chickasaws in one republic, the Cherokees, Creeks, and Seminoles). Once these peoples were brought under the Dawes Act, most of their land would be thrown open for non-Indian settlement. In 1889 the U.S. Congress acceded to the newcomers' demands and opened land in Indian Territory in the first of a number of land runs that eventually included lands originally assigned to the Plains tribes of the Southwest. Nine years later, the Curtis Act swept away the laws and courts of the Five Tribes and brought all residents of Indian Territory under federal jurisdiction. It also replaced communal landholding with allotment for the first time.[27] The story of events after the Five Tribes were terminated as autonomous republics was, in this context, the next topic that Debo began investigating.

Debo's new topic was timely since the administration of Indian Affairs was undergoing a sweeping change. John Collier, a former social worker and activist since the 1920s, had seen in the commitment to tradition and land among the Pueblo Indians of New Mexico a healthy counterpoint to the materialism and individualism of the United States.[28] Appointed commissioner of Indian Affairs in 1933 during

President Franklin Delano Roosevelt's New Deal, Collier won passage of the Indian Reorganization Act a year later. That legislation, by reversing the Dawes Act, sought to revitalize Indian tribal governments and give them control over vital services. In addition, a revolving loan fund permitted tribes to rebuild their landholdings.[29]

In the context of this changing Indian policy and with a grant from the Social Science Research Council, Debo traveled to Oklahoma City and Muskogee in Oklahoma and to Washington DC.[30] Her archival research indicated that, in 1900, seventy thousand Indians had still retained "the eastern half of the area that now constitutes the state of Oklahoma, a territory immensely wealthy in farmland and forest and coal mines, and with untapped oil pools of incalculable value."[31] Now they had little left of their land and its rich resources. Debo wanted to know why they had suffered such monumental losses after the Curtis Act had terminated their existence as separate republics. So far, the only published study was *Oklahoma's Poor Rich Indians,* a pamphlet that had appeared in 1925 and was written by Gertrude Bonnin (Zitkala-Ša), a Yankton Sioux writer and research agent of the Indian Welfare Committee of the General Federation of Women's Clubs; Charles H. Fabens, lawyer for the American Indian Defense Association; and Matthew K. Sniffen of the Indian Rights Association. Published by the Indian Rights Association, the pamphlet contained excellent analysis. The Five Tribes had accepted the Curtis Act reluctantly but with the belief that the federal government would protect them in their reduced holdings. Instead, when statehood was achieved, the management of Indian affairs was turned over to Oklahoma courts. That left the fullbloods of the Five Tribes vulnerable to those who wanted control of Indian land, its resources, and the ways the Indian land could be used.

Debo had encountered treachery in her earlier work, but nothing had prepared her for her newest discoveries. As she explained in a 1981 oral history interview, "I had grown up while that was happening." Her local newspaper had carried news of the Russian Revolution of 1905 but had largely ignored the fate of the Five Tribes. There was, Debo noted, "no spot on the globe that is as far away from my knowledge and understanding as the Indian Territory was when I was growing up in the Territory of Oklahoma."[32]

To accomplish their aims, the "grafters" (people who used public office or connections for personal gain) had used "the legislative enactment and court decree of the legal exploiter, and the lease, mortgage, and deed of the land shark." Debo now confronted a period that historians of the westward movement had overlooked. This part of the process of incursion into Indian lands was important because, in Debo's view, "the reaction of this process upon the ideals and standards of successive frontier communities is a factor in the formation of the American character that should no longer be disregarded by students of social institutions."[33] In reality, Debo was studying what New Western historians today characterize as "the legacy of conquest." Moreover, she was evaluating it in the context of what scholar Patricia Limerick calls "the unbroken past of the American West," or in the light of the problems that arose after the closing of the frontier in 1890. In a very real sense, Debo was a practitioner of the New Western history long before the field received a name. The methods of the grafters included, Debo found, not only court decree and legislative enactment but also intimidation, kidnapping, and murder. By winning guardianship rights over children and adults decreed incompetent by compliant courts, the exploiters obtained access to Indian land and resources, including oil.[34]

Darcy McNickle, noted Flathead author and administrative assistant to Commissioner Collier, evaluated Debo's manuscript for the University of Oklahoma Press. In a field "neglected by serious students" he had encountered "nothing quite so ambitious" before. To attract the wide audience it deserved, he suggested "careful pruning."[35] Joseph Brandt, head of the University of Oklahoma Press, agreed.[36] Debo was amenable but demanded that the extensive Indian testimony remain intact. "For more than forty years nobody has paid the slightest attention to what the Indians themselves thought about a matter so vital to their existence," she explained. Now, she insisted, their voices would finally be heard.[37]

By mid-March 1937, Debo impatiently awaited her second reader's report. A year earlier, Oklahoma had passed the Oklahoma Indian Welfare Act. A modified version of the Indian Reorganization Act, it allowed groups of ten or more Indians to form cooperatives and apply for loans to purchase land from a $2 million fund. Many members of the Five

Tribes—especially the elite—were of mixed-blood ancestry and favored assimilationist policies. They opposed the Indian Reorganization Act, including the Oklahoma version. Businessmen and politicians, who objected to removing Indian land and subterranean resources from the state tax rolls, joined forces with them.[38] Given this controversy, Debo wanted her work published quickly. Although she had included "no propaganda" for Collier or his Indian Reorganization Act, it was "the only scientific study that has ever been made of the question about which such a bitter fight has raged for the past four years, and it would please me to think that sincere people on both sides could have some facts available as a basis for their arguments."[39] If the "despoilers of the Indians" were to triumph again, it should not occur because of "lack of knowledge."[40] Shortly afterward, Debo received another glowing review from the press's second reader and relaxed. Publication was set for October 1, 1937.

That spring, Debo, impoverished and dependent on her parents for food and housing, wrote Dale, asking him to consider her for one of two vacancies in his department. She could not have replaced the Latin American scholar, but she might have filled in, at least temporarily, for Morris Wardell. After receiving his doctorate from the University of Chicago, Wardell was leaving the classroom to become assistant to the university's president, William Bizzell. The University of Oklahoma Press would soon publish his dissertation as *The Political History of the Cherokees*. Thus, Wardell's field was similar to Debo's. Angie suggested that Dale bring her into the department as an adjunct, and "the future would take care of itself." Admittedly, she had "one disqualification," or "defect." She was a woman, few of whom, she noted, "were employed on history faculties." Perhaps, however, her "productive scholarship" and record as a teacher could offset this weakness.[41]

Dale replied by assuring her that he was aware of her many fine qualifications. He devoted most of his letter, however, to explaining why he had to hire a Latin American historian. He never referred to the possibility that Debo might replace Wardell, even on a part-time basis, and gave her no encouragement that he would ever consider her for a teaching position in his department.[42]

While respectful and courtly toward women, Dale, in a Harvard seminar paper written in 1913, had displayed a bias that probably still colored his feelings about women as potential colleagues. In "Woman's Influence on the French Revolution" he had asserted that women had influenced the revolution mainly because the male revolutionaries were, at times, "imbued with a 'fatal feminism' a strange sentimentality that causes them to act more like excited, hysterical women than like sober law-givers to whom has been entrusted the task of creating a new form of government for France." Elaborating further, he argued, "They waste time on trifles, they talk endlessly, and they show in many ways incapacity for business, sentimentalism, a failure to 'make the head rule the heart,' and other characteristics which we in America usually regard as peculiarly feminine. Thus," he concluded, "not only did the women of France have a large share in the Revolution but there was also apparently a strain of 'femininity' or at least a lack of masculinity in the men of the period."[43]

If these biases remained a part of his thinking, they explained, in part, why Dale had brought Wardell, a former high school teacher, into his department even before he earned his doctorate and yet gave Debo's request for part-time employment no consideration. Dale, moreover, had carefully mentored Wardell as he advanced toward tenure and promotion. Despite Debo's prestigious award from the American Historical Association and her production of another manuscript on a very complex subject, involving the fate of five Indian peoples, plus her reputation as an "excellent" teacher in the classroom, Dale would never do for her what he had done for his male friend.[44] As for Debo, although Dale referred to her in correspondence as his "best student" and wrote letters of recommendation for her when she applied for positions at other institutions, she knew that he did not want her in his department even as an instructor or adjunct.

In reading Dale's rejection of her request to be considered for a teaching position, Debo must have felt acute embarrassment. By the spring of 1937, however, she had a larger concern. She worried that her forthcoming work on the termination of the republics of the Five Southern Tribes in Oklahoma might bring retaliation against the University of Oklahoma Press. After all, she had identified prominent individuals in the state as exploiters of Indians.[45] At her urging, Brandt submitted her manuscript to President Bizzell.[46] Bizzell, in turn, ordered his assistant—none other than Wardell—to evaluate the manuscript. Wardell issued a negative report in which he questioned Debo's impartiality and fairness. If the press published the work it could expect to generate criticism, libel suits, and retaliation against itself and the university.[47] Predictably, Debo soon received her canceled contract in the mail.[48]

Not knowing that Wardell had written this latest and very negative appraisal, Debo assumed instead that Dale was responsible. The recent exchange of letters between them may have predisposed her to form that opinion. More likely, Debo remembered that although Dale had told his classes of the treachery whites had practiced against Indians, he had left such incidents out of his publications. In the end, Debo's manuscript, titled *And Still the Waters Run*, was not published until Princeton University Press, having wooed Brandt away from the University of Oklahoma Press, brought it out late in 1940.

Although the academic reviews were excellent, Debo's work received little attention in the popular press.[49] With the eruption of World War II in Asia and Europe, public attention had turned to foreign affairs. In this context, the voices of intellectuals who saw in American Indian culture and traditions an antidote to their nation's materialism and intense individualism were muted.[50]

Despite the frustrations and disappointments of bringing *And Still the Waters Run* into print, Angie, having received a grant from the Social Science Research Council, produced another work in 1941, this time on the history of the Creek Nation. Again, she uncovered a chronicle of white deceit and, once more, told her story from the Indian perspective. While researching and writing this new work, Debo took temporary employment with the Indian-Pioneer Project of the Works Project Administration. In interviewing Creek Indians, she discovered that their oral history traditions were remarkably close—at least for one hundred years—to the documentary evidence her friend Grant Foreman had uncovered in his 1934 book *Indian Removal: The Emigration of the Five Civilized Tribes of Indians*. Debo now gained heightened respect for Indian oral tradition. It was a source that one compared to other documents or testimony to determine its congruity with other evidence. One weighed it in that light, rather than rejecting it out of hand.[51]

Again Debo's research revealed a story of years of broken treaties and betrayed trust. At last, when southern whites were determined to take their land in the Southeast, the Creeks were "dragged from their ancient homes and flung down upon a raw western frontier to conquer it or die."[52] In Indian Territory, nonetheless, the Creeks reconstructed their lives and their republic, retaining those Euro-American ways they found serviceable while steadfastly maintaining their traditions. They also struggled to work out their relations with neighboring western tribes. Despite the pain of adjustment and lingering divisions over removal, the Creeks prospered until the American Civil War intervened. That conflict, as the pioneering scholar in American Indian history, Annie Heloise Abel, had shown earlier in her pathbreaking works on the Five Southern Tribes during the Civil War and Reconstruction, sowed new dissension among them, pitting Creeks against one another as some supported the Confederacy and others, who became fugitives, supported the Union cause.[53]

After the war, like all the Five Tribes, the Creeks faced continuing dissension. They also confronted "the encircling menace of a new frontier" in the continuing encroachment of newcomers on their land. Despite their fierce attachment to their old ways, the Creeks were forced to capitulate to federal demands. Yet, even as the majority accepted the Curtis Act, shattering their tribal lands into "deeds and land titles," some under Chitto (Snake) Harjo resisted until their leaders were brought to trial in 1901.[54]

Among the Creeks, Pleasant Porter impressed Debo the most, mainly for his leadership immediately after the passage of the Curtis Act. As he counseled his people to move beyond their lost hopes and into the future, he understood the continuing importance of the Creek heritage to Oklahoma and the nation. Fittingly, Debo ended her work with his moving statement to the Creek Council in 1900: "The vitality of our race still persists. We have not lived for naught. We are the original discoverers of this continent, and the conquerors of it from the animal kingdom, and on it first taught the arts of peace and war, and first planted the institutions of virtue, truth and liberty." Those achievements, Porter maintained, taught Europeans "that it was possible for men to exist and subsist here." His people had bequeathed to them "our thought forces—the best blood of our ancestors having intermingled with [that of] their best statesmen and leading citizens. We have made ourselves," he was certain, "an indestructible element in their national history."[55]

Debo named her work *The Road to Disappearance*, a title she had chosen because no one, she thought, would read a book called *The History of the Creek Nation*.[56] Her decision was ironic and, in the end, a mistake, for one of her goals in her work was to resurrect the Creek spirit, their accomplishments, and their contributions. Although their republic had vanished, Porter's words said it all; "The race that has rendered this service to the other nations of mankind cannot utterly perish."

When the University of Oklahoma Press, short of funding due to the Great Depression, was finally able to schedule a publication date for *The Road to Disappearance*, Debo was employed in Oklahoma City as head of the Oklahoma Writers' Project for the Works Progress Administration (WPA). The job had come barely in time to save her from dire poverty. To travel to her interview at the state capital she had been reduced to borrowing the fifty-cent train fare from a friend and, armed with sandwiches from home, had stayed at the local Young Women's Christian Association overnight. Her WPA duties included overseeing the production of a state history and guide. Although she welcomed the relief from penury, she soon found that working for a bureaucracy and supervising what she saw as largely inept writers was difficult. Not surprisingly, within a year she resigned.[57]

In 1941, when she received a copy of the WPA state guide to Oklahoma, Debo was appalled. She and John M. Oskison were listed as coeditors of the volume, but the chapter on the history of Oklahoma was not hers. Her opening sentence had been, "Although Oklahoma is young as a state, the region came early within the scope of the white man's imperial ambitions." The substitute chapter made no reference to imperialism; instead, it emphasized Oklahoma's transformation from a place that once nurtured the aspirations of farmers to one that now served businesses and corporations. Debo resented being censored; worse yet, the chapter contained numerous errors, leaving her deeply embarrassed.[58]

That same year, John Collier, still commissioner of Indian Affairs, asked Debo to critique a speech he was giving. Afterward, she sent him a draft of "Indian Policy as a Problem in Colonial Administration," in which she argued that although Great Britain and, later, the United States recognized the sovereignty of Indian tribes and dealt with them as nations, these two powers sought, in reality, to add Indian land to their holdings. Debo's topic was not about colonial administration, Collier responded, but rather concerned imperialism. Doing justice to that subject meant examining Indian-white relations "in the context of national development." That required writing a book, not an article.[59]

Debo, with other projects under way, could not begin such an ambitious study for some time. In 1943 she published *Tulsa: From Creek Town to Oil Capitol*, and, a year later, *Prairie City: The Story of an American Community*, a history of a composite town. If Turner's 1893 "On the Significance of the Frontier in American History" presented individualism, democracy, and pragmatism as traits arising from the frontier experience and pivotal to the formation of the American character, Debo's study of a pioneer settlement told instead of the erosion of an earlier sense of community among the population.

At the same time, Debo demonstrated how the larger world, with its cycles of boom and bust and war and peace, increasingly shaped and reshaped the lives and fortunes of citizens in a Great Plains hamlet. Ending the work with young people were leaving home to participate in World War II as soldiers or defense workers, Debo predicted that Prairie City would endure but in a different form. "Why not a new village of farmers, citizens of the world through schools and radio and space-consuming transportation, grouped together in friendly sociability, building directly upon the soil?"[60] Although *Prairie City* had disappointing sales in 1944, it gave Marshall, Oklahoma—its chief inspiration—a measure of immortality. By the 1980s the book had entered the curriculum for Oklahoma's schoolchildren.

During World War II, Debo, like many other women over thirty-five in the United States, found new employment opportunities—but not in higher education. In addition to teaching high school history in Marshall, she served as a lay minister for the local Methodist church.[61] Nonetheless, with peace in sight, she wrote Savoie Lottinville, Brandt's replacement as director of the University of Oklahoma Press, to ask if he would consider a study of America's "real imperialism," its treatment of its Native peoples. If her country could not overcome its past mistakes in this era, "we may as well admit that the colonial problems that will be left from this present war are beyond our solving," she added. Lottinville, seeing little market for such a book, suggested another topic. She might write a history on the Indians of North America, something the press had long wanted to add to its listing. Debo responded that if the press would settle instead for a history of the Indians of the United States she might one day tackle that subject.[62]

In 1947 Debo received a Rockefeller grant from the University of Oklahoma Press and began working on *Oklahoma: Foot-loose and Fancy Free,* an interpretative history of Oklahoma. After weaving into this book the chapter that an unknown person had replaced in the WPA state guide in 1941, she also included examples of the discrimination blacks had experienced in Oklahoma.[63] Professor Dale, one of the readers for the press, objected to her discussion of race relations, since the subject was "hot." Debo adamantly refused to delete it, arguing that her views on this subject were "vital to the integrity of my interpretation."[64]

In that same year, Debo became curator of maps at the Oklahoma A&M (now Oklahoma State University) Library in Stillwater. Almost simultaneously, she received an offer to teach in that institution's history department. In the end, Debo wanted to write more than she wanted to teach history. As she confided to Carolyn Foreman, the wife of Grant Foreman and a historian in her own right, she would keep the library position because its hours were limited to those spent in her office. Besides, President Henry Bennett promised her a paid leave in the summer to continue researching and writing.[65]

In 1951, Debo completed a slim volume for the Indian Rights Association that examined the situation of the full-blood Indians of the Five Southern Tribes in the aftermath of the passage of the Oklahoma Indian Welfare Act. It found that although the act had assisted them, they still lived in poverty. She also edited Oliver Nelson's reminiscences as *The Cowman's Southwest,* which appeared in 1953. Nonetheless, personal responsibilities impeded her academic work.[66] Her mother, suffering from atherosclerosis and diabetes, succumbed to dementia, and as the surviving child (her brother Edwin had died in 1933), Angie was her caretaker, a role that would have befallen her as a daughter anyway. That exhausting job brought sleepless nights and little freedom to research or write.[67] When her mother died on June 11, 1954, Debo was relieved that her "long nightmare" was finally over but deeply depressed. She had lost not only her mother but also her closest friend, and she saw "creative work" as the "only antidote to grief and loneliness." For her that meant writing history.[68]

When Debo retired from the library at the then-mandatory age of sixty-five, her desire to devote herself entirely to research and writing met a new obstacle. Indian policy had changed again in the United States. In 1953 Congress had passed a concurrent resolution declaring its intent to terminate its relations with Indian tribes as soon as it decided they could stand on their own. Additionally, the new policy encouraged residents of reservations to move to cities, where they would supposedly make new and more prosperous lives for themselves. Behind these changes lay a cold war ideology which held that Indians had been "wards" of the government too long, relying on it for services in health and education and failing to learn the virtues of individualism and self-reliance. Congress followed its resolution with Public Law 280, which allowed states to unilaterally assume control over civil and criminal affairs on Indian reservations, thereby bringing Indian peoples under state rather than tribal jurisdiction.[69]

Debo was appalled. This was simply a return to the "bad old days" of the Dawes Act, which, in her view, had failed miserably before and would do so again to the detriment of America's Native peoples. Echoing the ideas of Felix Cohen, one of the nation's foremost authorities on Indian and federal relations and law, Debo saw Indians not as "wards" but as Native peoples who had entered into "contractual agreements" with the federal government. In those treaties they had relinquished vast holdings with the understanding that the federal government would abide by its promises—federal protection for their remaining land and fulfillment of the promised services, especially in health care and education. To Debo, the United States as trustee was required "to protect the property, but has no control over the person of the beneficiary."[70]

Incensed over the policy of termination, Debo denounced it in churches, schools, and community centers throughout Oklahoma and into Kansas and other states. She also wrote articles describing its impact on Native peoples for *Indian Affairs*, the newsletter of the Association on American Indian Affairs, a group that had originated in the 1920s to protect the land rights of the Rio Grande Pueblo Indians. As Debo noted in letters and Christmas correspondence to her wide circle of friends, she still longed to research and write, but until termination was defeated she would remain primarily an activist.[71] She relaxed when John F. Kennedy, the newly elected president in 1960, appointed Representative Stewart Udall, environmentalist and Indian advocate, as secretary of the interior. Surely now the policy based on termination and relocation to urban centers would be reversed.

In 1967 Debo taught a summer National Defense Institute–sponsored class at the University of Oklahoma for teachers of American Indian children. Her syllabus emphasized that the course would be "presented *from the Indian point of view*. This will apply to the geographical setting; for example," she explained, "Lewis and Clark did not *go out* from St. Louis and encounter Indians, but the Indians saw the explorers *coming up* the Missouri River to them."[72] Afterward she expanded her lectures into a book. Additional motivation came from her anger over her country's continuing involvement in the Vietnam War. As she wrote Professor Dale at Christmas in 1967, President Lyndon Johnson and his generals regretfully knew no Indian history: "The best hardware of the time didn't help much when the Seminoles hid out in the Everglades or the Apaches in the mountains."[73] In a roundabout fashion, she had begun her history of "America's true imperialism."

As she had in earlier books, Debo sought to write a work that would affect policy. The chapter that covered the background and current situation of the indigenous people of Alaska and the question of Native land claims legislation was titled "The White Man Gets a New Chance." Congress, she argued, should award the Native peoples of Alaska forty million acres of land, rather than the originally proposed ten million acres. Debo was determined that the Native peoples of Alaska would retain enough land to continue a way of life based on hunting wildlife in a tundra environment. In September 1970 she testified before Congress on behalf of her vision of justice for Alaska's Eskimos, Aleuts, and Indians.[74] Throughout the next year she sent her ever-growing network of supporters extensive mailings with information about members of both houses of Congress and suggestions about points they might make in writing, telegraphing, or calling them. As James Ralph Scales, then president of Wake Forest University in North Carolina, noted: "I am sure that Senators Sam Ervin and Everett Jordan thought that a college administrator from North Carolina had developed a curious enthusiasm for Eskimos, but I did as I was told."[75] When President Richard Nixon signed the Alaskan Native Claims Settlement Act into law on December 18, 1971, giving Alaska's Native peoples forty million acres of land and an additional award of almost a billion dollars, Debo knew that her network had played a strong role in that victory.

Indians of the United States was Debo's best-selling book, partly because it appeared in 1970 at an opportune time. The civil rights movement of the 1960s had alerted the nation to the injustice African Americans suffered from segregation and disfranchisement in the South. The Civil Rights Act of 1964 and the Voting Rights Act of 1965 had revitalized the Fourteenth and Fifteenth Amendments for blacks by outlawing racial discrimination and removing the barriers to black voting in southern states.

Despite becoming citizens in 1924, American Indians had also endured severe discrimination and disfranchisement, and in this way they were similar to African Americans. They were different, however, in important ways. Indians wanted their rights, both as U.S. citizens and as members of tribes. They also wanted to retain their cultures and attain self-determination as separate peoples within the United States. In 1968 they made strides toward achieving these goals with the passage of the Indian Civil Rights Act, which spelled out the constitutional rights Native peoples enjoyed under both federal and tribal governments. That act also prevented states from assuming jurisdiction over Indian lands without tribal consent, thereby modifying Public Law 280, the most threatening aspect of the hated policy of termination. In doing so, the act created a foundation on which Native peoples could pursue self-determination.[76]

Debo's work helped Americans understand these issues by explaining the historical context out of which they had arisen in American Indian history. When it came to self-determination, Debo explained that whether American Indians—as tribes or as individuals—sought to maintain their separate identity and traditions or advocated assimilation, these matters should be left to them to decide. In her view, the best federal policy would assure Native people the right to control and maintain their land, water, and resources. At the same time, it would assure American Indians the education and training they needed at a level "equal to that of other citizens" and sufficient to allow them to leave their communities if they so desired or to remain in them if they preferred. Again, the conditions should allow them to make either decision.[77]

With her royalty checks, Debo continued her work as an activist, copying articles on injustice toward Indians and buying stamps "like wallpaper." At night, when long-distance rates were reduced, she called individuals asking them to contact their legislators. Among the Native peoples she championed, the Havasupais of Arizona faced potential loss of their land, and the Papagos (Tohono O'Odhams) confronted the possible loss of their water rights in that same state. Debo defended her activism in "To Establish Justice," written for the *Western History Quarterly* in 1976. Once she had thought that when her published works exposed injustice, her task was done. Now she realized that, like "the farmer, the dentist or anybody else," she had a responsibility to fight against injustice.[78]

At eighty-two, Debo shifted her scholarly interests from the Five Tribes to the Indians of the Southwest when she began working on a full-scale biography of Geronimo (Goyathlay). She had conducted interviews in the 1950s with Apaches who had known the Chiracahua leader, either as children or from accounts of their parents or relatives. Most of those she interviewed had since died, and she was determined that their stories would not die with them. Where Debo lacked historical facts regarding Geronimo's childhood, she incorporated the insights that anthropologist Morris Opler had provided, thereby fleshing out the culture in which Geronimo had come to maturity.[79] Above all she sought to be fair to the Chiracahua by placing him in the context of his own world with its long-standing disputes with Mexican and

U.S. citizens. *Geronimo: The Man, His Time and His Place*, Debo's first biography, won three national prizes, including the Wrangler Award. It was her last book, for two years after its publication her health began deteriorating as she experienced the excruciating pain of osteoporosis, the loss of sight in one eye, and increasing deafness.

In 1981 Debo began submitting to extensive oral history interviews, due to the efforts of historian Glenna Matthews and Gloria Valencia-Weber, later a law professor at the University of New Mexico. These interviews provided the basis for the film *Indians, Outlaws, and Angie Debo*, produced by Barbara Abrash and Martha Sandlin, which appeared on the premier season, in fall 1988, of *The American Experience*. Debo never lived to see that film, but she experienced, in April 1985, the placing of her portrait in Oklahoma City's capitol rotunda. It hangs alongside those of the Cherokee scholar Sequoyah; the Indian athlete Jim Thorpe; humorist Will Rogers; Robert Kerr, former governor of Oklahoma; and Carl Albert, former speaker of the House of Representatives.

Shortly before her death on February 21, 1988, Debo received the lifetime achievement award from the American Historical Association for her thirteen books, numerous articles, and extensive work on behalf of Native peoples. Although she is buried in a cemetery not far from the small Oklahoma town she entered first in 1899, her journeys through historical archives and her wanderings over the back roads of Oklahoma to interview Native peoples had taken her a long way from her own origin myth, the uncritical celebration of the westward movement of Euro-Americans and Anglo-American culture into the American West.[80]

Debo had anticipated many of the changes in writing Indian history that scholars associate today with the period after World War II. The growth of ethnohistory, generally perceived as emanating from the formation of the Indians Claims Commission in 1946, brought historians and anthropologists together. That collaboration meant that the methods of the field-worker, compiling ethnographies and analyzing similarities and differences, could be reinforced with the knowledge of documents and Indian-white relations and the understanding of change over time that are the tools of the historian.[81] Since then the field of ethnohistory has become increasingly sophisticated, as scholars incorporate further insights from archaeology, linguistics, demographics, environmental studies, and gender analysis.

Ethnohistorians remain committed to writing a fuller history of the peoples of this earth who have had their stories subsumed under the narratives of more powerful groups, an endeavor—that Angie Debo had been involved in from the 1930s until the end of her life. She had sought to tell the story of Native peoples by placing them in their culture and telling their stories from their point of view.

Debo knew the role she had played. In 1979, nine years before her death, she had written Ed Shaw, the third director of the University of Oklahoma Press, noting the development of the new field. "Sometimes," she mused, "I play with a half-formed conviction that Savoie Lottinville invented the word 'ethno-history' and that I invented [that] kind of writing."[82]

Notes

1. *Oklahoma Times*, March 29, 1958. This chapter is based on research I conducted for *Angie Debo, Pioneering Historian*, vol. 18 in the Oklahoma Western Biographies (Norman: University of Oklahoma Press, 2000).

2. Richard White, *It's Your Misfortune: A New History of the American West* (Norman: University of Oklahoma Press, 1991); Patricia Limerick, *The Legacy of Conquest: The Unbroken Past of the American West* (New York: Norton, 1987); Donald Worster, *Dust Bowl: The Southern Plains in the 1930s* (New York: Oxford University Press, 1979).

3. Richard White, review of *Indians, Outlaws and Angie Debo, Journal of American History* 76 (December 1989): 1010. White wrote that Debo "invented the 'new' Indian history long before there was a name for it."

4. Angie Debo, "The Debo Family," Angie Debo Papers, Special Collections and University Archives, Edmon Low Library, Oklahoma State University, Stillwater [hereafter cited as ADP].

5. Typescript of interview conducted by Glenna Matthew, Gloria Valencia Weber, and Aletha Rogers with Angie Debo in Marshall, Oklahoma, January 20, 1982, 5–6. These interviews, conducted between 1981 and 1985, are located in ADP and are hereafter cited as ADT with the dates following this citation.

6. Debo, "The Debo Family," ADP; ADT, January 20, 1982, 5–6; Angie Debo, "Manuscripts of Family Stories," ADP.

7. Debo, "The Debo Family"; ADT, October 23, 1981, 5.

8. Angie Debo, "Edward Everett Dale: The Teacher," in *Frontier Historian: The Life and Work of Edward Everett Dale*, ed. Arrell Gibson (Norman: University of Oklahoma Press, 1975), 28–29.

9. Edward Everett Dale, "Turner—The Man and Teacher," *University of Kansas City Review*, Autumn 1951, 25.

10. ADT, November 20, 1981, 2–3, August 15, 1983, 9.

11. ADT, November 20, 1981, 4–5.

12. Marion Talbot, *More Than Lore: Reminiscences of Marion Talbot* (Chicago: University of Chicago Press, 1936), 127–43, 146–47. See also Rosalind Rosenberg, "The Limits of Access: The History of Coeducation in America," in *Women and Higher Education in American History*, ed. John Mack Faragher and Florence Howe (New York: Norton, 1988), 118–20; Ellen Fitzpatrick, "For the 'Women of the University': Marion Talbot, 1858–1948," in *Lone Voyagers: Academic Women in Coeducational Institutions, 1870–1937*, ed. Geraldine Joncich Clifford (New York: The Feminist Press at The City University of New York, 1989), 117–22; Ellen Fitzpatrick, *Endless Crusade: Women Social Scientists and Progressive Reform* (New York: Oxford University Press, 1990), 72.

13. James Fred Rippy and Angie Debo, "The Historical Background of the American Policy of Isolation," *Smith College, Studies in History* (Northhampton MA) 9 (April–July 1924): 71–165.

14. ADT, December 12, 1981, 1–2, August 17, 1983, 2, 9–10. Although Debo did not name the female professor in oral history interviews, Ada Knox was the sole female professor of history in the University of Chicago catalog for 1923–24.

15. ADT, December 16, 1981, 3–4.

16. West Texas State Teachers College (Canyon TX) *West Texas State Teachers College Quarterly*, bulletins nos. 39–69, 1925–1933.

17. Debo, "Edward Everett Dale: The Teacher," 35–36; ADT, June 8, 1985, 17.

18. Angie Debo, "Edward Everett Dale: Historian of Progress," unpublished seminar paper for the University of Oklahoma, ADP. In all fairness to Dale, as Ellen Fitzpatrick notes, his ideas began to expand after he participated in the Meriam Report. See *History's Memory: Writing America's Past, 1880–1980* (Cambridge: Harvard University Press, 2002), 128.

19. *Canyon (Texas) News*, June 1, 1933; Ima Barlow interviewed by A. K. Knott, November 24, 1978, Austin, Texas. This oral history tape is located in

Panhandle Plains Museum Research Center, Canyon, Texas, as part of the museum's oral history collection. Ruth Lowes, one of Debo's former colleagues at West Texas, termed Debo an "excellent" teacher. Ruth Lowes, telephone interview with Shirley A. Leckie, Ware Memorial Care Center, Amarillo, Texas, July 1, 1996. B. B. Chapman, former professor of history at Oklahoma State University, whose courses Debo took over in 1957 and 1958, gave the same evaluation. B. B. Chapman, telephone interview with Shirley A. Leckie, Orlando, Florida, October 24, 1994.

20. Debo to Dear Dr. Dale, June 19, 1937, Edward Everett Dale Collection, Western History Collection, University of Oklahoma, Norman [hereafter cited as EEDC].

21. Connie Cronley (close friend to Angie Debo) to Shirley Leckie, October 8, 1996, and December 28, 1998, author's private collection.

22. Angie Debo, "History of the Choctaw Nation from the End of the Civil War to the Close of the Tribal Period" (PhD diss., University of Oklahoma, 1933), 1.

23. Angie Debo, *The Rise and Fall of the Choctaw Republic* (Norman: University of Oklahoma Press, 1934), 1.

24. Lewis Meriam, ed., *The Problem of Indian Administration* (Baltimore: Johns Hopkins University Press, 1928).

25. Robert Utley, *The Indian Frontier of the American West, 1846–1890* (Albuquerque: University of New Mexico Press, 1985), 211–26. For a moving chronicle of an Indian school for Kiowas, see Clyde Ellis, *To Change Them Forever: Indian Education at the Rainy Mountain Boarding School, 19893–1920* (Norman: University of Oklahoma Press, 1996). Karen Anderson masterfully describes the turmoil Indian women experienced because of the Dawes Act, which threatened their ability to raise their children according to Indian traditions. See *Changing Woman: A History of Racial Ethnic Women in Modern America* (New York: Oxford University Press, 1996), 37–66.

26. Debo, *Rise and Fall of the Choctaw Republic*, 228–44.

27. Debo, *Rise and Fall of the Choctaw Republic*, 245–90.

28. Robert L. Dorman, *Revolt of the Provinces: The Regionalist Movement in America, 1920–1945* (Chapel Hill: University of North Carolina Press, 1993), 62–66, 79.

29. Graham D. Taylor, *The New Deal and American Indian Tribalism: The Administration of the Indian Reorganization Act, 1934–45* (Lincoln: University

of Nebraska Press, 1980), 12–13; see also Donald L. Parman, *Indians and the American West in the Twentieth Century* (Bloomington: Indiana University Press, 1994), 76. Excellent works on this period are Lawrence Kelly, *The Assault on Assimilation: John Collier and the Origins of Indian Policy Reform* (Albuquerque: University of New Mexico Press, 1983); and Kenneth Philp, *John Collier's Crusade for Indian Reform, 1920–1954* (Tucson: University of Arizona Press, 1977),

30. ADT, November 20, 1981, 14; Angie Debo to Dear Mr. [Walter] Campbell, March 24, 1935, Walter Campbell Collection, Western History Collection, University of Oklahoma.

31. Angie Debo, *And Still the Waters Run: The Betrayal of the Five Civilized Tribes* (1940; reprint, Norman: University of Oklahoma Press, 1986), ix. The subtitle was added in 1973.

32. ADT, June 8, 1985, 2. Articles on the Russian Revolution of 1905 appeared intermittently from January 6 to December 28, 1905, in the local newspaper, the *Kingfisher Free Press*.

33. Debo, *And Still the Waters Run*, ix–x.

34. Debo, *And Still the Waters Run*, 61–180.

35. D'Arcy McNickle, "Reader's Report on As Long as the Waters Run," included in Joseph A. Brandt to Dear Miss Debo, September 15, 1936, Joseph A. Brandt Collection, Western History Collection, University of Oklahoma [hereafter cited as JBC]. (The different title was the original one Debo gave her work.)

36. Brandt to Dear Miss Debo, September 15, 1936, JBC.

37. Angie Debo to Dear Mr. Brandt, November 7, 1936, JBC.

38. Taylor, *The New Deal and American Indian Tribalism*, 35–36; Peter W. Wright, "John Collier and the Oklahoma Indian Welfare Act of 1936," *Chronicles of Oklahoma* 50 (Autumn 1972): 347–71.

39. Debo to Dear Mr. Brandt, March 10, 1937, JBC.

40. Debo to Dear Mr. Brandt, March 10, 1937, JBC.

41. Debo to Dear Dr. Dale, June 19, 1937, EEDC.

42. Dale to Dear Dr. Debo, June 23, 1937, EEDC.

43. E. E. Dale, "Woman's Influence on the French Revolution," 6–7, unpublished paper from the seminar with Frederick Jackson Turner, "History of the West," fall 1913 through spring 1914, EEDC.

44. E. E. Dale to Professor M. L. Wardell, June 11, 1930, EEDC; see also Rich-

ard Lowitt, "Regionalism at the University of Oklahoma," *Chronicles of Oklahoma* 73 (Summer 1995): 170 n. 19.

45. Angie Debo to Dear Mr. Brandt, July 16, 1837, Angie Debo Collection, Western History Collection, University of Oklahoma [hereafter cited as ADC].

46. ADT, December 12, 1981, 10.

47. "Miss Debo, As Long as the Waters Run," review by Morris Waddell. Although the review is unsigned, an accompanying letter from William Bizzell to Joseph A. Brandt, dated July 20, 1937, indicates that the enclosed review is Waddell's and that because of that review the University of Oklahoma Press should not publish this work. University of Oklahoma, Office of the President, W. B. Bizzell, Correspondence, Box 124, Western History Collection, University of Oklahoma [hereafter cited as WBBC].

48. W. B. Bizzell, President, to Dear Mr. Brandt, July 20, 1937, WBBC; ADT, December 12, 1981, 10–11; Joseph A. Brandt to Dear Miss Debo, July 26, 1937, JBC.

49. ADT, December 11, 1981, 10, June 8, 1985, 14. The better-known publications reviewing the work were *Christian Century*, November 20, 1940, 1451; *Nation*, January 4, 1941, 26; Stanley Vestal, "Despoiling the Indians," *New York Herald Tribune*, January 5, 1941, 3.

50. Dorman, *Revolt of the Provinces*, 303–6; ADT, December 12, 1981, 10–11.

51. ADT, May 4, 1983, 9.

52. Angie Debo, *The Road to Disappearance: A History of the Creek Indians* (Norman: University of Oklahoma Press, 1941), vii.

53. See Annie Heloise Abel, *The American Indian as Participant in the Civil War* (Cleveland: Arthur H. Clark, 1919).

54. Debo, *The Road to Disappearance*, viii, 376.

55. Debo, *The Road to Disappearance*, 377.

56. ADT, December 16, 1981, 8.

57. Angie Debo diary entry, March 11, 1940. Debo kept diaries briefly as a child, then again in the early 1940s, and finally more regularly from 1947 until months before her death in 1988. These diaries are located in the ADP [hereafter cited as ADD]. Mary Ann Slater, "The Oklahoma Writers' Project: 1935–1942" (master's thesis, Oklahoma State University, 1985), 109–12; Angie E. Debo to My dear Dr. Dale, January 17, 1941, EEDC; ADT, May 4, 1983, 5–6.

58. Angie Debo to Dear Dr. Dale, January 11, 1942, EEDC.

59. Collier to Dear Miss Debo, December 8, 1941, ADC.

60. Angie Debo, *Prairie City: The Story of an American Community* (New York: Knopf, 1944), 245. Patricia Limerick sees a disconnect between Debo's work on Indians and Prairie City. See "Land, Justice, and Angie Debo: Telling the Truth to—and About—Your Neighbors," *Great Plains Quarterly* 21 (Fall 2001): 261–73. While Prairie City pays no attention to Native peoples, Debo is critical of this composite town. She laments the way technology leads to a decline in community. She also notes that town leaders, searching for profits, sell city plots to outsiders with little interest in the town, an action that truncates future growth. She also discusses the Ku Klux Klan, which in Oklahoma often warred against Catholics. Finally, she states that newly opened regions often attracted deviants.

61. *A Statistical Portrait of Women in the United States*, Current Population Reports, Special Studies, Series P-23, no. 58, U.S. Department of Commerce, Bureau of the Census (Washington DC: Government Printing Office, 1976), 31, cited by Carl Degler in *At Odds: Women and the Family in America from the Revolution to the Present* (New York: Oxford University Press, 1980), 511 n. 1; Gloria Valencia-Weber, "'Eulogy,' Angie Debo, 1890–1988," 5, ADP; The Methodist Church, Local Preacher's License for Miss Angie Debo, November 21, 1944, ADP; H. R. Doak, Ted Merrell, Raymond Bryson, Bert Burlew to Dear friends, September 26, 1946, ADP.

62. Debo to Dear Savoie, September 27, 1944, Savoie Lottinville to Dear Angie, September 30, 1944, and Debo to Dear Savoie, October 3, 1944, Savoie Lottinville Collection, Western History Collection, University of Oklahoma [hereafter cited as SLC].

63. E. E. Dale, "Reader's Report," Debo Manuscript, January 13, 1947, SLC; undated and unintelligibly signed "Reader's Report," Debo Manuscript, [Winter 1948], SLC; Savoie Lottinville to Dear Angie, January 15, 1948, SLC; ; E. E. Dale, undated memorandum on Angie Debo's Oklahoma: Where the Tall Superlatives Grow, EEDC.

64. E. E. Dale, undated memorandum on Angie Debo's Oklahoma: Where the Tall Superlatives Grow, EEDC; Debo to Dear Savoie, September 10, 1948, ADC.

65. Debo to Dear Mrs. Foreman, December 15, 1947, Grant Foreman Collection, Oklahoma State Historical Society, Oklahoma City [hereafter cited as GFC].

66. Angie Debo, *The Five Civilized Tribes: Report on Social and Economic*

Conditions (Philadelphia: Indian Rights Association, 1951); Angie Debo, ed., *The Cowman's Southwest: Being the Reminiscences of Oliver Nelson, Freighter, Camp Cook, Cowboy, Frontiersman in Kansas, Indian Territory, Texas, and Oklahoma, 1878–1893*, vol. 4 of the Western Frontiersman (Glendale CA: A. H. Clark, 1953).

67. Excerpts from Angie Debo's diary entries for July 11, September 8, 9, December 11, 1952, April 1953, June 25, 26, 27, 1953.

68. ADD, June 11, June 13, 1954; Angie Debo to My Dear Friend, Mrs. Foreman, May 7, 1953, GFC.

69. Angie Debo, *A History of the Indians of the United States* (Norman: University of Oklahoma Press, 1970), 304–5; Parman, *Indians and the American West*, 136–37.

70. Debo, *Indians of the United States*, 302.

71. Robert A. Hecht, *Oliver La Farge and the American Indian: A Biography* (Metuchen NJ: Scarecrow Press, 1991), 52–55, 115–120; ADD, July 7, 11, 13, 18, 19, 21, 22, 1955; Angie Debo, "Termination and the Oklahoma Indians," *Indian Affairs* 7 (Spring 1955): 17–22; Angie Debo, "What Oklahoma Indians Need," *American Indian* 7 (Winter 1956): 13–20; Angie Debo to "My very dear friend" [Carolyn Foreman], Christmas letter, 1956, GFC.

72. Angie Debo, "A Proposal to the U.S. Office of Education for an NDEA Institute for Advanced Study," University of Oklahoma, Norman, May 6 to July 21, 1967, Fred Harris Collection, Western History Collection, University of Oklahoma.

73. Angie Debo's Christmas letter, 1967, ADC.

74. Angie Debo, Statement Concerning the Alaska Native Claims Settlement Act of 1970, given in September 1970 and reprinted in *Congressional Record*, Senate, 92nd Cong., 1st sess., March 23, 1971, 7408–9.

75. Dr. James Ralph Scales's comments, Angie Debo Portrait Unveiling, April 8, 1985, Hugh and Ramona O'Neill Personal Collection, Marshall, Oklahoma.

76. Francis Paul Prucha, ed., *Documents of United States Indian Policy*, 2nd. ed., exp. (Lincoln: University of Nebraska Press, 1990), 249–52; see John R. Wunder, *"Retained by the People": A History of American Indians and the Bill of Rights* (New York: Oxford University Press, 1994), 124–46, 175–76.

77. Debo, *Indians of the United States*, xi–xii.

78. Angie Debo, "To Establish Justice," *Western Historical Quarterly* 7, no.

4 (1976): 405–11. The late Heather Lloyd, librarian in the manuscript room at the Edmon Low Library, recalled that Debo used the phrase "like wallpaper" to refer to the way she bought stamps.

79. Angie Debo, *Geronimo: The Man, His Time, His Place* (Norman: University of Oklahoma Press, 1976); ADD, November 13, 1971; ADT, February 16, 1984, 10–11.

80. Leckie, *Angie Debo, Pioneering Historian*, 174–91.

81. See Francis Jennings, "A Growing Partnership: Historians, Anthropologists, and American Indian History," *Ethnohistory* 29, no. 1 (1982): 21–34; Calvin Martin, "Ethnohistory: A Better Way to Write Indian History," *Western Historical Quarterly* 9 (January 1978): 41–56.

82. Angie Debo to Mr. Edward A. Shaw, September 2, 1979, JBC.

3

MARI SANDOZ

Historian of the Great Plains

John R. Wunder

HISTORIAN OF THE GREAT PLAINS, especially Nebraska's Sand-hills and upper Niobrara River valley region, Mari Sandoz embodied her home region. She was a perceptive commentator on culture change and the impact of people on the environment, and her fierce rhetoric and compulsion to write made her a survivor in her own time as well as a forerunner of today's New Western history and ethnohistory. Sandoz was blunt and confident about her historical contributions: "It's true that I'm not afraid of the evaluation posterity will put upon my nonfic-tion. . . . [G]ood or bad it is unique in its field and those who come after me will have to depend upon it to a very large extent. These books have always had critical acclaim even if not always understanding."[1] Such is the labor of a pathbreaker.

Although Sandoz wrote both history and fiction, she wrote history with a passion seldom exhibited before or since, and her work has withstood time's assessment. Indeed, as Stephen B. Oates comments in his introduction to the fiftieth-anniversary edition of *Crazy Horse*, Sandoz's biography of the Lakota patriot remains one of the finest lit-erary accomplishments of modern historical writing. During her life, Sandoz was thrilled when this book was named one of the Ten Best Serious Books ever published on the American West in 1954. And her biographer, Helen Winter Stauffer, concludes that as a historian, San-doz "fused her skill as a writer, her mastery of historical research, and her empathy for her subjects to create works of unique and lasting value."[2] For Sandoz, this was not an easy path.

4. (*Opposite Top*) Mary Fehr Sandoz with children Jules Sandoz Jr. (*left*), James Sandoz, and Mari Sandoz (*right*). Photograph taken in 1901 by Henry Surber. *Courtesy of Mari San-doz High Plains Heritage Center, Chadron* NE. *Accession no. 2003.001.0032, Caroline Sandoz Pifer Col-lection.*

5. (*Opposite Bottom*) Mari Sandoz in 1958. *Courtesy of Mari Sandoz High Plains Heritage Center, Chadron* NE. *Accession no. 2003.001.00314, Caroline Sandoz Pifer Collection.*

Early Life in the Sandhills

Born to Jules Ami Sandoz and Mary Fehr Sandoz in May 1896 at their homestead near the Niobrara River, Mari Susette Sandoz was first named Mary after her mother. As a baby and young child, her parents called her Marie. As a young adult she opted for a third spelling and pronunciation, Mari, with the "ari" phonetically pronounced as "are" and "E". Her mother spoke German, her father, French. Mary did not know when she married this gruff homesteader of the plains in 1895 that three other wives preceded her and one was still legally his wife. By the time she discovered her dilemma, she was dependent upon Jules financially and pregnant.[3]

Mary and Jules had more children (Jule and James within three years), and each new child brought new responsibilities for Mari. Because Mary's Swiss mother came to help with the babies, Mari had a brief childhood until she turned six. Her grandmother, having developed cancer, died in 1903 just as Fritz was born. At seven, Mari had total responsibility for Fritz, and at ten she cooked, baked, cleaned, and cared for all her siblings while her mother farmed. All the while Mari lived in terror of her father. Once, while beating her, he broke her hand, leaving her with an injury that never healed properly.[4]

Shortly before her ninth birthday, in 1905, Sheridan County officials required Mari and Jule to attend school. Mari spoke German, a little French, and a smattering of Polish gleaned from a neighbor girl, but no English. Although her first year of schooling lasted only six weeks, school quickly became a sanctuary. As Stauffer notes, "Mari wanted desperately to learn and school was the most interesting place in the world."[5] But it was not overly pleasant; Mari endured abuse, including being ostracized because she was not being reared religiously and her clothing was made from burlap sacks. Still, she learned to speak, read, and write English by the time she turned twelve and began to write as soon as she could read. Her teacher sent one of her first essays to the *Omaha Daily News*, which published it in April 1908 on the Junior Writer's Page. When she showed it proudly to her family, her father beat her mercilessly, dumped her into a cellar crawling with snakes and mice, and left her screaming until he let her out. Although this incident left an indelible mark, she kept writing but used pseudonyms. Jules "consider[ed] writers and artists the maggots of society," and he banned most books from his home, especially fiction. He only became reconciled to Mari's writing on his deathbed, when he asked her to write his biography.[6]

The day after her eleventh birthday, a new sister was born; Mari named her Flora. It was another very difficult birth and Mari served as midwife, another life-changing experience. Flora soon became Mari's "child," and they remained close for life. Three years later, when Caroline was born, Jules decided to move. He filed on another piece of land with a small lake, claiming 640 acres under the Kinkaid Act of 1904, four times the acreage allowed under the original Homestead Act. This somewhat isolated location, south of the Sandoz homestead, did not appeal to Mary, who refused to move. After a series of lean-tos were constructed on the site, Jules sent Mari and Jule to establish residency, "proving up" this new homestead. Fourteen-year-old Mari was on her own, a watershed moment in her life that afforded her an intimate knowledge of her homeland. Sandoz, the person and her writings, remained forever anchored in the soils of the Sandhills.[7]

These survival skills were needed after a late-May blizzard struck the Sandhills in 1910. The small herd of cattle Jules had been cultivating got lost in the catastrophe. Mari and Jule, sent on horseback, dug them out, but the adventure proved very costly. Mari collapsed upon their return and was bedridden for six weeks suffering from sunstroke. Although she eventually recovered sight in her right eye, the left was permanently blinded.[8]

Mari, however, was not about to stay put. At age seventeen she passed her eighth-grade exams. For her parents, Mari's education was over, but Mari secretly rode a horse to Rushville in July and, by passing the teacher's certification examination, earned a third-class teaching certificate, which enabled her to teach in rural schools. This represented independence and a major step toward realizing her dreams.

In her first timid steps, Mari initially taught classes in the Sandoz barn and lived at home. Then she met Wray Macumber, who had moved to the Sandhills in 1909. On May 29, 1914, they were married, and for five years they lived together on his ranch. In August 1919 she obtained a divorce on charges of extreme mental cruelty. Although Mari never publicly discussed the reasons for her divorce, it proved devastating for her relationship with her mother. Mary disapproved of divorce, especially for her daughters. The tensions were so difficult that in September, Mari moved to Lincoln to seek an education.[9]

A Historian in the Making

Barriers encountered by aspiring female historians in the twentieth century all too often limited their productivity and creativity, particularly in their early years. Personal lives were frequently conflicted, as many people believed that, for women, having a profession precluded marriage and children. When women did pursue a profession they were seen as feminine failures and, hence, suspect. They had few role models in professional female historians, since universities and colleges—the most likely places to employ historians—preferred to hire men, whom they believed brought greater prestige to departments and institutions. Often female scholars were forced into fallback positions, such as librarians, research assistants, or historical society staff, rather than university professorships. Lacking institutional support, these marginalized professionals often specialized in what many male scholars considered less important topics: the histories of Native peoples, local and regional history, and women. Often, too, they turned to popular rather than scholarly presses, as men controlled publication selection committees of the latter.[10]

But none of these barriers seemed to affect Sandoz unduly. In some ways, she had dealt with these roadblocks earlier in her life. She had taken care of a home and children during her childhood and had married and divorced at a young age. These experiences left her with no romantic illusions about marriage as a way to achieve personal fulfillment. She also learned that how she looked and what she did were not important to her; she wanted to write good history and engaging fiction. Later she readily embraced what to her were great opportunities—working in the Nebraska State Historical Society, conducting research for other scholars, and taking classes from noted literature and history professors. For Sandoz, the struggles in her later professional life paled in comparison to her early years in the Sandhills and her pursuit of an education. By 1920 she found that more learning was imperative for any writing success.

When she arrived in Lincoln in the aftermath of World War I with no savings and needing work, Sandoz took courses at a business school and learned secretarial skills that proved invaluable in her later research activities. To support herself she typed a manuscript for a retired University of Nebraska English professor and worked briefly at the Polk County courthouse in Osceola, Nebraska, before returning to the Sandhills to teach school and save her earnings to go to college.[11]

Luckily, Mari was determined, for persistence was needed even to be admitted. As she remembered later, "I came to Lincoln and sat around in the anterooms of various deans for two weeks between conferences with advisers who insisted that I must go to high school. Finally bushy-haired [Education] Dean [William E.] Sealock got tired of seeing me waiting and said, 'Well, you can't do any more than fail,' and registered me." But she thrived at the University of Nebraska, and as she studied "history and geology, [and] anthropology, the area we had explored as children took on greater significance." She also wrote "seventy-eight short stories (and didn't sell one), won honorable mention in a Harper's Intercollegiate Contest in 1926, and wrote a bad novel that, fortunately, no one would publish."[12] From 1923 to 1932 she took courses whenever she could afford to, never expecting to receive a degree. She also worked at the Nebraska State Historical Society, where she learned the archival techniques her works would eventually showcase.

Three history professors influenced Mari significantly. In her second semester she took a Western civilization survey from Professor Fred Fling, who had a doctorate from the University of Leipzig and had been hired in 1892 to anchor European history. Sandoz said that Fling was "the henniest, fussiest man imaginable . . . but his approach to historical fact was impeccable."[13] In his classes, he perfected his ideas on historical methodology. He published numerous handbooks and pamphlets on his "Nebraska Method," which profoundly influenced Sandoz. He frequently challenged teachers to use original sources in teaching history at the secondary level, which also appealed to her.

Mari excelled in his class and implemented his ideas rigorously as she set about collecting historical evidence. Her passion for historical accuracy and her "elaborate filing system" of cross-indexing were directly attributable to Fling.[14]

Another historian who influenced Sandoz was John Andrew Rice, the demanding head of the Classics Department. Rice, a native of the South Carolina upcountry, held an undergraduate degree from Tulane University and as a Rhodes Scholar obtained a Classics PhD from Oxford. Sandoz took his course on ancient Greek philosophy and history and acquired an abiding love of Greek tragedies and the comedies of Aristophanes.[15]

A semester of Fling and Rice surely challenged Sandoz, but her quest to learn and write could not sustain her. Without the resources to continue at the university, she grew dangerously thin and preoccupied. Rather than engage in self-pity, Sandoz continued to write and finally placed some of her fiction. She built a supportive community of other local artists, such as Weldon Kees, Loren Eiseley, and novelist Bess Streeter Aldrich. Mari published her first story in a new journal, *Prairie Schooner*, started in 1927 by the Department of English and Professor Lowry C. Wimberly. Sandoz also wrote and published two historical essays, one in the *North American Review* and another in *Folk-Say: A Regional Miscellany*.[16]

The late 1920s were very difficult for Sandoz. Her fiction continued to be rejected as she fiercely debated with editors over the nature and causes of their rejections and her use of "westernisms"—their term for her colloquial expressions. The painful criticisms only strengthened her resolve. With the onset of the Great Depression and a return to the poverty of her youth, she started in earnest to research the history of the Sandhills as context for her father's biography.

Sandoz sustained her confidence because she concluded that she had a unique understanding of both local American Indians and pioneering farmers and ranchers, a claim few others could make. Moreover, life brightened after she spent the summer of 1931 with her friend Eleanor Hinman, who had grown up on the Pine Ridge Reservation and was interested in Native Americans. Together they traveled more than three thousand miles in a Model T, visiting Northern Plains reservations and interviewing Indians.[17] Sandoz meticulously documented her expedition for future reference.

Returning to Lincoln, Sandoz finally experienced two strokes of good luck. The superintendent of the Nebraska State Historical Society, Addison E. Sheldon, hired her as his research assistant. The paycheck allowed her to return to the university to hone her history skills, apply her own experience, and contextualize Niobrara Country in its broader historical situation. She wanted to refine her Old Jules manuscript and anticipated returning to school to take a class on the trans-Mississippi West. Her sister Caroline later recalled that Mari was not sure "whether she was sufficiently schooled to write *Old Jules*" but had concluded that more education would help. Early in February, Sandoz wrote to Benjamin Botkin, a friend at the University of Oklahoma, that she had finished what she hoped was a final draft of "Old Jules" and that she was delighted to be back at the university, taking fourteen hours, including "a very promising course under Hicks, just returned from Harvard, I believe, The West after 1829, in which he offers to follow the frontier line across the continent."[18]

Professor John D. Hicks had arrived in Lincoln in 1923 and quickly climbed the academic ladder, becoming chair of the new Department of History in 1925. When the dean of the College of Arts and Sciences left in 1929, Hicks assumed the position until 1932, when he left for his graduate school alma mater, the University of Wisconsin. Throughout his administrative years he primarily taught surveys of American history, recent American history, and the history of the trans-Mississippi West while writing *The Populist Revolt,* a classic study that remains the starting point for all scholars studying Populism.[19]

Hicks considered himself a Turnerian, as did most American historians in 1932. In his "History of the West" course he "followed the pattern that [Frederick] Paxson had laid out at Wisconsin, beginning with the colonial frontier of 1763, and following the frontier across the continent, step by step, until 1893, the date Turner delivered his famous paper on 'The Significance of the Frontier in American History.'" Hicks used as texts Paxson's Pulitzer Prize–winning *History of the American Frontier, 1763–1893* and Turner's collected essays, but he deviated from a strict Turnerian interpretation, noting that the Turner thesis was "not always accurate (Nebraska, for example)." Regions did not always mature in an orderly fashion. Hicks "threw in a few extra lectures at the end in order to bring in the four states admitted [to the Union] later [than 1890]: Utah, Oklahoma, New Mexico, and Arizona."[20] He also raised issues comparing Canadian and American frontiers and, like Walter Prescott Webb, interjected concepts of a world frontier into his class.

Hick's Populism, which had once burned brightly in the soul of Mari's father and her own beliefs in the validity of her own experiences, kindled Sandoz's manuscript revisions. Hicks recalled that Sandoz visited him later and told him that "I had commented favorably on a term paper she wrote for me, noting her admirable understanding of frontier conditions." Hicks, writing after Sandoz's death, asserted, "I'm sure she merited whatever compliments I paid her; her *Old Jules* is one of the most moving narratives of the frontier that I have ever read."[21]

Given the achievements in western and American history at the University of Nebraska–Lincoln must have been exciting for Mari. The Nebraska State Historical Society (NSHS), moreover, was an epicenter of historical activity. In 1907 Clarence Paine, the new NSHS secretary, had invited six historical societies to send representatives to organize a new historical association. They had responded by adopting a constitution on October 17–18, 1907, forming the Mississippi Valley Historical Association (MVHA), the antecedent of today's Organization of American Historians. Paine became their secretary-treasurer, a position he held until his untimely death in 1916, whereupon his widow, Clara, a librarian at the NSHS, assumed his position.

Because of her sex, Frederick Paxson, the MVHA's president, tried to prevent Clara Paine from assuming the secretary-treasurer duties. She responded fiercely and prevailed. Possessing a "passion for history, literature, and genealogical research," Paine stabilized the association and saw to it that women achieved membership on committees. In 1930 her counterpart at the Wisconsin Historical Society, Louise Kellogg, became the MVHA's first woman president. Paine worked closely with Hicks and evidently did not hold Paxson's sexism again him. Hicks became president the very year he had Sandoz in his "History of the West" class.[22]

As she did in the budding national history association, Paine helped ensure that women scholars would be welcome at the NSHS, and director Addison Sheldon supported her. Sheldon had homesteaded in western Nebraska in 1886 and edited a newspaper until 1898, when he was elected to the state legislature as a Populist. He did not personally know Jules, but had corresponded with him. One of Sheldon's greatest acquisitions for the NSHS was Judge Eli Ricker's huge collection of documents and miscellanea from northwestern Nebraska; he hired Sandoz to organize it, re-sparking her long-held interest in American Indian historical research.[23] It was the first of many projects at the NSHS for her.

While Sandoz organized files and went to classes, she kept writing. She successfully published a literature review on the "New Regionalism" in the *Prairie Schooner*. Then she sent *Old Jules* to Atlantic Press for a nonfiction book contest in October 1932. After eight months the press rejected it, just as her job at the NSHS ended. Dejected after reading a reviewer's note saying the book was a boring one about "a dirty old man," she began revising it and sent it to Alfred A. Knopf, Houghton Mifflin, and other houses, but without success. By the fall of 1933, prepared to quit, she headed home to the Sandhills. Depressed and suffering from severe migraines, she realized she could not stop writing. When Sheldon wrote in December that he might have another job for her, she returned and assumed a position funded by a New Deal federal program for humanists.[24]

Mari's duties at the NSHS expanded. She became director of personnel, supervising forty to fifty employees; chief archivist for several collections; binder of the newspaper collection; and associate editor of *Nebraska History*. As a research assistant she helped Sheldon write a book on Nebraska land practices as part of another New Deal grant. With a modest salary, she began to regain her confidence. A revised *Old Jules* was unsuccessfully submitted to more New York presses and even Idaho's Caxton Printers, which asked her for a subvention she could not afford. In April 1935 she submitted it to the Atlantic Press nonfiction contest again, and this time she won. A telegram read: "Happy to announce that your manuscript wins the Atlantic contest. . . . Acknowledge this wire, hearty congratulations. Edward Weeks."[25] She could not believe it. Mari realized she now would pursue her professional dream: to write history and fiction of her beloved Sandhills.

The Works of Mari Sandoz

Mari Sandoz proved a prolific writer. Starting with *Old Jules* in 1935, she published eleven histories as well as a variety of historical essays and reminiscences; her loyalty to the Westerners, a club-like group of academics and the general public who shared a desire for quality history of the American West, also resulted in several articles and notes published in chapter "brand books." A writer to the end, she corrected the page proofs for her last book, *The Battle of the Little Bighorn*, as she valiantly fought cancer.[26]

Sandoz's legacies to the history of the American West are legion and profound; her corpus establishes her as a clear antecedent of the recent New Western history movement. To read Sandoz is to collide face-to-face with a place, the Great Plains. There was nothing particularly significant to her about 1890, the year the U.S. Census Bureau had declared the frontier closed and which Turner saw as the end of western history. Her frontiers knew no artificial time line. She embraced topics few historians of her time tackled, subjects that are now central to an understanding of the American West. Like Kansas historian James C. Malin, she paid attention to environmental history, tracking the changes of the land and the peoples drawn to the land. She readily wrote people of color and women into her histories; their voices are strong and their lives multidimensional. In essence, Sandoz's frontier did not match Turner's.

Like Annie Abel and Angie Debo, Sandoz treated Native American history and culture very seriously and respectfully. Four of her books and a number of essays directly embrace the methodology of what later anthropologists and historians would label "ethnohistory." Sandoz conducted both extensive fieldwork and archival research. She interviewed many who had either participated in historic events or were only one generation removed from them. She understood intuitively that cultural changes in Indians' lives were part of the dynamics of history, paving the way for modern scholarship. To study Lakota and Cheyenne history today requires reading Sandoz and consulting her extensive archival research files and maps.

Although Sandoz sought to describe for posterity the complex history of the Great Plains and the Sandhills, her historiography addresses a wide range of subjects. For the purposes of this analysis, I have divided her histories into two general categories that chronicle the history of the Great Plains: American Indian history and the history of Euro-American migration and settlement. Plains indigenous histories include four books (*Crazy Horse: The Strange Man of the Oglalas, Cheyenne Autumn, These Were the Sioux,* and *The Battle of the Little Bighorn*) and five essays ("There Were Two Sitting Bulls," "The Search for the Bones of Crazy Horse," introduction to *The Cheyenne Indians: Their History and Ways of Life* by George Bird Grinnell, introduction to *A Pictographic History of the Oglala Sioux* by Bad Heart Bull and Blish, and "The Great Council"). Settlement histories include five books (*Old Jules, The Buffalo Hunters, The Cattlemen, Love Song to the Plains,* and *The Beaver Men*) and six articles ("The Kinkaider Comes and Goes," "The New Frontier Woman," "The Neighbor," "Some Notes on Wild Bill Hickok," "Look of the Last Frontier," and "The Homestead in Perspective").[27]

NATIVE AMERICAN HISTORIES

Fundamental to an understanding of Sandoz's indigenous histories is the ethnohistorical process by which she composed her work. Sandoz relied upon a plethora of sources that few writers of her time consulted or even attempted to command. These reflected her earlier experiences and her times. First was the matter of her birth and having grown up on the post-Turnerian frontier. She and her family counted as personal friends a number of Lakotas and Cheyennes, who often visited their former campsites on Sandoz and adjacent lands. Mari remembered frolicking with Lakota children during the summers when the visits were most frequent. To hear her tell it, she was a youngster who nearly walked in more than one cultural world; but once she assumed more family responsibilities, there was less time for cultural exchange with her Lakota neighbors. He Dog, brother of Crazy Horse, nevertheless, called Sandoz his "granddaughter" until he died in 1937.[28]

Second, Sandoz knew the land, as did her Indian subjects, and she often visited places where crucial historical events had transpired. Her appreciation for the nuances of the physical environment permeates all her work, but it is most effective in the Crazy Horse biography and her chronicle of the Northern Cheyennes' return to their homelands. She understood the impact of place on the social and geopolitical history of the Native American West.

Third, Sandoz talked to people to obtain their versions and perspectives. Before she began her indigenous histories, she took a number of research trips on which she interviewed tribal elders and relatives of her primary subjects. Mari not only took copious notes and drew many original maps based upon indigenous descriptions; she conscientiously attempted to understand Indian language inflections, tones, and meaning. In her later writings she provided settings for the integration of history, folklore, and linguistics that previously had not been a centerpiece of American scholarship. In the process of describing Indian life and seeking indigenous historical viewpoints, Sandoz retraced the Cheyenne diaspora and the military ebbs and flows of the Battle of the Little Bighorn, and she personally walked and camped where Crazy Horse and his people had. Beginning in the summer of 1930 Sandoz often traveled to Indian Country to immerse herself in the cultures and oral histories of Plains peoples.[29]

Fourth, Sandoz was conscious of proper, modern ethnohistorical ethics, even before the methodology was codified. She gave primacy to Indian voices in her writings and did so in a respectful manner, acknowledging rights to cultural knowledge. She sought permission from the appropriate tribal keepers of history and understood restrictions they placed on information. She also respected the sacredness of place and accuracy; she focused on meticulous and precise descriptions of settings, using direct quotes and imagery. But her unrelenting quest for accuracy gained through extensive probing occasionally earned her the enmity of Lakotas, especially when she worked closely with the families of Crazy Horse, Man Afraid of His Horses, and He Dog. When she openly wrote of the weaknesses of Red Cloud and Spotted Tail in the political history of the Siouan struggle to retain their sovereignty, their relatives were offended since their stories were not told. This is a common problem for all ethnohistorians writing biographies.[30]

Sandoz outlines how she thought indigenous history should be written in her introduction to the 1962 reprinting of George B. Grinnell's *The Cheyenne Indians*. Blunt and unforgiving, she opens with a critique of capitalistic colonialism: "Buffalo still moved in vast dark herds over the prairies, and no Teton Sioux or Northern Cheyenne had ever set his moccasin upon the humiliating earth of an Indian reservation." There is no doubt where Sandoz stands. Grinnell "had the forthrightness, the scholarly open mindedness and training in investigation and evaluation, the firsthand knowledge and experience, the warmth of understanding and the prophetic vision." These traits were essential for the writing of successful Indian history. But the historian also must respect limits on knowledge. She complimented Grinnell for "keeping back only those rare bits of revelation that are of the innermost sacredness of a people, revelations permitted him because he could keep a confidence 'deep in the heart.'" His Cheyenne history also took into account culture change because he "approached them with the reserve and dignity that the Indians appreciated. . . . He studied their history as a warrior people, but he was even more concerned with the organization of Cheyenne life, the significance and essence of it, from the simplest comings and goings in the village circle to their deep sense of identification with all the things around them."[31]

Sandoz also described what made for a quality Sioux historian. In her introduction to *A Pictographic History of the Oglala Sioux* she listed the attributes of a good Native historian: "First there must be objectivity, the ability to be in a fight or a ceremonial or hunt and yet view it beyond the purely personal involvement, observe what happened all around, see it with the eye of the people as well as an individual." For Sandoz, history required accurate, detailed, honest reporting. She detested overly biased accounts and diatribes. Following Lakota concepts, she concluded that a writer needed to subsume his or her ego in order to be objective: "The second requirement was the artistic ability to portray the event or the incident so others could grasp the action and the meaning, with something beyond the factual content, something broader, more, as the Sioux liked to say, of the sky and the great directions, a meaning more elevated, more profound." As Patricia Nelson Limerick articulated later, Sandoz believed it was essential for Native historians to "say something," creatively and artistically. Moreover, Sandoz noted that formal band histories required the approval of a headman and had to be above the challenge of anyone involved. Oglala society had culturally appropriate quality control mechanisms that must be honored.[32]

Sandoz followed these principles in her joint biography of Dull Knife and Lone Wolf, Cheyenne leaders who had led their people from an Oklahoma exile back to their homeland, only to be imprisoned and murdered as they escaped from Fort Robinson. Her plan to write a full-length history of the Cheyennes abruptly changed when Simon and Schuster announced they had retained Howard Fast to do a "quickie" book on the Cheyennes. Extremely unhappy with this turn of events, Sandoz thought she might fashion serialized stories to scoop Fast but opted instead to wait until the Fast book could only be found "in the garbage dumps."[33]

She turned back to Crazy Horse when Eleanor Hinman, realizing she could not do him justice, offered her research materials to Mari. Although Sandoz had declined a similar offer in 1938, she now accepted the generous gesture and, combining it with her own extensive materials, began writing her greatest work. The execution took much labor because she wanted the book to be as perfect as possible. Fretting over virtually every sentence and word, she wrote and rewrote, sometimes revising a page fifty times. From 1939 until it appeared in print in 1942, Sandoz lived night and day with her manuscript. In the process, she went to Denver to consult relevant archives and returned to the Sandhills to trace the paths walked by Crazy Horse.

Judging from contemporary reactions and recent evaluations, Sandoz accomplished near perfection. Stephen Oates describes her "towering achievement" as filled with "literary gems," descriptions of Crazy Horse, the Lakota people, and their times. More recently, Vine Deloria Jr., after rereading *Crazy Horse*, wrote that "Sandoz had presented a masterful and wholly authentic account of the struggle for the northern plains during the 1850s through the 1870s in which almost every line rang true. I was stunned at the wealth of detail contained in each line of text—material that must have come from her conversations over time with a large number of elders, filed then in some great and efficient memory bank, and later skillfully woven into a chronicle of the times that overflows with authenticity." It is in *Crazy Horse* that Sandoz quotes a Sioux elder's observation that still remains haunting to all who write indigenous history: "A people without history is like the wind on the buffalo grass."

Wallace Stegner extolled the book in *Atlantic Monthly*; Sandoz wrote "with scrupulous regard to truth and history." Not everyone praised Sandoz, however. One rather sick literary critic, Clifton Fadiman, intoned that Sandoz "has been carrying on a fervent historico-literary affair with a dead Indian, the consequence of which is a curious, half-interesting, uneven book." Fadiman could not understand this "half history, half historic epic" work. He concluded that it would be unsuccessful because it was on a subject that was unimportant and of no interest to the average reader.[34]

For Sandoz, validation came during a 1943 incident after she had moved to New York City to be closer to the editors who seemed to be the primary bane of her writing career. A number of young Northern Sioux and Flathead men, none of whom Sandoz had met before, came to her apartment unannounced after attending a powwow. One had *Crazy Horse* with him, and "while they all sat around my apartment he gave an old-time harangue, in the sense of the word French traders speaking of Sioux orators used." Because not everyone understood Lakota, sign language was employed, and the speaker then dramatically read sections of the biography. "All the while that circle of dark eyes never left my face," Sandoz noted. When this event encapsulating laughter and solemnity concluded, each man offered Mari a double handshake and left. Sandoz treasured this moment. "It was the finest thing that could ever happen in my house," she penned, "and I felt terribly small and insignificant for a week."[35]

The 1940s and 1950s brought more Indian history and speaking out about Indian issues. Sandoz favored parts of the Indian New Deal, but she criticized John Collier on his rigidity and vehemently opposed termination policies of the post–Collier era. She buttonholed senators and representatives and wrote them often. An activist at heart, Sandoz traced her "liberalism" to "a childhood of living in the midst of poverty." The Sandoz homestead had entertained "the world's disinherited," who taught us "the history of rapacious empires." She logically concluded that "having at an early age become aware of the long struggle to obtain and defend a small and decent portion of individual liberty and of the recent pressures against this liberty—as society becomes more and more complex—the development of my social consciousness was logically inevitable." A second "determining factor" was "the daily presence of an expropriated race, the American Indian. I was attracted to them very much, as children are always attracted by men of grand bearing, graciousness, and wisdom." From a close friend He Dog "and others like him, I developed a feeling of the brotherhood with all the things on earth which is the essence of the ancient philosophy of the Sioux, and the foundation of the deep sense of responsibility which each Sioux feels for each member of his community."[36]

Sandoz's other indigenous histories all made their mark. *Cheyenne Autumn* received more praise than *Crazy Horse*. In some ways, Sandoz became radicalized as she traced the Cheyennes' flight from Oklahoma to their homeland on the Northern Plains. In this process she discovered the Sappa Massacre site. In 1875 the U.S. Army and several buffalo hunters attacked a Cheyenne village in northern Kansas, killing Chief Bad Heart and the keeper of the sacred arrows, Stone Forehead, along with dozens of villagers. Sandoz proved that the army account of the event was fabricated. She also documented the Cheyennes' retaliatory 1878 killings of nineteen settlers.[37]

Sandoz's biographer notes that while Mari was writing *Cheyenne Autumn* she read Franz Kafka's *The Castle* and Adolph Hitler's *Mein Kampf.* She saw parallels between Hitler's persecution of Jews and federal Indian policies. It did not surprise her when Cheyennes told her that their parents and grandparents believed the United States intended to kill all Cheyennes. As a result, Sandoz interpreted their flight "not as an isolated incident but as a typical result of colonization that might have happened at any place in the world to which settlers were sent to convert a wilderness into a market for capital and manufacture." Sandoz sets this tone in her preface. America's war on American Indians "is unrivaled in history: the destruction of a whole way of life and the expropriation of a race from a region of 350,000,000 acres in so short a time." How was it accomplished? "It entailed first of all a tremendous job of public conditioning. In the 1830s and 1840s the buffalo Indians were considered the most romantic of peoples, drawing visitors from everywhere. . . . But that was before the white man wanted these Indian lands. . . . By 1864, with the nation at war ostensibly to free the black man from slavery, the public had been prepared to accept a policy of extermination for the red."[38]

Why had people not stood up to this calamity? "All this time a few humanitarians were complaining against such treatment of the Indian, but no voice was loud enough to be heard above the drumbeaters for the railroads, the cattlemen, the miners, and the army contractors." Sandoz granted that Generals John Pope and George Crook protested these war tactics and regretted the extermination policy, "but their voices were like the wind on the buffalo grass." Thus, to Sandoz, the Cheyennes' flight was both "the epic story of the American Indian, and one of the epics of our history." She humbly concluded: "I hope that I have not failed my friends, both the Cheyennes and the whites, too greatly in the telling here."[39] Sandoz did not.

What Sandoz had not anticipated were attacks from Hollywood, where producers wanted to depict the Cheyennes' flight. On several occasions they sent her scripts. The first ones were predicated on Fast's book, which she could not abide, appalled by its lack of cultural and historical accuracy. Eventually, she agreed to a movie of her book, but soon found all she legally had done was to sell her title. John Ford made *Cheyenne Autumn*, with a script that amazingly interjected a contrived white love story between a cavalry captain and a Quaker schoolmarm who were conveniently along for the escape. Always disturbed by this treachery, Sandoz forbade any further films based on her work.[40]

Sandoz wrote two brief Indian histories in the 1960s. *These Were the Sioux* in many ways represents her ethnohistorical synthesis. One particularly pungent section confronts the sexist myth that Sioux women were oppressed and had no place within their society and that Sioux men were laggards. "The arrogant and superior white traveler, the superficial observer," she notes, "assumed that the Sioux woman was a drudge, the Indian man a lazy dog—but not too lazy to make a living for his people with crude bow and lance for thousands of years, not too lazy to humiliate the United States Army with the only two wipeouts on its record—at Fort Phil Kearny and on the Little Big Horn." Both, she continued, "were largely Sioux triumphs if one can call these victories triumphs when it seems that not only the Sioux but all the Indians are never to be done paying for their success." Sandoz explained how central to Sioux life women are. But why are these myths repeated? Sandoz thought too many historians were lazy and that information about Indians was controlled by "a petty political tyrant called an Indian agent."[41]

Sandoz's *The Battle of the Little Bighorn*, published posthumously, in many ways represented the logical conclusion to her pathbreaking Indian histories. Although an editor worried about her anti-Custer rhetoric, the publisher moved with uncommon speed and made it possible for Sandoz to correct page proofs before she died. Upon reviewing the book, Alvin Josephy Jr. remarked that much had been written about Custer's demise, but Sandoz provided more clarity and accuracy than historians had previously done.[42] The proof came in the detailed maps based upon Sioux and Cheyenne interviews.

In 1970 Dee Brown published *Bury My Heart at Wounded Knee*, which pricked America's conscience and helped initiate a renewed interest in Native American history. In many ways it proved a simple book, but like Harriet Beecher Stowe's nineteenth-century story of slavery, it had the ability to remake an entire discipline. New perspectives, questions, answers, and narratives elicited a new history. Of course, Sandoz had already covered this ground, including her analysis of Wounded Knee. She described this darkest of times in the American West as no mere "battle" but rather "the shocking butchery of Wounded Knee in 1890, when women and children were mowed down by Hotchkiss guns in the freezing cold of a late December day."[43] Thus, Sandoz's American Indian histories constitute an early building block upon which the resurgence of today's indigenous history stands. A moral compass, encouraging indigenous scholars to record their peoples' pasts, oral history and Native voices as requirements for quality history, and ethnohistory as an essential methodological approach—all of these were essentials of Sandoz's world.

Equal to Sandoz's commitment to uncover and explain Native American history was her desire to correct and trace the history of Euro-American settlement on the Great Plains. Sandoz's treatment of westward expansion involved a complex evolution of ideology filtered through personal experience. While she sought to portray immigrants to the American West realistically, she also recognized the boundaries of this endeavor. Historiographically, Sandoz vacillated between adopting a Turnerian approach, the only analytical framework applied to western history at the time, and acting as a catalyst for new paradigms that emerged after her death.

Sandoz's first major work in this area was *Old Jules*. Her father's biography captured the struggles invested in successful pioneering. It included biography, drama, storytelling, regional descriptions, violence, cultural exchange, family crises, women and men hard at work, and historical and environmental context. The portrait of her father and those who lived with him is unusually textured. Her historical technique, which still causes uneasiness among historians, involved massive research in traditional sources, extensive oral interviews, personal experiences and reflections, and reconstruction of historic moments and conversations based upon the general record. What *might* have been—the object of some historians' strong criticism—is accorded historical legitimacy in Sandoz's histories.[44]

Jules Sandoz is realistically presented; the triumphal homesteader and community builder from the 1880s to the 1920s stands side by side with the man who participated in such violent events as a lynching, child and spousal abuse, frequent gunplay, and verbal assault. One might not like much about Old Jules, but he earns a grudging respect by the end of the biography. Commenting near the end of her career, Sandoz observed: "There was, of course, no training school for the pioneer. He went out and was one or wasn't." What Sandoz achieves historically is the recording of settlement on an isolated frontier in a context "beyond the foibles of the Turner thesis."[45]

Throughout November and December 1935, Sandoz received more than a thousand letters from readers of *Old Jules*. Some empathetic fans mentioned her abuse at her father's hands (she referred to him almost always as only Old Jules). They praised her and condemned the family violence. Mari answered those letters, revealing her own understanding of the strength required for pioneering and personal survival. "Don't be too disturbed about Old Jules," she wrote in one reply. "Perhaps it is because of the historian in me that I would not have him different at all—a man of less impatience and less violence could not have come from his sheltered and safe environment and stood alone, cap to his brows, gun across his forearm, against his entire world. Such ego, such courage is given to but few of us." Later, responding to another person, Sandoz becomes harsh: "The world is full of ordinary women and children to be sacrificed. And by one of life's paradoxes, we [Sandozes] were not sacrificed at all. Instead we were given a close look upon the lightning such as is granted to few. I, for one, have no complaint to make over my singed eyebrows." Because he blazed the frontier trail, Old Jules could be forgiven.[46]

Sometimes Mari had to explain that there were two kinds of pioneers: those who arrived first on the frontier, like her father, and those who followed and reintroduced civilization. Unlike the Turnerian claim that all pioneers went through a metamorphosis requiring a transition from civilization to savagery to a new civilization, Sandoz suggested that the first settlers might never have evolved into a new civilization, since their sacrifices kept them stuck in the frontier's savagery stage. It fell to later pioneers to restart civilization. "Pioneers could be softer," she observed, if "they came after, and settled after the first battle for water and land had been fought. But the frontier[smen] were a long, lean, hard breed, with finger[s] on the trigger."[47]

Were Americans ready to read *Old Jules* when it came out? Some thought no. Arthur Maurice, who reviewed *Old Jules* for the *New York Sun*, noted the well-written book was too crude, "racy," and violent: "The book is strong meat; not merely that, but strong meat with a decidedly gamy flavor." Bernard DeVoto, who became a longtime friend of Mari's, wrote, "I am afraid for this book." Even though he praised Sandoz for "a magnificent job," he worried that her presentation of Great Plains history might be rejected by too many Americans reading *Old Jules*: "It is achingly, glaringly necessary to get the High Plains written about and understood, to force a realization of them and their place in our culture and our problems on the national mind. But Miss Sandoz is a native and a literary artist and, I suspect, disqualified on both counts. Her accents and rhythms, her assumptions, even her vocabulary, are alien." His concerns about her subjectivity proved unfounded; the book's prize-winning popularity and Book-of-the-Month Club selection contributed to its strong and consistent sales.[48]

Old Jules embodies Sandoz's multilayered commitment to exploring what Turner saw as the trans-Mississippi West's economic frontiers. Within her body of work are four separate characteristics that epitomize her contributions to the modern history of the American West. First, Sandoz believed history required the truth. It should not be watered down. In particular, western history needed to show the toughness that was required of all of its participants. Call it a strict sense of realism, but Sandoz did not appreciate glossy, feel-good approaches to what she personally witnessed as the hardships of life on the frontier. She never met a "myth" she didn't seek to debunk. Her anti-romanticism simply did not permit her to prop up "Wild West" personalities.

Second, Sandoz informed her settlement histories with storytelling. She often portrayed herself sitting in the kitchen of the Sandoz homestead watching most of northwest Nebraska drop in for a chat or advice or to pick up mail. She saw pioneer history as the history of the personal, frequently telling audiences that "I lived in a storyteller region." She treasured her time with "all the old traders, the old French [fur] trappers, all the old characters who had been around the Black Hills . . . [who] told grand stories of their travels and experiences." She successfully incorporated these stories into her histories, for as a friend remarked, "You have never forgotten anything you have ever seen or heard."[49]

Third, Sandoz's presettlement and settlement histories embraced a modified Turnerian narrative structure, replicating the human wave of activity necessary for the conquering of Turner's wilderness. Sandoz followed the classic Turnerian economic frontiers model with books focused on buffalo hunters, cattle raisers, and fur traders but injected Native American history liberally and on a par with pioneer history. However, she found ways to deviate. She extended economic history into both the future and the deep past in her planned volumes on the oil industry and precontact indigenous history, subjects not generally perceived as a valid part of Turner's West. In essence she historified a place, not a process, while paradoxically contradicting the Turner thesis. Sandoz's place is appreciated, described with awe, and learned from rather than incorporated into a celebratory despoliation dedicated to "progress."

Finally, Sandoz emphasized the diversity of peoples and processes without the single-mindedness of Turner's march of history. This reflects her dedication to elucidating the history of cultural exchanges. People learned from each other in order to survive. She also paid much more attention to gender than did Turner. She balanced her biography of her father with a biographical article of her mother.[50]

Sandoz believed she created a realistic picture of pioneering, one not for the timid. Sod houses were not pristine prairie apartments but filthy, mice-ridden hovels. All homesteaders had three basic needs: shelter, food, and water. Once one achieved these fundamentals, one could survive. But other challenges dealt cruel blows. Sickness, death, poverty and bankruptcy, isolation, drought, dust storms, and arguably the most deadly of all—blizzards and prairie fires—confronted everyone. Those who survived seemed toughened to Sandoz, maybe even grizzled. Only one in four homesteaders patented claims on the "easy" land; on marginal farmland, one in ten proved up.[51]

Her quest for realism meant Sandoz did not abide contrived heroes, particularly the plains antihero. When Mari saw the movie *The Plainsman* she felt compelled to comment on its inexactness: "If Wild Bill, Calamity Jane and Buffalo Bill hadn't been labeled, I wouldn't have recognized them. They did not one thing that was historically true." She particularly delighted in debunking "the two Bills." When the New York Westerners Posse invited Sandoz to present a program, she responded by offering a stinging critique of Frank J. Wilstach's *Wild Bill Hickok: The Prince of Pistoleers* (1926). Line by line she unveiled the historical inaccuracies, which the author later admitted editors had added to increase sales. In another essay, Sandoz wrote that "From the ranks of such young horse tenders at Nebraska stations rose both Wild Bill Hickok and Buffalo Bill Cody, the two most glamorized figures of the old wild West. Both are still widely advertised as killers—Hickok of white men, Cody of Indians." The trouble for Sandoz was that Hickok cowardly murdered his neighbor, and the only killing Cody ever did was shooting buffalo. When Cody visited her father to go hunting, a youthful Mari accidentally went into Cody's bedroom and saw his long, blond curls resting on the dresser.[52] Buffalo Bill's rug, to her, symbolized the problem of combining reality with mythology.

The Buffalo Hunters followed the structure Sandoz had employed in her other histories. Working chronologically, she used stories and personal experiences to trace the history of the bison and their interactions with humans on the Great Plains. She explained how, in Pawnee cosmology, the buffalo were present at the creation of the world. The Pawnees were careful to use bison in a sustainable fashion. While she wrote glowingly of Indians, her disapproval of Euro-Americans' wanton destruction of bison knew no bounds. She lashed out at Hickok, George A. Custer, Philip H. Sheridan, and Cody, and reported that one bone-purchasing company in a seven-year period bought nearly six million bison skeletons. By 1890 an estimated fifty million buffalo had dwindled to approximately 250. Tracing the buffalo's demise over the entire breadth of the Great Plains, she concluded with an emotional comparison of the massacre at Wounded Knee to the extermination of the bison. Sandoz dramatically described the quiet after the Hotchkiss machine guns stopped in the assault on Big Foot's people: "[I]n the afternoon snow began to fall, running in thin grey curls over the desolated ground at Wounded Knee [Creek], settling in little white drifts behind the bodies of the dead, the women and children, the chief and his men. As the snow deepened, they seemed more and more like great whitened carcasses scattered where they fell over the prairie. Now the dream of the buffalo, too, was done."[53]

Her longest book, The Cattlemen, which proved equally challenging to write, covered terrain familiar to western historians but provoked controversy. It followed her standard format; she carefully explored the grasslands, from the Rio Grande to the Canadian border, and considered cattle's history. She told stories and documented abuses of power, including the murderous treachery involved with the early cattle business such as the misdeeds of the Niobrara Country's Print Olive family.

This caused considerable comment and eventually led the Nebraska Supreme Court to reclaim the Olive murder trial records placed in the Nebraska State Historical Society (which Mari had liberally consulted) in an attempt to stop her research. Sandoz responded with acerbic confidence. She had carefully weighed her sources, and "nobody will drag me into court for fear I'll tell the rest."[54] The controversy was quelled when relatives of the Olives' victims came to Sandoz's defense.

A number of Texas ranching historians objected to *The Cattlemen* and held that Sandoz, a farmer sympathizer, had stepped outside her gender to write cow history. Horace Reynalds maintained that Sandoz "does not write like a woman—I can find no evidence in this book that it was written by a woman—and that, of course, is not all compliment." Lewis Nordyke, J. Frank Dobie, and C. L. Sonnichson ganged up on her, citing a variety of issues: historical turf, specific factual details, and her supposed imbalanced commentary. Mari thought she had written the history of the cattlemen with considerable fairness. After all, cattlemen had gunned down her own uncle, and she had firsthand knowledge of their fraudulent landholdings and the hardships they had deliberately perpetrated on the first generation of plains farmers. With each review, Sandoz responded, holding her own but growing increasingly irritated. Knowing she would receive heavy criticism, she had softened her approach by searching for cattlemen to admire, and to compensate for her potential biases she had undertaken even more comprehensive research. Byron Price summarizes: "Her quest for source material . . . eventually led from the New York Public Library to the renowned western history collections of a host of libraries, archives and museums in Nebraska, Colorado, Kansas, Texas, and Oklahoma." Sandoz also interviewed many involved in the cattle business, including former cattle-trail drovers and participants in the Johnson County War in Wyoming and the Lincoln County War in New Mexico. Several old cowboys even came to New York to talk with her. In particular, she consulted five brothers and sisters ranching in the Sandhills, who reminded her that not all cattle raisers had oil wells and bank stock.[55]

But *The Cattlemen* held up to scholarly scrutiny. Victor Hass wrote in 1958 that "Here, tough as whang leather, nourishing as pemmican, turbulent as Dodge City on a Saturday night in the late 1870s, is what time may well decide is the definitive history of the founding and flourishing of the cattle industry on this continent." Nearly forty years later, Price concluded that Sandoz had "succeeded in fashioning a coherent narrative on an epic scale. . . . Although often critical of the ranching clan, Sandoz's even-handed text celebrated her subject as well."[56]

Sandoz published *The Beaver Men* in 1964. Once again she prepared meticulously even though her health was deteriorating. She traveled to numerous American historical societies and Canadian repositories in Ottawa and Montreal, and she recalled the many stories she heard in childhood. To Sandoz, all these old stories contextualized the fur trade and the extinction of the beaver from the region. The resulting book covered the history of the Great Plains from 1630 to 1834, divided into three parts: "Soft Blood," "The Rise of the Company," and "The Fiercer Rivalries." In each section, Sandoz deals with environmental exploitation, the human cost of this extractive industry, and the international disruption of North America. She lists the fur trade's hallmarks: "price-cutting, ruthless trade practices, incitement of Indians, subsidization of upstart rivals, bribery, piracy and general corruption, as well as suspicion of murder." She dedicated it to the *coureurs de bois*, who "penetrated the farthest wilderness, perhaps escaped to it, and lost themselves among the Indians who welcomed them, gave them friendship, family and position, and, in the end, mourned them as of the People, with no memory that their skin had been alien." Sympathetic to the workers and their mixed-blood families while critical of corporate elites, particularly the French, Sandoz creatively invoked metaphors to explain the demise of the beaver.[57]

Historians embraced Sandoz's fur-trade history much more than her other economic frontier treatments. One review in *Colorado Magazine* summarized: "This book is not so much an historical study as a careful and intelligently drawn portrait of a world . . . that of the Great Plains during the period 1630–1834." Her "essential concern is ecological: the relations of living creatures with each other and with their physical world. It is this perspective, unique among chroniclers of the fur trade, that gives the book its very considerable value."[58] Interestingly, of all Sandoz's histories, this book has engendered the least comment. As her most ignored book, perhaps it represents an acceptance by those critics who had learned to appreciate the Sandoz historical take on the American West.

Sandoz's settlement histories are particularly reflective of treatments of cultural exchange and diversity, gender history, and the history of the environment. She appreciated the tremendous cultural variation on the Great Plains and integrated this factor into virtually everything she wrote. For her, it was a reflection of reality. After all, her neighborhood featured Czechs, Poles, and Germans; her own family included a French-speaking father and a German-speaking mother. "We tend to forget that the homesteaders were not a type," observed Sandoz, "not as alike as biscuits cut out with a baking-powder can." Homesteaders came in all shapes and sizes and different languages and hues. Sandoz wrote of Mennonites, Russian Jews, and Hutterites; Irish, Swedes, and Bohemians; African Americans, Dutch, and French. Through her stories, she accessed individual groups to determine the tensions and the divisions. She was particularly successful in doing so with the Lakotas in pathbreaking ways. Throughout her descriptive diversity, Sandoz also noticed the cultural exchanges that were taking place. People, she constantly enjoined her readers, had to survive, and it did not matter from whom you borrowed in order to harvest a crop successfully or trap a rabbit for a timely meal.[59]

The treatment of women in Sandoz's work has generated some discussion. In 1958 Sandoz penned a letter expressing her thanks for the inclusion of *The Cattlemen* on a list of outstanding books written by women: "It is true that I'm not much of a feminist. I'd rather be very far down in the whole human race than pretty high up in fractions of it." Precisely how Sandoz defined *feminist* is not known, but she seemed to equate it with wealthy women who were unconcerned about the women of the frontier. When pressed about gender in her settlement series, she noted that "This was a man's world but women were full time partners." Sandoz believed that the women in her works played important roles. "Although woman today has a far easier life and sometimes 'bosses' the family, she doesn't command the respect of the pioneer western woman," she pointedly observed.[60]

Sandoz wrote about many women in her essays and books. Although she did not perceive the "female frontier" that modern scholarship has afforded, she did not ignore women. Sandoz never portrayed women as an afterthought, like Turner's sole reference to women ("Kit Carson's mother was a Boone") in his exalted thesis. In fact, Sandoz showed women as frontier actors, full participants in homesteading, the cattle business, and fur trading as well as in Indian communities. Their triumphs also came with personal violence. In fact, Sandoz was one of the first western historians to describe the brutality women faced in the settlement of the American West.[61]

Prescient on issues of diversity and gender, Sandoz can also claim early recognition of the importance of land and the environment to western history. Her entire understanding of history began and ended with the land. "The place called the Great Plains," she writes at the beginning of *Love Song to the Plains*, "spreads southward from the upper Saskatchewan River down to the Rio Grande—a high country, a big country of vast reaches, tremendous streams, and stories of death on the ridges, derring-do in the valleys, and the sweetness and heartbreak of springtime on the prairies."[62] Life, death, history, and the land for Sandoz were inseparable.

Ecologically, Sandoz recognized the environmental disasters that accrued from Anglo-American settlement, especially the extreme impact of the beaver and buffalo slaughters. There were heroes and villains in these stories. Betsy Downey observes that "Sandoz rarely seems to have questioned the long range consequences that the successful ranchers and farmers had on the land, especially with their irrigation practices."[63] But Downey sees in Sandoz's last writings hints that she was starting to change her mind about ecological change. What might Sandoz have written in her final book in the trans-Missouri series, knowing of the draining of the Ogallala aquifer or the drying up of the Arkansas and Platte rivers on the Great Plains?

Thus, Sandoz's settlement histories represent significant accomplishments in the history of the American West. They percolate a style that combined a pithy earthiness with stories and a clear perspective on the economic frontiers of the Great Plains. Each established her expertise in another aspect of the westering experience, and each challenged conventional treatments of the topics at hand. Sandoz seemed to walk a complicated path, taking subjects occupied by antiquarians and Turnerians while bringing to them new life and interpretations.

Conclusion

In 1950 the University of Nebraska bestowed upon Mari Sandoz an honorary doctorate of literature. With this degree she joined the Omaha anthropologist Francis La Flesche, Russian musician Sergei Rachmaninoff, her good friend and Nebraska writer Bess Streeter Aldrich, and Milton Eisenhower. Louise Pound, who engineered the award, had to prove to a university administration that Mari had indeed taught at a number of writing institutes. The citation reads: "Mari Sandoz, distinguished Nebraska *historian, biographer, novelist, story writer, authority on Indians of the Nebraska territory and neighboring states . . .* [and] widely known teacher in creative writing at several state universities." Here a woman who made her living by writing history and novels of the Great Plains with an attitude had achieved some level of greatness. Being accorded recognition as a historian was quite pleasing to Sandoz, and her biographer Helen Winter Stauffer allowed that Sandoz "took special pleasure in her recognition as a storyteller."[64]

Sandoz had indeed come a far distance. Born into difficult circumstances on a Sandhills homestead in the late nineteenth century, she had survived a brutal childhood only to recapture and perhaps exorcise it in her writings. She had ventured to Nebraska's capital city to gain an education, learn how to write, study history, and immerse herself in the archives of her region. All the while, she continued to probe, to analyze, to create, and to type her stories and books. She believed in her abilities to find the truth, to right the wrongs of the past, and to compose "good history."[65]

In many ways, Sandoz was a part of the creation of a new approach to the history of the American West. No one can doubt her influence in writing quality Native American history. Her works are still revered by the very people whose stories and histories she sought to impart. In addition, her portraits of settlement and the coming of Euro-Americans to the High Plains remain largely consulted for the New Western history. Sandoz easily takes a place among prominent historians of the American West, perhaps sitting on an imaginary stage between Sandra Myres on her right and Patricia Nelson Limerick on her left. Had this gathering happened, the conversations could easily have been both salty and scintillating.

In 1971, five years after her death, the Mari Sandoz Heritage Society was established. Over the years this group of committed readers of Sandoz has awarded scholarships and funded oral history projects, published booklets and newsletters, and championed Mari Sandoz for induction into the Nebraska Hall of Fame and as namesake of the highway that runs from Gordon to Ellsworth, Nebraska, past her gravesite and the Old Jules homestead. It has also helped raise several million dollars to build a center to study Sandoz history and literature. Today on the campus of Chadron State College can be found the Mari Sandoz High Plains Heritage Center, which contains many Sandoz artifacts and records and hosts an annual spring conference dedicated to further explorations of the work of Sandoz and other Great Plains writers.[66]

Mari Sandoz, historian, profoundly influenced the way we perceive and interpret the American West and her Great Plains.

Notes

1. Mari Sandoz to Virginia Faulkner, August 10, 1957, quoted in Virginia Faulkner's introduction to Mari Sandoz, *Hostiles and Friendlies: Selected Short Writings of Mari Sandoz* (Lincoln: University of Nebraska Press, 1959), xii. For an assessment of the New Western history, see John R. Wunder, "What's Old about the New Western History? Part 1, Race and Gender," *Pacific Northwest Quarterly* 85 (April 1994): 50–58; John R. Wunder, "What's Old about the New Western History? Part 2, Environment and Economy," *Pacific Northwest Quarterly* 89 (Spring 1998): 84–96; and John R. Wunder, "What's Old about the New Western History? Part 3, Law," *Western Legal History* 10, nos. 1–2 (1997): 85–116.

2. Helen Winter Stauffer, *Mari Sandoz: Story Catcher of the Plains* (Lincoln: University of Nebraska Press, 1982), 1; Mari Sandoz, *Crazy Horse: The Strange Man of the Oglalas*, 50th Anniversary Edition, intro. Stephen B. Oates (Lincoln: University of Nebraska Press, 1992), vii–xxi; Sandoz, *Hostiles and Friendlies*, 247–48.

3. Stauffer, *Mari Sandoz*, 19–21. Confusion exists over the basic facts of

Mari's life, including her birth date. See "Mari Sandoz" by R. E. in Howard R. Lamar, ed., *The New Encyclopedia of the American West* (New Haven: Yale University Press, 1998), 1007–8. R. E. asserts that Sandoz was born in 1907, when she was actually eleven, and glibly describes her career as one in which she "gradually drifted into a life of editorial work, historical research, and freelance writing" (1008). The publication date for *Crazy Horse* appears as 1949 instead of 1942.

4. Stauffer, *Mari Sandoz*, 21–27.

5. Stauffer, *Mari Sandoz*, 27–29, quote on 28; Sandoz, *Hostiles and Friendlies*, xii. The family could not afford shoes. Small wonder Mari began her life-long suffering from migraines at this time.

6. Mari Sandoz, *Old Jules* (Boston: Little, Brown, 1935), foreword, viii and 419; Stauffer, *Mari Sandoz*, 69. See also Mary S. Sandoz, "The Broken Promise," *Omaha Daily News*, April 26, 1908.

7. Stauffer, *Mari Sandoz*, 30–32; Sandoz, *Old Jules*, 268–89.

8. Stauffer, *Mari Sandoz*, 33.

9. Stauffer, *Mari Sandoz*, 37–41.

10. For a discussion of the problems professional female historians confronted in this era, see chapter 8 in Patricia Loughlin, *Hidden Treasures of the American West: Muriel H. Wright, Angie Debo, and Alice Marriott* (Albuquerque: University of New Mexico Press, 2005).

11. Stauffer, *Mari Sandoz*, 43–45.

12. Quotes from Sandoz, *Hostiles and Friendlies*, xvii; Stauffer, *Mari Sandoz*, 49–70.

13. Robert E. Knoll, *Prairie University: A History of the University of Nebraska* (Lincoln: University of Nebraska Press, 1995), 62, 64, quote on 64; Robert E. Carlson, "Professor Fred Fling: His Career and Conflicts at the University of Nebraska," *Nebraska History* 62 (Winter 1981): 481–96; Betsy Downey, "'She Does Not Write Like a Historian': Mari Sandoz and the Old and New Western History," *Great Plains Quarterly* 16 (Winter 1996): 10; R. McLaren Sawyer, *Centennial History of the University of Nebraska*, vol. 2, *The Modern University, 1920–1969* (Lincoln: Centennial Press, 1973), 26; John D. Hicks, *My Life with History: An Autobiography* (Lincoln: University of Nebraska Press, 1968), 132–33.

14. Particularly noteworthy was Fling's *Outline of Historical Method* (Lincoln: J. H. Miller, 1899). See Stauffer, *Mari Sandoz*, 50–51; Knoll, *Prairie University*, 64–65; "Grade Listing," file 1, 1925, Personal Correspondence, box 1, Mari San-

doz Papers, University Archives/Special Collections, Love Library, University of Nebraska–Lincoln [hereafter cited as Sandoz Papers]; Caroline Sandoz Pifer, ed., *Gordon Journal: Letters of Mari Sandoz* (Crawford NE: Cottonwood Press, 1991), 4–5.

15. Sawyer, *Centennial History*, 12–13, 40; Knoll, *Prairie University*, 57–58; Hicks, *My Life with History*, 131; Stauffer, *Mari Sandoz*, 51; "Grade Listing," file 1, 1925, Sandoz Papers. See excerpt from *Time*, November 23, 1942, Autobiographical File, John A. Rice Collection, University Archives/Special Collections, Love Library, University of Nebraska–Lincoln. Like John D. Hicks, Rice published an autobiography, *I Came Out of the Eighteenth Century* (New York: Harper & Brothers, 1942).

16. Stauffer, *Mari Sandoz*, 52–63; Mari Sandoz, "The Vine," *Prairie Schooner* 1 (January 1927): 7–16, under pen name Marie Macumber, reprinted in Sandoz, *Hostiles and Friendlies*, 117–25; Mari Sandoz, "The Kinkaider Comes and Goes," *North American Review*, April 1930, 422–31, May 1930, 576–83, reprinted in Sandoz, *Hostiles and Friendlies*, 3–23; and Mari Sandoz, "Sandhill Sundays," in *Folk-Say: A Regional Miscellany*, ed. B. A. Botkin (Norman: University of Oklahoma Press, 1931), 291–303.

17. Stauffer, *Mari Sandoz*, 69–83.

18. Sandoz to Botkin, February 6, 1932, in Pifer, *Gordon Journal*, 21.

19. Stauffer, *Mari Sandoz*, 84–87. Hicks, *My Life with History*, 132–33, 141; Sawyer, *Centennial History*, 10–11; Knoll, *Prairie University*, 69; Gerald D. Nash, "John D. Hicks," in *Historians of the American Frontier: A Bio-Bibliographical Sourcebook*, ed. John R. Wunder (Westport CT: Greenwood Press, 1988), 306–15; John D. Hicks, *The Populist Revolt: A History of the Farmers' Alliance and the People's Party* (Minneapolis: University of Minnesota Press, 1931).

20. Hicks, *My Life with History*, 134–35, 141–42; Tully Hunter, "Frederick Logan Paxson," in Wunder, *Historians of the American Frontier*, 458–59; Richard White, "Frederick Jackson Turner," in Wunder, *Historians of the American Frontier*, 663–65; Thomas C. McClintock, "Frederick Merk," in Wunder, *Historians of the American Frontier*, 426–39.

21. Hicks, *My Life with History*, 135.

22. Debra Brookhart, "Managing Turbulent Times," *OAH Newsletter*, November 2003, 1–3, at aoh.org/pubs/nl/2003nov/brookhart.html; Minnie Prey Knotts, "Clarence S. Paine: In Memoriam," *Nebraska Territorial Pioneers' Association*, 2 vols., 1:53, at rootsweb.com/ ~neresour/pioneer/ntpa/voli/pages/

ntpav109.htm. In 1914 the MVHA launched the *Mississippi Valley Historical Review*, precursor to the *Journal of American History*.

23. Stauffer, *Mari Sandoz*, 84–85.

24. Stauffer, *Mari Sandoz*, 91–95.

25. Stauffer, *Mari Sandoz*, 94.

26. Mari Sandoz, *The Battle of the Little Bighorn* (Philadelphia: Lippincott, 1966). For a complete listing of Sandoz publications by 1982, the date of publication of her biography, see Stauffer, *Mari Sandoz*, 289–94. Subsequently, Mari's sister, Caroline Sandoz Pifer, has edited and privately published more of Sandoz's work. See Mari Sandoz, *The Great Council*, ed. Caroline Sandoz Pifer (Crawford NE: Cottonwood Press, 1970, 2nd ed. 1982); Mari Sandoz, *Victorie and Other Stories*, ed. Caroline Sandoz Pifer (Crawford NE: Cottonwood Press, 1986); and Pifer, *Gordon Journal*. Also see Mari Sandoz, "Some Notes on Wild Bill Hickok," *Westerners Brand Book* (New York Posse), Winter 1954, 8; "Search for the Bones of Crazy Horse," *Westerners Brand Book* (New York Posse), Autumn 1954, 4–5; "Some Oddities of the American Indian," *Westerners Brand Book* (Denver Posse), 1955, 17–28; "Climber of Long's Peak," *Westerners Brand Book* (New York), 1961, 70–71; and "Unavailable Documents," *Westerners Brand Book* (New York), 1962, 47. In addition, the Mari Sandoz Heritage Society publishes booklets based upon keynote lectures at its annual meeting held each year in Chadron, Nebraska, on the campus of Chadron State College at the Mari Sandoz High Plains Heritage Center. See Helen Winter Stauffer, "Sandoz, Neihardt, and Crazy Horse" (1992); Fr. Peter J. Powell, "The Killing of Morning Star's People" (1993); B. Byron Price, "'She Doesn't Write Like a Woman': Mari Sandoz's The Cattlemen" (1994); Linda M. Hasselstrom, "A 'Love Song to the Plains'" (2002); and Susanne George-Bloomfield, "'Absolutely No Manners': On Having the Audacity to Write Biography" (2003). See also Glenda Riley's keynote in "Mari Sandoz's *Slogum House*: Greed as Woman," *Great Plains Quarterly* 16 (Winter 1996): 29–41.

27. The structures and characters of Sandoz's novels and short stories are largely predicated upon historical sources. Two collections—*Hostiles and Friendlies* (1959) and *Old Jules Country: A Selection from Old Jules and Thirty Years of Writing since the Book Was Published* (New York: Hastings House, 1965)—include essays and excerpts that transcend the two categories. Sandoz originally integrated her indigenous and settlement histories into a planned series. As early as her teens, she conceived of a trans-Missouri series, a project

of seven planned books. Five—*Old Jules* (1935), *Crazy Horse: The Strange Man of the Oglalas* (1942), *Cheyenne Autumn* (1943), *The Buffalo Hunters: The Story of the Hide Men* (1954), and *The Cattlemen: From the Rio Grande across the Far Marias* (1958)—constituting volumes 2–6, were published by the time of her death in 1966. The bookends, an untitled volume 1 on the coming of iron and gunpowder to Stone Age societies of the Great Plains and an untitled volume 7 on oil and energy in the Great Plains region, were partially researched. In 1964 Sandoz added *The Beaver Men: Spearheads of Empire* to her projected series. All her histories are currently in print.

28. Sandoz, *Hostiles and Friendlies*, 30–31; Stauffer, *Mari Sandoz*, 80–82. See also Mari Sandoz to George Lorimer, editor of the *Saturday Evening Post*, July 23, 1932, in Personal Correspondence, file 25, box 1, Sandoz Papers; and Pifer, *Gordon Journal*, 18–19.

29. Undoubtedly she intuited many Lakota phrases. Mari Sandoz to George Horace Lorimer, editor of the *Saturday Evening Post*, January 13, 1932, in Personal Correspondence, file 4, box 1, Sandoz Papers; Stauffer, *Mari Sandoz*, 79–90, also 4–6.

30. When she submitted her articles for publication, Sandoz encouraged illustrations by Indian artists. She urged other scholars to consult Indians in writing their histories and often provided reservation contacts. Stauffer, "Sandoz, Neihardt, and Crazy Horse," 2–11; Sandoz to Lorimer, July 23, 1932, postscript hinting that Indians should be chosen as illustrators; and Sandoz, introduction to Amos Bad Heart Bull and Helen H. Blish, *A Pictographic History of the Oglala Sioux* (Lincoln: University of Nebraska Press, 1967), xix–xxii.

31. Mari Sandoz, introduction to George Bird Grinnell, *The Cheyenne Indians* (New York: Cooper Square Publishers, 1962), v–xiii, quotes on v, xii, xiii.

32. Mari Sandoz to Charles Sears, January 23, 1931, in Pifer, *Gordon Journal*, 23–24; Sandoz, introduction to *Pictographic History*, xxi; Stauffer, *Mari Sandoz*, 102–13, 145–46, 168–71, 222–23; Patricia Nelson Limerick, "What on Earth Is the New Western History?" in *Trails: Toward a New Western History*, ed. Patricia Nelson Limerick, Clyde A. Milner II, and Charles E. Rankin (Lawrence: University Press of Kansas, 1991), 81–88.

33. At this time she also considered writing biographies of two Lakota leaders, Young Man Afraid of His Horses and Crazy Horse. Stauffer, *Mari Sandoz*, 133–62, quote on 134. Fast later had legal troubles concerning plagiarism. Stauffer, *Mari Sandoz*, 149.

34. Oates, introduction to *Crazy Horse*, xv, xviii; Vine Deloria Jr., introduction to the most recent Bison edition of Mari Sandoz, *Crazy Horse* (Lincoln: University of Nebraska Press, 2004), vi (quotation on Indians and history is on page xvi; Stegner's praise is on page xix); Stauffer quotes Fadimer's comments in *Mari Sandoz*, 159.

35. Sandoz, *Hostiles and Friendlies*, 108–9, quotes on 109.

36. Sandoz publicly spoke out against fascism and supported the U.S. entry into World War II. Shortly after World War II, in 1947, she published a controversial novel, *The Tom-Walker*, which centered around the authoritarian tendencies of American society during wars and the danger to civil liberties. Mari Sandoz, *The Tom-Walker* (New York: Dial Press, 1947). The quotes are from pages 30–31.

37. While living on the Northern Cheyenne Reservation in Montana conducting research, she encountered the overwhelming poverty of the Cheyennes and vowed never to forget. Stauffer, *Mari Sandoz*, 176–78. During this time Sandoz wrote two historical essays on indigenous topics, "There Were Two Sitting Bulls," *Blue Book*, November 1949, 58–64; "The Search for the Bones of Crazy Horse"; and two novels, *The Horse Catcher* (Philadelphia: Westminster Press, 1957), and *The Story Catcher* (Philadelphia: Westminster Press, 1963).

38. Stauffer, *Mari Sandoz*, 191; Sandoz, *Cheyenne Autumn* (New York: McGraw-Hill, 1953), v–vi.

39. Sandoz, *Cheyenne Autumn*, vi–vii.

40. *Cheyenne Autumn* starred Sal Mineo, Karl Malden, Ricardo Montalban, James Stewart, and Edward G. Robinson plus a number of Navajo extras playing Cheyennes, who spoke Navajo, generally making fun of whites who did not know what was being said. Stauffer, *Mari Sandoz*, 246–47.

41. Mari Sandoz, *These Were the Sioux* (New York: Hastings House, 1961), 102–3.

42. Sandoz, *The Battle of the Little Bighorn*; Stauffer, *Mari Sandoz*, 260–61.

43. Dee Brown, *Bury My Heart at Wounded Knee: An Indian History of the American West* (New York: Holt, Rinehart & Winston, 1970); Sandoz, introduction to *Pictographic History*, xxi.

44. Sandoz might not have been able to convince publishers to print her American Indian works had she not already proven she could write good American history. See Downey, "'She Does Not Write Like a Historian.'" Downey is highly critical of Sandoz's historical methodology, objecting to her "fictional

devices" and "glaring departures from the norms of professional documentation" (11).

45. Sandoz, *Hostiles and Friendlies*, 1, quoting an essay signed as Marie Macumber, "What Should Be Considered When Choosing a Profession?" *Daily Nebraskan* (University of Nebraska–Lincoln), April 3, 1932.

46. Sandoz to Herbert Cushing, January 6, 1936, in Pifer, *Gordon Journal*, 97–98.

47. Sandoz to Alice Brown, Selah, Washington, January 6, 1936, in Pifer, *Gordon Journal*, 101.

48. Arthur Maurice, "Book of the Day," *New York Sun*, October 31, 1935; Bernard DeVoto, "A Violent, Fighting Pioneer," *Saturday Review of Literature*, November 1935, 5. Both are quoted in Stauffer, *Mari Sandoz*, 104.

49. Sandoz, *Hostiles and Friendlies*, xv, xvi; Elmer Sturgeon, Hay Springs, Nebraska, to Sandoz, December 16, 1935, in Pifer, *Gordon Journal*, 91.

50. See Mari Sandoz, "The New Frontier Woman," *Country Gentleman*, September 1936, 49, 65, reprinted in Sandoz, *Hostiles and Friendlies*, as "Marlizzie," 60–66. Sandoz echoed her father's and her neighbors' prejudices against ranchers. Ironically, ranching dominates economically and culturally much of the Sandhills today.

51. Mari Sandoz, "The Homestead in Perspective," in *Land Use Policy and Problems in the United States*, ed. Howard W. Ottoson (Lincoln: University of Nebraska Press, 1963), 48, 52, 59–61.

52. Sandoz to Fred Ballard, Peterborough, New Hampshire, January 23, 1937, in Pifer, *Gordon Journal*, 162; Sandoz, "Some Notes on Wild Bill Hickok," manuscript, December 7, 1953, in Article Publications, file 13, box 3, Sandoz Papers. This appeared later as "Some Notes on Wild Bill Hickok" in the *Westerners Brand Book*; Sandoz, "Nebraska," *Holiday*, May 1956, 105; Stauffer, *Mari Sandoz*, 26.

53. Mari Sandoz, *The Buffalo Hunters: The Story of the Hide Men* (New York: Hastings House, 1954), vii–x, 200–201, 358, 367; Price, "'She Doesn't Write Like a Woman,'" 1. Sandoz wrote *The Buffalo Hunters* in the midst of personal crises. A dear friend, hounded by Senator Joseph McCarthy, committed suicide, and Sandoz learned she had cancer.

54. Price, "'She Doesn't Write Like a Woman,'" 7, quoting Mari Sandoz to Ed Sutton, November 29, 1959, in Stauffer, *Marie Sandoz*, 347.

55. Price, "'She Doesn't Write Like a Woman,'" 2–3, 8–13; Horace Reynalds,

Christian Science Monitor, June 12, 1958, 7; Mari Sandoz to Editorial Offices, *Harpers Magazine*, June 10, 1932, in Pifer, *Gordon Journal*, 34–35. This section relies on the thorough research and excellent writing of B. Byron Price, who gave the keynote address at the 1994 Mari Sandoz Heritage Society conference on *The Cattlemen*.

56. Victor P. Hass, *Chicago Sunday Tribune*, May 25, 1958, 1, quoted in Price, "'She Doesn't Write Like a Woman,'" 8–9.

57. Mari Sandoz, *The Beaver Men: Spearheads of Empire* (New York: Hastings House, 1964), vii, 310, see also ix–x; Stauffer, *Mari Sandoz*, 232, 240, 249–51. In the foreword Sandoz lays out her plans for two additional volumes of her history of the Great Plains. She also separates herself forever from the Turner thesis: "When the series, now grown to seven volumes, is done, I hope to understand something of the white man's incumbency on the Great Plains from Stone Age Indian to the present, to understand something of what modern man does to such a region, and what it does to him" (xv).

58. Mari Sandoz, *The Beaver Men: Spearheads of Empire* (Lincoln: University of Nebraska Press, 1978), back cover.

59. Sandoz, "The Homestead in Perspective," 49, 47, 55; Downey, "'She Does Not Write Like a Historian,'" 17, 25; Sandoz, *Hostiles and Friendlies*, 17; Sandoz, "Nebraska," 111; Pifer, *Gordon Journal*, 140.

60. Sandoz to Fred Babcock, October 26, 1958, in *Letters of Sandoz*, ed. and intro. Helen Winter Stauffer (Lincoln: University of Nebraska Press, 1992), 325, quoted in part in Price, "'She Doesn't Write Like a Woman,'" 10, quoting remarks by Sandoz, April 17, 1958, Benn Hall Associate File, Sandoz Papers.

61. Sandoz, *Hostiles and Friendlies*, 45; Sandoz, "The Homestead in Perspective," 57–58, 62; and Sandoz, "The New Frontier Woman," 49, 65; see Downey, "'She Does Not Write Like a Historian,'" 17–19, who is particularly effective in her gender assessment.

62. Mari Sandoz, *Love Song to the Plains* (New York: Harper and Row, 1961), 1; Sandoz, "Dakota Country," 43–45; see Sandoz to Paul Hoffman, New York City, September 24, 1936, in Pifer, *Gordon Journal*, 147, for a description of autumn on the plains.

63. Downey, "'She Does Not Write Like a Historian,'" 23, and generally 21–25.

64. Sawyer, *Centennial History*, 265–68; Stauffer, *Mari Sandoz*, 181, emphasis added.

65. Additional in-depth discussion of Sandoz and her writings can be found in John R. Wunder, "Some Notes on Mari Sandoz," *Prairie Schooner* 80 (Winter 2006): 41–54; and John R. Wunder, "Writing of Race, Class, Gender, and Power in the American West: Mari Sandoz, Precursor to the New Indian History," in *North America: Tensions and Re(solutions)*, ed. Raili Poldsaar and Krista Vogelberg (Tartu, Estonia: University of Tartu Center for North-American Studies, 2007), 266–83.

66. Ron Hull, "A Brief History of the Sandoz Society," cited by George-Bloomfield in "'Absolutely No Manners,'" 29.

4

ISABEL T. KELLY

A Life in the Field

Catherine S. Fowler and Robert Van Kemper

ISABEL TRUESDELL KELLY'S distinguished career in anthropology spanned some fifty-five years of concentrated work as an ethnographer, archaeologist, and applied anthropologist. An avid field-worker, often in very rigorous situations, she pursued research topics in several locations in the western United States and Mexico as well as in Colombia, El Salvador, Ecuador, Chile, Puerto Rico, Bolivia, and Pakistan. Trained as an academic anthropologist at the University of California, Berkeley, she entered the field at a time when women were beginning to seek and expect full recognition of their professional abilities and with it, full-time appointments. Although she was consistently employed in a professional capacity throughout her career, it was largely in non-academic positions pursuing an impressive series of fellowships and grants. This led Mary Ann Levine to characterize her as a person with "a career trajectory defined by itinerancy."[1]

Part of Kelly's employment history was a result of her choice, early in her career, to live in Mexico and devote considerable time to intensive fieldwork there. But part may also reflect the difficulties women faced in finding full-time institutional positions at the time Kelly graduated in the 1930s. The career she put together and her body of professional work is impressive nonetheless, a legacy to her determination to be an anthropologist and to work in interesting places on interesting problems of her choosing.

This chapter will focus on Kelly's early years, highlighting her ethnography and archaeology in western North America: California, the Great Basin, and western Mexico. These early experiences set the pattern for much of her later orientation to anthropology, which was always intensely descriptive, placing value on collecting thorough and detailed data as the key to making sound analytical and theoretical

6. (*Opposite*) Isabel T. Kelly lived a life of itinerancy, traveling back roads, often in unreliable cars. Here she is loading her 1932 Ford for a trip to the Kaibab Southern Paiute in 1932. *Courtesy of Robert Van Kemper.*

statements. We will also outline some of the rigors Kelly faced in her life in the field, largely in her own words, gleaned from her extensive correspondence. Her later years, which she spent working in social and applied anthropology in Mexico and beyond, reflect her other deep commitment: to people and their well-being.[2]

Early Life and Education

Isabel Kelly's early life and education are summarized in four biographical essays. Two by Jean Knobloch provide broad profiles, while the third is an assessment of her graduate student work at Berkeley by Grace Wilson Buzaljko. The fourth focuses on the context of her first fieldwork, among the Coast Miwoks of California in the early 1930s, and is also by Buzaljko.[3] Important sources to Kelly's biographers are not only publications but also her detailed and often "spirited" correspondence with her mentors and colleagues.[4]

Isabel Kelly was born on January 4, 1906, to Thomas William Kelly and Alice Gardner Kelly in Santa Cruz, California. The elder of two daughters, she grew up in a household of strong women, including her mother's spinster sister, Louise Gardner, who lived to be one hundred. An excellent student, Isabel also excelled in sports during her high school years and intended to pursue a career in physical education when she entered the University of California, Berkeley. Due a mix-up in student records, however, and a delayed registration because of illness, she was denied admission into the Physical Education Program. She registered for an anthropology course instead, and by the end of the semester she had decided to pursue anthropology as her major. Her family soon moved to Berkeley, where she and her sister, Evelyn, who followed her to the university, were able to enjoy a home environment while they attended school.[5] Her parents were apparently very supportive of a university education for their daughters, including graduate study. Kelly graduated with her bachelor's degree in anthropology in 1926 and was then accepted into graduate school in the discipline that same year.

Kelly's mentors at the university were Alfred L. Kroeber, Robert H. Lowie, and Edward W. Gifford in the anthropology department and

Carl O. Sauer in geography. Kroeber was a student of Franz Boas, and his own research focus at the time was the ethnography and ethnology of California's indigenous peoples. Having already worked in several areas of the state, he was in the process of producing his monumental compilation *Handbook of the Indians of California*.[6] Kroeber felt considerable urgency in surveying and salvaging as much as possible of indigenous lifeways and languages, and he directed as many students as he could into the work. The products of his and their efforts are in part contained in the many papers and monographs published in the *University of California Publications in American Archaeology and Ethnology*, a series he founded in 1903, and later the *University of California Anthropological Records*, founded in 1937 (and completed in 1999).

Robert Lowie, another Boas student, had focused his attention on the ethnography of peoples of the Great Plains, particularly the Crows. However, he was a strong comparativist, with particular interests in social organization and religion.[7] He also had wide experience in comparative material culture, interests that fitted nicely with those of the university's Museum of Anthropology. Lowie, along with Kroeber and Gifford, encouraged students to take advantage of the impressive collections, to help to gather more, and to work on museum-related problems.

Edward Gifford, initially hired as an assistant curator in the museum, was largely self-taught. Encouraged by Kroeber to study California Indian cultures, he had by the time he met Kelly produced several monographs, particularly on the Sierra Miwoks of central California.[8] He became a lecturer in the department in 1920 and continued to pursue wide-ranging research interests in the field, including in archaeology. Of the three scholars, graduate students found Gifford the most approachable; many turned to him for advice and counsel.[9]

Carl Sauer was Kroeber's counterpart in the geography department. Interested in both cultural and physical geography, he used a broad-based approach to human history that included prehistory, and his work, like that of his colleagues, combined well with the approaches used in anthropology. Sauer and Kroeber taught joint seminars during the mid-1920s and 1930s, and Sauer's and Lowie's interests in diffusionist themes were parallel. Sauer's fieldwork interests in Baja California and western Mexico may have been particularly appealing to Kelly. Together with historian Herbert E. Bolton, Sauer and Kroeber formed (during the late 1920s and early 1930s) what would later be referred to as the "Berkeley School" of Latin American studies, exemplified by the monographs and papers published in their jointly edited journal, *Ibero-Americana*, founded in 1932.[10]

Kelly's experiences in graduate school included courses from all four of these noted scholars. Kelly entered graduate school with a keen interest in archaeology, although there was little emphasis on it in the department, and no formal courses were offered.[11] She followed the departmental paradigm, stressing a broad-based disciplinary education with an emphasis on ethnology and comparative studies. Lowie taught linguistics, although not much beyond a single course. Very little attention apparently was paid to field methods of any kind, although broader comparative analyses were stressed. Sauer's willingness to provide field classes in local geography may have been particularly important to those in anthropology interested in more specific field techniques. Kelly and several other anthropology students minored in geography on the graduate level and greatly appreciated these perspectives.[12] Kelly also developed interests in western Mexico through the Sauer-Kroeber-Bolton connection.

Anthropology graduate students at Berkeley with whom Kelly developed close ties included Anna O. Gayton, Lila M. O'Neale, Dorothy D. Lee, Cora Du Bois, Julian Steward, Charles Voegelin, Ralph Beals, Forrest Clements, and Lloyd Warner. The situation for female graduate students was mixed, with Kroeber less inclined than Lowie to endorse them wholeheartedly. Kroeber felt that there would be few academic jobs available to them if they finished. He was apparently especially unsympathetic to women who wanted to be archaeologists, suggesting that their reasons likely had more to do with pursuing male archaeologists than with genuine field interests. Once they showed ability and a firm commitment to the discipline, however, Kroeber helped in many ways. Lowie, on the other hand, felt that women deserved equal opportunities and favored their continuing with graduate studies. Gayton, O'Neale, and Lee finished their dissertations before Kelly (in 1928, 1930, and 1931, respectively), while Du Bois and Voegelin finished with Kelly (in 1932).[13]

Kelly actively sought archaeological field training in 1929 by applying for the summer program at the newly founded Laboratory of Anthropology in Santa Fe. Kroeber served on the founding board of trustees for the "LAB," as it became known, and taught a field course in ethnology focused on the Walapai people of Arizona.[14] Alfred V. Kidder, the dean of southwestern archaeology, headed the archaeology field school, with a plan that included an initial three weeks at Pecos Pueblo, a large, important site he was excavating, and then five weeks on a smaller, single-component site in the vicinity of Santa Fe.[15] In a letter to Kidder, Kroeber assessed Kelly as a candidate for the archaeological field school:

> The first [candidate] is Isabel Kelly, who wants definitely to do archaeology and not ethnology. She has had a full undergraduate major with us and during the past two or three years has usually done graduate work one semester each year, working at a job the other semester. This year she is with us for the full year. She is an excellent student, not theoretical minded, but interested, hard working, exact, accurate, and reliable in every way. With all these good qualities however she inclines too much to think of herself as an inferior sort of person. You would find that she would execute admirably any task set to her. What she needs is training in initiative.[16]

In his letter's final paragraph, Kroeber indicated that he was "still voting for an all-man's school this first year, if there are enough good men to go around," to which Kidder replied that he could "see no good excuse for not having them [women] at Pecos, except that it might be difficult to make up parties for the independent investigations" he was planning for the second month. "According to the above scheme I could only use women if I had two or three of them so that I could have them make up a straight female party."[17] As it turned out, Kidder had an all-female crew that year—four women, including Kelly. The separate excavation was conducted at Tecolote Ruin, near Las Vegas, New Mexico, and the field party attended the second Pecos Conference held at Pecos Ruin in August.[18]

Kelly returned to Berkeley that fall, ready to finish her coursework. During that year she completed and published three studies based on museum collections: a comparison of designs on Peruvian ceramic bowls, a study of the wood and horn carver's art among northeastern California tribes, and a description of the basketry tradition of the Yuki Indians of northwestern California.[19] The study of the carver's art was her master's thesis, a topic Kroeber assigned her based on his collection supplemented by other specimens that had been accumulating in the museum.[20] Good grounding in material culture was considered very important to develop a student's observational and analytical skills, and thus the department favored these types of studies. Also required was ethnographic field experience, preferably in California, and continuing Kroeber's salvage orientation. Because of this Kelly conducted her first Great Basin fieldwork among the Northern Paiute people in Surprise Valley in extreme northeastern California in the summer of 1930, and perhaps also her work with the Coast Miwoks north of San Francisco, in late 1931 and early 1932 (see below).

Dissertation requirements for anthropology students at Berkeley in the 1920s and early 1930s focused on broad comparative topics from the literature rather than on specific data from the student's own field-work. Kelly's dissertation topic, following departmental guidelines, was a comparison of the growth and development of Great Basin cultures, titled "Fundamentals of Great Basin Culture." In it she explored basic aspects of hunter-gatherer lifeways, including territoriality, subsistence, material culture, social organization and religion, against the backdrop of a semiarid environment. Kelly completed the work in the spring of 1932. Kroeber, Lowie, and Sauer served on her dissertation committee.[21]

Northern Paiute Fieldwork

As we have noted, graduate students at Berkeley were required to conduct ethnographic fieldwork as part of their general requirements for graduation, and Kelly worked on this in the summer of 1930. Although Kroeber apparently gave her little direction about where to go or which group to work with, she chose a Northern Paiute group living in Surprise Valley in extreme northeastern California. She recalled later that she made her choice because a friend of her mother's ran a boarding-house in the valley and knew that there were some Indian people in the vicinity.[22] A week after arriving, Kelly wrote to Kroeber about her inadequate preparations for linguistic fieldwork: "It aggravates me horribly to see all this good linguistic material going to waste. I am simply butchering it. The glottal stop completely eludes me. . . . The good people are sympathetic and consequently bellow on the whispered syllable for my benefit. A good linguist could get absolutely an[y]thing. . . . Language aside, things are not going too badly." Kelly ended her letter by noting: "I almost forgot to tell you that archaeology is my first love and my only love."[23]

Kelly spent the summer in Fort Bidwell (the reservation community) and returned to Berkeley in the fall with a thorough ethnographic sketch and a large collection of mythological tales. She reported that Kroeber was surprised at her success, telling her that work with Great Basin Shoshoneans, in his experience, was particularly difficult. (He later characterized them as "superficial[ly] lack[ing] amiability," and not without "churlish incivility.") Kelly responded that they had "sicced the dogs on me" a couple of times but that, given her lack of ethnographic experience, she assumed that that was the normal course of all fieldwork.[24]

Kelly prepared her Northern Paiute ethnography for publication in the departmental series that fall and the next year, while also working on her dissertation.[25] She discussed her results with fellow graduate student Julian Steward, who had worked among the linguistically and culturally related Owens Valley Paiutes in southeastern California in the summers of 1927 and 1928. Later, she published her collection of Northern Paiute tales as a separate monograph.[26]

Coast Miwok Fieldwork

Kelly's Coast Miwok fieldwork, also undertaken and completed before she finished her doctorate, has been described and assessed by Buzaljko in a 1991 work and by Collier and Thalman on the occasion of the posthumous publication of Kelly's extensive ethnographic notes on the group.[27] Although the exact impetus for the work is unknown, Kroeber apparently assigned Kelly to study the group after plans for her to work with the Death Valley Shoshones in the fall of 1931 failed to materialize.[28] Following his common practice with promising students working in California ethnology, Kroeber provided Kelly with a small departmental stipend for living and travel expenses and an additional small amount for consultants' fees.

After two initial visits in December 1931 to Bodega Bay in west-central Marin County, north of San Francisco and Berkeley, Kelly settled into a small rented cottage in that area in late January and remained there for roughly four months.[29] While there she worked with Tom Smith, an elderly Coast Miwok man very knowledgeable in the old ways. She wrote Kroeber not long after she had begun her work:

> My informant is one of the world's nicer people and we are on excellent terms with each other. The poor chap works about as hard as I do, and it is just impossible to hold more than half-day sittings. He spends his evenings singing, so that he may remember things to tell me the following day. It provokes him frightfully when he cannot remember. He is extremely conscientious, but also agreeable, and I have constantly to guard against putting my words into his mouth.[30]

Prefiguring a research interest and approach that would remain with her throughout her career, Kelly went on to say:

> I think I have some nice concrete material on ethno-geography. The territory is remarkably compact, and one can travel over the greater part by car. I have the important boundary lines exact I think. Also a very great deal on the localization of various subsistence items. The exact rocks where they got seal; which flat yielded which clams; just which hills formerly bore oak trees; and the like. I shall never cease to be grateful for the joint seminar; the concept of land utilization is a very handy one in ethnography.[31]

Kelly's reference to the "joint seminar" was to a Kroeber-Sauer class that stressed the importance of an on-the-ground orientation to geography and subsistence. This orientation would also be one of Kelly's primary interests in her subsequent work with the Southern Paiutes, for which she was preparing a funding request while she was in the field with the Coast Miwoks. It was likewise related to her interests in archaeology, as these types of specific data are exceedingly useful for relating archaeological sites to one another.

In addition to working with Tom Smith, Kelly conducted extensive interviews with Maria Copa, a descendant of a different Coast Miwok subgroup. The material she obtained from Copa was equally rich and provided a valuable woman's perspective on all topics. The only difficulties Kelly reports in her field correspondence is that Smith was cautioned by his half brother not to reveal too much about things that might reflect negatively on the people, specifically, things that might be interpreted as "magic" or "superstition." Smith, however, seemed determined to describe things in his own way, including controversial aspects of religion and ceremonialism.[32]

Partway through the field experience, nonetheless, Kelly began to worry about her masses of data and how to interpret the materials. "I have a horrible feeling that I am accumulating concrete description without the underlying significance," she wrote to Kroeber. "It is like having the pieces to a patchwork quilt but not knowing how to put them together. I suppose anything is better than nothing, it worries me that I cannot visualize the socio-religious mechanism as a working unit."[33] A few weeks earlier she had written to Gifford, who was interested in Miwok religion, to complain of the richness of the data she was getting and the unhappy prospect of "putting all this lovely ceremonial into skeletonized form."[34] For Kelly, it was the detail that made the picture complete. To break it down into a preestablished outline, as was the procedure of the day for comparative purposes, was to make it lose its meaning and appeal.

Upon her return from the field, Kelly wrote to Kroeber (who had been on leave for the semester) that she hoped he would not send her to the field again after her upcoming Southern Paiute work, as she would need considerable time to work over all the Coast Miwok material. For various reasons, she did not return to the data until the early 1970s, when she was asked to write the ethnographic sketch on the Coast Miwoks for volume 8 (*California*) of the Smithsonian Institution's massive *Handbook of North American Indians*. The original field data, recorded in eleven handwritten field journals (eight for Tom Smith and three for Maria Copa), later were carefully excerpted and categorized by Kelly according to George P. Murdock's popular *Outline of Cultural Materials* scheme. Eventually, Mary E. T. Collier and Sylvia B. Thalman compiled and edited Kelly's ethnographic notes in a handsome volume published by the Miwok Archaeological Preserve of Marin. The initial printing in 1991 sold out, and a second printing was issued in 1996.[35]

Southern Paiute Ethnography

Although it is unclear from the correspondence whether Kelly actively sought an academic position after she finished her dissertation, she was apparently eager, with the support of her mentors, to continue to support herself through grants for more fieldwork. On February 9, 1932, while still at Bodega Bay, she received word that the National Research Council had granted her a fellowship in the biological sciences for a one-year study titled "A Determination of the Ethnic Groupings of a Great Basin Tribe, with Special Reference to the Geographic and Subsistence Bases." This project was an outgrowth of her dissertation work. With its comparative emphasis on the subsistence systems and fundamental adaptations of Great Basin peoples, it was designed to gather specific data on the relationship of cultural variation and environmental variation. The field orientation was to be ethnogeographical, involving the gathering of highly specific data on boundaries, settlements, economic cycles, and the utilization of natural resources, which would then be analyzed against the backdrop of different environments. The original proposal did not specify a group to be the focus of the field efforts, but sometime during that spring, perhaps in consultation with Kroeber and particularly Lowie, who had done fieldwork among the Shivwits Southern Paiutes, Kelly chose to work with the Southern Paiute people of the southern Great Basin.[36]

She chose wisely, as this ethnic group spans two major geographic provinces (the Basin and Range and the Colorado Plateau) as well as several different environmental zones with local variation. She also was interested in ethnic boundaries in hunter-gatherer groups; in her dissertation research she had found them characterized in the literature as having "weak localization," which she thought questionable.[37] Kroeber and Lowie, as well as A. V. Kidder of Harvard University, guided her in her project. The Laboratory of Anthropology in Santa Fe (directed by

Jesse Nusbaum), where she had been a fellow in archaeology in 1929, administered her funds.[38]

In mid-June 1932, Kelly arrived in Santa Fe to take up the National Research Council fellowship. She had been granted $1,800 for the one-year study, which was to include collecting all of the types of data her proposal had specified, plus a few months for writing up the results. Although she had completed her dissertation at Berkeley, she was still affiliated with the institution, and this allowed Kroeber to supplement her field account for the year with an additional $250 of university funds.[39] She also had almost another $400 from the Laboratory of Anthropology, Harvard's Peabody Museum, and the American Museum of Natural History to purchase ethnographic collections for their museums.[40] This level of funding ($2,450 for the year), even though partly committed to purchases, seemed adequate, particularly considering the scarcity of funding during the Great Depression. Kelly would spend roughly fifteen months in the field over the next two and a half years, however, which required a second-year National Research Council grant. The extension in field time was due partly to the difficulty of the field situation and partly to an auto accident she suffered in the field and the recovery time that followed. She finished the project nonetheless, amassing large amounts of primary data on Southern Paiute ethnogeography and ethnography throughout their precontact territory. Unfortunately, because of the delays almost no time was allotted for synthesis and write-up, and she was unable to publish the bulk of the data.[41]

Kelly's correspondence is invaluable to discussing her fieldwork experiences as well as her methods. Kelly arrived in Santa Fe in her single-seat 1932 Ford with fellow Berkeley student Jane Gabbert, whom Kroeber sent as a companion.[42] They departed Santa Fe on June 26 for Kaibab, Arizona, the first stop in Kelly's field circuit. They drove via northern New Mexico and southern Colorado, passing Mesa Verde, then into Utah and northern Arizona. After a few harrowing adventures on the roads in northern New Mexico (she comments that due to mud and rain they denuded several juniper trees to extricate themselves), they arrived at their destination on July 1 and were able to camp in the luxury of the school kitchen. Shortly thereafter,

We discovered that Dr. [C. Hart] Merriam had been there only three days ago. Last evening his informant presented himself, unsolicited, and was engaged. The very thought of a Paiute who volunteers services as an informant makes me cross my fingers. This morning I tore over hill and dale with him and his wife, and we collected thirty or so plant specimens. The entire camp takes a flattering interest in our activities, and we are continually receiving impromptu calls, and what not. About fifteen perch outside the door and, all told, things are quite different from the surly Northern Paiute.[43]

Her initial enthusiasm was tempered somewhat when the person she had chosen as a consultant turned out to be too young for, as she later characterized her field approach, the "unabashedly how-it-was-in-your-grandfather's-day" approach.[44] She wrote about three weeks later:

From the expressions of sympathy, I judge that my letter to Dr. Mera must have been highly lugubrious. I am famous for the mournful letters which I send in from the field. Since I wrote, I have changed informants and am now working with a man who claims to know everything. Although he falls some-what short of his modest claim, he is really an excellent informant, and I am genuinely pleased with the material that is accumulating. I am trying to do the Kaibab rather thoroughly in order to supplement the nucleus that Sapir has. With the other Paiute I shall confine myself more to straight ethnogeography.[45]

Since Kelly was also collecting Southern Paiute material culture for various museums, she was eager to learn what was available and what the museums were expecting. She wrote Nusbaum about the desires of the American Museum of Natural History: "We have been offered the usual buckskin gauntlets, etc., but I have wind of a seed gathering apparatus which might be nice. I suppose Dr. Wissler would prefer a somewhat bedraggled but genuine article to a neat looking model?"[46] When she still had not heard from Wissler by month's end, Kelly devised her own plan.[47] Ultimately, during the course of her field studies she acquired some 325 items of material culture from twelve Southern Paiute/Chemehuevi subgroups for several museums. The collections are similar in depth and breadth, are very well documented, and form an excellent corpus for comparison.[48]

Kelly remained at Kaibab for roughly two months, working with people she termed the "last four of the old Kaibab." When Gabbert returned to school, Kelly was on her own with her trusted Ford and her camping tent. But, she added in a letter to A. V. Kidder, "I just can't tell you how splendidly things have gone so far. Really, life is good. I have been getting good material, so good that my fingers have been crossed since the first week out."[49]

In mid-September 1932, Kelly moved to Cedar City, Utah, where she worked with several individuals originally from different bands in that vicinity. She deemed them the "last survivors" of their particular groups. She wrote to Kidder, "The past week I have been camped in the wilds at Indian Peak, sixty miles from here, on exceedingly chummy terms with 7 Paiute, 9 horses, and countless canines resident there. This does not include the amiable bobcat which wandered into my tent one moonlight night."[50]

In early October, Kelly backtracked to Navajo Spring, near Marble Canyon, in search of elusive Paiute people who lived south of the Colorado River in what is now called the Navajo Strip. There she had great difficulty finding families, and once she did she could not enlist a satisfactory interpreter. However, she persevered and managed to collect considerable material on this then-unknown group. Another challenge was inclement weather and lack of paved roads: "Winter draws on apace and I am still trailing gayly over the Plateau, flirting with the chance of a snowstorm that will close the roads. As a matter of fact, the road here from Kanab was quite washed out in spots, and there was a heavy downpour of rain last night. My trusty tent is still flapping in the breeze, dry inside thank heaven."[51] After her sojourn at Navajo Springs, Kelly moved on to Santa Clara, Utah, near the Shivwits Reservation. By the time she finished at Santa Clara, she could say that she had relatively full ethnographies in addition to ethnographies of the Shivwits and St. George Paiutes.

In mid-November, Kelly returned to Berkeley to consult with Kroeber and prepare the specimens she had collected for the museums for photographing, illustration, and shipment. She had intended to spend December back in the field at Moapa, Nevada, but was unable to do so because of a flare-up of back troubles exacerbated by travel over rough roads. As she wrote Nusbaum on December 20:

I have been obliged to take an enforced vacation which Harold Hitch-cock, the famous bone specialist, claims has been brought on by too much Ford-driving. He insists that everyone who drives a Ford must pay a penalty sooner or later and that account is being taken of me because of my having averaged something like 2000 miles monthly since June. At any rate, I must confess that although I have always been a rugged and hearty soul, the last few weeks have been made miserable with a stiff back—all of which involves sleeping on planks, sporting 20 inches of adhesive tape, and desisting from driving. All of this is a perfect nuisance.[52]

After field study from late December 1932 through January 1933 in Moapa, where again Kelly received excellent cooperation and data, she returned to Berkeley to begin writing up her materials. In the process, she prepared a paper on comparative Southern Paiute shamanism for an anniversary volume for Robert Lowie.[53] In addition, she applied for a renewal of her National Research Council fellowship for a second year to concentrate her work among the westernmost Southern Paiute groups in southern Nevada and California: the Las Vegas band and the Chemehuevis, their close linguistic and cultural kinsmen. Both groups, along with the Moapa people, are in the Mojave Desert, an area of considerable interest to Kelly for comparative ethnogeographic purposes. She was granted the extension the following June, and after time in Santa Fe working on her field notes from the previous year she again set out for the field. This time, however, her spirit of adventure led to difficulty. While in Santa Fe, she had met two Harvard students working in the Southwest on Rockefeller fellowships, who had asked if they could join her on her trip to southern Nevada by way of the Grand Canyon. She agreed, and after picking them up in Flagstaff they headed out in her trusty one-seat Ford. One of the men drove and, apparently unfamiliar with the hazards of dirt roads, rolled the car, ejecting the three and all of their belongings.[54] After a four-hour wait for help, the three were taken to Flagstaff, where Kelly spent the next two months hospitalized with several broken vertebrae. Her most immediate concern was her field notes from the previous year's work. Despite her immediate fear that the accident had destroyed them, they were ultimately recovered in her battered trunk.

After recuperating in Berkeley, Kelly returned to the field in mid-November, first at Moapa and then at Parker, Arizona, and Las Vegas, Nevada, for Chemehuevi fieldwork. The comparative ethnographic problems and the more recent history of at least some Chemehuevi people's move to the floodplain of the Colorado River, where they were influenced by the "virile and distinctive Mohave river culture," had peaked her interest. She remarked on conditions in Parker: "Parker is pleasant as regards temperature, but the town itself is about as dismal, dusty, and uninviting as anything I have seen in years. Work is coming on satisfactorily, but not with such success that I am frenzied with enthusiasm. My Las Vegas informant is a more satisfactory informant than the local people—but he is blind and 200 miles from his native hearth. However, the local material is supplementing his very nicely."[55] Kelly refers as well to very pleasant nights spent stargazing with the Chemehuevis. She regretted being unable to spend another couple of months there, as the materials were continuing to "roll in most satisfactorily."[56] In all, she spent some five months in the low desert areas.

After her Southern Paiute field sessions, Kelly turned her attention to western Mexico and her first love, archaeology. Nevertheless, she published three important papers from her Southern Paiute research: first, a paper on the distribution and territories of the fifteen Southern Paiute groups she was able to visit and identify; second, a paper on Chemehuevi shamanism, which focused on the data she collected in late 1933 and 1934, in a volume honoring Kroeber; and third, a short but rich monograph overview of Southern Paiute shamanism, in which she combined the data from both the Lowie and Kroeber volume treatments.[57] The remainder of her Southern Paiute ethnography would be set aside—but not forgotten—for some three decades.

Initial Archaeological Fieldwork in Western Mexico

While Kelly was still working among the Chemehuevis, her mentors Kroeber and Sauer were arranging for a short-term grant from the university's Institute of Social Sciences that would take her to Mexico for the first time. It would also change forever her life and her place in the anthropological world. In a letter to Kroeber before she departed for

Mexico, Kelly expressed her apprehension about being the right person for the assignment: "What with knowing practically nothing about archaeology and absolutely nothing about Mexico, I should be in a fair position to muddle the works! And with so much capital involved!"[58] This capital was $3,600 to cover her salary, travel expenses, and the cost of field laborers.

Kelly headed off to Culiacán, in the state of Sinaloa, to learn if "prehistoric cultures of the coast plain of Sinaloa . . . may prove to be a link between the ancient and native cultures of Mesa Central of Mexico and the culture of the Pueblo Indians of the southwestern part of the United States," a topic that Sauer and Kroeber had long found intriguing.[59] From January to May 1935 she made extensive surface collections and carried out excavations at mounds in five sites in the region, particularly along the course of the Rio Culiacán. Physical anthropologist Frederick S. Hulse helped her deal with the large number of skeletons—190 in *ollas* (large jars) and another 62 in free burials—encountered in all five sites. Kelly stretched her funding with assistance from the Sud Pacífico de México railroad company, which provided "transportation, storage, and a variety of extremely helpful incidental services."[60]

Toward the end of the field season at Culiacán, Kelly left Hulse to finish the site excavations and took part of the field crew to Chametla, in the southern part of Sinaloa, using a small amount of the University of California, Berkeley, monies. She made a "brief investigation" for three weeks, working systematically but at an energetic pace. In a letter to Sauer, Kelly described her typical day: "Up at 5:30; to work by 7:30; home at 4:00; cataloguing, writing notes, counting sherds until 11 and later every night. As our factotum says, 'The days are too long and the nights are too short.' Right now a really tough ethnological trip would seem a positive relaxation. But it is a swell country; I like the people, and I like the country, and I can hardly remember having lived in Berkeley."[61] A prophetic statement, indeed. Kelly remained in Mexico to do the preliminary data analysis of the materials collected in Culiacán and Chametla. In November and December 1935 she stayed at the home of Mesoamericanist George Vaillant in Colima, where "she helped out caring for the children by singing German lullabies to them." Subsequently, she was assisted by Irmgard Weitlaner (Johnson) "in labeling and mending the collection while it was being studied in Mexico City."[62]

Perhaps because of the smaller amount of materials recovered at Chametla, Kelly decided to write up this material first. She soon completed her report, with its emphasis on pottery typology and chronology, and submitted it to Sauer and Kroeber for their approval. The final report, transmitted to the University of California Press for publication in the Ibero-Americana series—which Sauer and Kroeber coedited with the historian H. E. Bolton—in 1936, was not issued until December 1938.

Kelly left Mexico and returned to Berkeley in January 1936 to serve as Sauer's teaching assistant, preferring this opportunity over Kroeber's suggestions.[63] Apparently, although permanent academic appointments were in short supply during the Great Depression, Kroeber and Sauer recognized her value and were determined to keep her employed in some manner.

Archaeological Work in Arizona

In due course, Kelly left Berkeley for another temporary position, this time in Tucson, Arizona. She took charge of the Hodges site excavations, a large Hohokam complex where archaeological work had begun in 1936 under the direction of Carl Miller, with the assistance and financial support of Mr. and Mrs. Wetmore Hodges. According to Gayle Hartmann, the archaeologist who played the major role in obtaining finances for the publication of *The Hodges Ruin*, "Digging continued through 1937 and 1938 still supported by the Hodges, but now under the auspices of the Gila Pueblo Archaeological Foundation in Globe, Arizona. . . . The late winter and early spring were devoted to fieldwork, the other months being taken up with laboratory analysis and preparation of the manuscript. Dr. Kelly's appointment with Gila Pueblo expired before she could complete her report and late in 1938 she turned to other research."[64] The "other research" to which Hartmann refers involved Kelly's return to Mexico, where she surveyed in Sinaloa, Nayarit, Colima, and Michoacán. Her notes, the unfinished report, and the collections from the Hodges site eventually found their way to the

Arizona State Museum in Tucson, where coincidentally Kelly later was affiliated as a research associate so that she would have a professional affiliation to publish her Mexican archaeology reports.

Nothing happened with the Hodges site materials until 1955, when Emil Haury asked James Officer, then a graduate student at the University of Arizona, to finish the Hodges site report. Officer advanced the analysis, but the final report was not yet ready for publication. Then, in the 1960s and 1970s, the Hodges site suffered obliteration at the hands of urban developers.[65] Coincidentally and concurrently, Stephen M. Larson, president of the Arizona Archaeological and Historical Society (1973–75), purchased a home near the Hodges site. He became enthusiastic about publication of the complete manuscript and urged the project on Hartmann and her colleagues at the museum. They, in turn, approached Kelly in 1975, who agreed despite the lack of cataloging and several other problems:

> A month ago, Arizona sent me the old report on the Hodges site, an ancient village on the outskirts of Tucson, where I excavated in 1937 and 1938. Report written in the latter year, but left unfinished because the Gladwins [of Gila Pueblo] and the "patrons" of the work had a fight. In cold storage nearly 40 years, the report has been fished out and the Arizona Historical Society threatens to publish. Quite disgraceful, I may say, to discover that much of the collection is missing—never catalogued by the Arizona State Museum—so my original layouts for illustrations could not be used. In 1955 or 1956, Haury asked Officer to complete the missing sections. With this ms off my desk and back on that of Haury, I decided to take a new squint at the Capacha ms. Have added a couple of new pages; corrected a few typing errors, but in general, I'm inclined to let it stand.[66]

But in 1939 Kelly's attention was focused on western Mexico, where she would continue to conduct some of the most significant research of her career.

Archaeological Fieldwork in Western Mexico

With a small grant from the University of California, Berkeley, and with Sauer's strong encouragement, Kelly returned to Mexico for another archaeological survey in early 1939. She spent January in Culiacán and then headed south by car and rail as far as Nayarit. From there, she and her companion, Marian Cummings, traveled for ten days by mule to Puerto Vallarta. Their field trip also included three weeks by horseback from Autlán to Tuxcacuesco. Eventually, Kelly and Cummings flew from Puerto Vallarta to Guadalajara and then onward to Mexico City, where they began to review some five tons of materials, mostly surface-collected ceramic sherds. This substantial collection was obtained by visiting and making surface collections at some two hundred sites located along the full length of the Nayarit, Jalisco, and Colima coasts.[67]

In the summer of 1939, Kelly presented her preliminary findings at the Twenty-seventh International Congress of Americanists in Mexico City. This short but suggestive paper appeared in the two-volume set of proceedings issued in Mexico City after the war and was also included in the volume published posthumously in her honor.[68] Kelly sent a report on her Culiacán excavations to Sauer and Kroeber, and they submitted the final version for publication in the Ibero-Americana series on July 18, 1940, although it, too, was not published until after the war—on September 20, 1945.

By this time, Kelly had committed herself to a career and life in Mexico. In 1940 she settled in the famous ceramic-producing village of San Pedro Tlaquepaque, located on the southeastern periphery of Guadalajara, Jalisco. She maintained a home there until 1945, while she continued her archaeological investigations in western Mexico begun in the summer of 1939 as she conducted surveys along the Jalisco-Colima border.[69]

With funds from the University of California, she traveled to Autlán on a five-day trip with Sauer and Bruman.[70] With a grant from the John Simon Guggenheim Memorial Foundation, she returned to the area in the fall and winter of 1940–41, making a twenty-day survey on horseback from Autlán to Tuxcacuesco, eventually going as far as Mazatlán, near the Colima border. She next surveyed the San Gabriel–Apulco–Tapalpa area in the spring of 1941, again under the auspices of the Guggenheim Foundation. The following spring (1942), with funding this time from the New York City–based Institute of Andean Research,

Kelly returned to Tuxcacuesco, extending the surface survey and making test excavations. Two reports based on these field sessions were published with a subsidy from the Institute of Andean Research. As happened to all publications during the war, it took several years for the works to appear.[71]

Kelly continued her archaeological investigations beyond the Jalisco-Colima border region into the coastal region of the state of Michoacán because it was "a zone where we still do not know all the answers. Many years of survey and excavation will be necessary before this happy goal is attained."[72] Her current project focused on the Apatzingán region with fieldwork financed by the Institute of Andean Research, under a grant nominally awarded to Kroeber and Sauer, while her own Guggenheim fellowship and a joint grant from the Carnegie Institution of Washington and the American Philosophical Society supported her report-writing activities during 1944.

With these extended projects in the Jalisco-Colima and Michoacán coastal regions, Kelly significantly expanded her horizon from Sauer and Kroeber's earlier concerns to establish cultural connections of western Mexico to the Mesa Central and the American Southwest. Now, she began examining the linkages between the preconquest cultural sequences and the postconquest period *within* the region of western Mexico. Her efforts to bridge the gap between archaeology and colonial history became a hallmark of her work for the remainder of her career in Mexico, a feature seen in the work of other women in this book.

Kelly made her initial analyses in terms of specific artifact types rather than a grand synthesis. For example, she published short notes on "Ixtle Weaving at Chiquilistlán, Jalisco" and "Worked Gourds from Jalisco."[73] The latter discussed gourd making in the communities of Ayotitlán, Sayula, and San Pedro Tlaquepaque, where she remarked: "Its gourd industry is so unobtrusive that, after three years of nearly continuous residence there, I was completely unaware of any such enterprise. Quite by chance my aide, José María Corona, noticed through an open doorway that a number of gourds were being packed; he made inquiry and determined that they had been prepared locally."[74] Kelly's eye for unexpected elements of material culture was never more important than in her visits to the town of Sayula, Jalisco, between 1941 and 1945.[75] While in Sayula she became aware of a Talavera-style ceramic tradition dating from the nineteenth and early twentieth centuries. She began acquiring pieces discreetly from the town's families, who had them sitting on their shelves or stored in their closets. Little by little she assembled a substantial collection of Sayula ceramics, which she eventually installed in a separate building at her home in Tepepan. Kelly's last will and testament donated the collection, estimated to contain no fewer than 550 pieces, to the BANAMEX Cultural Foundation. BANAMEX published a book about the Kelley Sayula Collection in 1984, and it still regularly sends the Kelly Sayula Collection on tour from its permanent location in their Guadalajara museum.[76]

Kelly's final contribution to western Mexican archaeology offers a window to her entire career. For more than three decades she conducted fieldwork in the state of Colima, starting with the preconquest cultures and moving systematically into a broader cultural chronology stretching to modern times. Her commitment to careful collection of data sufficient to establish a "convincing chronology" led her to store her early collections with the Instituto Nacional de Antropología e Historia (INAH) for more than two decades, while she shifted her career to social anthropology (see below).[77] Eventually, with grants from the Rockefeller Foundation (for the 1966 and 1967 field seasons) and from the National Geographic Society and the Wenner-Gren Foundation for Anthropological Research (for fieldwork in 1968 through 1971 and 1973), she returned to Colima to research problems about regionalism she felt she had not completed.

After years of careful analysis of the several tons of sherds and related materials on loan to her from INAH, Kelly eventually identified what she called the Capacha phase, "after the ex-hacienda from which came the first material to permit its recognition as an entity."[78] Published later, when funding became available, as "Ceramic Sequence in Colina: Capacha, an Early Phase," her work not only describes the ceramic sequence in Colima, with a focus on the Capacha phase, but also discusses Capacha relationships with the rest of Mesoamerica and even northwest South America. In his foreword, Emil W. Haury observed of Kelly's work:

An argument can be made for in-depth investigation and immersion in regional archaeology, for without it the Capacha complex might not have been so convincingly recognized and its implications understood. Another fact emerges too. The breakthroughs, the insights that come from investigation, are usually not instantaneous. They result from long hours of plodding and tedious work. The Capacha Phase, though based largely on ceramic evidence and dating from about 1870–1720 B.C., is an example of that, as Dr. Kelly will be the first to admit.[79]

Kelly also would have admitted to serious distraction while completing the Capacha report. In mid-1973, as she was preparing her Coast Miwok article for the *Handbook of North American Indians*, she learned of the unauthorized publication of her Coast Miwok field notes by the Treganza Museum of San Francisco State College. Kelly had placed these field notes with the Department of Anthropology at the University of California, Berkeley, for safekeeping when she went to Mexico in the late 1930s. Their unauthorized publication greatly distressed her, and she wrote to numerous university administrators and anthropologists asking them to investigate the situation. At the same time, she was trying to concentrate on her Colima archaeological research.[80]

Six months later, still seeking satisfaction about her Coast Miwok field notes (which she never obtained), she wrote to George Foster that work was going "slowly but well enough." Checking and rechecking sherds to enable her to make conclusive statements about Colima and its ceramic complexes was taking up most of her time. As she usually did, she was working on more than one monograph at a time, never quite content with what she had produced. "The Capacha monograph was finished some months ago, but I've been horsing around, trying to whip up an introduction which would provide some perspective on Colima archaeology, as I see it at present. Also, a conclusion which looks at Colima in Mesoamerican context, and so on. More ambitious than I should attempt. But I've been doing some readings—catching up after 15 years in Public Health and Community Development. And it is great fun to charge off on assorted tangents. Am having a fine time."[81] Having finally come full circle in her western Mexico work, Kelly demonstrated yet again that archaeology was her first love. At the same time, she began important and innovative work in social anthropology. So, we return to that critical moment in 1945 when necessity and opportunity merged into serendipity.

Social Anthropological Research in Mexico

At the time Kelly moved permanently to Mexico City in 1945, she was running out of funding for her research.[82] Through her friend Bertha Harris she obtained a job at the Biblioteca Benjamin Franklin, operated by the U.S. Information Service. In 1946 she was able to return to anthropological work when she received a recommendation from social anthropologist George Foster to take over his position as ethnologist in charge of the Smithsonian's Institute of Social Anthropology (ISA) office in Mexico City.[83] In assuming the role of senior ISA representative, Kelly began to teach courses at the Escuela Nacional de Anthropología e Historia (National School of Anthropology and History) and also take students into the field for ethnographic training (of the sort that she had decried never having received from Kroeber).

Curiously, Kelly did not take students to western Mexico for field training; instead, she went east to Sierra de Puebla, in the area where the states of Veracruz, Puebla, and Tlaxcala converge. There she initiated a study among the Tajín Totonacs living in the communities of El Tajín and San Marcos Eloxochitlán. Between 1947 and 1951 her students included many men and women who would become the cornerstone of Mexican anthropology: Gabriel Ospina, José Luis Lorenzo, María Cristina Alvárez, Roberto Williams García, Florencia Muller, and especially Angel Palerm, with whom she coauthored the well-known ethnography *The Tajín Totonac: Part I. History, Subsistence, Shelter, and Technology*.[84] Kelly's rationale for shifting attention from western Mexico reflects a sophisticated and ethical understanding of the relationship between field-workers and their communities:

> In recent years, other individuals and institutions have concentrated on the Tarascan zone, with the result that knowledge of this area is comparatively full, at least in contrast to other parts of Mexico. Under the circumstances, it seemed both expedient and humane to relieve the

long-suffering Tarascans from the pressure of a protracted open season; and, in 1947, with the concurrence of the Escuela, it was decided to shift the scene of field activities from highland Michoacán to the Gulf coast of Mexico in the vicinity of Papantla, in the State of Veracruz.[85]

Explaining in more detail her choice of a field site, Kelly shows her archaeological colors:

[T]he deciding factor was that Tajín was the seat of the famous archaeological site of that name. There, for many years, the Instituto Nacional de Antropología had maintained a Totonac care-taker and, from time to time, had undertaken excavations of major proportions. Accordingly, we assumed that the local population would not be unduly alarmed by a group of students which arrived under the aegis of the Instituto; and the caretaker, long accustomed to note-taking and to queries, might be able to explain our activities in innocuous terms to his neighbors.[86]

The Tajín Totonac materials are substantial: more than eight thousand original data sheets, as well as a comprehensive ethnographic census of some 187 households in the two communities, several hundred pages of typed life histories, thirty-eight rolls of black-and-white print film negatives and contact print sheets, more than 450 slides, and a forty-minute silent color motion picture film (depicting courtship and wedding dance scenes).[87]

Applied Anthropological Activities in Mexico and Beyond

When the ISA shifted its priorities from teaching and ethnographic training toward more practical projects, Kelly began a series of short-term studies of health-related problems in urban and rural Mexico. These projects continued when the ISA was folded into the new Institute of Inter-American Affairs (IIA, the forerunner of the United States Agency for International Development), where Kelly worked until her retirement in 1960.

The constraints imposed by numerous short-term assignments meant that Kelly and her colleagues usually had only the briefest periods for direct fieldwork and study of the available historical, geographical, and ethnographical literature before submitting a report to the agency sponsoring a particular project. In some ways, the training she had received at the University of California served her well in doing what now would be called "rapid assessments."

Her first study, carried out during 1951 and 1952, involved the Centro de Salud Beatriz Velasco de Alemán (Beatriz Velasco de Alemán Health Center) in the Federal District and a companion health center located in suburban Xochimilco. Kelly also made brief field trips to Union de San Antonio, Jalisco, and to Teposcolulua, Oaxaca, to gather additional data on medical beliefs and practices. At the same time, she conducted fieldwork in Cadereyta, Querétaro, regarding the feasibility of installing a culturally appropriate potable water system. There she surveyed 288 households about their water-use patterns. She also gathered a broad range of data on social and economic activities throughout the community, on the use of domestic animals, and on folk medicine. Putting her archaeological field skills to good use, Kelly mapped the town in terms of current activities related to water use, then coded these maps in terms of potential sites for the proposed potable water system.

In 1953, under the sponsorship of the IIA, Kelly conducted survey research in the communities of El Cuije and El Duraznito, both located in the Laguna region of Coahuila. The project concerned housing conditions at these ejido settlements based on a sample of fifty-four households, each of which was administered a questionnaire. Kelly completed three technical reports for the IIA and eventually prepared a manuscript in 1957, but "publication has dragged while awaiting official clearance from the Mexican ministry of Public Health."[88]

In 1954 Kelly carried out a short-term investigation of the pilot project of the Bienestar Social (Social Welfare) rural program in the community of Villa José Cartel, Veracruz. The following year she worked with Hector García Manzanedo on the relationship of culture and health in Santiago Tuxtla, Veracruz. They gathered ethnographic data, made maps, and developed analytical charts to summarize major features of folk medical beliefs, folk remedies, and mortality statistics. In 1955 and 1956 Kelly did additional research by herself in the community of Villagrán, Guanajuato, before continuing her collaboration with

García Manzanedo on a study of health practices in the region of the Isthmus of Tehuantepec, Oaxaca, in 1956 and 1957. The ethnographic coverage is extensive, with an emphasis on folk medical practices and spiritualism.

Beyond her applied ethnographic research in Mexico, during the 1950s Kelly collaborated with other anthropologists who were studying public health practices throughout Latin America. In 1955 she traveled to Puerto Rico and collected general ethnographic information that resulted in an unpublished paper titled "Puerto Rican Observations." In 1958 and 1959 she researched and lectured in Bolivia, gathering information on the status of agricultural extension projects and public health issues. In 1959 and 1960 she traveled far from her Latin American base to engage in work on community development in Pakistan. She visited Chichawatni, Panjab, East Pakistan, Karachi, and Quetta.

Along with anthropologists such as Dorothea Leighton, George Foster, Benjamin Paul, and Richard Adams, Isabel Kelly became a pioneer in the emerging specialty of medical anthropology. In a sense, her applied work with the IIA redirected her attention to problems of health, housing, and survival among marginal populations. These, of course, complemented her earliest fieldwork among the Coast Miwoks and the Southern Paiutes, where she had been interested in the relationship between culture and environment, especially material culture and foodways, health and healing, and technology and housing.

Returning to the American West

In the 1950s, with the initiation of the Indian Claims Commission in the United States and suits for land compensation to indigenous groups for early illegal appropriations, several anthropologists turned their attention to preparing briefs in cases for both sides in the disputes: the Indian tribes and the Department of Justice. Attention also turned to unpublished data that might be of use in these cases. Among these materials were Kelly's unpublished Southern Paiute and Chemehuevi materials. In 1955, Julian Steward, who was working for the Justice Department on the Southern Paiute case, wrote to Kelly inquiring about access to her field notes still stored in the Berkeley's anthropology department archives. A few weeks later, Kroeber, who was busily at work on several California cases, including the tribal side of the Chemehuevi case, also wrote requesting access to her Chemehuevi field notes.[89]

Kelly originally discouraged Steward, but in her reply granting Kroeber access she suggested that, to be fair, both sides should be able to see the materials. However, she asserted her ownership, as well as the need for copying them to secure against any data losses. She also spoke of her earlier intentions to publish on some of the rich data on Chemehuevi springs that she had obtained, lamenting that, "as usual in those days, there always was a bit of money for field work but mighty little for living expenses, while preparing [a] manuscript."[90] Kroeber, apparently sufficiently impressed by the depth and completeness of her Chemehuevi data, soon proposed that they write a joint publication on Chemehuevi–Las Vegas, and further, that "you really ought to come back to it sometime."[91] They decided to move forward with the joint publication effort, but only after Kroeber finished his Claims Commission work and Kelly was relieved of some of her other commitments. In August, Kroeber sent her a manuscript copy for comment of his "Desert Mohave: Fact and Fancy," in which he cited some of her data, with the statement: "The enclosed is not—or I might say not yet—the first installment of our joint manuscript on the Chemehuevi."[92] Their ultimate collaboration was not finalized before Kroeber's death in 1960.

Kelly also returned to her other unpublished western U.S. ethnographies in the 1960s, with additional requests to consult her materials for Claims Commission cases, an offer to publish some of her data in connection with the Glen Canyon Archaeological Project, and the announcement of the Smithsonian's plans to publish a massive twenty-volume *Handbook of North American Indians*. In 1961 attorneys for the Navajo claim requested access to her Southern Paiute field notes still at Berkeley. Omer Stewart, involved with the tribal side of the Southern Paiute claim, also was interested in consulting them. This provided her with the opportunity to request again that copies be made of all of her materials on deposit there and that a complete inventory be taken.[93] This was accomplished in December 1961. In 1963, when J. D. Jennings of the University of Utah's Glen Canyon Archaeological Project expressed an interest in citing more of the materials, Kelly indicated her willingness to publish a manuscript she had prepared in the 1930s on the easternmost Southern Paiute groups, those adjacent to the Glen Canyon area in southern Utah and northern Arizona.[94] With an agreement reached, and in order to prepare the publication, in 1963 Kelly requested that most of her Southern Paiute materials in Berkeley be microfilmed and the originals returned to her in Mexico. She then submitted the manuscript on the easternmost bands for publication in the Utah series, thereby relieving her of roughly one-third of the burden she felt regarding her unpublished Southern Paiute materials.[95] She then intended to work on the remainder, but other tasks intervened.

In the early 1970s, Kelly was approached to write an overview article on the Southern Paiutes (and another on the Coast Miwoks) for publication in volumes in the Smithsonian's series. This occasioned her review of all of her Southern Paiute materials, and she reorganized and synthesized them onto some fifteen thousand cards and a whole series of charts that would facilitate accurate band-by-band comparisons. She apparently did much the same for her Coast Miwok materials, which were finally published in the *California* volume of the *Handbook* in 1978.[96] Her Southern Paiute article was published in the *Great Basin* volume after her death.[97]

Conclusion

Isabel Kelly followed a career trajectory defined by itinerancy. Without permanent ties to an institutional research base, she made do with an impressive series of short-term grants and fellowships. This situation enabled her to remain professionally active but limited her influence in the discipline.[98] If by "itinerancy" one means that a scholar follows opportunities to do research on diverse problems in different places, then Kelly certainly was itinerant. Plotting her fieldwork creates quite a map:

- research among the Coast Miwoks of northern California in 1931 and 1932
- ethnographic and ethnohistoric research among some twenty groups of the widely dispersed Southern Paiutes (from California to Nevada, Utah, and Arizona) from 1932 to 1934

- archaeological investigations in Culiacán and Chametla in the state of Sinaloa, Mexico, in 1935 and 1939
- archaeological work at the Hodges Ruin, a Hohokam site in the Tucson Basin, Arizona, in 1937 and 1938
- archaeological investigations in Sinaloa and southward to Nayarit, Colima, and Michoacán in 1939 and 1940
- ethnographic research among the Tajín Totonacs of the Sierra de Puebla, Veracruz, from 1947 to 1951
- diverse public health and applied anthropology projects in rural and urban Mexico from 1951 to 1957
- research on public health issues in Latin America (El Salvador, Ecuador, Colombia, Chile, and Peru) in 1951 and 1952
- a research trip to Puerto Rico in 1955
- a research and lecturing trip to Bolivia in 1958 and 1959
- a trip to investigate community development in Pakistan in 1958 and 1959
- archaeological investigations in Colima in 1966 and 1967, from 1968 to 1971, and in 1973

The results of these many field trips and research projects in the Desert West, not circumscribed by international borders, are found most obviously in Kelly's professional publications: a dozen monographs and dozens of articles, including major surveys on the Coast Miwoks and the Southern Paiutes in the *Handbook of North American Indians* and on the Totonacs in the *Handbook of Middle American Indians*. This is *not* the profile of a scholar with "limited influence in her discipline," as some might argue because she never held a professorial position. Far from it.

Kelly was highly regarded in Mexico and among a broad spectrum of U.S., European, and Latin American archaeologists and social anthropologists. She was always very modest about her accomplishments, proclaiming that she was just working carefully through her accumulated materials—whether that involved thousands of pages of ethnographic field notes or tons of potsherds. Not having a tenure-track university position gave her a measure of freedom that many of her colleagues envied.

Kelly designed her home in Tepepan around her research activities.

The downstairs area of the two-story main house was for living and entertaining. Upstairs she had her office, where she maintained her voluminous correspondence, field notes, and related ethnographic materials. The older, original house on the north side of the property was filled with one of the finest personal libraries on anthropology in North America.[99] A large laboratory building (which Kelly called the *troje*) in the central section of the property was filled with tables laid out with potsherds, especially those from Colima which were on permanent loan from INAH, and the accompanying documentation. A structure located across the formal gardens to the west housed her unique collection of Sayula ceramics, donated after her death to the BANAMEX Cultural Foundation.

Throughout her career, Kelly was a superb letter writer. Her voluminous correspondence with her friend and mentor Carl Sauer and her letters to and from A. L. Kroeber, A. V. Kidder, and Jesse Nusbaum detail her descriptions of the rigors of life in the field in western North America and her struggles to obtain and maintain funding for her many projects.[100] Their replies often reflect their sincere efforts on her behalf as well as their deep respect for her abilities and accomplishments. In her later years, as she suffered from arthritis, she shifted from a manual to an electric typewriter so that she could keep up with her network of correspondents in Mexico, the United States, and beyond.[101] Those who corresponded with Kelly were blessed with her wonderful sense of humor as well as her acerbic comments on her own work. In a letter to George and Mickie Foster, Kelly offers a serious reflection on the choices available to her in her waning years:

> The trade-bead study should have been finished long ago, but there have been interruptions—hospitalization, for example. Also, I became interested in the selection of data by the different sources and so reworked the historical material quite completely. This has slowed matters depressingly, and there still are a couple of major chapters left. Am becoming bored and wish I'd devoted the time to Coast Miwok or Tajín; archaeology has been out the question, because my hands and wrists could not support the weight of a bag of sherds.[102]

And then again in yet another letter to the Fosters, sent about six weeks later:

Glad you liked the little blurb re jet. Both you and [Woodrow] Borah remarked that it contained "unusual" material. A few kind words were welcome, for I sent one copy to a friend, who wrote: "A Bead Journal My God, what next?" Another little paper on beads is about ready to be submitted, but a few details must be checked. It will be published jointly with Irmgard [Weitlaner-Johnson].

The more ambitious monograph on Beads and the Conquest of Mexico, or whatever it will turn out to be called, has become a great bore. I have to force myself to work on it. But not much remains to be done, so that is a relief. From Tucson comes word that galleys are ready on the site report I turned in in 1937! Apparently to be published by public subscription, with donations by all Tucsonians interested in the history of their fair city. As for the Capacha (Colima) report that has been there two years—no, 2.5 years—the editor writes that she now is resuming work on it.[103]

In sum, Isabel Kelly's life as an anthropologist is reflective of a career of total engagement in the discipline—creative field research and writing in archaeology, ethnography, ethnohistory, and social and applied anthropology. In many ways Kelly had it all and did it all, and did it her way, at a time when few options were available to a woman who wanted a full-time career in the discipline. By combining small amounts of monies from grants and fellowships with some full-time employment with federal and national agencies, and living frugally but well, she achieved a lasting place in the history of the discipline and earned major respect from her many colleagues and friends, especially in the United States and Mexico. The role of her mentors and friends in helping her achieve her goals she always acknowledged; but in the last analysis, the satisfaction as to so much research accomplished and so many jobs well done had to be her own.

Notes

1. Mary Ann Levine, "Presenting the Past: A Review of Research on Women in Archaeology," in *Equity Issues for Women in Archaeology*, ed. Margaret C. Nelson, Sarah M. Nelson, and Alison Wylie, Anthropological Papers no. 5 (Washington DC: American Anthropological Association, 1994), 30.

2. For additional information on her numerous projects beyond western North America, consult particularly "The Isabel T. Kelly Ethnographic Archive: A Descriptive Guide," prepared by Robert V. Kemper, Department of Anthropology, Southern Methodist University, Dallas; and Robert V. Kemper and John Marcucci, "The Isabel T. Kelly Ethnographic Archive: A Descriptive Guide," in *Homenaje a Isabel Kelly*, Yoloti González, coordinadora, Colección Científica no. 179 (Mexico, D.F.: Instituto Nacional de Antropología e Historia, 1989), 59–70. Kelly's extensive archives, held in the DeGolyer Library at Southern Methodist University, are administered by Robert Van Kemper, Department of Anthropology, Southern Methodist University.

3. Patricia Jean Knobloch, "Isabel Truesdell Kelly (1906–1983)," in *Women Anthropologists: A Biographical Dictionary*, ed. Ute Gacs, Aisha Khan, Jerrie McIntyre, and Ruth Weinberg (New York: Greenwood Press, 1989), 175–80; Patricia Jean Knobloch, "Isabel Truesdell Kelly," in *Homenaje a Isabel Kelly*, 11–21; Grace W. Buzaljko, "Isabel Kelly: From Museum Anthropologist to Archaeologist," *Museum Anthropology* 17, no. 2 (1993): 41–48; Grace W. Buzaljko, "Isabel Kelly and the Coast Miwok: A Biographical Introduction," in *Interviews with Tom Smith and Maria Copa: Isabel Kelly's Ethnographic Notes on the Coast Miwok Indians of Marin and Southern Sonoma Counties, California*, ed. Mary E. T. Collier and Silvia B. Thalman, MAPOM Occasional Papers no. 6 (San Rafael CA: Miwok Archaeological Preserve of Marin, 1991), xi–xxiii.

4. See Buzaljko, "Isabel Kelly and the Coast Miwok," xiii. Kelly's correspondence is contained in her files at the DeGolyer Library and in the personal files of Robert V. Kemper, Southern Methodist University [hereafter cited as RVK-SMU]; at the Laboratory of Anthropology, Museum of New Mexico, Santa Fe; and in the Bancroft Library, University of California, Berkeley (Department of Anthropology Archives, A. L. Kroeber Papers, and Carl O. Sauer Papers). All were consulted for this chapter. Permission to quote from the correspondence courtesy of DeGolyer Library, the Laboratory of Anthropology, and the Bancroft Library.

5. Knobloch, "Isabel Truesdell Kelly (1906–1983)," 173; Buzaljko, "Isabel Kelly and the Coast Miwok," xi.

6. A. L. Kroeber, *Handbook of the Indians of California*, Bulletin 78 of the Bureau of American Ethnology of the Smithsonian Institution (Washington DC: Government Printing Office, 1925).

7. See the following articles by Lowie: "Social Life of the Crow Indians,"

American Museum of Natural History Anthropological Papers (New York) 9, no. 2 (1912): 179–248; "Societies of the Crow, Hidatsa and Mandan Indians," *American Museum of Natural History Anthropological Papers* (New York) 11, no. 3 (1913): 143–358; "Crow Indian Art," *American Museum of Natural History Anthropological Papers* (New York) 21, no. 4 (1922): 272–322; "The Religion of the Crow Indians," *American Museum of Natural History Anthropological Papers* (New York) 25, no. 2 (1922): 309–444; "Notes on Shoshonean Ethnography," *American Museum of Natural History Anthropological Papers* (New York) 25, no. 3 (1924): 185–314.

8. Gifford pursued interests in a variety of topics beyond anthropology (ornithology and conchology): "Miwok Moietes," *University of California Publications in American Archaeology and Ethnology* 12, no. 4 (1916): 139–94; "Miwok Myths," *University of California Publications in American Archaeology and Ethnology* 12, no. 8 (1917): 283–338; "Miwok Cults," *University of California Publications in American Archaeology and Ethnology* 18, no. 3 (1926): 391–408.

9. George M. Foster Jr., "Edward Winslow Gifford, 1887–1959," *American Anthropologist* 62, no. 2 (1960): 327–29.

10. James J. Parsons, Obituary: Carl Ortwin Sauer 1889–1975, *Geographical Review* 66, no. 1 (1976): 86.

11. Virginia Kerns, *Scenes from the High Desert: Julian Steward's Life and Theory* (Urbana: University of Illinois Press, 2003), 84.

12. Parsons, Sauer obituary, 85; see Kerns, *Scenes from the High Desert*, 88, for its effect on fellow graduate student Julian Steward.

13. Buzaljko, "Isabel Kelly and the Coast Miwok," xiii.

14. Alfred L. Kroeber, *Walapai Ethnography*, Memoirs of the American Anthropological Association no. 42 (Menasha WI: Anthropological Association, 1935), 7.

15. Alfred V. Kidder to Alfred L. Kroeber, January 15, 1929, Laboratory of Anthropology Archives, Museum of New Mexico, Santa Fe [hereafter cited as LAB].

16. Kroeber to Kidder, January 9, 1929, LAB.

17. Kidder to Kroeber, January 15, 1929, LAB.

18. Jesse L. Nusbaum, 1934 Report of Activities, LAB; Richard B. Woodbury, *Sixty Years of Southwestern Archaeology: A History of the Pecos Conference* (Albuquerque: University of New Mexico Press, 1993), 106.

19. Isabel T. Kelly, "Peruvian Cumbrous Bowls," *University of California*

Publications in American Archaeology and Ethnology (Berkeley) 24, no. 6 (1930): 325–41; Isabel T. Kelly, "The Carver's Art of the Indians of Northwestern California," *University of California Publications in American Archaeology and Ethnology* (Berkeley) 24, no. 7 (1930): 343–60; Isabel T. Kelly, "Yuki Basketry," *University of California Publications in American Archaeology and Ethnology* (Berkeley) 24, no. 9 (1930): 421–44.

20. See Buzaljko, "Isabel Kelly: From Museum Anthropologist to Archaeologist," 43. For further details see Ira Jacknis, "Carving Tradition of Northwest California," in *Carving Traditions of Northwest California with a Reprint of "The Carver's Art of the Indians of Northwestern California" by Isabel T. Kelly* (Berkeley: Phoebe Hearst Museum of Anthropology, 1995), 1–73.

21. Kearns, *Scenes from the High Desert*, 90; Isabel T. Kelly, "The Fundamentals of Great Basin Culture" (PhD diss., University of California, Berkeley, 1932).

22. Kelly to Catherine S. Fowler, personal communication, 1978.

23. Kelly to Kroeber, May 27, 1930, Department of Anthropology Archives, Record Group CU-23, The Bancroft Library, University of California, Berkeley [hereafter cited as DABL].

24. Kroeber, *Walapai Ethnography*, 9; Kelly to Fowler, personal communication, 1978.

25. Isabel T. Kelly, "Ethnography of the Surprise Valley Paiute." *University of California Publications in American Archaeology and Ethnology* (Berkeley), 31, no. 3. (1932): 67–210.

26. Julian H. Steward, "Ethnography of the Owens Valley Paiute," *University of California Publications in American Archaeology and Ethnology* (Berkeley), 33, no. 3 (1933): 233–350; Isabel T. Kelly, "Northern Paiute Tales," *Journal of American Folk-Lore* 51, no. 202 (1938): 363–438.

27. Buzaljko, "Isabel Kelly and the Coast Miwok," xi–xxiii; Collier and Thalman, *Interviews with Tom Smith and Maria Copa*.

28. Kelly to Howell, September 27, 1931, Isabel T. Kelly Archives, Degolyer Library, Southern Methodist University, Dallas, Texas [hereafter cited as KADL].

29. Buzaljko, "Isabel Kelly and the Coast Miwok," xiv.

30. Kelly to Kroeber, January 24, 1932, DABL.

31. Kelly to Kroeber, January 24, 1932, DABL.

32. Kelly to Kroeber, March 5, 1932, DABL.

33. Kelly to Kroeber, March 5, 1932, DABL.

34. Kelly to Gifford, February 20, 1932, DABL. Gifford wanted to compare Kelly's data to his own on the Sierra Miwok. Fellow students and faculty, including Carl Sauer and his family, visited Kelly in the field. The long-lasting ties led to an active correspondence with the Sauers and others. See Buzaljko, "Isabel Kelly and the Coast Miwok," xiv.

35. Isabel T. Kelly, "Coast Miwok," in *Handbook of North American Indians*, vol. 8, *California*, ed. Robert Heizer (Washington DC: Smithsonian Institution, 1978), 414–25; George P. Murdock, *Outline of Cultural Materials* (New Haven CT: Human Relations Area Files, 1957); Collier and Thalman, *Interviews with Tom Smith and Maria Copa*, xi–xxiii.

36. Robbins to Isabel T. Kelly, February 9, 1932, KADL; Isabel T. Kelly, "A Determination of the Ethnic Groupings of a Great Basin Tribe, with Special Reference to the Geographic and Subsistence Bases," unpublished manuscript, March 1, 1933, KADL; Lowie, "Notes on Shoshonean Ethnography."

37. Kelly, "A Determination of the Ethnic Groupings of a Great Basin Tribe."

38. During the 1930s, one of the few sources of funding available for anthropological fieldwork was the National Research Council. Kroeber and Kidder had both supported her proposal.

39. Kroeber to Jesse Nusbaum, June 2, 1932, LAB.

40. Clark D. Wissler to Jesse Nusbaum, June 15, 1932, LAB.

41. The Kelly Southern Paiute archive is being processed for publication by the senior author through the permission of Kelly's literary executor, Robert V. Kemper.

42. This new field requirement stemmed from the murder of a female Columbia University graduate student on one of the Western Apache reservations (Schmerler tragedy) the previous summer. All field-workers and officials worried about having a lone woman in the field. See Nancy J. Parezo, ed., *Hidden Scholars: Women Anthropologists and the American Southwest* (Albuquerque: University of New Mexico Press, 1993), 361–62. Nusbaum and Kroeber corresponded during 1931 and 1932 about the situation, and both felt that if Kelly had a companion, the Bureau of Indian Affairs area director might be more easily persuaded to give permission for her to be on reservations. Nusbaum Papers, LAB.

43. Kelly to Nusbaum, July 2, 1932, LAB.

44. Isabel T. Kelly, *Southern Paiute Ethnography*, University of Utah Anthropological Papers no. 69, Glen Canyon Series 21 (Salt Lake City: University of Utah Press, 1964), iii.

45. Kelly to Nusbaum, July 27, 1932, LAB. Mera was director of the LAB. Kelly had written to Sapir about working among the Kaibab in 1932, and he had kindly sent his unpublished notes based on ethnographic data received from Tony Tillohash when he was interviewing him on the language. See the following works by Edward Sapir in the *Proceedings of the American Academy of Arts and Sciences* (Boston) 65, no. 1 (1930–31): "Southern Paiute, a Shoshonean Language," 1–296; "Texts of the Kaibab Paiutes and Uintah Utes," 297–535; and "Southern Paiute Dictionary," 537–730. Kelly used the notes for comparison and refers to them continually in her Kaibab monograph, *Southern Paiute Ethnography*. The full text of Sapir's notes with comments was published by Catherine S. Fowler and Robert C. Euler as "Kaibab Paiute and Northern Ute Ethnographic Notes" in *Southern Paiute and Ute Linguistics and Ethnology*, ed. William Bright (Berlin: Mouton de gruyter, 1988), 779–922, vol. 10 of the *Collected Works of Edward Sapir*.

46. Kelly to Nusbaum, July 2, 1932, LAB.

47. Kelly to Nusbaum, July 27, 1932, LAB.

48. Kelly's Southern Paiute material culture collections are at the following institutions: American Museum of Natural History; Museum of Indian Arts and Cultures (for the Laboratory of Anthropology, Museum of New Mexico); and the Peabody Museum of Archaeology and Ethnology, Harvard University.

49. Kelly to Kidder, September 19, 1932, KADL.

50. Kelly to Kidder, September 19, 1932, KADL.

51. Kelly to Nusbaum, October 2, 1932, LAB.

52. Kelly to Nusbaum, December 20, 1932, LAB.

53. Isabel T. Kelly, "Notes on Southern Paiute Shamanism," in "Anthropological Essays Presented to Robert H. Lowie in Honor of His Birthday, June 12, 1933, by His Students," typescript, The Bancroft Library, University of California, Berkeley.

54. Nusbaum to Kidder, Wissler, and Kroeber, September 15, 1933, LAB.

55. Kelly to Nusbaum, January 29, 1934, LAB.

56. Kelly to Kroeber, March 14, 1934, KADL; Isabel T. Kelly, "Final Report" [on Chemehuevi fieldwork], unpublished manuscript, I. T. Kelly Archive, KADL.

57. Isabel T. Kelly, "Southern Paiute Bands," *American Anthropologist* 36,

no. 4 (1934): 548–60; Isabel T. Kelly, "Chemehuevi Shamanism," in *Essays in Anthropology Presented to A. L. Kroeber in Celebration of His Sixtieth Birthday*, ed. Robert Lowie (Berkeley: University of California Press, 1936): 129–42; Isabel T. Kelly, "Southern Paiute Shamanism," *University of California Anthropological Records* (Berkeley), 2, no. 4 (1939): 151–67.

58. Kelly to Kroeber, April 7, 1934, KADL.

59. President Robert G. Sproul, University of California, to Ministry of Public Education, Mexico, D.F., KADL; Carl Sauer and Donald Brand, *Aztatlán: Prehistoric Mexican Frontier on the Pacific Coast*, Ibero-Americana no. 1 (Berkeley: University of California Press, 1932).

60. F. S. Hulse, "Appendix III.—Skeletal Material," in Isabel Kelly, *Excavations at Culiacán, Sinaloa*, Ibero-Americana no. 25 (Berkeley: University of California Press, 1945), 187–98.

61. Kelly to Sauer, February 24, 1935, Carl Ortwin Sauer Papers (I. T. Kelly Correspondence: BNeg 1366: 1), The Bancroft Library, University of California, Berkeley [hereafter cited as BL-COS].

62. Knobloch, "Isabel Truesdell Kelly," in *Homenaje a Isabel Kelly*, 13; Isabel Kelly, *Excavations at Chametla, Sinaloa*, Ibero-Americana no. 14 (Berkeley: University of California Press, 1938), 3. Irmgard Weitlaner, the daughter of Robert J. Weitlaner, became Irmgard Weitlaner-Johnson after her marriage.

63. Sauer refers to the job offered by Kroeber as involving "element statistics," thus suggesting that Kroeber was going to employ Kelly in some capacity in analyzing materials from his Culture Element Distribution Survey project. Sauer to Kelly, November 5, 1935, BL-COS.

64. Gayle Hartmann, preface and acknowledgments, in Isabel Kelly, *The Hodges Ruin: A Hohokam Community in the Tucson Basin* (with the collaboration of James E. Officer and Emil W. Haury), Anthropological Papers of the University of Arizona no. 30 (Tucson: University of Arizona Press, 1978), vii.

65. As Hartmann reports, "Most of it is under residential subdivisions; the ball court and adjacent portions were bulldozed in 1972 during construction of a trailer park south of Ruthrauff Road and west of La Cholla Boulevard." Kelly, *The Hodges Ruin* , viii.

66. Isabel T. Kelly to George and Mickie Foster, September 9, 1975, RVK-SMU.

67. Knobloch, "Isabel Truesdell Kelly (1906–1983)," 176; Isabel T. Kelly, *The Archaeology of the Autlán-Tuxcacuesco Area of Jalisco, I: The Autlán Zone*, Ibero-

Americana no. 26 (Berkeley: University of California Press, 1945), 10. From her work in western Mexico, Kelly made three contributions to the Anthropology Museum at the University of California. In 1943 she contributed 15 maize samples from the Jalisco and Zacatecas regions (Accession 824). In 1944, with funds from a university appropriation, she delivered 3,370 items, including pottery, shell, lithics, and spindle whorls (Accession 828). Finally, in 1945, with another university appropriation, she delivered 630 pieces of pottery, shell, lithics, and spindle whorls (Accession 855).

68. Isabel T. Kelly, "An Archaeological Reconnaissance of the West Coast: Nayarit to Michoacán," *Actas de la primera sesión celebrada en la ciudad de México en 1939*, International Congress of Americanists (Mexico, D.F.: Instituto Nacional de Antropología e Historia, 1947), 74–77; Isabel T. Kelly, "An Archaeological Reconnaissance of the West Coast: Nayarit to Michoacan," in *Homenaje a Isabel Kelly*, 71–73.

69. After completing the surveys, Kelly moved her household and several tons of sherds and artifacts to Tepepan, a suburban village southeast of Mexico City on the road to Xochimilco in 1945.

70. Kelly, *The Archaeology of the Autlán-Tuxcacuesco Area of Jalisco*, I, viii.

71. Isabel T. Kelly, *The Archaeology of the Autlan-Tuxcacuesco Area of Jalisco, II: The Tuxcacuesco-Zapotitlan Zone*, Ibero-Americana no. 27 (Berkeley: University of California Press, 1949). Part I was sent to Sauer and Kroeber in 1942, submitted by them to the press on September 11, 1942, but not issued until September 7, 1945. Part II was submitted by the editors to the press on November 16, 1943, but did not appear in print until June 30, 1949. Her physical anthropologist on this last trip was James Gavan of the University of Chicago. His report on the skeletal material appeared in part II, as appendix II.

72. Isabel T. Kelly, *Excavations at Apatzingán, Michoacán*, Viking Fund Publications in Anthropology no. 7 (New York: n.p., 1947), 189, 5.

73. Isabel T. Kelly, "Ixtle Weaving at Chiquilistlán, Jalisco," *Notes on Middle American Archaeology and Ethnology*, Carnegie Institution of Washington, Division of Historical Research no. 42 (1944): 106–12; Isabel T. Kelly, "Worked Gourds from Jalisco," *Notes on Middle American Archaeology and Ethnology*, Carnegie Institution of Washington, Division of Historical Research no. 43 (1944): 113–26.

74. Kelly, "Worked Gourds from Jalisco," 120.

75. Kelly undertook several seasons of archaeological survey work in the region of Zacoalco, San Marcos, and Sayula, during 1941 and in 1945.

76. Otto Baumbach Schöndube, "La colección Kelly de loza sayulteca," in *Homenaje a Isabel Kelly*, 275–82; BANAMEX, "Lozoda Sayala—Coleccion de Isabel Kelly (Presentacion de Fernando Solano: Colaboracion de Otto Schondube)" (Mexico, D.F.: Fomento Cultural Banamex, 1984).

77. Isabel T. Kelly, *Ceramic Sequence in Colima: Capacha, An Early Phase*, Anthropological Papers of the University of Arizona no. 37 (Tucson: University of Arizona Press, 1980), ix. During the initial phase of her reinvigorated research in 1966, she was accompanied to the field by Otto Schöndube, a museum archaeologist for the Instituto Nacional de Antropología e Historia.

78. Kelly, *Ceramic Sequence in Colima*, 1. This publication was dedicated "To the memory of Carol Ortwin Sauer and Lorena Schowengerdt Sauer."

79. Kelly, *Ceramic Sequence in Colima*, vii.

80. For example, Kelly began a letter to George Foster with a paragraph about the Treganza affair and then wrote in the second paragraph: "Little to report here. Made a hasty trip to Colima and actually bagged a carbon sample. Now am working hard on the Capacha paper but have bogged down when it comes to comparisons with Tlatilco." Kelly to Foster, June 14, 1973, RVK-SMU.

81. Kelly to Foster, January 30, 1974, RVK-SMU. In a letter to George and Mickie Foster, Kelly offered a final comment about the Capacha report: "A long silence—and even so, nothing very cheery to report, except that I finally finished the eternally-dangling Capacha report. Took same personally to Tucson (by train, so I'd not have to remove my eyes from the baggage)." Kelly to George and Mickie Foster, May 14, 1975, RVK-SMU.

82. Kelly bought a house and property in suburban Tepepan.

83. Foster had known Kelly from his time at Berkeley when he was doing graduate work and she was a teaching assistant for·Sauer. He, too, had been a student of Kroeber and Sauer and had done his dissertation fieldwork in Mexico. See George M. Foster, *A Primitive Mexican Economy*, American Ethnological Society Monograph 5 (New York: J. J. Augustin, 1942). Foster's recommendation was sent to Julian H. Steward, the outgoing director of the ISA in Washington DC, who knew Kelly very well from her Berkeley days and her work in the Great Basin. Kelly was hired to replace Foster just as Foster was moving to Washington to replace Steward.

84. Isabel T. Kelly and Angel Palerm, *The Tajin Totonac: Part 1. History, Subsistence, Shelter, and Technology*, Institute of Social Anthropology, Publication no. 13 (Washington DC: Smithsonian Institution, 1952), ix.

85. Kelly and Palerm, *The Tajin Totonac*, ix.

86. Kelly and Palerm, *The Tajin Totonac*, ix.

87. Kemper and Marcucci, "The Isabel T. Kelly Ethnographic Archive." In addition, all of the background data analysis for the Kelly-Palerm monograph still exists.

88. Isabel T. Kelly, *Folk Practices in North Mexico: Birth Customs, Folk Medicine and Spiritualism in the Laguna Zone*, Institute of Latin American Studies, Latin American Monograph no. 2 (Austin: University of Texas Press, 1965), viii.

89. Kroeber to Kelly, March 30, 1955, KADL.

90. Kelly to Kroeber, April 15, 1955, KADL.

91. Kroeber to Kelly, May 2, 1955, KADL.

92. Kroeber to Kelly, August 20, 1955, KADL; Alfred L. Kroeber, "Desert Mohave: Fact or Fancy," *Ethnographic Interpretations 7–11*, University of California Publications in American Archaeology and Ethnology 47, no. 3 (1959): 294–307. In a letter to Kroeber, Kelly (May 4, 1955, KADL) outlines ten field projects that she needs to finish, including her western North American ethnography, Tucson archaeology, and various archaeological and ethnographic projects in Mexico. She adds: "I'll never be able to liquidate all that, if I live to be 150, for I write very slowly and painfully." Ultimately, she finished or made substantial progress on all of them before her death in 1982.

93. Kelly to Robert Heizer, September 15, 1961, KADL.

94. Kelly to J. D. Jennings, January 16, 1963, KADL.

95. Kelly, *Southern Paiute Ethnography*.

96. Collier and Thalman, *Interviews with Tom Smith and Maria Copa*.

97. Isabel T. Kelly and Catherine S. Fowler, "Southern Paiute," in *Handbook of North American Indians*, vol. 11, *Great Basin*, ed. Warren d'Azevedo (Washington DC: Smithsonian Institution, 1986), 368–97.

98. Levine, "Presenting the Past."

99. In her last will and testament, Kelly donated her library to the Instituto de Investigaciones Antropológicas at the Universidad Nacional Autónoma de México, in Mexico City, where generations of students, faculty, and visiting scholars continue to make use of her collection. She also donated a large collection of textiles to the Textile Museum in Washington DC. The several tons of potsherds and the associated field notes were returned to INAH after her death. Her ethnographic field notes and related materials were willed to Rob-

ert V. Kemper and now form the Isabel T. Kelly Ethnographic Archive at the DeGolyer Library, Southern Methodist University.

100. Carl Ortwin Sauer Papers (Isabel T. Kelly Correspondence, BNeg 1366:1, 2), The Bancroft Library, University of California, Berkeley; A. L. Kroeber Papers, BANC MSS C-B925, BANC FILM 2049, The Bancroft Library, University of California, Berkeley; A. V. Kidder Collection and Nusbaum Papers, Laboratory of Anthropology, located at the Museum of New Mexico, Santa Fe.

101. Kelly used humor effusively. In a two-page screed (one of her favorite words) to George and Mickie Foster she warned about "my semi-new electric machine. Trouble getting set on the proper spot of the keyboard and I may write a complete line of gibberish before I realize the error. So gird your loins." Kelly to George and Mickie Foster, September 9, 1975, RVK-SMU.

102. Kelly to George and Mickie Foster, July 10, 1977, RVK-SMU.

103. Kelly to George and Mickie Foster, August 24, 1977, RVK-SMU. Her study of trade beads was published posthumously. Isabel T. Kelly, *Trade Beads and the Conquest of Mexico* (Windsor, Ontario: Rolston-Bain, 1992). The Capacha report was not published until 1980, two years after the volume on the Hodges site.

5

MARJORIE FERGUSON LAMBERT

Including American Indians and Hispanic Peoples in
Southwestern Anthropology

Shelby Tisdale

IN A BRILLIANT CAREER spanning more than six decades, Marjorie Ferguson Lambert left her imprint on southwestern anthropology, archaeology, and history.[1] She devoted her life to the study and advancement of our understanding of the presence of humans upon the landscape of the American Southwest in the past, as well as to the preservation of the arts and cultures of the living Native Americans and Hispanic peoples of New Mexico. She became a professional archaeologist and museum curator at a time when relatively few women were establishing full-time careers in either profession. When Marjorie joined the Museum of New Mexico staff in 1937, she was well on her way to being an established southwestern archaeologist and was, according to Cynthia Irwin-Williams, "one of the first women to occupy a major curatorial position in the country."[2]

Marjorie authored almost two hundred articles for *American Antiquity*, *El Palacio*, *New Mexico Anthropologist*, and *New Mexico Magazine*; two monographs for the School of American Research; and several review articles and forewords to books. In addition to her numerous publications, as Barbara Babcock and Nancy Parezo inform us, she gave "countless lectures and organized many exhibits introducing New Mexico's Indian and Hispanic peoples to the general public."[3] It was important to Marjorie that anthropology and archaeology be accessible to the general public. Unfortunately, this form of popularizing of the discipline was generally undervalued in academia, and those who attempted to introduce anthro-

7. (*Opposite Top*) Marjorie Ferguson (*top left*) while instructor and supervisor of a summer archaeology class at New Mexico Normal School (now New Mexico Highlands University) at Tecolote Ruin LA 296 in 1932. She is pictured with her field crew, which included Rose and Joe Aguilar of Santo Domingo Pueblo. *Courtesy of Marjorie Lambert Collection, Archives, Laboratory of Anthropology, Museum of Indian Arts & Culture, Santa Fe NM.*

8. (*Opposite Bottom*) Marjorie Ferguson Lambert (*left*) and her husband, Jack Lambert, with Helen Cordero of Cochiti Pueblo at the Wheelwright Museum of the American Indian, ca. 1980. *Marjorie Lambert Collection, Archives, Laboratory of Anthropology, Museum of Indian Arts & Culture, Santa Fe NM.*

pology to a nonprofessional audience generally tended to be marginalized by their colleagues and the discipline as a whole.[4]

Marjorie's life experiences were intricately involved with the development of southwestern archaeology and its supporting institutions, including the University of New Mexico, the School of American Research, and the Museum of New Mexico. The choices Marjorie made throughout her career were influenced early on by an intriguing cast of characters, in particular, Edgar L. Hewett, Sylvanus G. Morley, Alfred V. Kidder, Kenneth Chapman, and Harry P. Mera.

Marjorie always had the deepest respect for and emotional attachments to the numerous Native Americans and Hispanics she knew and worked with throughout her career, many of whom became lifelong friends. These friendships were strengthened through her interest in and concern for the preservation of their arts and cultural traditions. Her active involvement in the Indian Arts Fund, the New Mexico Association on Indian Affairs (now the Southwestern Association for Indian Arts, or SWAIA), the annual Santa Fe Indian Market, the Spanish Colonial Society, and the Spanish Market also brought her into contact with numerous artists and their supporters and patrons.

One of the early pioneers of ethnohistorical and ethnoarchaeological techniques, Marjorie hired American Indian and Hispanic men as crew members on her excavations. She also consulted them about her findings and incorporated their oral traditions and histories into her analyses and interpretations of the past. Her approach was much different from that of other archaeologists at the time.

Since the beginning of American archaeology as a discipline, the relationship between archaeologists and American Indians has been essentially one-sided. Archaeologists study the past, and in the Southwest they study the past of present-day Native peoples. Unfortunately, the opinions and oral traditions of these living Native peoples were often overlooked by archaeologists in their interpretations of the past.[5] Only in the past two decades has American archaeology recognized the importance of including American Indians in a dialogue about the past, something that Marjorie had been doing from the beginning.

Throughout her career Marjorie had to overcome and maneuver around many obstacles that would have discouraged—and probably did discourage—many young women from pursuing a career in south-western archaeology. Like other women in anthropology and the sci-ences, Marjorie experienced a disparity in her career opportunities and pay.[6] Even her mentor, Edgar Lee Hewett, who recognized Marjorie's intellectual superiority, supervisory skills, and organizational abilities, did not pay her the same salary that her male colleagues received. He often made comments about her domestic skills when touring impor-tant visitors around the museum, thus comparing her curatorial duties to housework. This always had a negative effect on her self-confidence and her status among her male peers. Margaret Rossiter discusses this double standard in which women in science were often relegated to positions that most resembled "women's work."[7] Marjorie quickly learned that women in the museum had to work harder for less pay and that they enjoyed fewer opportunities for advancement than their male colleagues in similar positions.

Having few intellectual limitations, Marjorie was clearly viewed as a threat by some of her male colleagues, while highly respected by nu-merous others. Her perseverance and strong desire to be a southwest-ern archaeologist kept her going. Later, her high regard for scholar-ship, professionalism, and collegiality elevated her standing with her male colleagues.

Marjorie was thankful to have the position as curator, and she cred-its Hewett with providing her the opportunity to be professionally em-ployed. Nonetheless, he moved her from an academic position at the University of New Mexico to the curatorial position in the Museum of New Mexico. Perhaps this was an intentional move on his part, since there were few women faculty members in anthropology departments across the country in the 1930s and Marjorie did not have a doctorate, which at the time was becoming the standard credential in academia. It is also possible that Hewett's male peers at the university pressured him to move her. We will never know why Hewett transferred Marjorie to Santa Fe to work in the museum, especially since it appeared that she was well on her way to a career in academic archaeology. There she would have continued to make a major contribution to our knowledge of southwestern archaeology, and she would also have had the chance to educate generations of young archaeologists.

Instead, Marjorie enjoyed a thirty-two-year career with the Museum of New Mexico, even though this limited her archaeological pursuits and the projects she worked on when compared to her earlier career development. Although she still found time to pursue fieldwork on occasion, she had little time to write up field reports or produce monograph-length texts. Instead, she turned her attention to public education and the preservation of the arts and cultures of the Native American and Hispanic peoples of New Mexico.

An Introduction to Southwestern Archaeology

While attending Colorado College from 1926 to 1930, Marjorie Elizabeth Ferguson was introduced to southwestern archaeology. At the time, Colorado College was a small liberal arts college in the Harvard Exchange Program, which included lecturers and visiting professors from Harvard University. On occasion scholars such as Sylvanus G. Morley and Edgar L. Hewett were invited to Colorado Springs to present lectures at the college. Both were associated with the School of American Research in Santa Fe, New Mexico, at the time. Marjorie was introduced to southwestern archaeology by two men—Hewett and Morley—who became her mentors and effectively directed her career.

Hewett, a key figure in southwestern archaeology and anthropology from 1905 to 1945, had the most influence on Marjorie's professional life. Much like Franz Boas at Columbia University, Hewett was instrumental in opening doors for women to study and work in southwestern anthropology, archaeology, and museums. At the time there were relatively few women mentors other than Ruth Benedict, Elsie Clews Parsons, and Ruth Bunzel. Although the writings of these early pioneer women in anthropology influenced Marjorie, they were not accessible as mentors to young women training as archaeologists in the Southwest.

Hewett is best known for his institution building. At the turn of the century, when his scientific ideas were developing, he proposed an interdisciplinary approach that he later termed the "Science of Man."[8] To further implement his ideas and broaden his vision, he next turned his energies toward leading an institution that would lend his projects

credibility and prestige. Such organizations were crucial to the development of careers in the new sciences of anthropology and archaeology.[9]
On December 30, 1907, the Archaeological Institute of America established the School of American Archaeology in Santa Fe under Hewett's
leadership. Ten years later it changed its name to the School of American Research (SAR).

The mission of the new research institution reflected Hewett's intellectual and education goals and allowed Hewett to pursue a vision
of archaeology and cultural preservation that he had developed over
the previous fifteen years.[10] Hewett had been working on a map of the
culture areas of the American continent and continued this concept as
director of SAR. One of the school's first projects was an investigation
of archaeological sites in the Pueblo region of the Southwest. In SAR's
early days, Hewett trained or worked with Alfred V. Kidder, Sylvanus
G. Morley, and Jesse Nusbaum, who became well-known southwestern
archaeologists and were instrumental in the development of the new
subdiscipline of southwestern archaeology.

Marjorie met Hewett during one of his lectures at Colorado College in the late 1920s. In all likelihood, when Hewett gave his lectures
he addressed the ideas he expressed in his 1930 work, *Ancient Life in
the American Southwest*. His ideas, while exceedingly idealistic, argued
for the importance of the Pueblo Indians in the "humanizing of the
continent" and asserted that archaeological surveys and excavations
could reveal much about their ancient way of life.[11] "The Pueblo is the
best surviving example of Native American culture," he maintained,
because "the physical, intellectual and spiritual elements that characterize the whole Native American race" are preserved in them.[12]

Hewett was disturbed by how poorly the ruins were being excavated
and by the removal and relocation of artifacts to eastern institutions
and Europe. It was a critical era for southwestern archaeology, a time
of amateur exploration that amounted to blatant pothunting. Even professional excavations were often destructive. Hewett was among many
who helped enact the Antiquities Act of 1906, the first law passed to
protect archaeological sites on federal lands.[13]

In the 1920s and 1930s Hewett focused his attention on preserving
the prehistory of the Pueblo cultures by training students in scientific

research and excavation techniques. He pointed out that researchers in the Southwest had the distinct advantage of having living Pueblo men working on their excavations, which helped in the interpretation of the sites and the material culture. Hewett shared his worldview with his students, and Marjorie absorbed everything her mentor taught her and later incorporated this into her own research and interpretations as an archaeologist and museum curator.

After earning her bachelor's degree in social anthropology from Colorado College in 1930, Marjorie was offered graduate fellowships at three universities—the University of New Mexico in archaeology, Smith College in social welfare work, and the School of Social Work at Columbia University. She had dreamed of working with someone like Ruth Benedict and possibly meeting Franz Boas, but Hewett, Morley, and W. W. Postlethwaite, director of the Colorado College Museum and member of the managing board of the School of American Research, convinced her that the Southwest was an ideal locale for her future studies. She had already expressed an interest in studying southwestern archaeology, and it was economically more feasible for her to stay in the Southwest since her family was not able to support her if she went to graduate school in the East. It was the depression, and the Fergusons wanted to provide a college education for their three children.

Hewett, in particular, may have been the most persuasive, because he saw in Marjorie an extremely intelligent and curious mind and no doubt wanted to be able to monitor her progress. Because Boas was against Hewett's appointment as director of the school in 1907, the two became enemies, and it is quite possible that Hewett did not want to lose this bright young student to Boas. By this time Hewett was directing both the School of American Research and the Museum of New Mexico, and he was head of the Department of Archaeology and Anthropology at the University of New Mexico.[14]

Marjorie accepted a research-teaching fellowship at the University of New Mexico and began graduate studies in the fall of 1930. She did not realize at the time that she held the only fellowship in the anthropology department. This created tension between Marjorie and the male students who were the other applicants. "There was some resentment," Marjorie recalled. "I didn't know why two of them didn't like me very well. I found out soon enough though. They were jealous."[15] Unfortunately, she often faced discrimination and other gender-related issues in a field where mediocre men have long resented outstanding women. Marjorie was faced with this during her first archaeological field school experience.

The summer prior to beginning her graduate studies, Marjorie accepted an invitation from Hewett to attend the Battleship Rock Field Camp in the Jemez Mountains. At the time Hewett was running two archaeological field camps in New Mexico during the summer, one in the Jemez Mountains and the other at Chaco Canyon. Students who had no field experience worked at Battleship Rock, while those with previous experience spent part of the summer at Chaco Canyon. The advanced students would generally spend six weeks at each field camp.

Many of Marjorie's lifelong friendships—both professional and personal—began at the Battleship Rock Field Camp. The camp was composed of students from both national and international colleges and universities. Marjorie's first real knowledge of American Indians came from this first field experience when she was introduced to Pueblo culture and ceremonies at Jemez Pueblo. In line with Hewett's philosophy, Marjorie always said that she learned mainly from the Native peoples she worked with. "I think Jose Rey Toledo was my real instructor," she recalled in a 1997 interview. "I think that whole summer working with Indians of different sorts and in different types of situations is how I really learned to be an archaeologist."[16] In addition to Jemez Pueblo, Hewett took Marjorie and the other students to ceremonies at Zia Pueblo, where she met Trinidad Medina's family and Florence Shije.

During this first archaeological experience Marjorie also learned that some men in the camp clearly did not want women in the field. In the early 1930s archaeology was considered the sacred domain of males, and women were not supposed to make it their career. While working at the site of Unshagi, the male crew chiefs, Gordon Vivian and Paul Reiter, refused to teach excavation techniques to the female students as a way of discouraging them from pursuing a career in archaeology. They would also assign the female students some of the most difficult excavation tasks, hoping they would fail.

Little did the men in this field camp know that when this petite young student with a head full of curls and huge brown eyes showed up they would be dealing with such a strong-willed, intelligent young woman who was determined to be a southwestern archaeologist. Unlike several of the other young women, Marjorie was not looking for a husband. Even though she stood her ground among the males in the camp, she always maintained her femininity and was considered a "lady" by her colleagues and friends. Marjorie was often dressed in southwestern-style adaptations of the "squaw dress" and several unusual pieces of Indian silver and turquoise jewelry, and the average person in the street would not know that she would rather be poking around in archaeological ruins wearing her denim jeans, white shirt, and concho belt. Marjorie belonged to a group of women archaeologists described by Florence Lister as being "those women whose femininity had not been compromised and who resented but quietly accepted male professional prejudice while still enjoying male social companionship." Throughout her career Marjorie did not compromise her femininity and had little tolerance for the women who fit in the other two categories described by Lister.[17]

Despite the difficulties she encountered with some of the male crew members, this first field experience had a dramatic effect on Marjorie. "Once I got my hands and feet in the dirt that was it," she later said in an interview. "I knew that I had come to the place that I wanted to be. I didn't want to leave the Southwest. I didn't want to go to New York. I didn't want to become a social studies person or a social welfare worker."[18] This first experience in the field as a dirt archaeologist led her down a very different path than she had anticipated. It was certainly different from what was expected of a young woman in the 1930s.

Upon completing her initial training at the Battleship Rock Field Camp, Marjorie headed south to Albuquerque to begin her graduate studies at the University of New Mexico. There she majored in anthropology and minored in southwestern and Latin American history. She also took a course in Indian art from Kenneth Chapman, which would prove to be extremely valuable when she started working in the museum.

While at the university she became friends with many Native American students, especially the Marmon sisters from Laguna and others from Isleta and Sandia Pueblos. At Cochiti she became close friends with the Cordero, Herrera, and Pecos families and was often invited to feast days and family gatherings. Through these friendships she embraced Pueblo culture and history and gained an appreciation and deep respect for the role of the Pueblo Indians in New Mexico's history.

During her second summer, Marjorie was one of Hewett's students who shuttled between the Jemez Mountains and Chaco Canyon. By the time she arrived at Chaco Canyon it was hot and both food and water were in short supply. Once the sun went down and the canyon cooled off, the students found ways to be entertained. If no evening lecture was scheduled they spent their time at the trading post going through the old pawned items and the Navajo rugs and blankets. If there was a full moon they went down to the Great Kiva at Chetro Ketl to sing and tell stories.

During the archaeological excavations, life among the Navajos living in Chaco Canyon carried on as usual, and in 1931 the students witnessed part of a healing ceremony. This occurred on the same day Marjorie was called into the excavation headquarters to take her oral exam for her master's degree. At the time, candidates for the master's degree whose theses related to the work of the region were given their oral examinations in the field by the graduate committee of the University of New Mexico. Marjorie recalled having an extraordinary experience during her oral exam: "I was kind of numb and I really didn't know if I was going to pass or not because the Navajos were having a sing for an old man who was completely covered with sores. . . . They had a Devil chase because they were sure that was part of the trouble. The Devil was in him in some way or another. Here came this screeching bunch of Navajos, the Devil just going like the wind on one horse, and the rest of them with whips cracking and screeching all around the building and up and down the canyon while my oral exam was going on."[19] What Marjorie may be describing here was part of the Evilway ceremony, characterized by techniques for exorcising Navajo ghosts and chasing away evil influences. According to Leland Wyman, "Evilway chants are used to treat disease traced to contact with Navajo ghosts and to combat the effects of witchcraft."[20]

Marjorie passed her oral exams and completed her master's thesis, "The Acculturation of Sandia Pueblo."[21] She felt that a study of Sandia Pueblo would be of interest to historians and archaeologists because there were questions concerning the exact location of the old pueblo. Due to the reluctance of some members of Sandia Pueblo to divulge cultural or religious information, Marjorie had to rely on accepted ethnographic techniques, including the collection of historical data, available statistical information, personal contact, and participant observation, to complete her thesis. Her goal was to bring about a better understanding of Native peoples in general and the contributions they had made throughout history. She noted that the biggest catalyst for change and acculturation was the establishment of a school in the pueblo. In the three quarters of a century since she wrote her thesis there is no doubt that acculturative pressures have succeeded in bringing about tremendous culture change among the Pueblos of New Mexico. At the beginning of the twenty-first century, Marjorie viewed Indian gaming as intensifying the acculturation process and having an overall negative impact on Pueblo communities.

After finishing her master's, Marjorie considered going on for a doctorate, but at the time the University of New Mexico did not have a doctoral program in archaeology or anthropology. Initially, she wanted to go to Columbia University, but Hewett wanted her to go to the University of Southern California, where he had just established a new anthropology department. Since this new department was just getting started, Marjorie did not see that going there would advance her career. Like many of Hewett's other students and staff, she considered him a father figure, but she did not always follow his advice and recommendations. She chose to remain in New Mexico to pursue a career in archaeology.

Professional Archaeologist

As an archaeologist, Marjorie was extremely meticulous in her systematic excavation techniques and record keeping. She also had a wonderful rapport with her students and work crews. From 1931 to 1936 she taught anthropology classes at the University of New Mexico and was the field supervisor of the university's archaeological field school. Marjorie gained many Pueblo friends when she became a field supervisor and hired them to work on her excavations in the northern Rio Grande Valley. Many of her crew members came from San Ildefonso Pueblo, and one in particular, Joe Aguilar, became a friend and was her assistant on several excavations.

During the summer of 1932 Marjorie was the instructor in charge of the excavation at Tecolote site for the New Mexico Normal School (now New Mexico Highlands University).[22] Her preliminary report on the ruins, located south of Las Vegas, New Mexico, was included in *El Palacio*.[23] She noted that the Tecolote Ruins contained a mixture of Plains and Pueblo characteristics. It was one of several sites in the Las Vegas area, and Marjorie was convinced that there was more evidence of Plains and Puebloan contact and exchange in the region.[24] Unfortunately, she never had the opportunity to conduct further investigation in the Tecolote area to support her theory.

In 1934 Marjorie worked on the School of American Research excavations at Puaray and Kuaua. These sites were principal towns in the ancient Tiguex Province and figured prominently in the historic entrada of Francisco Vásquez de Coronado in 1540 and in the expeditions of Antonio de Espejo in 1582 and Juan de Oñate in 1598. They also played a major role during the Pueblo Rebellion of 1680.

Marjorie and Gordon Vivian worked at both Puaray and Kuaua, spending two days a week at one site and three days at the other. This arrangement often led to confusion as to what each was doing on the ground. There may have been some tension between the two as a result of their earlier work at Battleship Rock when Vivian was crew chief. In any case, the excavations at Puaray and Kuaua were poorly carried out and recorded. Marjorie viewed the whole project as a hodgepodge and concluded that it could have been better excavated and that information could have been recorded in more detail. She also felt that Vivian and some of the crew members had little interest in Puaray.[25] Vivian may have been more interested in Kuaua, known to Coronado as Tiquex, where large murals were found in a square kiva.

Marjorie was in charge of the study of the cultural and skeletal material derived from the two excavations. Because materials were so poorly documented by the time they reached the lab, her job was more difficult. She had six museum assistants employed by the U.S. government's Federal Emergency Relief Administration program at the university to assist her with the cleaning and analysis of the excavated materials. These assistants were advanced or graduate students who had field and laboratory experience. She reported on the progress of this work in 1935.[26]

In 1936 Marjorie wrote of her concerns about making assumptions about the locations of sites in the Tiguex Province, in particular Alameda, Puaray, and Sandia. She noted that the location of Puaray assigned by Adolph F. Bandelier was accepted by some but "heartily denied" by others, in particular, Frederick Webb Hodge, Charles W. Hackett, and Hubert Howe Bancroft.[27] Until the excavations were more advanced and the data could be matched to the historical records, she argued, the locations of some of the towns visited by Coronado in 1540 had been identified based on insufficient data. She surmised that more than likely the whole story of the Tiguex Province would never be entirely known because most of the tangible evidence of human occupation had been destroyed.[28] Marjorie repeated her concern about the proper identity of Puaray in a subsequent report in 1939.[29] Unlike the mystery of Puaray's exact location, the identification of Kuaua seems to have been less problematic. The descendants of the original inhabitants of Kuaua are the present-day peoples of Isleta and Sandia Pueblos.

In the fall of 1936, Marjorie's interests shifted when Hewett asked her to take charge of the second season's excavation at the Paa-ko site. The ruin was located on the east side of the Sandia Mountains near San Antonito. Her salary was $146 a month, from which Marjorie paid for the excavation supplies. She had a crew of primarily Hispanic men from San Antonito working for her, even though her colleagues told her that, because she was a woman, she could never persuade a Native American or Hispanic crew of men to work for her.[30] Marjorie always believed that this was a rumor spread by one of her jealous male colleagues at the University of New Mexico. Paa-ko was the first excavation in which she was left absolutely alone to develop the project's research design and to lead her own crew.

Marjorie also learned rather quickly that Hewett was stubborn and contentious and that his management style was highly personal and authoritarian. His adversaries referred to him as "El Toro." Hewett is often remembered as a flamboyant, innovative figure who left his mark on the preservation of prehistoric and historic sites.[31] In later years, however, his critics objected to his excavation methods, which had aroused Alfred Tozzer's opposition during the 1908 excavation at El Rito de los Frijoles. Even his students and supporters agreed that Hewett showed little interest in the increasingly technical and scientific aspects of archaeology, including such basic field methods as taking meticulous notes in the field and using stratigraphic excavation techniques for dating sites and artifacts.[32] Stratigraphy, the study of the contents of strata or levels, is the foundation upon which archaeology everywhere has been built.

While working at Paa-ko, Marjorie experienced firsthand Hewett's lack of systematic scientific methodology and site documentation. She was convinced that stratigraphic testing was important, and while at Paa-ko she excavated a large test trench. When Hewett visited the site he told her that she was wasting time and was not uncovering enough artifacts. She was taken aback by his comments because she thought that she was there to obtain information, not whole pots. Ignoring his objections, she continued her trenching and proved to herself the value of simple stratigraphy as a relative dating method in determining the various occupations of a site, as well as how valuable scientific methods are to interpreting the past.[33]

Although all the projects she worked on contributed importantly to New Mexico prehistory, Linda Cordell writes that "Lambert is best known for her work at Paa-ko," which "exemplifies the particular kind of research for which she is known."[34] Marjorie managed to produce four brief reports on Paa-ko in 1937 and 1938, but it was always a struggle to balance her museum work with analysis and writing. She remarked that she preferred "to finish an account of an excavation as soon as the field work was done, but with Paa-ko there were years of interruptions before the final monograph was published."[35] This 1954 published site report, according to Cordell, "achieves a high level of excellence in descriptive reporting, synthesis of detail, and clarity that remains a model today."[36]

During the early 1930s Marjorie excavated in the fall and winter and worked in the University of New Mexico's archaeology lab the rest of the year, using museum techniques to catalog and restore the materials that had been recovered. She also taught her students proper collections care and preservation techniques. Later, she conducted surveys and test excavations in 1944 at sites in the northern Rio Grande Valley such as Yuque Yunque, the first known Hispanic settlement in New Mexico, which was referred to as San Gabriel by Oñate.[37] In 1960, with Richard Ambler, she conducted the first fieldwork in Hidalgo County.[38] There, in one of the caves, a hunting net of human hair—the largest of its kind in the world—was discovered. She also conducted sporadic research in Mexico and Central America.

The Museum of New Mexico Years

In 1932, while Marjorie was at the University of New Mexico, Hewett sent her to Santa Fe to work temporarily for the Museum of New Mexico. Five years later he transferred her permanently to Santa Fe, where she was appointed the chief preparator for archaeology for a couple of months before being promoted to curator of archaeology. First she worked on the exhibits, and then she was charged with the care and interpretation of the archaeological collections. She spent the next thirty-two years in the Museum of New Mexico. During that time—from 1938 to 1969—she was curator of archaeology; in charge of Palace of the Governors from 1955 to 1964; curator of anthropology and exhibits from 1959 to 1963; and curator of the research division from 1963 to 1969. Given her position and the collections she worked with, she had the opportunity to meet and work with several Native and Hispanic peoples.

Often invited to feast days, christenings, and family celebrations, Marjorie helped her American Indian and Hispanic friends in any way she could. She even helped them file their yearly income taxes, something her male colleagues would never consider given their status in the community and the museum hierarchy. Of these relationships she recalled, "I wouldn't exchange those contacts for anything and I think I am a better person for having had those contacts. I think it's been wonderful and I think there would be more understanding in this country if we all had the opportunity to work closely with people of different ethnic backgrounds."[39] For Marjorie, this was a natural process in that she did not distinguish whether her friends were from the pueblos or the surrounding Hispanic villages. They were employees as well as neighbors, and these cross-cultural friendships, to which she was open, enriched her as a scholar. She was an early proponent of cultural diversity and inclusion.

As the curator of archaeology at the Museum of New Mexico, Marjorie met the Pueblo artists who sold their wares under the portal of the Palace of the Governors. Several American Indian teachers and students at the Santa Fe Indian School became her close friends, including Helen and Kenneth Shupla of Santa Clara Pueblo, Geronima Montoya (P'otsúnú) of San Juan Pueblo, and Alan Houser, a Chiricahua Apache, as well as numerous others who were training under Dorothy Dunn and the other art instructors.

Marjorie met numerous artists, in particular Pueblo potters, while on collecting trips for the Indian Arts Fund. She knew Maria Martinez, the famous potter from San Ildefonso, primarily through Martinez's promotion by Harry P. Mera and Hewett. Mera and Hewett played a major role in the popularization of American Indian art forms, in particular the work of Maria and her husband, Julian. Others, including Kenneth Chapman, Wesley Bradfield, and Elizabeth Shepley Sergeant, shared Mera and Hewett's desire to preserve the arts of the Pueblos with the founding of the Pueblo Pottery Fund in 1922. Over the next three years the original group was joined by numerous others, including Mary Austin, Andrew Dasburg, Alfred Kidder, Mabel Dodge Luhan, Sylvanus Morley, Charles Springer, and Amelia Elizabeth White. All continued the important work of the fund and renamed it the Indian Arts Fund in 1925. The fund's purpose was to collect the finest examples of historic and contemporary Indian arts and crafts in the Southwest for the scholarly purpose of cultural preservation. Marjorie had the opportunity to work with these interesting luminaries and with this superb collection of Southwest Indian pottery, textiles, baskets, jewelry, paintings, clothing, and other ethnographic objects. This collection is now housed at the School of American Research.

When Marjorie became involved with the New Mexico Association on Indian Affairs (now the Southwestern Association for Indian Arts, or SWAIA) in the late 1930s, their main event was the annual Fiesta Indian Market, now the Santa Fe Indian Market. For the first few years a major concern was finding a suitable place for the Indian artists to camp. Initially, many camped in a parking lot on Marcy Street where there were no facilities. Marjorie and Margretta Dietrich worked with the market, the museum, and local businesses to provide accommodations for the Indian artists.[40] They also collaborated with several gallery owners to raise funds for prizes.[41]

Marjorie started judging Pueblo pottery in 1938, an activity she continued for the next thirty years. During this time she successfully encouraged the museum staff to become involved in the market and the judging as well. One staff member in particular, Nancy Fox, became very involved in judging, and several staff members at the Museum of New Mexico continue to serve as judges and volunteers at this annual event in Santa Fe.

The Pueblo peoples, both male and female, were willing to take Marjorie under their wing and teach her about aspects of their cultures. They respected her as much as she respected them. Individuals from the pueblos would come to the museum to see what information and objects might be in the collections. Often they brought artifacts to Marjorie for identification, or she visited them to see if they knew what purpose an object served. As an ethnoarchaeologist, Marjorie felt it was important to consult with the Pueblo peoples about the identification and use of objects found in an archaeological context. Although museum curators, like archaeologists, work more collaboratively with the Native peoples today, this was not common practice at the time. Marjorie especially depended on the advice of her American Indian friends in planning and installing exhibits in the museum. She never put anything on exhibit that might be culturally sensitive, such as religious material or human skeletal remains, without going to San Ildefonso or Santo Domingo to consult with trusted Pueblo elders. At the time there was little concern for intellectual property rights or the display of human remains or sacred material, but Marjorie always felt better if she had the elders' permission to put such materials on exhibit. She was especially concerned that the interpretation of the material represent the Puebloan worldview in an appropriate and respectful manner. Marjorie was at the forefront of concerns about the representation of Native Americans in museums, and in many ways she was much ahead of other scholars at the time.

Throughout her career, Marjorie also worked as an advocate for Native Americans whenever she could. During World War II numerous Pueblo men, as well as Navajos and Apaches, joined the military and went overseas. Several of them were recruited through the Santa Fe post office, and when they received their final papers they would march around the plaza and get on a bus for the train station at Lamy, New Mexico. Marjorie recalled seeing a group of Jicarilla Apaches on the plaza: "They had long, shiny black hair. Some of them had braids, others had it growing long. Some of them still wore moccasins. . . . And here they went along marching. . . . I knew they had very little schooling and that it would be a very scary experience. They looked frightened. They looked like cattle being rounded up."[42]

Witnessing this was very difficult for Marjorie because she knew they would not come back as "Indians"—if they came back at all. She recognized the tremendous impact their participation in World War II would have on their families as well as their cultures. Her concerns were well founded. Several Native American troops returning after the war found few job opportunities on their reservations and were forced to find employment elsewhere. As noted by Donald Fixico, many "left their reservations and rural homelands for the first time, and the late 1940s and early 1950s witnessed their migration to the cities."[43]

Marjorie was part of a group of Santa Feans concerned about the welfare of the Indian soldiers. They set up a community center in an old filling station on the corner of Washington and Palace where the troops could get a cup of coffee and a doughnut and sit and talk with one another. She became acquainted with many soldiers and corresponded with them while they served overseas. In 1943 Marjorie devoted many evenings helping the Red Cross Motor Corps by transporting patients and nurses to and from Bruns Army Hospital. She also volunteered her time and services to the Red Cross War Fund Drive.

One memorable moment during the war occurred when Marjorie took an old friend back to his pueblo home. Santiago Naranjo of Santa

Clara Pueblo was an old friend of Hewett's and had worked as his foreman at the Puye Cliffs and the Rito de los Frijoles excavations. When Hewett was in his eighties and in frail health, Santiago would walk from Santa Clara to Santa Fe to see him, and it often fell on Marjorie to make sure that Santiago got back to the pueblo. One time during World War II, Hewett's housekeeper came to the museum to give Marjorie enough coupons to buy gas to take Santiago home. They had just received word that the first atomic bomb had been detonated at the Trinity Site.[44] Santiago, who was one of Marjorie's dearest friends, blessed her when they learned about the scientific experiments that had been taking place up the road from the pueblo in Los Alamos. The mystery behind the Manhattan Project had finally been revealed. When Marjorie and Santiago arrived in Santa Clara Pueblo he asked her to take him to his old home, where he had lived with his late wife before moving in with his daughter and her family. When they arrived, Marjorie recalled, Santiago walked over to a dresser that had an abalone shell with carnelian fetishes in it and said prayers and waved his hands above them. He then walked toward Marjorie and put his hands on her head and said a prayer for her. This experience touched Marjorie very deeply.

In the 1950s, Margretta Dietrich, president of the New Mexico Association on Indian Affairs, asked Marjorie for her help.[45] The federal government was planning to construct dams along the Rio Grande, and Marjorie was to find out what the Pueblo peoples were saying about the construction of the Cochiti Dam. Marjorie found that the members of Cochiti Pueblo were concerned that they were going to lose their farmland and that the dam was being constructed to help the efforts at Los Alamos and not them. The association raised enough money to send a delegation of Pueblo Indians to Washington DC, and Marjorie wrote letters on their behalf. Unfortunately, the dam was built and their predictions came true.

Marjorie was often asked for assistance in the development of tribal museums in New Mexico. In the 1970s she played an active role in the planning and development of a museum for Picuris Pueblo. Marjorie, Al Schroeder, Geronima Montoya, and the Bureau of Indian Affairs staff served as members of the planning committee. Because Picuris is located away from any urban area or main highway, the BIA and the Eight Northern Pueblos Indian Agency viewed a tribal museum as a means for economic development by encouraging tourism and the sale of local arts and crafts. Herb Dick was excavating in the old pueblo, and the plan was to build the museum next to the site. The museum would act as a repository for the materials excavated, and the exhibits would relate to the prehistory of the area. This was the first instance of archaeological materials remaining in a home community. Again, Marjorie was ahead of her time.

In addition to her daily activities at the museum, Marjorie was responsible for organizing all of the lectures for the museum, the School of American Research, and the state's archaeological and historical societies. This often involved traveling around the state giving lectures at branch museums and to different civic organizations. All of these additional activities cut sharply into her scholarship time.

As the curator of archaeology, Marjorie was the de facto secretary of the Archaeological Society of New Mexico, a post she held from 1943 to 1956. One of her responsibilities as curator of archaeology and secretary of the society was the annual lecture series. Her male colleagues in the museum and in the Archaeological Society never offered to help her to arrange lectures, set up the projectors, or entertain the speakers, generating a lot of resentment on her part. As far as Marjorie was concerned this duty was relegated to her because she was a woman, and it frustrated her throughout her career. Unfortunately, she was made to feel that if she did not do it no one else would, and she felt obligated as the curator of archaeology to ensure the success of the program for the museum and the society.

A Fulfilling Career and a Pioneer in Including the
Voices of Native and Hispanic Peoples

Despite some frustrations throughout her long and productive career, Marjorie had made important contributions to the development of New Mexico archaeology and the preservation of Native American and Hispanic art and culture. She had also been recognized for her interest in the history of Santa Fe, as well as her support of the Museum of New

Mexico and the School of American Research. Most scholars would agree with Cordell that Marjorie "was best known among southwestern archaeologists for being a meticulous and successful fieldworker."[46] Through her field excavations and historic research she had added to our knowledge of the long history of human occupation in New Mexico.

Marjorie had numerous achievements to her credit, not only in archaeology but also in the history and ethnology of the Southwest and its relationship to Mesoamerica. She was listed in *American Men of Science, Who's Who in the West, American Women Who's Who,* and the *International Directory of Anthropologists.* In 1985 she was the recipient of the Society for American Archaeology's Fiftieth Anniversary Award for Outstanding Contributions to American Archaeology, and in 1996 she received the Byron S. Cummings Award from the Arizona Archaeological and Historical Society. In 1988 she received the New Mexico Heritage Preservation Award from the Office of Cultural Affairs in Santa Fe. That same year, she and her second husband, Jack V. Lambert, were named Santa Fe Living Treasures in recognition of and appreciation for their participation in the life, heart, and spirit of the Santa Fe community.

Marjorie worked her entire career for the University of New Mexico, the Museum of New Mexico, and the School of American Research, and she began serving on the latter's board of managers in 1969. Whether she was in the field or in the museum laboratory, she loved her work; nevertheless, the two areas that annoyed her throughout her career were the inequity in her salary and the resentment some of her male colleagues harbored toward her. During her career Marjorie was often subject to sexual harassment by co-workers and men in powerful positions. She remained married to George Tichy for eighteen years even though they had lived together for less than one year, feeling that it was safer to remain in a bad marriage than to live as a single woman. Her second marriage, to Jack Lambert, proved successful and was more of a partnership where they shared a similar passion for the history and traditions of New Mexico.

As to why she chose a career in anthropology and archaeology, Marjorie explained, "I just like the challenge that prehistory seemed to give, the mystery of it, and finding out about people—why they think the way they do, and what makes history." She embraced the cultural diversity of the Southwest, and her friendships with the Native Americans and Hispanics with whom she worked enriched her life. "My archaeology would be nothing without the present-day Indians," she said. "The whole thing makes a complete picture in my mind. I do not look on archaeology as something separate. It's part of the whole picture."[47]

Marjorie Lambert passed away on December 16, 2006, at the age of ninety-seven in Santa Fe. When she went to the spirit world she left a lasting legacy to the people of New Mexico, the professional fields of archaeology, anthropology, history, and museums, and those interested in the arts and cultures of the American Indian and Hispanic peoples of the Southwest.

Notes

1. The author is currently writing a biography on Marjorie Ferguson Lambert. Most of the information in this chapter is based on tape-recorded interviews with Marjorie Lambert from 1990 to 1997 and archival research. Some information comes from a 1985 taped interview with Jennifer Fox as part of the Daughters of the Desert Project carried out by Barbara Babcock and Nancy Parezo at the University of Arizona, Tucson. This research resulted in a conference, an exhibit, and publication by Babcock and Parezo of *Daughters of the Desert: Women Anthropologists and the Native American Southwest, 1880–1980: An Illustrated Catalogue* (Albuquerque: University of New Mexico Press, 1988).

2. Cynthia Irwin-Williams, "Women in the Field: The Role of Women in Archaeology before 1960," in *Women of Science: Righting the Record*, ed. G. Kasa-Simon and Patricia Farnea (Bloomington: Indiana University Press, 1990), 25.

3. Babcock and Parezo, *Daughters of the Desert*, 131.

4. Shelby J. Tisdale discusses how women anthropologists who attempted to educate the public about anthropology and the Southwest through popular writings were stigmatized and marginalized by the discipline in "Women on the Periphery of the Ivory Tower," in *Hidden Scholars: Women Anthropologists and the Native American Southwest*, ed. Nancy J. Parezo (Albuquerque: University of New Mexico Press, 1993), 311–33.

5. This issue is addressed in more depth in a series of articles based on three sessions organized for the 1996 annual meeting of the Society for American

Archaeology that examined the relations between Native Americans and archaeologists. See Nina Swidler, Kurt E. Dongoske, Roger Anyon, and Alan S. Downer, eds., *Native Americans and Archaeologists: Stepping Stones to Common Ground* (Walnut Creek CA: AltaMira, 1997).

6. Margaret W. Rossiter writes about this lack of career opportunities in the sciences, including anthropology, as well as other gender-related issues in the sciences in *Women Scientists in America: Struggles and Strategies to 1940* (Baltimore: Johns Hopkins University Press, 1982).

7. Rossiter discusses the development of the concept of "women's work" and the numerous problems women encountered while trying to enter the male-dominated sciences in *Women Scientists in America*, 51–72.

8. Edgar L. Hewett, *Ancient Life in the American Southwest: With an Introduction on the General History of the American Race* (Indianapolis: Bobbs-Merrill, 1930).

9. Curtis M. Hinsley Jr., "Edgar Lee Hewett and the School of American Research in Santa Fe, 1906–1912," in *American Archaeology Past and Future*, ed. David Melzer, Don Fowler, and Jeremy Sabloff (Washington DC: Smithsonian Institution Press 1986), 231.

10. Malinda Elliott, *The School of American Research: The First Eighty Years* (Santa Fe: School of American Research, 1987), 11.

11. Hewett discusses the role of the Pueblos and other Indian cultures in "the humanizing of a continent" in chapter 1 of *Ancient Life in the American Southwest*, 21–32.

12. Hewett, *Ancient Life in the American Southwest*, 44, 45.

13. The Antiquities Act of 1906 was a direct consequence of the controversy surrounding the excavations of Richard Wetherill and the Hyde Exploring Expeditions sponsored by the Museum of Natural History at Chaco Canyon. This act also established Mesa Verde National Monument in 1906 and Chaco Canyon National Monument in 1907.

14. Hewett did not limit his energies to building institutions in New Mexico. He had also directed the exhibits at the San Diego Panama-California Exposition from 1911 to 1915 and was director of the San Diego Museum of Man and professor of anthropology at San Diego State Teachers College from 1915 to 1928. In 1934 he helped found the anthropology department at the University of Southern California. Don D. Fowler discusses Hewett's activities in greater detail in *A Laboratory of Anthropology: Science and Romanticism in*

the American Southwest, 1846–1930 (Albuquerque: University of New Mexico Press, 2000), 261.

15. Marjorie Lambert, interview with Jennifer Fox, Tucson, Arizona, September 2, 1985.

16. Marjorie Lambert, interview with Shelby Tisdale, Santa Fe, New Mexico, August 6, 1997.

17. Florence C. Lister observed three different groups of female archaeologists. Marjorie fit into one group, and the other two groups included, first, those women who had the "anything you can do I can do better" attitude. Lister describes these as primarily "appearing as masculine as possible in their dress and grooming, defiantly hanging tough under field conditions that would have devastated most of the so-called weaker sex, and cultivating aggressive, roustabout behavior and vocabulary," which she points out was "window dressing totally unrelated to their scientific accomplishments." Lister's third group "was composed of the neutral mousy creatures who retreated into their working realms without concern for the real world, much less for the men who dominated it." *Pot Luck: Adventures in Archaeology* (Albuquerque: University of New Mexico Press, 1997), 19.

18. Lambert interview with Jennifer Fox.

19. Marjorie Lambert, interview with Shelby Tisdale, Santa Fe, New Mexico, July 25, 1990.

20. Leland C. Wyman, "Navajo Ceremonial System" in *Handbook of North American Indians*, vol. 10, *Southwest*, ed. Olfonso Ortiz (Washington DC: Smithsonian Institution, 1983), 542.

21. Marjorie Ferguson, "The Acculturation of Sandia Pueblo" (master's thesis, University of New Mexico, 1931).

22. The earliest documented archaeological fieldwork at Tecolote was by Isabel Kelly, Francis Watkins, and Eva Horner from July to August 1929. This field research was sponsored by the Laboratory of Anthropology in Santa Fe and was supervised by Alfred V. Kidder. Kidder and such colleagues as Harry P. Mera and Charles Amsden periodically visited the site while the archaeological team was conducting its investigations. After Marjorie's fieldwork at Tecolote in 1932, there is no record of any formal archaeological investigation until 1959. Ownership of the site was transferred from the Tecolote Land Grant to the Las Vegas Historical Society in the early 1900s and was transferred to the state of New Mexico in 1959. The New Mexico Normal School (New Mexico Highlands University) was charged with its stewardship.

23. Marjorie Ferguson, "Preliminary Report on the Tecolote Ruin," *El Palacio* 34, nos. 25–26 (1933): 196–98.

24. Research after 1950 revealed that the site appears to be a multi-storied pueblo that was occupied between 790 c.e. and 1570 c.e. by people who were contemporaries of the Ancestral Puebloans. Due to the massive erosion from the river and persistent pothunting activities, most of the irreplaceable archaeological information has been destroyed.

25. Lambert interview with Shelby Tisdale, August 6, 1997.

26. By this time Marjorie was married to her first husband, George Tichy, and her publications from 1932 to 1950 are listed under Marjorie Ferguson Tichy.

27. Marjorie Ferguson Tichy, "Observations on the Mission Uncovered at Puaray," *El Palacio* 41, nos. 11–13 (1936): 63.

28. Tichy, "Observations on the Mission," 66.

29. Marjorie Ferguson Tichy, "The Archaeology of Puaray," *El Palacio* 46, no. 7 (1939): 154.

30. Lambert interview with Shelby Tisdale, August 6, 1997.

31. Fowler, *A Laboratory of Anthropology*, 261.

32. Elliott, *The School of American Research*, 28.

33. Lambert interview with Shelby Tisdale, August 6, 1997.

34. Linda Cordell, "Sisters of Sun and Spade: Women Archaeologists in the Southwest," in *The Archaeology of Gender: Proceedings of the Twenty-second Annual Conference of the Archeological Association of the University of Calgary*, ed. Dale Walde and Noreen D. Willows (Alta, Calgary: University of Calgary, 1991), 505.

35. Lambert interview with Shelby Tisdale, August 6, 1997.

36. Cordell, "Sisters of Sun and Spade," 505.

37. Marjorie Ferguson Lambert, "Exploratory Work at Yunque-Yunque," *El Palacio* 51, no. 11 (1944): 2–7.

38. Marjorie F. Lambert and J. Richard Ambler, *A Survey and Excavation of Caves in Hidalgo County, New Mexico*, School of American Research Monograph no. 25 (Santa Fe: Museum of New Mexico Press, 1961).

39. Lambert interview with Jennifer Fox.

40. Margetta Dietrich was a wealthy widow who moved to Santa Fe in 1928 from Nebraska, where she had been a leading organizer of women's suffrage groups. In New Mexico she devoted herself to the cause of Indian rights.

41. In the 1930s Indian Market was held in the patio and under the portal of the Palace of the Governors; it has since grown to include Santa Fe's plaza and surrounding streets.

42. Marjorie Lambert, interview with Shelby Tisdale, Santa Fe, New Mexico, July 31, 1997.

43. Donald Fixico, *The Urban Indian Experience in America* (Albuquerque: University of New Mexico Press, 2000), 9.

44. The world changed with the explosion of the first atomic bomb on July 16, 1945. The explosion took place at the Trinity Site, on what is now the White Sands Missile Range in southeastern New Mexico.

45. The New Mexico Association on Indian Affairs was founded in 1922 to help fight the U.S. Senate's proposed Bursam Bill, which would have illegally given an enormous amount of Pueblo land to Hispanic and American squatters. In 1936 the association took over the Indian Fair, which is now the Santa Fe Indian Market, organized by the Southwestern Association for Indian Arts.

46. Linda Cordell, "Women Archaeologists in the Southwest," in Parezo, *Hidden Scholars*, 214.

47. Lambert interview with Jennifer Fox.

6

ALICE MARRIOTT

Recording the Lives of American Indian Women
Patricia Loughlin

"ALL YOUR ACCOMPLISHMENT DEPENDS on your ability to detach yourself from your own culture," Alice Marriott states in *Greener Fields: Experiences among the American Indians* (1953), an ethnographic memoir in which she shares her personal observations as an anthropologist with the reader based on her fieldwork experiences. "Mentally, emotionally, or in some other inner way you are a displaced person, or you would not have found interest in or satisfaction from the study of other cultures. This is your lack—or your great good fortune. Face it squarely, admit it honestly, take advantage of it."[1]

And take advantage of it she did. Eschewing the traditional approaches of her discipline (the formal, authoritative style of anthropological texts), Marriott wrote books that read like fiction. She allowed much of her personal observations and daily living into her texts and, at the same time, revealed the ethnographic dialogue of her fieldwork experiences with American Indian people. Many anthropologists during the 1930s and 1940s considered such an approach feminine and unscholarly, but anthropologist Barbara Tedlock, among others, has identified anthropologists such as Marriott, Gladys Reichard, Ruth Underhill, and Ruth Landes as the forerunners of this method, now referred to as "narrative ethnology."[2] By writing in an interesting and accessible way and revealing something of herself in her works, Marriott hoped that her books would appeal to a general readership, both to educate readers about Native communities, especially American Indian women, and also to interest them in anthropology.

Born in 1910 to a middle-class family in a Chicago suburb, Marriott as a child explored with her grandfather the Field Columbian Museum, a natural history museum featuring anthropological exhibits from the

9. (*Opposite Top*) Alice Marriott and an unidentified male in front of a tipi. *Courtesy of Western History Collections, University of Oklahoma Libraries, Norman OK.*

10. (*Opposite Bottom*) Maria Martinez making pottery as Alice Marriott looks on, 1946. *Courtesy of the Western History Collections, University of Oklahoma Libraries, Norman OK.*

1893–94 Chicago World's Fair. When she was seven, her family moved from Chicago to Oklahoma City in search of economic opportunities. Her father had accepted a position as the treasurer of an insurance company, and her mother worked as a certified public accountant. The Great Depression had dramatic consequences for Marriott, as it did for other women public intellectuals, guiding career choices, education, and relationships. To save money she lived at home and pursued her college degree at nearby Oklahoma City University. In 1930 she graduated magna cum laude with a double major in English and French. For the next two years, she cataloged literature of the Five Southern Tribes—the Cherokees, Creeks, Choctaws, Chickasaws, and Seminoles, known originally as the "Five Civilized Tribes"—at the Muskogee Public Library.[3] She had always wanted to attend graduate school, and her interest in anthropology intensified following her library work.

With bachelor's degree in hand, Marriott believed she could attend the University of Oklahoma as a graduate student, only to discover that the new program in anthropology offered no advanced degree. Since she lacked prior coursework in this discipline, her adviser, Forrest Clements, a Berkeley graduate who had studied with Alfred Kroeber, one of Franz Boas's best-known students, enrolled Marriott in freshman anthropology courses. Marriott attended the University of Oklahoma "out of sheer necessity," she later stated, because the depression left her unable to go elsewhere.[4] In addition to her entry-level courses, she conducted laboratory work in pottery restoration and library research on the archaeology of eastern Oklahoma.[5]

In 1934 Marriott returned to the University of Oklahoma after summer fieldwork in Oregon as part of anthropologist Leslie Spier's team working with the Modocs. This experience renewed her enthusiasm for ethnology, particularly working with Indian women. As she explained in *Greener Fields*, "I am a woman and I talk to women."[6] Her emphasis on the importance of women and their roles could be seen as her greatest contribution to anthropology. Most anthropologists at the time—except for Gladys Reichard, Ruth Underhill, and Ruth Landes—neither worked with women respondents nor documented their lives in American Indian communities. Marriott, by contrast—and like Reichard, Underhill, and Landes—not only employed women respondents but wrote numerous books and articles on American Indian women. To understand Alice Marriott, one must examine the two books for which she is best known, *The Ten Grandmothers* (1945) and *Maria: The Potter of San Ildefonso* (1948), and her employment as a field representative for the Indian Arts and Crafts Board.

Marriott's *The Ten Grandmothers*, published by the University of Oklahoma Press as the twenty-sixth book in the Civilization of the American Indian series, became one of the press's most successful productions, going through numerous reprintings. Telling stories of Kiowa life spanning almost a century—from the buffalo days of the mid-1840s to World War II—the work also exposes the intense cultural incursions Kiowa people faced: the growing presence of the federal government, encroaching westward settlement, and the decline of the buffalo.[7] It also covers the traumatic adjustments of reservation life, and assimilationist policies such as the advance of Christianity and the creation of boarding schools for American Indian children.

Throughout these many changes, Marriott insists, the Grandmothers—ten medicine bundles—remained a stabilizing force among the Kiowas. Not only did the Kiowas she interviewed support her research, but they viewed *The Ten Grandmothers* as a way of preserving their stories. Marriott considered this book an ethnological achievement because, she noted, younger members of the tribe consulted it to learn more about their history. By utilizing *The Ten Grandmothers* and *Greener Fields* as well as correspondence and field notes, we have a window through which to view the ethnographic process between anthropologist and respondents and the published text as the tangible product of that process.

As an anthropology student preparing for fieldwork at the University of Oklahoma, Marriott surveyed the existing literature on Plains Indians' material culture. In her reading she became fascinated with social anthropology, a developing field during the 1930s that challenged anthropologists to explore social structure in new ways through the examination of family and kinship. As her reading of the secondary literature deepened, she grew disturbed by what was left out of the narratives—principally American Indian women's stories and activities. She attributed this oversight to male anthropologists who had used only male collaborators in past studies.[8] Thus began her pursuit of Kiowa women's narratives. She focused on "women's life, women's ways, women's tricks" when she interviewed Kiowa women.[9] But she did not view her research as exclusively about Indian women. Rather, she was examining the missing link to a fuller understanding of Kiowa society. "I just felt that the audience for anthropology was going unsatisfied, so to speak," Marriott maintained. "Because half of everything was being left out. It became a kind of challenge, an 'I'm as good as you are' way of proving to everybody I knew that women did have a life."[10] After only one year of anthropological study, Marriott had located an important untapped resource in the lives of women. She had uncovered material that had been invisible in prior anthropological research. Marriott became committed to working with women collaborators and women interpreters in order to reveal women's culture within Kiowa society.

After she received permission to conduct ethnological research from the Bureau of Indian Affairs superintendent for the Kiowa agency at Anadarko in southwestern Oklahoma, Marriott visited George Hunt and his family—the family that would become her primary collaborators and interpreters—during Thanksgiving in 1934. Orphaned as a boy, Hunt had lived with his uncle, I-see-o, a Kiowa scout at Fort Sill, and had attended school at the post, where he had learned to speak and write English. In his youth during the mid-1890s, Hunt was "perhaps the only Kiowa," according to historian Wilbur Sturtevant Nye, "then able to interpret properly for James Mooney," the noted government ethnologist for the Bureau of American Ethnology under the Smithsonian Institution.[11] With interests in Kiowa and frontier history, Hunt, as a tribal historian who worked both as an interpreter and secured collaborators for historians and anthropologists, had served as Nye's principal collaborator and interpreter for two texts, *Carbine and Lance: The Story of Old Fort Sill* (1937) and *Bad Medicine and Good: Tales of the Kiowas* (1962).[12]

In 1897, George Hunt eloped with Julia Given, daughter of Kiowa chief Sitting Bear, also called Satank. Given received her early education at Fort Sill and then attended Carlisle Indian School in Pennsylvania, where she became a Christian and studied domestic arts as part of the federal government's larger assimilation program. After ten years away from home, she returned to Rainy Mountain as an interpreter and missionary helper for the Woman's American Baptist Home Mission Society. At Rainy Mountain she taught missionaries the Kiowa language and also translated portions of the New Testament into Kiowa. Hunt worked as farm agent for the Indian Service conducting business from the Anadarko office and dispensing annuity checks to the Kiowas.[13] Marriott's contact with the Kiowas was through the Hunt family. Their Baptist commitment, experience with boarding school education, and willingness to welcome Marriott into their family influenced the ethnographic process and the production of *The Ten Grandmothers*.

That Thanksgiving weekend in 1934, Hunt not only welcomed Marriott into his home but introduced her to potential collaborators. He also suggested that Marriott talk to older women and preserve their stories for young members of the tribe.[14] Hunt and his family were Marriott's point of contact with the larger Kiowa community. He even recruited his daughter, Ioleta Hunt McElhaney, the first Kiowa woman college graduate and a Christian missionary, to become Marriott's principal interpreter. In addition, his other daughter, Margaret Tsoodle, and McElhaney and Hunt introduced Marriott to other potential collaborators, all drawn from the older members of their families. These relationships indicate that Marriott's fieldwork was conducted entirely with Hunt's extended family, a common practice in ethnographic situations. The Hunts' commitment to Christianity, education, and Kiowa history influenced the production of Marriott's texts as well as her ability to access certain Kiowa people and tribal information.[15]

Although Marriott conducted the bulk of her research on the Kiowas during the summer months of the mid-1930s, she continually returned to Kiowa country throughout her life. Initially, she lived with the Hunt family in a room she rented while conducting her research. During her first summer of fieldwork with the Hunts, McElhaney's maternal grandmother adopted Marriott in a ceremony attended by Marriott's parents. After completing her fieldwork, Marriott joined the Hunts when they camped together at Kiowa gatherings and addressed her correspondence to George Hunt as "Dear Father." During an oral history interview in 1986, she stated: "If you establish that kind of relationship, a rapport, with an Indian group, it will spread from one person to another. You will eventually find that you have much more in common with them, than you have with people in your own age group, in your own culture."[16] Her emotional attachment to the Kiowa people, particularly the Hunt family, never waned throughout her life. In many ways, Marriott was more at home in their community than in her own.

Although she learned to say a few Kiowa phrases, Marriott never pursued the study of their language. This was in contrast to principles espoused by Boas, who argued that learning the language deepened one's understanding of a culture, though not all of Boas's students did so.[17] Marriott contended that the Kiowa language, a five-toned pitch language, was too difficult for her to learn. "I have no ear, none whatever, for pitch," she claimed.[18] Most of her fieldwork was conducted with older people who spoke only Kiowa. Therefore, the quality of Ioleta Hunt McElhaney's work as interpreter was of paramount importance.

In tracing the life of Ioleta, a teacher and social worker for the Indian Service, one quickly finds that she was an exceptional individual. Born near the Wichita Mountains at Saddle Mountain in 1908, she was raised by her father to be mindful of Kiowa history and its ramifications. Since her birth occurred shortly after the cutoff date of the Jerome Treaty, she would not receive an allotment of 160 acres. "Poor little Ioleta—no land," her father would say. So at an early age, Hunt reinforced to his daughter the importance of education as a tool of economic advancement and stability in her life. Educated in public schools at Rainy Mountain and Mountain View to fifth grade, she then attended Bacone College, the Northern Baptist School for American Indians (at Muskogee in eastern Oklahoma), through high school and two years of junior college. For her final two years of study she attended Keuka College, a women's college in upstate New York, and majored in sociology.[19]

McElhaney, in her late twenties, was Marriott's age. Speaking English and Kiowa, she became, in Marriott's words, her "dearest friend," and for the next three summers they did everything together. Marriott commented on their relationship: "She was the interpreter, I was the recorder, and anybody we could put our hands on, our four hands, was the informant! Most of them were in the family."[20] Marriott recognized the importance of McElhaney, upon whom "fell the burden of the work, not only as interpreter, but as contact woman. Her great knowledge of both English and Kiowa and her painstaking care in translation made it possible to be sure of accuracy of spirit, as well as meaning, throughout the work."[21]

The Ten Grandmothers is based on Kiowa oral traditions passed down through tribal members. Older Kiowa men had lived as buffalo hunters on the Great Plains before the reservation period. Women's work had included preparing the buffalo meat and hide, sewing essential items such as tipi coverings and moccasins, and caring for children, although men also assisted in child care. Two of Marriott's principal interviewees were McElhaney's grandmother and her uncle, both in their mid-nineties in the mid-1930s. Marriott considered herself fortunate to have had this opportunity to work with them, for within the next five years their entire age group had passed away.[22]

From her discussions with elders, Marriott concluded that she could not make generalizations about Kiowas during a period that lasted from the days of the buffalo hunt to acculturation under the Bureau of Indian Affairs. "While each person acted within the general pattern of the culture he knew," she states in the preface of *The Ten Grandmothers*, "the pattern itself was changing too rapidly and too radically to be absolutely defined."[23] Therefore, although the sketches illustrate individual behavior, they reveal what it meant to be Kiowa, since "no one but a Kiowa would have behaved in that way, at that time, under those conditions." Finally, Marriott noted that, rather than embellishing, "I have tried to tell these stories as much as possible as they were told to me," she concluded in the book's preface.[24]

Marriott sought to obtain from the older Kiowas what anthropologists describe as "salvage ethnography" of the late nineteenth and early twentieth centuries, or as Louise Lamphere defines it, "the collection of myths, tales, details of kinship and social organization, items of material culture, details of phonology and grammar, and accounts of ritual practices and belief systems before cultures 'died out.'"[25] Marriott obtained collaboration by prompting the elders to "think of the children who will grow up not knowing what their grandparents lived. It's cheating the grandchildren."[26] At the same time, her approach adhered to the tenets of cultural relativism made popular by Boas and his students by the 1920s and 1930s. She did not evaluate Kiowa culture according to her own experiences or culture; instead, she described and interpreted Kiowa traditions and kinship on their own terms, according to their own standards.

The Ten Grandmothers presents thirty-three short stories, each associated with a year in the Kiowa calendar. Beginning in 1832, the Kiowas kept a calendar that recorded the major events each summer and winter in the tribal year pictographically. Marriott consulted Mooney's *Calendar History of the Kiowa Indians* (1898), a record the ethnologist made from a monthly and yearly calendar that Kiowa artist Anko composed on paper and that spanned almost thirty years. At Mooney's request, Anko re-created his original yearly calendar on buckskin and in color.[27] For comparative purposes, at the back of her book Marriott placed Mooney's calendar alongside George Poolaw's continuation of the Mooney calendar to 1939 and George Hunt's and Mary Buffalo's respective calendars. Examining the four calendars together, she found few discrepancies in memory and interpretation, calling them "surprisingly consistent."[28]

The result is a series of chronological sketches under four headings: "The Time When There Were Plenty of Buffalo," "The Time When Buffalo Were Going," "The Time When Buffalo Were Gone," and "Modern Times." In the sketch "Hanging the Red Blanket" in the Year of the Power Contest (1881–82), for example, Spear Woman contemplates the changes in Great Plains life and thinks to herself, "It wasn't so much having the soldiers come that changed things . . . as having the buffalo go."[29] Facing an altered Plains landscape no longer capable of sustaining them left the Kiowas in a tragic situation. As Spear Woman observes, the departure of the herds was painful, for much of their culture centered on buffalo.

Another theme includes the shift from "old ways" to the ways offered by the federal government, missionaries, and reformers. In "Allotments" (1900), Marriott discusses the family's encounter with the assimilative process at the turn of the century. When a missionary asks Hunting Horse if he is ready to follow the Jesus road, he replies that he is following it now. The missionary shakes his head and tells Hunting

Horse that he cannot follow the Jesus road with two wives. Hunting Horse needs time to think this over.

Hunting Horse wants to follow the Jesus road, but what about his two wives, Spear Woman and Bow Woman? All three start to cry, and through the weight of his tears, Hunting Horse says: "I want to take the Jesus road. That's the only way to go. It's what we know all our lives is right. But," he adds through his tears, "it isn't right to hurt somebody, even to take that road. . . . Seems like I'm being pulled in two, two ways at once."[30]

Spear Woman decides to make it "easy" for Hunting Horse and Bow Woman. She tells them in a cross tone—Marriott implies that she is sounding cross deliberately to convince herself and convince them—that she will leave the marriage. "I've had all of it I can stand," she says. "I was married to you at first, and I've had to stand it longer than my sister has." They will each receive an allotment and select them side by side, ensuring water at the creek and limited fencing. In Marriott's subtle way, at the end of the sketch she adds the response to Spear Woman's decision: "They were understanding what she was saying, all right. In another moment they would understand what she wasn't saying, and then the worrying would start all over again. She turned her back on them and walked off, leaving husband and wife alone."[31] Within this short, six-page story, Marriott conveys the powerful forces of the assimilation process at the individual and family level. Their lives were changing from the "old ways" of polygamy and the days of following the buffalo, to the Jesus road and the new problems of allotment, especially when one had more than one wife.

Marriott intended her story to be told as some Kiowas would tell it, as she explained in a letter to her parents regarding her decision to send her future manuscript to the University of Oklahoma Press: "If I have anything to say about it, it will go as it is, literally transcribed, without any English to come between the real life and the reader."[32] This method, a recent trend, appeared first in Paul Radin's *The Autobiography of a Winnebago Indian* (1920) and *Crashing Thunder: The Autobiography of an American Indian* (1926), then later in Leslie Spier's *Yuman Tribes of the Gila River* (1933), Ruth Underhill's *Autobiography of a Papago Woman* (1936), and Ruth Landes's *Ojibwa Woman* (1938).[33]

Marriott, influenced by Spier and Underhill, referred to *Papago Woman* as her bible.[34] In addition to literal transcription methods, Marriott also rejected the organization of the traditional ethnography, which begins with the larger community and narrows in focus to the family and individuals. Instead, her text emanated from the family to the larger community in a circular approach that reflected the way Kiowas perceive the world.

Although Marriott included her collaborators in her texts, often giving the impression that they were speaking in the first person, she arranged and edited the material into a book marketable to a primarily white general readership. She wrote the work in a "brief, Kiowa manner," as one reviewer noted, thereby reaffirming her claim that she was merely the recorder of stories that were told to her.[35] Marriott and other anthropologists during the 1930s and 1940s may have claimed they were merely recorders of American Indian stories or autobiography; however, they often reshaped or modified the final draft of the manuscript to conform to their objectives and to accommodate editorial or publishing requirements.

In part 4, "Modern Times," in *The Ten Grandmothers*, Marriott again illustrates assimilation on a personal, individual level. "Back to the Blanket" (1928) involves an educated Kiowa woman, Leah, returning to her home and her people after being away at an eastern boarding school. Despite her intention to teach her people "civilized ways" she learned in the East, she feels the pull of the traditional ways that the boarding schools had tried to erase.

The story begins with Leah traveling west by train in a first-class sleeping car. School administrators send the students home in style, and "people knew you amounted to something." What follows is a description of Leah's "civilized" attire: "Girdle, brassiere, bloomers, slip, blouse, skirt, jacket. Her hair braided, and the braids twisted around her head. A pin at the throat of her blouse, and then her hat and gloves. She looked at herself and pulled her veil down. The outfit was really stylish. Now that you couldn't see the color of her skin, she could pass anywhere for a white girl."[36] In this discussion of civilized ways and dress, Marriott directs the reader to the subtleties and the overt displays of identity. In this attire, with her hat and veil covering her face and her gloves pulled up covering her hands, Leah's identity as a Kiowa woman is masked.

By extension, as the reader walks through this process, Leah becomes increasingly uncomfortable with her new masked identity: "It was hard coming back to this life. The missionaries made it sound easy. You went away for most of your life and forgot your own language, but you learned lots of other things to take the place of it. Then you went back and taught all the new things to the people at home, and they did better and lived better, like you. There was just one danger that you had to look out for. That was going back to the blanket. If you ever went back to the blanket, you were lost. Then there was no hope for you any more. You would be just Indian all your life."[37]

Her father, stepmother, and sister, Jane, meet Leah at the station with their "ugly" wagon and their sluggish ponies. Leah climbs aboard the wagon and they head for home. She grimaces as she looks in the wagon bed and sees a slab of beef, a sack of flour, and a can of coal-oil alongside her trunks. Seeing the beef "lying out like that with the flies all over it" especially pains her. She has learned at school the importance of cleanliness and the dangers of germs. She must tell her mother about the "proper" handling of meat. And didn't her parents know to keep coal-oil separate from the other items? One of the aims of her eastern education was to return home to educate her people on the domestic arts such as housework, mending, and food preparation.[38]

But on their day-long trip home in the heat and the dust from the red dirt, Leah starts to get restless in her fancy clothes and longs for the comfort of a shawl and breathable cotton dress. She speaks more Kiowa to her parents and Jane. And when they stop for lunch, she is impressed with her mother's deftness at preparing the beef. The fire smells like perfume and the smoke smells sweet, but because of her eastern training she is reluctant to eat the meat.

When they arrive home after the long journey, Leah strips off her fancy clothes and borrows one of Jane's cotton dresses to keep cool in the summer heat. Her sister hands her the dress. "Sure is funny," Jane says. "You go away, learn to be white woman. First thing when you come back, you put on Indian clothes." The missionaries arrive to check on Leah and to make arrangements for her work as interpreter at the church. The white woman missionary is horrified to see Leah wearing a "squaw dress." Jane defends her sister. "She's Indian," Jane says. "She's just educated Indian."[39]

The transition from eastern boarding school to home is far more complicated than Leah had imagined. "She thought she would come home, go to the mission, work to uplift her people. It would all be easy. Then she would marry some good young man, not an Indian, a missionary, and go away and do good all her life. And here was her own sister calling her Indian."[40]

Many themes are wrapped up in this short yet telling story. The most pervasive is Leah's struggle to find balance as a Christian missionary among her own people. The reader participates in her internal struggle to at once reject Kiowa culture and participate in it. Leah thought she had immersed herself in the Christian ways of boarding school, only to find that many of her Kiowa ways—the cotton work dress, the language, curing beef over an open fire—made sense to her in this place. The story offers a glimpse into the life of an educated Kiowa woman and her personal conflict with her mission to "uplift" her people and, simultaneously, to defend her culture to white missionaries.

Kiowa consultants often discuss anthropological texts by noting which Kiowas worked with the anthropologist. "They do not," states noted anthropologist Luke S. Lassiter, who worked for years with the Kiowas, "talk about Maurice Boyd's *Kiowa Voices* (1981, 1983) or Alice Marriott's *Ten Grandmothers* (1945), for example, as a definitive representation of Kiowa culture. Instead, they explicitly point out that these books reflect the opinions and viewpoints of the particular Kiowa people who worked with the authors of those books."[41] Marriott worked specifically with the Hunt family, and this family could not speak for all Kiowas and thus would not be representative of "Kiowa culture." Instead, *The Ten Grandmothers* offers one family's account of their lives and connects their stories to the larger tribal experience from the times of the buffalo to World War II.

The Ten Grandmothers received praise from those close to Marriott. Her adviser at the University of Oklahoma, Forrest Clements, one of the reviewers for the University of Oklahoma Press, was pleased with Marriott's "brain child" and complimented its organization. In his view, it "gives the book a vitality," he wrote to Marriott, "which would have been absent had you followed the orthodox ethnographic report style and this method is particularly effective when dealing with a culture which is cracking up."[42] Clements's "cracking up" comment reflects the assumptions of "salvage ethnography," or the idea that Indian cultures were disappearing or being altered by Western civilization. It also indicates that he did not spend much time with Indian people. After reading *The Ten Grandmothers*, Ioleta Hunt McElhaney's husband, Louis, commended Marriott for "writing a book about Indians which is, so far as I can tell, utterly devoid of prejudice, and which reveals a genuine desire on your part to get at the simple truth." Having expected to read a "coldly-analytical, test-tube treatment" of the Kiowa people, he was surprised that the book read like a novel.[43]

Some professional reviews were less favorable, since Marriott deliberately broke scholarly conventions. In addition, she was battling professional territoriality in these reviews, with academic historians and anthropologists evaluating her work and in a sense jettisoning her from the profession because she did not possess the doctorate. For example, Ernest Wallace, Texas historian and a specialist in Southern Plains studies, commented that the "scholarly reader may be disappointed that the author has not cited her authorities as the story progresses, and consequently may wonder at times if there is any departure from fact to fiction."[44] Wallace's claim is valid, for Marriott did not document her sources. In addition, her writing style is fluid and fiction-like, which could cause people like Wallace to question the book's credibility. On the other hand, historian Angie Debo, who also targeted a broad audience for her books, sent Marriott a note of praise, stating that *The Ten Grandmothers* was a "once in a blue moon kind of book. I have no words to tell you how much I enjoyed it. I read it slowly savoring every word to make it last longer."[45]

Although *The Ten Grandmothers* was published in 1945, Marriott had completed her fieldwork with the Hunt family and other Kiowas earlier. After receiving her bachelor's degree in anthropology from the University of Oklahoma in the mid-1930s, she had begun working as a field representative for the Indian Arts and Crafts Board (IACB). Created by Congress in 1935, the IACB reflected the important changes occurring in federal Indian policy during John Collier's tenure as commissioner of Indian Affairs in the 1930s and early 1940s. Collier actively campaigned for economic revitalization among American Indian communities, and one of the ways was through the production and sale of Native arts and crafts. The IACB served as an important part of his larger "Indian New Deal," a program designed to halt the long-standing policy of assimilation in favor of a return to semi-sovereign tribal status by restoring communal land tenure and revitalizing traditional religions, ceremonies, and arts and crafts.[46] The board placed representatives such as Marriott in the field to improve the quality of Indian goods and broaden the market. This would be one of the only "regular jobs" she would hold. She would spend the remainder of her life as a historical consultant, adjunct instructor of creative writing and folklore at the University of Central Oklahoma, and freelance writer whose finances were linked to successful book sales and fellowships. Moreover, she only took jobs that truly benefited the people she studied. She lived on the margins of conventional society, and she preferred it that way.

Despite her maverick qualities and independence, Marriott shared some of the gender assumptions that undergirded the structure and strategies of the IACB. First, the board assumed a natural association between women and arts and crafts. The board also argued that most Indian women could not be employed outside the home, but could supplement household income through the production of arts and crafts. Marriott agreed with this approach based on her experiences in the field: "The work of the Indian Arts and Crafts Board in Oklahoma has been principally concentrated on the development of home industries; both in traditional tribal crafts and in introduced handicrafts. We find that the majority of the crafts workers are women, who are anxious to earn extra money at home in their spare time."[47] Given these assumptions, it is no coincidence that the IACB's first field representatives were all female anthropologists.

Initially, Marriott's assignment was to research the Southern Cheyenne women's crafts guild as part of the board's preliminary research for the Oklahoma region. Later, her study "The Trade Guild of the Southern Cheyenne Women" became the IACB's first "purely ethnological paper."[48] During the first six months of her employment as a participant in the board's preliminary survey of American Indian communities in Oklahoma, Marriott also conducted extensive research concerning the material culture of the Plains tribes and an overview of the Five Southern Tribes. Her reports detailed not only arts and crafts but also the tribes' living and economic conditions, customs, traditions, and beliefs.[49]

Following these initial surveys, the board decided to begin its work with Kiowa, Cheyenne-Arapaho, Shawnee, and Five Tribes people. For example, the IACB encouraged the Kiowas and Shawnees to pursue silver work, especially jewelry making. Marriott and other field representatives relied on contacts within the tribes to serve as intermediaries to promote and implement the federal government's plan to revive Native arts and stimulate tribal economies. The board, furthermore, mirroring the prevailing anthropological view of the early twentieth century that older Indians equaled traditional or "real" Indians, employed only respondents over sixty with some knowledge of traditional arts and crafts.[50]

Marriott faced the challenge of educating potential consumers about the value of local Indian arts and the achievements of individual artists; this was especially true for products from Oklahoma, for which there was no market. Through public exhibits like Tulsa's American Indian Exposition in 1937 and later the San Francisco World's Fair in 1939, the IACB labored to generate greater public awareness of quality Indian arts and crafts. By showing potential buyers—especially white, middle-class buyers—how to use these arts and crafts as decorative accents in the home, the IACB hoped to stimulate demand.[51]

In preparation for the San Francisco World's Fair in 1939, Marriott traveled to the Great Lakes area and Florida to meet Indian artists and collect arts and crafts for the IACB Indian exhibition in the Federal Building located on Treasure Island in San Francisco Bay. The American Indian exhibit was one of ten sponsored by the federal government.[52] During much of 1938 and 1939 the IACB channeled most of its energies into this "grand endeavor," which attracted some 1.5 million visitors. Indian artists demonstrated their talents before audiences, and arts and crafts were also available for purchase.[53] "The exhibit depicted Indians as vital and dynamic, not as dying or vanishing people," notes Susan Labry Meyn in *More Than Curiosities*, "by showing their cultural products as art."[54]

From May to September 1939, Marriott worked in the exhibition and sales rooms with Indian artists. She assisted approximately forty Indian demonstrators who had come to San Francisco for a specified time, and usually at Indian Service expense.[55] They included, among others, a totem-pole carver from British Columbia and Julian and Maria Martinez, a couple from San Ildefonso Pueblo, New Mexico, famous for their black-on-black pottery.

Marriott's work with the IACB ended in 1942 when, due to U.S. involvement in World War II, the board's field operations were suspended and only nominal work continued at the Washington DC office. Marriott evaluated the work of the IACB and her participation in it as a success: "As nearly as we could estimate, the Indians were doing a two million dollar a year business in fine arts—instead of twenty thousand a year in curios" they had done earlier.[56] She characterized working with the IACB as "heaven" and maintained that her position with the board never took her away from anthropology, since she used her training as an anthropologist in the field.[57]

Another benefit Marriott derived from working for the IACB was the opportunity to meet Margaret Lefranc, a painter who had studied with Andrew L'Hote in Paris. The two became acquainted in 1940 at the Museum of Modern Art in New York City at the Indian arts and crafts show, actually a modified version of the 1939 world's fair exhibit. Following World War II, Marriott moved with Lefranc, who was recently divorced, to New Mexico. There they purchased a house in Nambé, a predominantly Indian and Hispanic community approximately twelve miles from San Ildefonso Pueblo, to be near Maria Martinez.[58] Marriott had decided that examining Martinez's life and career as a Pueblo artist would be the focus of her next scholarly work. In Nambé, Marriott and Lefranc led a contented life, with Marriott working on the book about Maria with support from a Rockefeller Foundation fellowship and Lefranc continuing with her art. Lefranc illustrated several of Marriott's books, including *Maria*, *The Valley Below*, and *Indians on Horseback*. They maintained an active social life and always welcomed the frequent guests who dropped by their adobe home.[59]

Disillusioned with an increasingly urbanized and industrialized world, Marriott and Lefranc were drawn to the "relatively untouched" condition of the Pueblos. There they participated in the "postwar back-to-the-soil movement," as Marriott put it.[60] Dissatisfaction with modern America was a common theme among many anthropologists, social critics, artists, and writers who flocked to the Southwest in droves at the turn of the century and then in the 1920s and again in the late 1940s as postwar responses. Historian William Leach has pointed out that the "simple-life movement" that swept through the United States at the turn of the century was intimately connected to the field of anthropology.[61] Leah Dilworth terms this "modernist primitivism," the search for the simple life and the idea that this life could be found in American Indian communities.[62] Women anthropologists, including Marriott and Ruth Underhill, participated in this critique of modern culture, contrasting the gender equality they perceived in Pueblo communities, particularly in terms of women's roles and the respect accorded women, with the gender inequities they experienced in their own society.[63] As Nancy Parezo points out, "Women anthropologists were drawn to matrilineal societies, where women were respected for their talents and it was felt they would have access to information and be treated better than in societies where women had low status."[64] Marriott's decision to live in Nambé and conduct fieldwork with Martinez fits into this larger movement of women anthropologists who critiqued their own culture through the study of American Indian people.

Historians and anthropologists have debated these critiques. Women's studies scholar Deborah Gordon argues that white women anthropologists such as Marriott, Underhill, and Ruth Bunzel "looked to Native Americans and Native American women for the reconstruction of themselves."[65] Bunzel, for example, in her research on Pueblo potters during the late 1920s, selected Maria Martinez and Hopi potter Nampeyo as artists who initiated innovative styles and made aesthetic decisions in keeping with traditional practices. She also discussed these potters as decision makers, as representatives of "the modern individual," attuned to the marketability of their craft. At the same time, as Dilworth explains, Bunzel studied Pueblo potters looking to "the primitive to find authenticity."[66] Following the anthropological literary tradition of women anthropologists before her, Marriott was engaged in modernist primitivism—that is, she was looking for some "purer" form of humanity to validate her own notions of human experience. She found it in American Indian societies. At the same time, she wanted to educate the larger Anglo-American public about American Indian people, especially American Indian women, and explained her objective as "making ethnographic reports human stories" for those who "didn't yet know much about Indian women."[67]

Before commencing the series of interviews with Maria in February 1946, Marriott needed the approval of Governor Dionicio Sanchez and the San Ildefonso council. San Ildefonso, like other pueblos, was a small, insular community with a population of approximately two hundred in the 1940s. Its population had increased in recent decades because of rising tourism, which brought more people employment within the pueblo. The council forbade Marriott and Martinez to discuss San Ildefonso government, clan, or religion. Martinez was not free to describe such matters as the selection of the governor and council or the division within the pueblo in 1925 that had led to the creation of a separate south plaza. Although the governor approved Marriott's research, he required her to abide by the same regulations. To ensure that Marriott honored these restrictions, he instructed her to show her field notes to Kenneth Chapman at the Laboratory of Anthropology in Santa Fe.[68]

Marriott spent the spring of 1946 conducting daily interviews with Martinez in preparation for the biography. As noted, they had met at the 1939 world's fair, where Marriott worked for the IACB and Maria and her husband demonstrated their pottery making. Julian and Maria had attended two world's fairs since their first as newlyweds at St. Louis in 1904, promoting their art in a "living museum" exhibit for the public. Fame was part of Maria's life—it made her neither happy nor unhappy. "She accepted it and she lived with it," Marriott observed; "she did not avoid visitors, and she never refused requests to pose for photographs, even holding babies. Many tourists interrupted our work, several for hours-long intervals. I grew impatient and ruffled of temper; Maria never did."[69]

Despite these interruptions, Marriott made progress toward understanding her subject's life. With no exact recollection of the year she was born, Maria guessed it was around 1881; her son later researched the year as 1887. Her parents, Reyes Peña Montoya and Tomas Montoya, lived in their adobe home at the north end of San Ildefonso Pueblo, located twenty-five miles northwest of Santa Fe in northern New Mexico. From their home they could look beyond the plaza to the west and see the Rio Grande and the Pajarito Plateau, where their Tewa ancestors resided long ago. During childhood Maria attended a nearby day school, followed by two years at St. Catherine's Indian School, a boarding school in Santa Fe that her parents had also attended. There she and her sister studied English and other subjects and received confirmation in the Roman Catholic Church.[70]

In 1907 the Museum of New Mexico began excavations on the Pajarito Plateau under the direction of archaeologist Edgar L. Hewett of the School of American Research in Santa Fe. Julian Martinez and other Indian laborers worked at the dig site and copied petroglyphs. Hewett commissioned Martinez to replicate a specific potsherd using the San Ildefonso methods she had learned; however, neither Hewett nor Martinez could describe the potsherd when Marriott asked about it in the summer of 1946.[71] With the assistance of Hewett and Santa Fe traders, Martinez "found an economic way out," Marriott argues in *Maria*, "first for her family and then for her village."[72] Julian and Maria Martinez were the leading figures in the revival of Rio Grande Pueblo pottery, and anthropologists and art historians have credited them with the economic regeneration of their community through the revival of pottery as art, particularly the black-on-blackware, an innovative technique they began about 1919. Working as a team, Maria shaped the pottery and Julian decorated it.

For her part, Marriott respected the privacy of the San Ildefonso community and did not use her association with Martinez to pry into sensitive matters. Acknowledging the gaps within the text, she explained to the reader in her preface, "I find the same blanks myself, and regret their presence as bitterly as anyone can."[73] Justifying her method, Marriott posited that white people who speak with authority on Pueblo religion and government were "either violating confidences or falsifying."[74] "The material," she maintained, "has been left in every regard as the people of San Ildefonso would have it presented to the reading public."[75] Marriott was well ahead of her time in respecting community intellectual property. Not everyone who read the biography approved the result. Working under such conditions, Ruth Underhill wrote in a review of *Maria*, "was like writing Hamlet with Hamlet left out"; nonetheless, "a clear but subtly shaded picture" emerged.[76]

Marriott and Maria established an orderly interview schedule. From 9 a.m. until noon they would sit in Martinez's living room and talk. Marriott paid her one dollar per hour—more than respondents received in Oklahoma during the mid-1940s, but adequate payment in the pueblos.[77] At Martinez's request, they talked alone during these meetings. "At first I tried asking questions," Marriott observed, "but I soon discovered that it was impossible for me to frame them so that they did not impinge on the forbidden topics."[78] Marriott's structured interview technique of question and answer required prompt modification to meet the council's requirements.

With notebook in hand, Marriott adopted what she called a "stream-of-consciousness" or unstructured interview technique, much like contemporary grounded theory. Under this method, Martinez would select a topic to discuss that day, and if anything were unclear, Marriott would ask the necessary questions.[79] Marriott had used this approach before with Kiowa respondents, but only with people she knew well. Martinez and Marriott were still on very formal terms with one another, and Marriott called her Mrs. Martinez.

After several months of morning interviews, Marriott recalled, "the day came when Maria said, gently, 'I think that's all I have to tell you.'" Since Martinez had come to the end of her story, Marriott returned to her home in Nambé to organize her field notes and "coax from them a coherent story of one woman's life."[80] Recent studies call for more collaborative efforts in the ethnographic process, whereby the anthropologist sends the manuscript to her collaborators for review and revision. As Luke Lassiter points out, although an ethnographer may intend to create a text that explores the dialogue between ethnographer and collaborators, the result is often a monologue about "the native point of view" written for a "nonnative" audience. "Control of this conversation," Lassiter concludes, "rests solely with the ethnographer."[81] Thus, like anthropologists of the 1930s and 1940s, Marriott might have claimed she was merely the recorder of an American Indian autobiography, but she often reshaped or modified the final draft of the manuscript to conform to her objectives.

Just before publication, however, at Martinez's request, Marriott read the book to Martinez. That action forced Marriott to participate in a more collaborative process, although only as an afterthought just before the text appeared in print. By recording this event later in *Greener Fields*, Marriott demonstrated her awareness that Martinez had prompted her to become more open to at least a degree of collaboration. That, in turn, was a departure from the often unconscious authoritarian posturing of anthropologists of that era.

In *Maria*, Marriott used the life history of Maria Martinez as an exceptional individual to explore a culture. In doing so, she continued an important southwestern literary and ethnographic tradition begun by Ruth Underhill in *Papago Woman*. At the same time, Marriott was continuing a practice she had inaugurated earlier. As she had used the Hunt family to examine Kiowa culture, so she was now using Maria to explore the cultural values and behavioral norms of the people of San Ildefonso. She realized the value of this method about halfway through her interviews with Martinez and justified it. "Only by knowing one person," she recalled in the 1980s, "can you even begin to picture a culture. I'm convinced of that."[82] This approach, however, had its own set of problems. Marriott, like any other writer, brought her own concerns to her work. Also, she had to organize the interviews so that the reader would have a narrative to follow. At the same time, she assured the reader that she was merely the recorder of Martinez's story.

From the outset, Marriott tells the reader that *Maria* is biography, not ethnography. She follows the story of Martinez's life as her subject remembers it and in her "own words" as much as possible, assuring the reader of its authenticity.[83] The book is divided into four sections that follow the biographical turning points of Martinez's life and also highlight specific themes, such as the importance of community in San Ildefonso Pueblo, the severity of Julian's alcoholism, the economic success of Maria and Julian's pottery, and finally, its beneficial effects on the entire Pueblo.

The book opens with Maria Martinez's early memories of being a good trader in the mid-1880s, at the age of five. Her mother often made cheese, and sometimes, instead of selling it as her mother instructed, Maria bartered with people in the pueblo to exchange it for other goods. "You are a good trader," her mother responded approvingly. With this exchange between mother and daughter, Marriott tells the reader that Pueblo children "definitely strived to learn and please their elders. They quickly became aware of the contributions they should make. The good opinion of the group was a potent motivating force and an effective instrument of social control."[84] This assessment of the process by which San Ildefonso adults socialized their children may be accurate, but as Deborah Gordon reminds us, it also reflects Marriott's postwar concerns regarding the nuclear family and its impulse to turn inward rather than embrace the larger community.[85]

The third and longest section of the book, "The Bowl Is Fired," discusses Maria and Julian's distinctive pottery-making process, black-on-black pottery, and the dramatic sales that followed. The black-on-black-ware began as a mistake during a firing sometime around 1919. Before this, the couple had been making redware and buffware. Julian, who fired and decorated Maria's pots, put too much manure on the fire, thereby turning all the pots black. Consequently, these early pieces featured a shiny black design on a matte black surface. The disappointed couple stored these "ruined" pots away, but a Santa Fe trader saw them and requested more pieces for his shop. He took all the black-on-black pots and marketed them as special items. When tourists fancied these unique wares, the trader quickly requested more. This style became known as San Ildefonso black-on-blackware—a shiny black surface with a matte black design—the inverse of the earlier attempt. The firing mistake produced a profitable product as people flocked to Santa Fe and San Ildefonso to purchase the pottery. Around 1923, Santa Fe traders persuaded Maria Martinez to sign her pottery, driven by market demand to identify the pottery with a specific artist. Breaking with tradition, she became the first Pueblo artist to do so.[86]

With the growing popularity of San Ildefonso pottery came not only greater prosperity for the pueblo's residents but also increasing contact with the attractions of modern life. Although Marriott resisted the romantic notion that "all was sweetness and light in San Ildefonso before the highway was built and there were cars, and tourists could come and go in the village at will and random," nonetheless she blamed the outside world for the vices that threatened to tear apart community life.[87] She spent little time in *Maria* discussing those evils, however, since she holds readers largely within the walls of the pueblo and takes them only on short excursions to world's fairs or the Museum of New Mexico in Santa Fe. To gain a broader perspective regarding the impact of modern incursions on San Ildefonso during the 1940s, one must read *Greener Fields*, where Marriott explains how Los Alamos and the development of the atomic bomb dramatically altered the people and the local environment.

Prior to the success of pottery, for example, most San Ildefonso men worked in the outside world as day laborers for archaeologists or the railroad crews, and many succumbed to the temptations of alcohol. In the case of Julian Martinez, alcohol ultimately destroyed him. The issue of his drinking has been a source of varying interpretations among scholars. Marriott links his drinking to the internal political dissension within San Ildefonso as well as the jobs he took with Anglos that sent him away from his family for long periods. Several times Maria joined her husband, as in the three years they spent together at the Museum of New Mexico performing janitorial duties and selling pottery, believing that her presence helped to curb his drinking. Barbara Babcock and Edwin Wade support Marriott's position that one of Maria's primary concerns was Julian's alcoholism, but they link the alcoholism of men like Julian to the economic success that women potters enjoyed, which subverted traditional gender roles.[88] Their argument offers a more critical evaluation of the effects of pottery revival in San Ildefonso than either Marriott or Maria was willing to give.

Julian's drinking, however, had begun before the couple experienced success as artists. Well known as a painter in his own right, Julian was instrumental in his wife's "image maintenance" and fame—promoting her pottery at world's fairs and selling it in the salesroom of their home. Still, having a strong role entirely his own might have helped him, for Maria maintains that he stopped drinking in his mid-fifties during his term as governor of San Ildefonso. Significantly, Julian resumed his alcohol abuse soon after his term ended. For a time, Maria tried to keep him occupied with decorating and firing pottery, but his addiction took him from his family for the last time. In 1943, at the age of fifty-eight, he was found dead on a nearby hill. *Maria* ends with Julian's death. Discussing his alcoholism and World War II in the same breath, Marriott concludes: "The world was sick and Julián was sick. There was no cure for either of them."[89]

The central unresolved issue in *Maria* arises not from the restrictions under which Marriott worked, the assumptions she brought to her research, or even her failure to confront all the possible consequences that economic success had on Julian and Maria Martinez and San Ildefonso, but rather from Marriott's desire to privilege community concerns over the individual while singling out one person in her story. By identifying Maria Martinez, the individual, as "the" famous potter, she is, in fact, placing the emphasis on the individual. Marriott claims that Martinez "does not regard herself as an exception to the general rule" of the community and that her life has been "the normal life of a woman of her culture" as much as possible.[90] Marriott also argues that Martinez "did not like being, even a little, different from the other women of her town."[91] These claims are difficult to reconcile with Martinez's well-recorded life. She was different: she was a guest at the White House several times, traveled extensively, and worked as a pottery demonstrator at several world's fairs between 1904 and 1939. She was the first in her community to own a car or purchase a sewing machine and a special stove. The idea that she was somehow representative of her culture flies in the face of this evidence. Was this Marriott's interpretation of Maria Martinez, or Martinez telling her own story, or both?

Ruth Underhill pondered these questions in her review of *Maria*. She wondered, for example, if Marriott had withheld negative information about the full character of the communalism of Pueblo life. "Recent investigators have brought out the fact that the neighborliness of the pueblos has its obverse side, often shown in virulent gossip and accusations of witchcraft," Underhill maintained. "No breath of such a thing appears in Maria's story. Was this ugly side suppressed, along with the mention of ceremony?"[92] She also questioned the lack of more personal or intimate details in Marriott's account. "Maria's sex," Underhill observed, "seems as deeply and painlessly suppressed as that of any Victorian lady. Is this the result of childhood training, or an unusual character, or of an adult decision in talking to a white woman? As such questions present themselves, we become avid for more biographies of Indian women."[93] Evaluating *Maria* alongside Marriott's field notes offers some clues to contributions and alterations made by recorder and collaborator. In many instances, Marriott's interpretation is dominant because in the field notes Martinez does talk about her skill and makes some modest self-celebratory claims. To her credit, however, Marriott stayed true to her field notes for the most part, describing events as Martinez described them.

Today, if you visit the San Ildefonso Pueblo visitors' center, you will find Marriott's *Maria* placed on a prominent shelf behind glass. It is not for sale, though the employees of the visitors' center maintain that visitors would like to purchase it. No other books on Maria Martinez are displayed there. Marriott's book on Maria and her Kiowa book, *The Ten Grandmothers*, preserve the memory and stories of tribal members, which was her goal. Marriott also wanted to broaden her reach as a public intellectual by writing readable stories for the communities she worked with as well as a general audience. Following the publication of *The Ten Grandmothers* and *Maria*, she continued to write numerous books for adults and children on American Indian topics.

In 1983 Marriott was an honored speaker at the dedication of the Kiowa Cultural Center in Anadarko, where her fieldwork had begun more than five decades earlier. The Kiowas were dedicating the center to the "old people who were dead but not forgotten," Marriott explained in her formal remarks.[94] She reminded her audience that the cultural center would encourage future generations of Kiowas to "learn what the old people tried to teach, and wanted to have known."[95] She viewed her presence in the Kiowa community as that of a lifelong collaborator, as one who was always welcome to return and participate in community events. When she died in Oklahoma City in 1992, she left behind a legacy of over twenty books and even more articles and short stories.

Examining Alice Marriott's two most significant texts—*The Ten Grandmothers* and *Maria*—in tandem helps us begin to understand the life of a woman anthropologist during the 1930s and 1940s. Marriott and many other women anthropologists in the Southwest during this era carved out new spaces for themselves in terms of private life, career, and writing for the public first rather than academic circles. While many academic anthropologists during the time rejected narrative ethnography as unscholarly and feminine, Marriott and other women anthropologists used it to provide the reader with a front-row seat from which to view their lives as anthropologists and their roles as participant observers in American Indian communities. Like many of her peers, Marriott reached audiences with her engaging narratives, inviting them to learn more about Native communities, especially the lives of American Indian women.

Notes

1. Alice Marriott, *Greener Fields: Experiences among the American Indians* (New York: Thomas Y. Crowell, 1953), 84. Portions of this essay appear in a more detailed examination of Alice Marriott in Patricia Loughlin, *Hidden Treasures of the American West: Muriel H. Wright, Angie Debo, and Alice Marriott* (Albuquerque: University of New Mexico Press, 2005).

2. Barbara Tedlock, "From Participant Observation to the Observation of Participation: The Emergence of Narrative Ethnography," *Journal of Anthropological Research* 47 (Spring 1991): 74–78; Ruth Behar and Deborah A. Gordon, eds., *Women Writing Culture* (Berkeley: University of California Press, 1995); Gladys Reichard, *Spider Woman: A Story of Navajo Weavers and Chanters* (New York: Macmillan, 1934); Ruth M. Underhill, *The Autobiography of a Papago Woman*, Memoirs of the American Anthropological Association no. 46 (Menasha WI: American Anthropological Association, 1936); Ruth Landes, *The Ojibwa Woman* (New York: Columbia University Press, 1938); Sally Cole, *Ruth Landes: A Life in Anthropology* (Lincoln: University of Nebraska Press, 2003).

3. The Five Southern Tribes were originally located in the southeastern United States. During the 1830s the federal government forcibly removed them to Indian Territory, located in present-day Oklahoma.

4. Alice Marriott, interview by Jennifer Fox for the Daughters of the Desert Oral History Project, March 13, 1986, Tucson, Arizona, audio recording, tape 1, side 1, Wenner-Gren Foundation for Anthropological Research, New York, New York; Theodora Kroeber, *Alfred Kroeber: A Personal Configuration* (Berkeley: University of California Press, 1970), 164. For graduate work in anthropology,

Marriott would have had to attend the University of Chicago, the University of California at Berkeley, or Columbia University, and traveling such a distance for school was not an economic option for her during the depression.

5. Alice Marriott to Miss E. Petty, August 12, 1937, folder 4, box 18, Alice Lee Marriott Collection, Western History Collections, University of Oklahoma, Norman [hereafter cited as AMC].

6. Marriott, *Greener Fields*, 79.

7. Alice Marriott, *The Ten Grandmothers* (Norman: University of Oklahoma Press, 1945).

8. Marriott, *Greener Fields*, 102.

9. Marriott interview, tape 1, side 2.

10. Marriott interview, tape 1, side 2.

11. Wilbur Sturtevant Nye, *Bad Medicine and Good: Tales of the Kiowas* (Norman: University of Oklahoma Press, 1962), xix. The Bureau of Ethnology became the Bureau of American Ethnology in 1894.

12. Wilbur Sturtevant Nye, *Carbine and Lance: The Story of Old Fort Sill* (1937; reprint, Norman: University of Oklahoma Press, 1969).

13. Claribel F. Dick, *The Song Goes On: The Story of Ioleta Hunt McElhaney* (Philadelphia: Judson Press, 1959), 22–23, 29, 53. See also Clyde Ellis, *To Change Them Forever: Indian Education at the Rainy Mountain Boarding School, 1893–1920* (Norman: University of Oklahoma Press, 1996).

14. Marriott, *Greener Fields*, 65.

15. Marriott, *Greener Fields*, 65.

16. Marriott interview, tape 1, side 1.

17. Murray B. Emeneau, "Franz Boas as a Linguist," *American Anthropologist* Memoir Series 45 (July–September 1943): 35–38; Gladys A. Reichard, "Franz Boas and Folklore," *American Anthropologist* Memoir Series 45 (July–September 1943): 52–57.

18. Marriott interview, tape 1, side 1.

19. Ioleta Hunt McElhaney, interview by B. D. Timmons, March 3, 1968, T-198–1, Doris Duke Oral History Collection, Western History Collections.

20. Marriott interview, tape 1, side 1.

21. Marriott, *Ten Grandmothers*, xi.

22. Marriott interview, tape 1, side 1.

23. Although Marriott principally researched and wrote about American Indian women, she often used the masculine pronoun "he" when making

general statements. I find this typical of her time and do not read additional meaning into it.

24. Marriott, *Ten Grandmothers*, xi.

25. Louise Lamphere, "Gladys Reichard among the Navajo," in *Hidden Scholars: Woman Anthropologists and the Native American Southwest*, ed. Nancy J. Parezo (Albuquerque: University of New Mexico Press, 1993), 159–60.

26. Marriott interview, tape 1, side 1.

27. James Mooney, *Calendar History of the Kiowa Indians*, Seventeenth Annual Report of the Bureau of American Ethnology, pt. 2 (Washington DC: Government Printing Office, 1898); L. G. Moses, *The Indian Man: A Biography of James Mooney* (1984; reprint, Lincoln: University of Nebraska Press, 2002), 100.

28. Marriott, *Ten Grandmothers*, x.

29. Marriott, *Ten Grandmothers*, 142.

30. Marriott, *Ten Grandmothers*, 220.

31. Marriott, *Ten Grandmothers*, 221

32. Alice [Marriott] to Darlings, July 13, [1936], folder 4, box 20, AMC.

33. Alice [Marriott] to Darlings, July 13, [1936]; Paul Radin, *The Autobiography of a Winnebago Indian*, University of California Publications in American Archaeology and Ethnology, vol. 16, no. 7 (Berkeley: University of California Press, 1920); Paul Radin, *Crashing Thunder: The Autobiography of an American Indian* (New York and London: D. Appleton, 1926); Leslie Spier, *Yuman Tribes of the Gila River* (Chicago: University of Illinois Press, 1933); Underhill, *Papago Woman* (1936); Landes, *Ojibwa Woman* (1938).

34. Alice [Marriott] to Darlings, July 13, [1936].

35. Newspaper clipping, n.d., folder 9, box 32, AMC

36. Marriott, *Ten Grandmothers*, 239.

37. Marriott, *Ten Grandmothers*, 244.

38. Marriott, *Ten Grandmothers*, 240.

39. Marriott, *Ten Grandmothers*, 246.

40. Marriott, *Ten Grandmothers*, 246.

41. Luke E. Lassiter, *The Power of Kiowa Song: A Collaborative Ethnography* (Tucson: University of Arizona Press, 1998), 13.

42. Forrest [Clements] to Alice [Marriott], January 28, 1943, folder 3, box 22, AMC.

43. Louis [McElhaney] to Alice [Marriott], March 7, 1945, folder 3, box 22, AMC.

44. Ernest Wallace, review of *The Ten Grandmothers*, by Alice Marriott, *Southwestern Sciences Quarterly* 26 (June 1945): 99–100.

45. Debo to Marriott, December 16, 1946, folder 9, box 32, AMC.

46. Susan Labry Meyn, *More Than Curiosities: A Grassroots History of the Indian Arts and Crafts Board and Its Precursors, 1920 to 1942* (Lanham MD: Lexington Books, 2001), 83. See also Robert Fay Schrader, *The Indian Arts and Crafts Board: An Aspect of New Deal Indian Policy* (Albuquerque: University of New Mexico Press, 1983).

47. Alice Marriott, Specialist in Indian Arts and Crafts, to Miss Conroy, [n.d., 1942?], folder 5, box 18, AMC.

48. Meyn, *More Than Curiosities*, 194.

49. Alice Marriott to Miss E. Petty, Indian Arts and Crafts Board, Washington DC, August 12, 1937, folder 4, box 18, AMC.

50. Helen Carr, *Inventing the American Primitive: Politics, Gender and the Representation of Native American Literary Traditions, 1789–1936* (New York: New York University Press, 1996), 203.

51. Meyn, *More Than Curiosities*, 174.

52. *Official Guidebook*, Golden Gate International Exposition World's Fair on San Francisco Bay (San Francisco: The Crocker Company, 1939), 72, folder 5, box 17, AMC.

53. Marriott, *Greener Fields*, 184–85.

54. Meyn, *More Than Curiosities*, 123.

55. "Alice Marriott—Case History," 1, [n.d.], folder 23, box 78, AMC; Alice Marriott to Miss Morrow, November 16, 1939, folder 3, box 22, AMC; Meyn, *More Than Curiosities*, 145.

56. Marriott, *Greener Fields*, 187.

57. Marriott interview, tape 2, side 1.

58. Marriott interview, tape 1, side 2.

59. Alice [Marriott] to Darlings, March 28, 1947, folder 2, box 21, AMC.

60. Marriott, *Greener Fields*, 10.

61. William Leach, *Land of Desire: Merchants, Power and the Rise of a New American Culture* (New York: Pantheon Books, 1993), 202–3; George Stocking, "The Ethnographic Sensibility of the 1920s and the Dualism of the Anthropological Tradition," in *Romantic Motives: Essays on Anthropological Sensibility*, ed. George W. Stocking Jr. (Madison: University of Wisconsin Press, 1989), 208–76.

62. Leah Dilworth, *Imagining Indians in the Southwest: Persistent Visions of a Primitive Past* (Washington DC: Smithsonian Institution Press, 1996).

63. Nancy J. Parezo, "Conclusion: The Beginning of the Quest," in Parezo, *Hidden Scholars*, 356.

64. Parezo, "Conclusion," 356.

65. Deborah A. Gordon, "Among Women: Gender and Ethnographic Authority of the Southwest, 1930–1980," in Parezo, *Hidden Scholars*, 130.

66. Dilworth, *Imagining Indians in the Southwest*, 171.

67. Marriott interview, tape 1, side 2.

68. [Kenneth Chapman] to Dionicio Sanchez, Governor, San Ildefonso Pueblo, February 5, 1946, folder 1, box 48, AMC.

69. Marriott, *Greener Fields*, 236.

70. Terry R. Reynolds, "Maria Montoya Martinez: Crafting a Life, Transforming a Community," in *Sisters: Native American Women's Lives*, ed. Theda Perdue (New York: Oxford University Press, 2001), 160–63.

71. Alice Marriott, *Maria: The Potter of San Ildefonso* (Norman: University of Oklahoma Press, 1948), xiii.

72. Marriott, *Maria*, xix.

73. Marriott, *Maria*, xii.

74. Marriott, *Greener Fields*, 162.

75. Marriott, *Maria*, xiii.

76. Ruth Underhill, review of *Maria*, by Alice Marriott, *American Anthropologist* 50 (October–December 1948): 670.

77. [Kenneth Chapman] to Dionicio Sanchez, Governor, San Ildefonso Pueblo, February 5, 1946.

78. Marriott, *Greener Fields*, 233–34.

79. Marriott, *Greener Fields*, 234–35; Marriott interview, tape 1, side 2.

80. Marriott, *Greener Fields*, 234.

81. Lassiter, *Power of Kiowa Song*, 236.

82. Marriott interview, tape 1, side 2.

83. Marriott, *Maria*, xii.

84. Marriott, *Maria*, 19.

85. Gordon, "Among Women," 138–40.

86. Marriott, *Maria*, 195–202.

87. Marriott, *Maria*, xx.

88. Barbara A. Babcock, "Marketing Maria: The Tribal Artist in the Age of

Mechanical Reproduction," in *Looking High and Low: Art and Cultural Identity*, ed. Brenda Jo Bright and Liza Bakewell (Tucson: University of Arizona Press, 1995), 128; Edwin L. Wade, "Straddling the Cultural Fence: The Conflict for Ethnic Artists within Pueblo Societies," in *The Arts of the North American Indian: Native Tradition in Evolution*, ed. Edwin L. Wade (New York: Hudson Hills Press in association with the Philbrook Art Center, Tulsa, 1986), 243–54.

89. Marriott, *Maria*, 276.

90. Marriott, *Maria*, xi.

91. Marriott, *Greener Fields*, 235.

92. Underhill, review of *Maria*, 670.

93. Underhill, review of *Maria*, 670.

94. Marriott interview, tape 1, side 1.

95. Marriott interview, tape 1, side 1.

7

ELLA CARA DELORIA

Telling the Story of Her People

Maria Eugenia Cotera

The modern questor now takes up the search
His quest the same, his methods only changed.
He studies, records; carefully he weighs
Each point, for light upon his inquiry:
"Whence came his people? Whither are they going?
What struggle have they known? What victories?"
Out of his notes, he weaves an epic story.

—Ella Cara Deloria, *The Modern Questor*

IN HER PRESIDENTIAL ADDRESS given at the one hundredth meeting of the American Anthropological Association, in 2003, Louise Lamphere called for a reassessment of the "official history" of American anthropology. Citing a past tendency to view the development of anthropology in the United States as a succession of "great men," Lamphere suggested that in the light of anthropology's changing face—its turn to cultural critique, its current interest in reconceptualizing fieldwork, and its recognition and embrace of the perspectival nature of ethnographic writing—scholars revisit the past and explore historical figures at the margins of the anthropological establishment. Lamphere focused her attention on anthropologists who labored at the margins of the discipline and who—perhaps because of their marginal status—introduced key innovations "that have resonance with our contemporary preoccupations." Among these innovations Lamphere noted "four sources of creativity": first, the rise of "Native ethnography" and the transformation of fieldwork, in particular the objectivist norms at the heart of participant observation; second, the development of "ethno-

11. (*Opposite Top*) Ella Cara Deloria wearing Native Yankton Sioux dress. No date. *Courtesy of the Dakota Indian Foundation in Chamberlain SD.*

12. (*Opposite Bottom*) Ella Cara Deloria in mid-life. No date. *Courtesy of the Dakota Indian Foundation in Chamberlain SD.*

graphic writing" from the "standard ethnographic present to more dialogical forms"; third, the interest in anthropology as a site of cultural critique; and fourth, the emergence of anthropologists as "public intellectuals" who artfully combine activism with their scholarly work.[1]

In her considerable contributions to the discipline, Dakota anthropologist Ella Cara Deloria quietly traversed all of these categories: she simultaneously embraced and transformed the still-evolving fieldwork methodologies of the 1920s and 1930s; she developed an ethnographic writing style that evoked the intersubjective and dialogic nature of the fieldwork experience; and she used her ethnographic research and writing as a forum for addressing the needs of indigenous peoples. At the heart of her interventions was not an argument with the anthropological establishment itself but rather a strategic plan to use the tools of anthropology (its emergent status as a forum for public debate and its credibility as a "science" of human nature and social relations) to tell the story of her people, the Dakotas.

That Deloria was even able to tell this story seems a minor miracle given the economic, social, and professional barriers that she and other Native intellectuals of her generation faced. But tell it she did, and in its telling she created a substantial body of ethnographic information that clarified major misconceptions about Plains Indian languages and cultures. I too wish to tell a story of survival, the story of Ella Cara Deloria's circuitous travels between the place she called "home" and the centers of metropolitan meaning-making about that place and the people who inhabited it. Not quite a tragedy, and somewhat less than a triumph, the story of Deloria's engagements with anthropology is one worth telling.

Native Speaker: Ella Cara Deloria among the Anthropologists

Ella Deloria was born on the Yankton Sioux Reservation in the middle of a driving snowstorm in January 1888. The blizzard that accompanied her birth was portentous. The winter of 1890 would bring not only another bitter storm but also the final, devastating blow to Sioux armed resistance against U.S. intrusion into their territories—the Massacre at Wounded Knee. The decades following would lead to dramatic

and painful changes in Sioux lifeways. As a child, Ella Deloria was witness to these heartbreaking transformations, and she made it her life's
work to intervene against the "storm" of colonialism by documenting
Dakota culture both before and after Wounded Knee.

In some ways, Deloria was destined for leadership among her people. She was descended from a long line of leaders among the Yankton band of the Dakotas: her paternal grandfather, Saswe, was a chief
among the Yankton and a medicine man widely recognized for both his
leadership and his supernatural powers. Her father, Philip J. Deloria,
was also a chief and a holy man, though his path took him to the Episcopal Church, where he rose to prominence as a priest and a spokesperson for his people. Although her mother, Mary Sully, was enrolled
as a Yankton, she was also connected through social kinship to the
Sans Arc band of the Lakotas and had a distinguished heritage in her
own right. Ella grew up at St. Elizabeth's Mission, near Wakpala, South
Dakota, where her father served as an Episcopal priest. After allotment
and the breakup of the *tiyospaye* (kinship-based tribal units), the mission became a social center, and as a child Ella became "acquainted
with many of the elders at Standing Rock and Yankton reservations
and learned firsthand from them the old Sioux ways."[2] Although her
parents stressed the need for Ella and her siblings to acquire the linguistic and social skills of Anglo-American culture, they also instilled
in their children a deep and abiding respect for the old ways. This dual
heritage would sustain Deloria as she made her way through the challenging landscapes of early-twentieth-century cultural politics.

Deloria attended school at the boarding school attached to her father's mission, and later at All Saint's Episcopal School in Sioux Falls,
South Dakota, where she took college preparatory courses from 1906
until her graduation in 1910. She began her university education at
Oberlin College in Ohio and later enrolled at Columbia University's
Teacher's College, where she met Franz Boas in the spring of 1915. Boas
desperately needed someone familiar with all three dialects of Dakota
to aid him in translating Lakota stories collected by George Bushotter
(a young Sioux educated at Hampton Institute in Virginia) under the
supervision of James Owen Dorsey, an anthropologist working for the
Bureau of American Ethnology in the late nineteenth century. During

the spring and summer of 1915, Deloria helped Boas and his students prepare a small portion of the Bushotter materials for publication. As she noted in a letter some years later, the money she received for her help was her first "real paycheck."[3]

Notwithstanding this early and positive exposure to the emerging discipline of anthropology, Deloria initially chose to apply her considerable talents to the field of education, taking a job at her alma mater, St. Elizabeth's, upon her graduation in 1915. She later worked as a national health education secretary for the YWCA, and in 1923 she took a job as a physical education instructor (for girls) at Haskell Institute in Kansas. At Haskell Deloria designed an innovative curriculum that combined physical activities and culturally relevant pageantry.

In April 1927, Boas renewed contact with Deloria. "I have thought of you very often," he wrote, "and wished to have a few weeks time to continue the little work that we did years ago. . . . I should enjoy very much working with you again for a little while. I am very anxious to get some good material on Dakota because what we have is not quite up to our modern scientific standards and I want your help."[4] That summer, Boas personally instructed Deloria in his method of phonetical transcription, leaving her a number of texts to translate. Deloria must have enjoyed the work, because by the end of the year she had decided to resign from her teaching position at Haskell to devote full time to her "Dakota work." As Raymond DeMallie notes, this was an intellectual collaboration founded on mutual respect: "For Ella Deloria, Franz Boas was a charismatic figure. She respected his integrity as well as his scholarship. . . . For Boas, Ella Deloria was the fulfillment of a long search to find a native speaker who could help him in his study of the Sioux language. With her command of Dakota, appreciation for scholarship, sharp intellect, and literary skills, she was the perfect collaborator."[5] Although Boas could be quite controlling with regard to her research, and, as he was with all of his female students, insensitive to the logistical difficulties she faced in her fieldwork, he gradually came to trust Deloria's personal and professional judgment.

By 1929 Boas had secured the funding to offer Deloria an appointment as "research specialist in Indian ethnology and linguistics" with the Department of Anthropology at Columbia University. For the next ten years Deloria worked for Boas and later Ruth Benedict in the Dakota field. During this period she generally divided her time between winters in New York and summers doing fieldwork in South Dakota. She was part of an emerging group of anthropologists, including Ruth Landes, Ruth Bunzel, and Margaret Mead, who spent increasing time on fieldwork. In addition to the linguistic research under Boas, Deloria received training in the emerging methodologies of fieldwork under the guidance of Ruth Benedict. Because she possessed not only the methodological and scientific training of an anthropologist but also an insider's knowledge of Dakota culture, Deloria was particularly well suited for the challenges of participant observation.

While Deloria's correspondence with both Boas and Benedict (who took over as her primary intellectual mentor after Boas died in 1942) in the 1930s and the 1940s reveals the degree of her involvement with the production of ethnographic knowledge about the Sioux, this involvement was not without its difficulties. Indeed, even as she agreed with many of the premises of Boasian anthropology, her relationships with Boas and later Benedict were by no means uncomplicated. Tensions often arose—especially with Boas—over Deloria's fieldwork methodologies. Boas was particularly nettled by her skeptical stance with regard to some of the nineteenth-century ethnological accounts of "Sioux"[6] mythology that he had assigned her to corroborate among her Dakota informants.[7]

Deloria also had trouble advancing professionally in the field. Possessing neither the financial resources nor the time to pursue a doctorate in anthropology, she found it difficult to secure sources of funding to support her independent research. While Boas and Benedict could always locate funding to support her research for their own linguistic and ethnographic projects, there is no evidence that they ever tried to help, or even encourage, Deloria to get a doctorate and become an independent anthropologist. This seems especially distressing because both Boas and Benedict had reputations for mentoring and finding financial support for other women interested in the field. Surely Boas could have arranged to fast-track her through the doctoral program at Columbia (as he had for Benedict some years before), especially since Deloria had more field experience than any of his other graduate students.

Benedict often arranged for scholarships for her favored graduate students. Could she not have found a way to enable this tremendously talented woman to acquire the credentials she so desperately needed for job security in the field? These questions must go unanswered, as neither Benedict nor Boas ever mentioned the possibility in their correspondence with Deloria. As for Deloria herself, she limited her commentary on the subject to a few rueful asides, made to Boas during the darkest days of her fieldwork, when both he and Benedict, faced with the tightening university budget during the depression era, could find no source of support to continue her research in the Dakotas.

Even though Deloria's lack of academic credentials undercut her status in the field of Plains anthropology, her collaborations with Boas and Benedict were certainly fruitful for the discipline. Deloria almost single-handedly collected all of the early-twentieth-century Dakota linguistic and ethnographic material currently housed in the American Philosophical Society's archive. These include some thirty boxes of ethnographic reports, linguistic data, and story transcriptions. Indeed, several scholars used Deloria's ethnographic and linguistic research among Dakota communities to advance their own careers in anthropology. Jeanette Mirsky wrote her article on the Dakotas in *Cooperation and Competition among Primitive Peoples* (1937) in consultation with Deloria, basing it almost entirely on Deloria's unpublished monograph. Ruth Bunzel (a classmate of Deloria's at Columbia) relied heavily on Deloria's unpublished ethnographic reports for "The Economic Organization of Primitive People" (1938).[8] Boas published several collaborative articles on Dakota linguistics with Deloria, and Benedict used some of Deloria's reports to think through her own comparative approach to culture and psychology.

Deloria's research was not confined to source material for her better-known colleagues. She also published her own work, texts that are recognized to this day as foundational in the study of Dakota language and culture. In 1929 she published "The Sundance of the Oglala Sioux" in the *Journal of American Folk-lore*, an article based on the ethnographic materials she had reviewed and translated for Boas, as well as some additional material she collected on her own. She followed this publication with *Dakota Texts*, a collection of her free translations of Teton-Dakota tales edited by Boas and published in 1932 by the American Ethnological Society. Her most enduring contribution to linguistics was *Dakota Grammar*, published in collaboration with Boas in 1941.[9] Although Boas and Benedict were generous with their time and expertise, apparently neither imagined that Deloria might become an anthropologist in her own right, an oversight that would limit her standing within the field. While her younger, less-experienced colleagues' careers were ascendant during this period, Deloria remained at the margins of the discipline, a "contract worker" for scholars who built their reputations on her research.

Kinship Ethnography: Ella Deloria's Decolonizing Methodology

Deloria's professional difficulties were due, in part, to her anomalous and somewhat contradictory position in early-twentieth-century anthropology. While Deloria had greater access to training in the theory and practices of anthropology and linguistics than Native informants of the nineteenth century (like George Hunt), she did not possess the credentials that would allow her to take full control of her ethnographic research. In short, she was neither a Native informant in the classic sense nor a fully accredited anthropologist. She was, instead, an "informed Native." Despite this in-between status—or perhaps because of it—early in her career, Deloria began to rethink some of the conceptual limitations and methodological norms that governed ethnographic practice in the 1920s and 1930s. Her methodological innovations and theoretical interventions are significant as they anticipate those of a generation of Native anthropologists who followed her into the field in the 1960s and 1970s. Because Deloria forced the discipline to confront some of its most cherished assumptions about participant observation and the role of the anthropologist in the ethnographic encounter, she represented a figure that was irreconcilable to the norms of anthropology as it became more bureaucratic and entrenched in male-dominated academia.

Deloria had always read the accounts of Dakota language and cultures produced by nineteenth-century ethnologists with a skeptical eye. Indeed, because she was raised in close proximity to traditional culture, she was quick to perceive the disconnect between overgeneralized ethnographic accounts of her people and her own experiences with Dakota culture. She attributed the misinformation that had passed as knowledge about the "Sioux" to Dakota reticence, and in particular their reluctance to share privileged information with individuals who were not Dakotas. As an anthropologist and a Dakota, Deloria understood that the kinship rules governing Dakota society drew stark divisions between relatives and outsiders. While it was permissible to share information about history, religion, and social organization with relatives, sharing such information with strangers was frowned upon. Deloria sensed that, unbeknownst to non-Indian ethnographers, these social strictures had determined the relations between Indian informants and non-Indian observers. Moreover, she suspected that the privileged informants who had provided information on the religious and cultural practices of the Dakotas to nineteenth-century ethnologists had either been intentionally misleading them or were themselves social outcasts.[10]

Deloria quickly realized that to be an effective recorder of tribal history and culture she had to abandon the objectivist norms guiding participant observation and devise a model of fieldwork that was more culturally appropriate to the social conventions of her community. Thus she crafted a methodology that embraced the rules of kinship and capitalized on her identity as a Dakota. Instead of approaching her informants as an "outsider," Deloria invoked the kinship system during her interviews, asserting her relatedness (as daughter, granddaughter, niece, sister, etc.) to respondents, and thus making the transmission of knowledge a "family affair."[11] This approach enabled her to circumvent Dakota reticence and negotiate the social strictures governing the transmission of information about Dakota life. For Deloria, then, kinship was not just a form of social organization; it was also an ethnographic practice—what one might call "kinship ethnography"—a neologism that captures both the practical aspects and political dimensions of her approach. By respecting the social conventions that governed the kinship relations between herself and the Dakota people she interviewed, Deloria was able to develop trusting and reciprocal relationships with them and gather ethnographic information generally withheld from outsiders. In so doing, she also made herself accountable to the people who shared their knowledge with her, something that was rarely a feature of the ethnographic encounter in the 1920s and 1930s.

On the other hand, Deloria negotiated her unavoidable outsider status among her people—as an unmarried woman and an educated and somewhat cosmopolitan figure among traditional Dakotas—by adopting the role of the "outsider within." According to Deloria, in Dakota society, unmarried women were suspect unless they were recognized "perpetual virgins"—women who, for higher purposes, had decided to forego marriage and dedicate themselves to other community-nurturing tasks, such as maintaining tribal artistic and storytelling traditions. As Dakota scholar Joyzelle Godfrey has noted, because perpetual virgins were not only "honored, but they were also considered repositories of tribal information," it was appropriate that they be recorders of tribal knowledge. Thus Deloria adopted this role not only to explain her unmarried status but also to situate herself as a "keeper of tradition" within the tribal communities she studied. Moreover, because the Dakotas frowned upon overt inquisitiveness, Deloria deployed her status as perpetual virgin to reframe her ethnographic inquiries in a socially acceptable way. Clearly, her status as perpetual virgin allowed her greater flexibility in her research, especially since the label gave her ethnographic inquiry a respectable cast.[12]

This was not simply a practical solution to the problems of fieldwork; it was a thoroughly developed theory of method. Throughout her correspondence with Boas and Benedict, Deloria cogently outlined her methodology and consistently argued for its appropriateness in the Dakota field. However, while both Boas and Benedict recognized the utility of her methods, their lingering doubts over Deloria's "objectivity"[13] often undercut her credibility as an ethnographer. Although he never clearly articulated his suspicions, Boas often implied in his letters to Deloria and to his colleagues that Deloria's research might be tainted by her personal prejudices. "While Boas valued the knowledge Deloria gained from her intimate connection to her informants," Janet Finn notes, "he presumed that as an objective researcher she [should] detach herself from the world she documented. . . . Deloria's correspondence with Boas posed an ongoing challenge to that belief."[14] Indeed, although Deloria's approach to fieldwork was effective, it unsettled the boundaries between insider and outsider that constituted the ground rules for participant observation. This naturally rattled Boas, who had modeled his vision of anthropology on the scientific method and thus had focused a good deal of energy on injecting more "objectivity" into the discipline.

Because of her perspective as a Dakota woman, Deloria's approach to fieldwork necessarily raised troubling questions about the nature of the ethnographic encounter. The decolonizing ethnographic methodology Deloria developed—her "kinship ethnography"—might thus be refigured as a critique of anthropology itself. By reframing the process of participant observation to take into account the relationship between observer and informant, and by pointing to the ways in which this relationship structured the ethnographic encounter, Deloria demonstrated, as Finn puts it, that "ethnographic truth was partial, perspectival, and embedded in social and material relations of power and obligation."[15] This sophisticated understanding of the intersubjective nature of fieldwork would return to trouble the waters as Deloria struggled to consolidate her copious ethnographic notes into a coherent monograph on Dakota social life.

Ruth Benedict, Ella Deloria, and Gendered Native Ethnographic Texts

Most of the published essays that address Deloria's collaborative ethnographic work—even those written by feminists—focus on her relationship with the father of modernist anthropology, Franz Boas. But it could be argued that Deloria's most refined ethnographic work emerged after Boas's death, under the tutelage of Ruth Benedict. Deloria's relationship with Benedict began in 1932 when Boas asked Benedict to design research plans for the ethnographic side of the linguistic investigations Deloria was carrying out for him. Although Deloria had a rocky start with Benedict, their relationship soon developed into a full-fledged and somewhat more equitable collaboration than the one Deloria had shared with Boas. Whereas Boas saw both Deloria and African American Zora Neale Hurston "more as 'native informants' than as scholars in their own right," Benedict, by contrast, granted Deloria more scholarly independence. Indeed, she helped Deloria produce her own ethnographic work, assiduously reading, editing, and promoting Deloria's ethnographic manuscripts.[16]

In fact, it was under Benedict's guidance that Deloria emerged as a Native ethnographic *writer*. More importantly, it was during their intense collaborative engagement that Deloria turned her keen ethnographic gaze to the lives of women in Dakota society.[17] As DeMallie notes, it was Benedict who first suggested that Deloria "work on the family and tribal structures, and examine kinship and the role of women, recording women's autobiographies as a source of insight."[18] While Deloria's early reports to Boas indicate that she had always included information from both male and female informants, it was under Benedict that she began to focus on women as interpreters of custom, preservers of tribal history and tradition, and educators within tribal communities.

By all accounts, the passage from ethnographic researcher to ethnographic writer was a difficult one for Deloria to navigate, primarily because she knew how much was at stake. Her training in anthropology had introduced her to a body of knowledge about the "Sioux," most of which was incorrect, and she was well aware of how this faulty information filtered into public policy and determined the lives of Indian peoples. Moreover, she had a vast collection of ethnographic notes to organize, some five hundred pages in total. Finally, she was deeply concerned about audience. To whom should she direct the monograph: anthropologists, government and church workers in the Indian field, the general public, or Indians themselves? Judging from her correspondence with Benedict during this period, Deloria began to have serious doubts about whether she could consolidate all of her knowledge about the Dakotas into a single manuscript that would satisfy her multiple audiences. She ultimately hit on a solution that seems unimaginable given the pressing economic (and time) constraints she faced: Deloria decided to write *three* books: an anthropological monograph titled "The Dakota Way of Life"; *Waterlily*, a novel documenting the experiences of three generations of Dakota women; and *Speaking of Indians*, an analysis of Dakota history and culture geared toward a general readership. For the next seven years—with help from a grant from the American Philosophical Society and the Missionary Education Movement of the National Council of Churches—Deloria labored on these three projects.

Only *Speaking of Indians* was published during her lifetime (in 1944; she died in 1971). Benedict worked with Deloria on "The Dakota Way of Life" and *Waterlily*, helping her to organize and edit both manuscripts. Unfortunately, Benedict's untimely death in 1948 deprived Deloria of the institutional leverage needed to push the manuscripts through to publication. Notwithstanding an enthusiastic letter of endorsement by Benedict's colleague Margaret Mead, "The Dakota Way of Life" ended up in the archives of the American Philosophical Society. *Waterlily* too languished in the files of the Oklahoma University Press, never to see publication during Deloria's lifetime.[19] While *Waterlily* has recently received some acclaim since its recovery and publication in 1988, "The Dakota Way of Life" remains ensconced in the archives of the Ella Cara Deloria Project in Chamberlain, South Dakota, a deeply unfortunate situation given its importance as a radically revisionary text in terms of both its ethnographic information and its style.

"The Dakota Way of Life" offers a unique picture of Dakota life drawn from more than a decade of research on five reservations: Pine Ridge, Rosebud, Lower Brule, Cheyenne River, and Standing Rock. While it conforms in some respects to the standards of ethnographic writing during the 1930s, it represents a radical departure from the schematized picture of "exotic others" that characterized ethnographic monographs of the period. Such modes of cultural description necessarily represented only partial views of complex cultures and were predicated on the ability of the "observer" to distance him-or herself from the "object of inquiry," something that, as an insider to Dakota culture, Deloria simply could not do. In a letter to friend Virginia Lightfoot Dorsey, who had provided both emotional and financial support during the writing process, Deloria speaks to the difficulties of "writing culture" from the inside:

> People who visit a country or a primitive race for a four or five-month field study are a lot better off than I. They get certain concrete facts and information and that is all they know, so it gets written down and finished fast enough. But with me it is different. I have been steeped in

Dakota lore and seen and felt it around me ever since childhood, it is in fact the very texture of my being. I can't just consult native informants, translate their contribution, and let it go at that. Almost always I know something in addition, or some more of the same thing not touched on by him. And I must include that, too.[20]

Indeed, by her own account, one of the most difficult aspects of writing an authoritative monograph on the Dakotas was establishing an authorial position from which to elaborate a text that would make sense to other anthropologists. Deloria had trouble conforming her vast knowledge of the Dakotas—based, on the one hand, on the ethnographic data she had "objectively" collected under Boas and Benedict, and on the other, on her "subjective" personal experience as a Dakota woman—to the rhetorical norms of a "classic" ethnographic text. In a letter to Benedict in February 1947, as she was finishing "The Dakota Way of Life," Deloria complained that she could not write in a "detached, professional manner": "I try to keep out of it, but I am too much in it, and I know too many angles. If the outsider investigator is like a naturalist watching ants, and reporting what he *sees*, and draws conclusions from that, I am one of the ants! I know what the fight is about, what all the other little ants are saying under their breath! I did think it would be such a cinch!"[21] Clearly, Deloria believed that in order to describe the internal dynamics of Dakota culture in an objective manner she had to adopt the distanced observational stance of an "outsider." However, she found it nearly impossible to adopt this "outsider" stance from the very beginning of her career as an anthropologist, because she had conducted her research among her people from the perspective of a cultural "insider." When the time came to write her authoritative account of Dakota culture, Deloria faced a frustrating contradiction. While she was more effectively placed to speak authoritatively about Dakota social norms than an "outside investigator" because of her familial, political, and social alliances to Dakota people, she simply could not assume the objective and distanced stance that would lend ethnographic authority to her text.

Deloria resolved these contradictions by self-consciously positioning herself within the text as a "mouthpiece" for the Dakota people. In her introduction to "The Dakota Way of Life" she states directly and without apology that her textual description of the Dakotas will represent a departure from the narrative norms of conventional ethnographies:

> For one speaking out of the culture, the position of an outside investigator observing an alien, primitive society with cool detachment, did not seem altogether becoming or desirable. Such a pose might not be impossible to assume, and sustain all the way, though perhaps only with considerable artifice. But since the struggle to remain consistently objective would be too preoccupying, whereas my real duty was to make my material available somehow or other, I chose the less exalted role of plain mouthpiece for the many who gave it to me, with such care for accuracy; and have tried to pass it along with the same care.[22]

This reversal of the ethnographer's conventional claim to authority—from "objective" outsider to "subjective" insider—transforms the ethnographic text in significant ways.

One of the most striking ways in which Deloria subverts the narrative conventions of the ethnographic text is found in her refusal to reduce the complex discursive situations of her fieldwork experiences in the interests of creating an authoritative account of the Dakotas. Cultural anthropologist James Clifford has noted that ethnographic writers of the classic period typically erased the messy polyphonic and dialogic realities of fieldwork in order to create a unified and "coherent" picture of "a people." Individual interlocutors—and, indeed, the very dialogic conditions of participant observation—were erased in place of narratives that posited a single "author" (individual informants are replaced, e.g., by the "the Sioux," "the Trobrianders," "the Nuer," etc.) and an integrated portrait of a distinct, isolated "Society."[23] Deloria deliberately resists such textual practices by stating in the first sentence of her introduction: "This writing is about the Dakota-speaking Indians of the Plains and all its material comes directly from them." Here and throughout the monograph, Deloria redistributes the authoritative power of the ethnographer among her interlocutors, granting them the agency to interpret their own social conditions. By placing herself at the center of the ethnographic text *among* the people she interviewed (many of whom were actual family members), Deloria simultaneously rejects the discursive erasure to which Clifford refers and transfers ethnographic authority from the anthropological community to the Dakota community. In a key reversal of ethnographic narrative conventions, "The Dakota Way of Life" allows Dakota people themselves to speak—through Deloria, the Native "mouthpiece"—as the "experts" on Dakota social life. In this manner, "The Dakota Way of Life" engages in a "defamiliarization of ethnography authority" that shares many of the innovative strategies of contemporary experimental ethnographies. Deloria's monograph is thus closely related to contemporary ethnographic texts that "conceive of ethnography not as the experience and interpretation of a circumscribed 'other' reality, but rather as a constructive negotiation involving at least two, and usually more, conscious, politically significant subjects."[24]

Deloria's rejection of anthropology's monologic and depersonalizing narrative practices moves beyond simply figuring "the native" as a key interpreter of "his" own reality. Perhaps the most interesting subversive act in "The Dakota Way of Life" involves the equal weight Deloria gives the voices of men and women in her polyphonic picture of Dakota social life. By recognizing women as conscious, politically significant subjects in Dakota society, Deloria subtly undermines the masculinist[25] bent of ethnographic representations that had focused on male informants and typically represented gender relations among the Dakotas as unequal in the best cases and brutal in the worst. Indeed, Deloria acknowledges in her letters to Benedict that her study defies the norms of ethnographic texts on the "Sioux" because it does not focus solely on men's activities. When Deloria submitted her monograph to the American Philosophical Society for final review, she worried that they would not consider it a truly comprehensive study of Dakotas because it did not include "male ceremonials" and war stories. Reminding Benedict that her stated purpose had been a study of Dakota family life (the domain of women in "traditional" Dakota culture), Deloria wondered nonetheless whether she ought to include more information on typically male activities. "But don't ask me to do anything on war, particularly. Religion, yes; ceremonial, yes. War—no! Anyway all the things that men have written have pointed war up so much, that if I omitted it, as a topic I mean, I think it would be missed. I talk mostly with women, you see. What I have gathered about war has been largely as an eavesdropper."[26]

Thus Deloria's ethnographic intervention also addresses what Chandra Mohanty has identified as one "of the major questions [of] feminist anthropology"—the politics of representation. If the "nature of anthropology during the colonial rule" has taken on a "fundamentally gendered and racial nature," then how does the feminist anthropologist go about "representing third world women in anthropological texts (as a corrective to masculinist disciplinary practices)" without replicating the erasure of third-world women so typical in anthropological discourse?[27] Deloria offers an interesting solution to the problems of representation that Mohanty outlines. By interweaving narrative accounts of the discursive situations of her fieldwork among Dakota women into her authoritative text, Deloria allows these women to speak through her. A most striking example is found in the way she describes a chance conversation with an elderly couple, Mr. and Mrs. Brown Elk:

After a long married life they were in their latter years. Mr. Brown Elk was a friendly, genial, soft-spoken man with a rare sense of humor. Long since, he had worked out a philosophy for living with his wife, who, though well meaning and likable—and as hospitable to his guests as he could wish—had the habit of snatching nearly every subject out of his mouth. And when she did so, he let her have it, and settled back to relax. Seeming not to hear, he sat with eyes shut and a hint of a smile around his mouth while puffing leisurely on a long-stemmed pipe; as if to say, "There she goes again . . . and it is all right."

Only rarely he teased her by boasting of his good luck in not having to do more than select and introduce a subject. There his responsibility ended, for she at once bit into it and shook it to shreds and did not let go until she had it completely exhausted. He would say this in the presence of his brothers or male cousins because they were his wife's joking relatives. "It must be great to have so capable a wife," they would comment, "for it releases you for more important things—like smoking and meditating and taking your ease." Mrs. Brown Elk appeared neither to hear what he said nor to react to the good-natured "ribbing" of those joking relatives; and there was no effect whatsoever on so fixed a habit. . . .

When there were men guests who sat with him in the honor place beyond the fire, he talked entertainingly and with more freedom because women did not properly interrupt such conversation. Nevertheless, from her own space near the entrance way, Mrs. Brown Elk kept up a steady stream which I might liken to a running commentary down the margin of the printed page. From long and close association both knew the same facts and stories so that she did not need to correct a detail or ask a question about the subject of the moment. It was her interpretation and opinion—the "woman's angle"—that she volunteered, in an endless muttered accompaniment; just loud enough to excite interest in her version too. One was hard put to follow both "text" and "commentary" at once, though one tried. But despite this habit, which the old man was used to, as one grows used to a periodic noise until it no longer exists, the Brown Elks were a happy and congenial couple.[28]

Deloria's keen sense for the subtleties of Dakota humor and, as Margaret Mead referred to it, her "literary abilities, unfortunately only too rare among ethnographers," works to render a scene that captures the artful use of language among the Dakotas even as it offers an undeniably touching picture of the necessary negotiations of married life.[29] The scene also seems to suggest a metaphor for the practice of feminist ethnography. Mrs. Brown Elk's "commentary"—"the woman's angle"—running alongside her husband's "text" would surely be excised from a masculinist anthropological account of the scene. In Deloria's text it openly competes for attention, and inevitably receives it. In fact, Mrs. Brown Elk may even be figured as feminist anthropologist in her own right, "snatching the words" from her husband's mouth, sitting alongside him and offering her own "interpretation" of his text.

Deloria's evident admiration for Mrs. Brown Elk's insistence that her "commentary" on her husband's "text" be heard reveals much about Deloria's own complicated relationship with Boasian anthropology. Deloria clearly believed that anthropology might offer an effective tool for correcting misconceptions about Indian life that had led to ill-advised solutions to the "Indian problem." Nevertheless, she found it nearly impossible to conform to the norms of research and writing that granted anthropologists an authoritative voice in public discourse. In "The Dakota Way of Life" this difficulty is most evident. Indeed, Deloria violates almost every ethnographic code of the classic monograph: she refuses key rhetorical strategies for claiming ethnographic authority over her subjects, includes "ways of knowing that are conventionally placed on the margins of the fieldwork narrative," and rejects abstractions and generalizations about Dakota culture by allowing multiple perspectives to emerge in the voices of her male and female informants.[30] This repudiation of the norms of ethnographic writing signaled Deloria's growing sense that an "authoritative" ethnographic account of the Dakotas could not possibly tell the whole story of her people.

Her frustration with the impersonal "objective" authorial voice of the standard ethnographic text was, no doubt, one of the reasons why Deloria felt the need to explore a variety of textual formats to bring her intimate knowledge of Dakota life to the public during this period. These texts incorporate elements of ethnographic detail within rhetorical and aesthetic forms that enable her to circumvent the ethnographic strictures that limited her expression. In *Speaking of Indians* we see her vast ethnographic knowledge of the everyday lives of Dakota people—their stories, histories, and lived experiences under the reservation system—adapted to a public statement that has distinctly political valences. In her ethnographic novel, *Waterlily*, we find an aesthetic rewriting of ethnography that rejects the typifications and analytical/objective perspective employed to grant textual authority to "classic" ethnographic description. But *Waterlily*'s intervention moves beyond the ethnographic realm: by focusing on the intimacies of women's lives in Dakota culture, *Waterlily* fundamentally redirects anthropology's quest for knowledge about the "other." As Beatrice Medicine (Sioux) has noted, most anthropological and sociological research on Indians has "glossed gender differences and presented a monolithic view of the indigenous people. These approaches have successfully covered the rich variation of gender differences in socialization patterns and actualization and continuation of native lifestyles which have been a part of the adaptive strategies of native peoples."[31] Deloria, too, recognized that in focusing on male subjects, anthropologists had (perhaps unwittingly) erased a key survival tool for Indian people struggling for "actualization and continuation" against the ravages of colonialism. In *Waterlily*, Deloria brought her ethnographic research to life in order to bring the lives of Indian women to the very center of a re-imagined discourse on Indian survival. In effect, *Waterlily* allows Mrs. Brown Elk's voice to move from the margins of the ethnographic monograph to the very center of the literary text.

Ella Deloria and the Politics of Invisibility

It is a telling irony that Ella Deloria, the primary recorder of Plains Indian ethnographic and linguistic data of the 1930s, is absent from the pages of *Indians and Anthropologists*, a 1988 volume edited by anthropologists Thomas Biolsi and Larry J. Zimmerman. This irony veers harrowingly close to insult when one considers the fact that *Indians and Anthropologists* was inspired by *Custer Died for Your Sins*, Vine Deloria Jr.'s piercing and hilarious indictment of white "Anthros" in Indian Country. It is an especially poignant irony because Ella Deloria was Vine Deloria's aunt, and in her time she was, like him, a widely recognized spokesperson for Indian people. Her invisibility in the volume speaks to a long-held assumption about radical difference in the ethnographic encounter, namely, that it is the Western interlocutor who bridges the gap of difference by translating the utterances of "primitive" informants and revealing the inner workings of their language, culture, and social organization to a cosmopolitan audience.[32] While Biolsi and Zimmerman's introduction to *Indians and Anthropologists* rightly claims that such translations have real material effects on the communities they seek to scrutinize and takes anthropologists to task for not being more accountable to the communities that they study, it does not address how anthropology *changes* when "native informants" take up the tools of analysis to develop their own visions of the aims and purposes of the ethnographic enterprise. In his coda to the collection, Vine Deloria, clearly irritated by the contributors' lingering assumptions about "who studies" and "who is studied," states:

> Since the publication of *Custer* there has been no concerted effort by the academic community, or by anthros themselves, to open the ranks

of the discipline to American Indians. Anthropology departments still cling fiercely to the belief that it is more valid and scholarly to have an Anglo study an Indian tribe than to have a member of that tribe trained in Anthropology.

Beneath this view lie alarmingly distressing attitudes that have not been plumbed. The basic message is that Indians, even Indians who are trained in Anthropology, cannot be trusted to be objective, to be analytical or to understand what is happening in their own communities.[33]

He might well have used his own aunt, Ella Deloria, as an example of this concern. The story of her engagement with the field of anthropology is at times exhilarating, at times distressing, but always complicated. It is the story of an American Indian woman of considerable talents who took on an emerging discipline that is capable of transforming the way we think about race, culture, and society yet somehow incapable of rethinking its own assumptions about identity and the ethnographic encounter. It is also the story of an American Indian woman's quest to tell the story of her people, the Dakotas, and to be the kind of anthropologist that Vine Deloria would call for in the 1990s.

Notes

1. Louise Lamphere, "Unofficial Histories: A Vision of Anthropology from the Margins," *American Anthropologist* 106, no. 1 (2004): 126–27.

2. Vine Deloria Jr., introduction to *Speaking of Indians*, by Ella C. Deloria (1944; reprint, Lincoln: University of Nebraska Press, 1998), xi.

3. Ella Deloria to Miss Beckwith, November 11, 1926, Ella Cara Deloria Project, The Dakota Indian Foundation, Chamberlain, South Dakota [hereafter cited as ECDP].

4. Boas to Deloria, April 27, 1927, Franz Boas Papers, American Philosophical Society, Philadelphia.

5. Raymond J. DeMallie, afterword to *Waterlily*, by Ella C. Deloria (Lincoln: University of Nebraska Press, 1988), 234–35.

6. Quotation marks are used here because the term *Sioux* is not a term of the Native peoples but rather one imposed on them by outsiders. The descriptive term *Dakota* was used in the classification of Indian languages during

the early development of anthropology and linguistics in the United States. In this early ethnolinguistic paradigm, the word *Dakota* was employed to identify those tribes who spoke one of three dialects: Dakota (Santee), Lakota (Teton), and Nakota (Yankton). In keeping with the linguistic and ethnographic norms of her period, Deloria employed the term *Dakota* to identify the people among the Siouan linguistic family who spoke one of the Lakota/Nakota/Dakota dialects. Deloria used the general term *Sioux* when referring to the larger classification of the linguistic stock, which included twenty-seven other forms of the Siouan language.

7. Deloria and Boas disagreed vehemently over J. R. Walker's account of Dakota mythology. For more information on this disagreement see Maria Cotera, "Native Speakers: Locating Early Expressions of U.S. Third World Feminist Discourse: A Comparative Analysis of the Ethnographic and Literary Writing of Ella Cara Deloria and Jovita González" (PhD diss., Stanford University, 2001), 185–229.

8. Jeanette Mirsky, "The Dakota," in *Cooperation and Competition among Primitive Peoples*, ed. Margaret Mead (New York: McGraw-Hill, 1937), 382–427; Ruth Bunzel, "The Economic Organization of Primitive People," in *General Anthropology*, ed. Franz Boas (New York: D. C. Heath, 1938), 327–408.

9. Ella Deloria, "The Sundance of the Oglala Sioux," *Journal of American Folk-lore* 42 (October–December 1929): 354–413; Ella Deloria, *Dakota Texts*, Publications of the American Ethnological Society 14 (1932; Freeman SD: Pine Hill Press, 1972); Ella Deloria, *Dakota Grammar*, with Franz Boas (Washington DC: Government Printing Office, 1941).

10. Dakota scholar Joyzelle Godfrey corroborates this assertion: "Beyond the language barrier, and unknown to the non-Indian, the traditional culture forbade the sharing of information about the culture and especially the religion and religious practices with anyone outside the tribe." Obviously, Ella, as "Dakota by blood" and speaker of "the language from birth," and as a woman "raised in the traditional kinship system," fully understood "that the Kinship System was the law that governed all interpersonal relationships socially, legally, religiously and most importantly, morally." Lying to a kinsperson violated the law. Lying to outsiders, however, "was not only acceptable, but was expected of all good Dakota people." Godfrey notes that one sees the importance of this in the labels for people who sought and gave information. They include *Wawiyuge-s'a*, one who "questions boldly and as a habit," or the derogatory term, a

"regular questioner." *Woyake s'e* "freely tells secrets to outsiders" and should be "avoided by all other tribespeople including one's own relatives" and is a person to be "ostracized by the entire tribe." Finally, *Wasloslol-kiye ktehci*, a very derogatory term, refers to a person who is always "bent on knowing everything." That person is not entitled to the truth. Joyzelle Godfrey, "Ella Deloria Research Project," *Insight Newsletter, Dakota Indian Foundation* 17, no. 2 (1998): 1–2.

11. Joyzelle Godfrey, interview by Maria Cotera, August 26, 1999, Dakota Indian Foundation, Chamberlain, South Dakota.

12. Deloria refers to herself as a "perpetual virgin" in a May 20, 1941, letter to Ruth Benedict. Ruth Benedict Papers, Vassar College. In an interview with the author, Godfrey corroborated Deloria's claim that she was recognized as a perpetual virgin among the Teton-Dakotas. Godfrey interview, August 26, 1999.

13. Quotation marks are placed around the words *objective* and *objectivity* because anthropologists in this era saw themselves as objective outsiders. Because of that outsider status they believed that they brought a non-biased view to their ethnography—that is, one that is unaffected by kinship, familiar, or social obligations in the society or individual. As this chapter explains, Boas and other "masculinist" scholars brought a number of unexamined and unquestioned biases to their ethnographical work, biases that many women later challenged especially as they began to record cultural differences based on gender.

14. Janet L. Finn, "Ella Cara Deloria and Mourning Dove: Writing for Cultures, Writing against the Grain," in *Women Writing Culture*, ed. Ruth Behar and Deborah A. Gordon (Berkeley: University of California Press, 1995), 138.

15. Finn, "Ella Cara Deloria and Mourning Dove," 140.

16. Ruth Behar, "Introduction: Out of Exile," in Behar and Gordon, *Women Writing Culture*, 18.

17. Benedict encouraged other women anthropologists to explore the central role of Native women in the production and continuation of tribal culture, including Deloria's accredited colleagues Ruth Landes and Ruth Underhill. In 1933 she wrote a foreword to Underhill's ethnographic life history, *The Autobiography of a Papago Woman* (1933), in which she celebrated Underhill's ability to render ethnographic knowledge from the "from the lips of an old woman," a "friend" and "confidante," and noted that such information revealed more about how Native men and women "live and die and pursue their goals" than the more "businesslike" accounts of cultures so typical in standard mono-

graphs. Benedict's enthusiastic support for the ethnographic life history may well have enabled women ethnographers like Landes, Underhill, and Deloria to focus their methodological and theoretical labors on the lives of women in the communities they studied. Ruth Benedict, foreword to *The Autobiography of a Papago Woman* (1933), in Ruth Underhill, *Papago Woman* (Prospect Heights IL: Waveland Press, 1985), vii.

18. DeMallie, afterword, 236.

19. Deloria mentions *Waterlily*'s fate in a November 23, 1952, letter to her friend Virginia Lightfoot Dorsey, ECDP.

20. Deloria to Dorsey, August 8, 1949, ECDP.

21. Deloria to Benedict, February 13, 1947, Benedict Papers.

22. Deloria, "The Dakota Way of Life," 17–18, manuscript, ECDP.

23. James Clifford, *The Predicament of Culture* (Cambridge: Harvard University Press, 1988), 40.

24. Clifford, *The Predicament of Culture*, 41.

25. I use the term *masculinist* rather than *sexist* or even *patriarchal* to define the ethos that suffused Boasian modes of ethnographic inquiry, because unlike other terms it points to the *discursive* marginalization of feminist anthropology. In other words, while the Boasian milieu did incorporate and even encourage women anthropologists' involvement in the development of its theoretical perspectives and methodological innovations (and thus, in the strictest sense, was not overtly "sexist"), the discipline was nevertheless founded on an assumption that anthropology was, in the end, a conversation between men about other "primitive" men. The "masculinist" bias of early-twentieth-century anthropology expressed itself in both its faith in the classic scientific norms of "objectivity" (presumably embodied in the non-subjective, non-emotional, non-female "observer") and its vision of the ethnographic encounter as an inherently male drama. See Behar, "Introduction: Out of Exile," 2–4, 17–23; Chandra Mohanty, "Cartographies of Struggle: Third World Women and the Politics of Feminism," in *Feminism without Borders: Decolonizing Theory, Practicing Solidarity* (Durham: Duke University Press, 2004), esp. 74–75. See also "Cartographies of Struggle: Third World Women and the Politics of Feminism," in *Third World Women and the Politics of Feminism*, ed. Chandra Talpade Mohanty, Ann Russo, and Lourdes Torres (Bloomington: Indiana University Press, 1991); Trin Minh-ha, *Woman, Native, Other: Writing Postcoloniality and Feminism* (Bloomington: Indiana University Press, 1989), esp. 85.

26. Deloria to Benedict, May 16, 1947, Benedict Papers.

27. Mohanty, "Cartographies of Struggle," 31–32.

28. Deloria, "The Dakota Way of Life," 142.

29. Margaret Mead, introduction to Deloria, "The Dakota Way of Life," ECDP.

30.Deborah Gordon, "The Politics of Ethnographic Authority: Race and Writing in the Ethnography of Margaret Mead and Zora Neale Hurston," in *Modernist Anthropology: From Fieldwork to Text*, ed. Marc Manganaro (Princeton: Princeton University Press, 1990), 156.

31. Beatrice Medicine, "Professionalization of Native American (Indian) Women: Towards a Research Agenda," *Wicazo Sa Review* 4, no. 2 (1988): 31.

32. For further discussion, see Mitsue Yamada, "Invisibility Is an Unnatural Disaster: Reflections of an Asian American Woman," in *This Bridge Called My Back: Writings by Radical Women of Color*, ed. Cherrie Moraga and Gloria Anzaldúa, rev. ed. (1981; New York: Kitchen Table, 1983), 35–40.

33. Vine Deloria Jr., "Anthros, Indians, and Planetary Reality," in *Indians and Anthropologists: Vine Deloria, Jr. and the Critique of Anthropology*, ed. Thomas Biolsi and Larry J. Zimmerman (Tucson: University of Arizona Press, 1997), 211.

8

ZITKALA-ŠA

A Bridge between Two Worlds

Franci Washburn

SCHOLARS AND INTERESTED OTHERS have long recognized that the accepted body of canonical written knowledge in the United States is skewed in favor of works produced by white males, while ignoring contributions from minority voices such as those of women, people of color, gays, lesbians, and bisexuals. The political climate of the 1960s, emphasizing equal rights for minorities and women, encouraged the recovery and reintroduction of works by non-mainstream writers, historians, political figures, scholars, and academics whose significant contributions to all aspects of knowledge and culture were buried beneath the overwhelming weight of mainstream culture.

Scholars more recently have recovered the works of many neglected writers and scholars, not only to honor their contributions but also to expose the unequal social system that had consigned these works, supposedly, to the dustbin of history. Essays, speeches, political tracts, literary works, and other information were reprinted, and new critical writings about overlooked writers and their work were published. Anthologies that had previously included only the works of an agreed-upon canon were revamped and reissued to include recovered works that more accurately represented the breadth and depth of female and minority writing and scholarship in many fields.

Gertrude Simmons Bonnin, or Zitkala-Ša (Red Bird), as she called herself after a family dispute, was overlooked for two reasons. She was a woman, and, as a Yankton Dakota from south-central South Dakota, was expected "to be invisible, silent, segregated, and submissive; instead," according to a preface in a popular anthology, "she became vis-

13. (*Opposite Top*) Zitkala-Ša (Gertrude Simmons Bonnin) in 1898. Photograph by Gertrude Käsebier. *Photographic History Collection, National Museum of American History, Courtesy of the Smithsonian Institution, Washington DC. Negative no. 83-904.*

14. (*Opposite Bottom*) William J. Hanson and Zitkala-Ša (Gertrude Simmons Bonnin). *Gertrude and Raymond Bonnin Collection. Courtesy of L. Tom Perry, Special Collections, Harold B. Lee Library, Brigham Young University, Provo UT.*

ible, vocal, intrusive, and aggressive in pursuit of her own development and the legal, and cultural rights of other native Americans."[1]
At times in her life, Bonnin had her closest relationships with those
who advocated that American Indians turn their backs on their cultural
heritage and adopt mainstream culture as the only means of survival
in a white-dominated society. At other times she appeared to ally herself with those who counseled that Indians should honor and maintain
their own lifestyles and religion with only minor concessions to the
white world. Bonnin's seemingly contradictory viewpoints can only be
understood in the context of the problems that Indian intellectuals—of
which she was an outstanding example—faced during her lifetime.

By the turn of the twentieth century, Native intellectuals like Bonnin
confronted tremendous problems as representatives of their peoples. By
passing the Dawes Act of 1887, which allowed for the breakup of Indian land and its allotment to "heads" of families according to various
formulas and the sale of "excess" land to outsiders with the proceeds
used for creating schools that sought to teach Indian children white
ways, the United States had embraced assimilationist policies designed
to destroy Indian cultures by transforming Native peoples into private
property–owning, Christian farmers with family gender roles and goals
mirroring those of middle-class Americans. The solution to the "Indian
problem," was, Washington bureaucrats thought, that Indians should
cease being Indians. After 1900, as Frederick Hoxie maintains, white
Americans became more ethnocentric in their views and more cynical in
their attitudes about the ability of people of color to participate equally in
American society.[2] In addition, the breakup of the Great Sioux Reservation in 1889 and the U.S. Supreme Court's 1903 decision in *Lone Wolf v.
Hitchcock* that Congress, through its "plenary power," had the right to ab-
rogate its treaties with Native peoples and dispose of their land as it saw
fit meant that American Indians faced not only a program of cultural
"cleansing" but also the large-scale dispossession of their land.[3]

As past Indian leaders had done, Native intellectuals sought varying
and often conflicting strategies to enable their people to endure the cultural and spiritual assaults on their ethnic identities and the material
impoverishment that assimilationist policies inevitably brought against
them. As the acculturated elite of the Five Southern Tribes of the south-

eastern United States—Cherokees, Creeks, Choctaws, Chickasaws, and Seminoles—had done decades earlier in their struggle against removal to Indian Territory west of the Mississippi, Indian intellectuals now often championed the acquisition of Euro-American education and skills and even the adoption of white middle-class family standards.[4] To varying degrees they saw such adaptations as tools and methods that would equip their people to survive in a new environment increasingly dominated by Euro-American market forces in an ever more industrialized and urbanized world. Indian intellectuals always faced a delicate balancing act, for the question inevitably arose: When did the acquisition of Euro-American education, skills, and family values themselves become threats to their cultural heritage, and when were they essential for the survival of Indian culture?

In such a context, Gertrude Simmons Bonnin was not inconsistent or vacillating but rather pragmatic, a complex person whose stance depended on the issues and what she believed was best for American Indians at any particular time and place. The core of her belief and work, however, remained consistent even when her strategies shifted. She held that American Indians are human beings whose cultures and histories are at least equal to those of Euro-Americans, and that given equal opportunity, American Indians can and will contribute to the larger society in all areas of endeavor.

These choices and attitudes grew out of Bonnin's own experience in negotiating her constantly changing geographical and social position between her Yanktonai Dakota upbringing with traditional cultural values and her education and career in white society and all the spaces between. The phrase "torn between two worlds" has become an often inaccurate cliché for American Indians, particularly in the early decades of the twentieth century. Cliché or not, it is accurate for Gertrude Simmons Bonnin. The difference is that she took the torn fragments of her life and stitched them, at times painfully, into a functioning, productive bicultural identity, dedicated to protecting and advancing the well-being of Native peoples.

Bonnin's life and work can be roughly divided into two periods. During her early career she wrote autobiography, autobiographical fiction, and poetry and transcribed versions of oral tradition stories from her Yanktonai Dakota heritage. Her major publications in these years consisted of short stories and autobiographical essays in magazines such as *Atlantic Monthly* and *Harper's Monthly* and publication of her first book, *Old Indian Legends* (1901), based on her writings in *Harper's*. During her later career, Bonnin worked largely on improving the legal, economic, and social status of American Indians in general and her own people in particular. She joined the Society of American Indians (SAI), and when that organization collapsed she founded the National Council of American Indians in 1926. Her writing during these years was less creative and more political. As a contributing editor for the SAI's *American Indian Magazine*, and later as its editor in chief, she encouraged American Indians to improve themselves through education and hard work. She also published some poetry in these journals, but even these creative works had underlying political motivations and themes. Her audience for these later publications was not the broad mainstream, as had been true for her early publications. Rather, she aimed her remarks at American Indians themselves and non-Natives capable of influencing pending legislation and the administration of Indian affairs and those who could improve the economic and social situation of American Indians in the United States.

Growing up Dakota

Gertrude Simmons Bonnin, or Zitkala-Ša, was born on February 22, 1876, on the Yankton Dakota (Sioux) Reservation in South Dakota. She was almost four months old when one of the last major confrontations between whites and Indians on the Great Plains occurred—the Battle of the Greasy Grass.[5] Very likely no one from her family participated in this event, since the Yankton Dakotas had been herded onto their reservations years before the western branch of the Sioux, the Lakotas, engaged in the last desperate battles for independence and survival of their way of life. However, all branches of the Sioux Nation knew of this event as well as the long history of land theft and oppression of all American Indians. Bonnin, then Gertrude Simmons, would have grown up hearing comments about the battle and its aftermath from Indian acquaintances and friends and her own family as well.

In one of her autobiographical short stories, "My Mother," Bonnin, writing as Zitkala-Ša, records some of her mother's bitter words. For example, she recalls her mother's comments when she asked why her mother was crying. Her mother pointed to graves on a nearby hill and said: "This is what the paleface has done! Since then your father too has been buried in a hill nearer the rising sun. We were once very happy. But the paleface has stolen our lands and driven us hither. Having defrauded us of our land, the paleface drove us away."[6] This quote, demonstrating the resentment of American Indians and of Gertrude's mother in particular toward white invaders, implies that her father was Yankton Dakota or at least an American Indian. He was not. Another man, John Haysting Simmons, of Euro-American heritage, has been mistakenly identified as her father, and Gertrude used his last name until a family dispute led her to rename herself. Others state that her father was another of her mother's husbands, who was said to have abused David, Gertrude's brother.[7] P. Jane Hafen notes that in private correspondence, Bonnin identified her father only by his last name, as a man named Felker.[8]

Zitkala-Ša explained something about the confusion over her father and her surname in one of the letters she wrote to her then-fiancé, Yavapai physician and activist Carlos Montezuma, during the summer of 1901:

> I have a half brother whose name is Simmons. Once my own father scolded my brother; and my mother took such offense from it that eventually it resulted in a parting—so as I grew I was called by my brother's name—Simmons. I have [had] it a long time till my brother's wife—angry with me because I insisted upon getting an education said I had deserted home and I might give up my brother's name "Simmons" too. Well—you can guess how queer I felt—away from my own people— homeless—penniless—and even without a name! That I choose to make a name for myself and I guess I have made "Zitkala-Ša" known—for even Italy writes it in her own language.[9]

The change of name from Gertrude Simmons to Zitkala-Ša came partly as a result of this family dispute and was used when she began writing for publication.

Despite her awareness of tension in the mixed community of Yankton people and non-Native people where she grew up, Bonnin apparently had a relatively happy early childhood. She characterized herself as "a wild little girl of seven," and "[l]oosely clad in a slip of brown buckskin, and light-footed with a pair of soft moccasins on my feet, I was as free as the wind that blew my hair, and no less spirited than a bounding deer. These were my mother's pride,—my wild freedom and overflowing spirits. She taught me no fear save that of intruding myself upon others."[10]

To modern sensibilities this passage seems overly romanticized and perhaps even pejorative in her description of her childhood self as "wild." This romantic style, typical of writing of the time, would, however, have appealed to a non-Native audience. Not that she pandered to her audience; on the contrary, she used Euro-American expectations of what Indian people were to subtly include information about Indian culture and advocate for Indian rights. At the same time, she knew that her literary accomplishments showed that Native peoples were as capable of meeting literary and intellectual standards as Euro-Americans.

Writing as Zitkala-Ša, Bonnin remembered her early childhood years as a pleasant time among her family and Dakota friends and relatives, in spite of the obvious cultural conflict occurring between the Yankton Dakotas and the local white residents. These relatively carefree days ended in 1884 when missionaries arrived to recruit Indian children to attend eastern boarding schools (although *impress*, in the sense that European sailors were captured and forced into navy service, might be a more accurate term). The children nearby had already primed young Gertrude for the idea of going to boarding school. Her brother, David, whom she would later call Dawee, had attended an eastern boarding school. Since all Indian children suffered intense cultural shock from this displacement, it seems odd that young Gertrude would be enthusiastic about going to boarding school herself. Very likely David and other returning Indian children concentrated more on whatever pleasurable aspects boarding school offered rather than divulging all of their painful experiences, for she writes: "I gleaned many wonderful stories from my playfellows concerning the strangers [missionaries]."[11] One of these stories came from a childhood friend whose words she recorded: "Judéwin had told me of the great tree where grew red, red apples; and how we could reach out our hands and pick all the red apples we could eat. I had never seen apple trees. I had never tasted more than a dozen red apples in my life; and when I heard of the orchards of the East, I was eager to roam among them."[12] The missionaries confirmed Judéwin's story of the red apples and added another incentive through the interpreter: "you will have a ride on the iron horse if you go with these good people."[13]

Obviously, a similarity exists between Zitkala-Ša's story of being tempted by the "red, red apples" held out in promise by her friend (and reiterated by the missionaries) and Eve's succumbing to the temptation to eat the apple in the book of Genesis. Certainly the reservation life of Gertrude's early childhood was no Garden of Eden, but it was a more comfortable place than she would find, at least initially, in the boarding school.

Gertrude's mother, Ellen, whose Yankton name was Taté I Yóhin Win, wanted her to stay home with her own people rather than attend the boarding school. Her desire arose not from a selfish wish to deny her daughter an education but stemmed from the pain that white society had inflicted on Indian people from the moment of first contact and the unenthusiastic stories of boarding school that David had told her. Ellen believed that protecting her daughter was more important than educating her. When Gertrude's aunt intervened to plead her cause, however, Ellen reluctantly relented.[14]

The reality for Bonnin at White's Manual Labor Institute in Wabash, Indiana, was similar to that of American Indian children at other boarding schools. The trip on the "iron horse" that she had so anticipated was not exciting but frightening and uncomfortable as passengers, particularly the children, stared rudely at her and the other Indian children. "Their mothers, instead of reproving such rude curiosity," she later wrote, "looked closely at me, and attracted their children's further notice to my blanket. This embarrassed me, and kept me constantly on the verge of tears."[15] Like all other American Indian children, Gertrude was first subjected to a bath and her long hair was shorn. Her own clothing was taken away, and she was issued the standard boarding school attire for girls: underwear, socks, dress, and stiff shoes, so unlike her own soft moccasins. The children were expected to conform to a closely regimented schedule with bells ringing to signal the end of one activity and the beginning of another. Forbidden to speak their Native languages, they were expected, unrealistically, to immediately begin communicating in English. But it was the cutting of her hair that provided the ultimate humiliation; in Dakota cultural practice, cowards were punished by having their hair cut short. When that happened, she recalled, "I then lost my spirit. Since the day I was taken from my mother I had suffered extreme indignities. . . . . And now my long hair was shingled like a coward's! In my anguish I moaned for my mother, but no one came to comfort me. Not a soul reasoned quietly with me, as my own mother used to do; for now I was only one of many little animals driven by a herder."[16]

After enduring the first year of boarding school, Gertrude returned home for three years and felt almost as uncomfortable among her own family as she did at school. The often brutally enforced cultural, educational, and religious practices that the boarding school insisted upon warred with the values, beliefs, and practices of the Yankton people. Her mother, not understanding her anguish, could not identify with Gertrude's internal confusion and cultural conflict, which arose from forced language change and the harsh discipline she had undergone. Modern psychiatry would probably diagnose her as suffering from depression and post-traumatic stress disorder.

After those years at home, where the comfort that she sought was not forthcoming, Bonnin fled back east again for more education, perhaps hoping that after this second session she could return home to a more comfortable situation with her own people. This was the pattern of her early life: she lived in the white boarding school world, trying to adjust by excelling at whatever tasks she was set until a particular term was ended, and then returned home hoping for a continuity and solace she rarely found.

After completing her course of education at White's boarding school, Bonnin enrolled in another Quaker institution, Earlham College in Richmond, Indiana, in 1895, again against her mother's wishes. Ill health, however, prevented her from finishing the course of study. The stress of the previous years had taken its toll, and she returned to her own people in South Dakota but again found no peace or stability. In 1897 she accepted an offer from Colonel Richard Henry Pratt, head of Carlisle Indian School in Pennsylvania, to teach there.[17]

Meeting Pratt when she first arrived, Gertrude seemed impressed and somewhat overwhelmed by both his physical and social stature and the force of his personality.[18] Disenchantment soon came, however, stemming from the incompetence and self-centered behavior of fellow teachers and personnel at Carlisle and extending eventually to Pratt himself. "As months passed over me," she wrote, "I slowly comprehended that the large army of white teachers in Indian schools had a larger missionary creed than I had suspected. It was one which included self-preservation quite as much as Indian education," she learned. "When I saw an opium-eater holding a position as teacher of Indians, I did not understand what good was expected, until a Christian in power replied that this pumpkin-colored creature had a feeble mother to support. An inebriate paleface sat stupid in a doctor's chair, while Indian patients carried their ailments to untimely graves, because his fair wife was dependent upon him for her daily food." In the midst of such incompetence, one male teacher, obviously a civil servant, "tortured an ambitious Indian youth by frequently reminding the brave changeling that he was nothing but a 'government pauper.' Though I burned with indignation upon discovering on every side instances no less shameful than those I have mentioned," she added, "there was no present help. Even the few rare ones who have worked nobly for my race were powerless to choose workmen like themselves."[19]

In addition to chafing under the appalling quality of staff at Carlisle, Bonnin disagreed with Pratt's views of Indian education. According to Mary Young, she saw them as limited to "a brief vocational training coupled with a plow," and to Bonnin, "a plow meant slavery."[20] In correspondence with Montezuma she described the plow as "drudgery," adding that "drudgery is hell—not civilization." She believed that if Pratt really wanted to assimilate Indians, he should be striving to bring college education to them instead.[21]

Exhausted, still in poor health, and discouraged by her inability to improve conditions for Indian students, she left Carlisle and in late 1898 entered the New England Conservatory of Music in Boston (one of the premier musical colleges in the country) to study violin. We can infer that she was quite accomplished, because all students were required to undergo a rigorous audition before they were allowed to enroll. Apparently, despite her disgust with Pratt and the teachers, she left Carlisle on good terms, probably by keeping her opinions to herself and focusing on her music. When the Carlisle Indian School Band toured the Northeast in the spring of 1900, she was the featured soloist. With Pratt's encouragement she wore Native clothing (a buckskin dress) in her stage appearances, which included not only performing on the violin but also dramatic renderings of the famine scene from *Hiawatha*.[22]

Becoming Zitkala-Ša

Around this time Gertrude Simmons's short stories and essays, published under her pen name, Zitkala-Ša, began appearing in print.[23] Pratt was furious that she wrote favorably of traditional American Indian culture as opposed to the "civilizing" influences of Christianity and that she indirectly criticized the boarding school methods by describing her childhood trauma.

Defiant now, her next step was bound to anger him more. Learning through her contacts at Carlisle and through her fiancé, Carlos Montezuma, about Pratt's public comments labeling her a pagan, Zitkala-Ša wrote "Why I Am a Pagan" in response.[24] Typical of her writing, this article does not directly criticize Christianity. The first part celebrates God as embodied in nature, which she holds up as the Indian belief in spirituality without directly describing the ceremonies of particular Native peoples. The latter portion of the essay contrasts Christian behavior with Native belief when she describes the visit of a Christian Indian relative who urges her to attend church with him. The main female character of the essay, who is certainly Zitkala-Ša herself, does not argue with this relative, but offers the traditional hospitality of a meal. After the relative leaves, the main character reflects upon "the copy of a missionary paper brought to my notice a few days ago, in which a 'Christian' pugilist commented upon a recent article of mine, grossly perverting the spirit of my pen. Still," she adds, "I would not forget that the pale-faced missionary and the hoodooed aborigine are both God's creatures, though small indeed their own conceptions of Infinite Love. A wee child toddling in a wonder world," Zitkala-Ša now concludes: "I prefer to their dogma my excursions into the natural gardens where the voice of the Great Spirit is heard in the twittering of birds, the rippling of mighty waters, and the sweet breathing of flowers. If this is Paganism, then at present, at least, I am a Pagan."[25]

Indeed, in her mild reproach of the "'Christian' pugilist" and her comment that both he and she are children of God, she emphasizes that, in her paganism, she is exhibiting the Christian value of forgiveness. The term "Christian pugilist" is a veiled reference to Pratt himself. The evidence exists in a letter to Montezuma, where she wrote: "I wish I could make reply to your philosophy but being neither a pugilist (like Col. Pratt) nor a debater (like you) I have to be content to do what I feel without explaining or justifying myself."[26]

About this time, her personal life also became more complicated. She had probably met Montezuma when both had been traveling with the Carlisle Indian School Band when Montezuma served as the touring boys' chaperone. At any rate, they had become engaged and had planned to marry in November 1901, but their relationship was tumultuous from the beginning.[27]

Originally named Wassaja, Montezuma, of Yavapai origins, was a child of six or seven when a band of Pima (O'odham) warriors kidnapped him and held him captive at the San Carlos Apache Agency. Carlos Gentile, an itinerant photographer, miner, and jack-of-all-trades, noticed him there, adopted him, and renamed him Carlos Montezuma. After traveling for a while with Gentile, Montezuma was placed under the care of a Mrs. Baldwin in New York City, where he was educated. Eventually, after earning a degree from the University of Illinois, he graduated from Chicago Medical College in 1889. Thereafter, he held positions as a doctor in the Indian Service at various agencies, eventually coming into contact with Pratt and serving as the school physician at Carlisle from 1893 to 1896. Perhaps because he had spent most of his life in white society, Montezuma enthusiastically supported Pratt's assimilationist policies, which were based on the slogan "Kill the Indian and save the man," and served as his poster child for those same policies.[28]

Pratt's diametrically opposite opinions of Montezuma and Zitkala-Ša caused friction between them, but perhaps the most serious cause of their breakup came from their dissenting views on how to better the lives of American Indians. Montezuma advocated the rejection of all Native culture and the total acceptance of white culture, while Zitkala-Ša believed in taking the best of both worlds—holding onto what was valuable in Native culture and adding what was useful and beneficial from the dominant white society. Montezuma was an assimilationist, while she believed in integration and syncretism; he subscribed to the white cultural concept of individualism, that the way to success must necessarily involve the egocentric value of placing oneself first and struggling for individual achievement, while she believed that each person must work for his or her own betterment, but it was also incumbent upon a Native person to assist other Native people in the upward struggle for economic and social achievement.

With that dual goal in mind, Zitkala-Ša returned to the Yankton reservation in the summer of 1901. In addition to feeling obligated to spend a year caring for her aging mother, she wanted to collect stories from her community to preserve oral traditions. It was not just a selfish desire to publish another book.[29] Instead, it was a way to follow her belief that Indians should not be sent to distant boarding schools but, whenever possible, should be educated on their own reservations where family and cultural ties could be maintained while avoiding the trauma that she and other Indian boarding school students had endured. By teaching at the Yankton Agency school, she lived what she believed, although it was difficult.[30] This personal belief in direct service to Indian people put her into further conflict with Montezuma.

By now Montezuma had left the Indian Medical Service to go into a successful private practice in Chicago. Zitkala-Ša, however, wanted him to give up this endeavor and return to the Indian Service as a physician on or near the Yankton Agency, something he refused to do. (One wonders if she would have been satisfied if he had given up his practice but went to work among his own people, the Yavapai, in Arizona, rather than working among her Yankton tribe.) Apparently, from her letters to him, upon marriage he expected her to give up her activism, if not her writing, and to become the proper supportive wife. She, by contrast, wanted to maintain her individuality. "I am too independent. I would not like to *have to obey* another—never!" she wrote to him.[31] They were pulling in opposite directions, a situation that did not bode well for a future life together. Their differences could not be resolved, and eventually the engagement was broken, although many years later they would join forces as friends and allies in mutual causes to benefit American Indians. As Leon Speroff states in his biography of Montezuma, "Both wanted the benefits of American life (technology, healthcare, education) for their people; they disagreed on the process."[32]

Zitkala-Ša's personal life at this time was stressful, but her career as a writer was on the rise. Besides the essays in *Atlantic Monthly* and *Harper's*, and even before she turned in her final corrections for her first book, *Old Indian Legends*, released in the fall of 1901, publishers wanted another volume of stories. In 1902, Zitkala-Ša's additional tales appeared in the *Boston Evening Transcript, Everybody's Magazine*, and *Atlantic Monthly.*[33]

In May 1902, Zitkala-Ša married Raymond Bonnin, also a Dakota Sioux from the Yankton Reservation. After the birth of their only child, Raymond Ohiya Bonnin, they moved to the Uinta Ouray Ute Reservation in Utah, where Raymond was employed as a purchasing and issue clerk. For most of the fourteen years they lived and worked in Utah, Zitkala-Ša practiced the community service she had advocated earlier for Montezuma. In addition to performing her duties as wife and mother, she taught cooking and sewing classes and organized a band.

She continued her literary writing during some of those years but published none of those stories at the time. A selection of those works, recovered by P. Jane Hafen, was published in 2001.[34] Most of the material appears to be transcriptions of stories from Yanktonai oral tradition, probably collected when she worked on the Yankton Agency in the summer of 1901. Hafen speculates that Zitkala-Ša intended to publish these stories, because word counts appear at the top of many of them. Perhaps, Hafen suggests, the magazines where she had previously published her stories were no longer interested.[35]

One cultural production that Zitkala-Ša created during her years in Utah that attracted attention is *The Sun Dance Opera*, which she cowrote with William J. Hanson, a white Mormon music teacher from the nearby town of Vernal.[36] Hanson taught music in the local schools, so they probably met while Zitkala-Ša was organizing the band for the Utes of the Uintah Ouray Reservation. Zitkala-Ša's early writings came out of her personal experience and knowledge and interest in the oral tradition stories of her culture. *The Sun Dance Opera*, however, marked the beginning of works written in response to contemporary political and economic issues for American Indians. The opera was one of her few art productions inspired by the injustices she perceived in contemporary Indian policy. Other than essays on Indian education, most of her writing from about 1913 on dealt with issues affecting Natives peoples and appeared in articles, letters, and reports.

For many years the federal government had tried to outlaw American Indian religious rituals and ceremonies, including the Sun Dance ceremony of the upper Plains tribes, on the grounds that they were barbaric, wild, and heathenish.[37] Some speculate that authorities were also concerned about the large numbers of Indians who congregated for these dances, which might have seemed threatening to non-Native people living near the areas where the rituals were performed. The commissioner of Indian Affairs banned the Sun Dance in 1883, and in 1884 a federal regulation made the practice of any Native American religion illegal. In 1904 the Department of the Interior found it again necessary to issue a ban on the Sun Dance, probably because it was still being covertly practiced. The Indian Reorganization Act of 1934 allowed the open practice of the dance, but even then the government insisted upon modifications to suit white sensibilities.[38]

Written over a period of approximately two years, *The Sun Dance Opera* utilized methods of Zitkala-Ša's early years—subverting white prejudice toward Indian culture by demonstrating the beauty and social value of Indian culture, not by confrontational political activism. In the plot, which involves a competition between two braves who hope to marry a chief's daughter, Zitkala-Ša not only supported the ritual but "translated its power for predominantly white audiences," according to Cathy N. Davidson and Ada Norris.[39] In addition, since she constantly sought to bring together the best of both Indian and white cultures, she and Hanson carefully wove "oral musical Indian traditions into a highly organized and acculturated Western musical form."[40]

The opera, first performed in February 1913 in Vernal for three nights, ran again in May and December of the following year. Whether or not Zitkala-Ša succeeded in educating non-Natives about Indian culture, she did sensitize some audiences to the injustices Indians had experienced. One reviewer of the opera, after noting the "color and variety of movement, [and] more vivid stage effects" than he had seen in previous operas, stated that it celebrated the "inner spiritual life of this much wronged and misunderstood people."[41]

A photograph, probably taken for publicity, shows Zitkala-Ša and Hanson in beaded buckskin costumes, typically Sioux in style and decoration. Zitkala-Ša stands slightly angled to the camera with a rather amused expression on her face, while Hanson, in contrast, faces the camera straight on. His facial expression seems sheepish, as if he felt as silly as he looked with his pale skin, short hair, and typical non-Native appearance, but dressed in American Indian attire like a child playing dress-up.[42]

The opera was performed several times in Salt Lake City and other towns in Utah during 1933, but after this brief local flurry, opera companies and guilds overlooked it for more than twenty years. It was performed twice in 1935 by the New York Light Opera Guild, an amateur company that focused its efforts on one or two light opera productions a year during the 1930s, and was revived again in 1938 as the company's opera of the year.[43] John Hand, director of the amateur theater group, had performed the lead role of Ohiya in an earlier production at Brigham Young University and was the driving force in these productions. Hanson's name appeared by itself on most programs and promotions for the 1938 production, with Zitkala-Ša identified in a few footnotes as a "collaborator."[44] Hanson claimed most of the credit for the opera for most of his life, even copyrighting it in his name only. He only assigned Zitkala-Ša half of the copyright when he became convinced that he would need further collaboration to improve the work. Late in his life he apparently had some regrets over his egotism.[45]

Some have suggested that the cultural contexts in the work and the lyrics came from Zitkala-Ša but that Hanson wrote the musical score. That does not seem likely. When they were collaborating, Zitkala-Ša had three years of classical training at the New England Conservatory of Music in Boston and had traveled as a performer. Hanson had only two years of general education at Brigham Young University with no music specialization, although he must have had some natural musical ability and Brigham Young did encourage the performing arts. Hanson did not receive further musical training until 1924 in Chicago, finally earning a master's in music from Brigham Young in 1937, only a year before the last performance of *The Sun Dance Opera*.

Strangely, in all the years during which Hanson and Zitkala-Ša worked on the opera and the years in which it was publicly presented, Bonnin made no mention of it in her letters, journals, or private papers. Perhaps she simply had more pressing issues on her mind. At the time she was concerned over the spiritual well-being of the Utes and was looking for a school for her son. According to Hafen, "Her distress over spiritual circumstances led her to ask the Catholic fathers to recommend a Christian boarding school for her son, Ohiya."[46] The closest she comes to mentioning anything about music is in a letter to Montezuma in 1913, after recently reestablishing their friendship. In the letter she notes that she is taking her son to "Spalding Institute for Small Boys, a Benedictine Sisters School, Nauvoo, Ill." Although she understood the necessity of giving him an education, "this knowledge does not make it any easier to leave him." Then, changing the subject, she states that while in Ohio she had "studied piano music at Otterbein University. I practiced 6 hours a day. . . . I am returning to Utah," she added, "because Mr. Bonnin insists upon it. I shall continue my study at home and try to go every summer to some place to study under a real first class teacher of music."[47]

Work on the opera with Hanson may have been the inspiration for her continuing to study music, but other events soon intruded on her plans. As a result of her appointment to the position of secretary for the Society of American Indians, Zitkala-Ša and her husband moved from Utah to Washington DC, where the SAI's offices were located. At this point she had several possible career choices: she could continue her work with her husband on the Ute reservation and work on her music career sporadically; she could defy him and pursue further music education on her own, or she could go back to her literary aspirations. Her acceptance of a more activist role as SAI secretary suggests that she might have concluded that the indirect route of gentle persuasion through music and literary writing was ineffective. But now she had a new quest.

While Zitkala-Ša actively promoted the Sun Dance as a viable and valuable Indian religious tradition, she adamantly opposed another Indian religious tradition: the use of peyote in the new Native American Church. Peyote is the small, buttonlike cap of a spineless cactus native to the southwestern United States and Texas. The active substance is mescaline. When ingested, peyote produces a hallucinogenic effect but no aftereffects, and the drug is not physiologically habit-forming.[48] Native peoples of the Southwest and Mexico have long used it in religious rites and ceremonies, but in the seventeenth century Native tribes in Texas adopted its use and further diffused it into the Oklahoma tribes in the late nineteenth century, where it became syncretized with Christianity. From there the use of peyote in what would become known as the Native American Church spread to other tribes across the United States. Zitkala-Ša, observing the use of peyote in ceremonial practice on the Uintah Ouray Ute Reservation, had become opposed to its increasing popularity. The reasons for her opposition to one American Indian religious ritual while supporting another were, nonetheless, complex.

Zitkala-Ša and the Fight over Peyote

First, the Sun Dance ritual, which uses no drugs or alcohol in any form, was part of her own Great Plains Dakota culture, so she would have been familiar with it from childhood. To Zitkala-Ša, peyotism was an unfamiliar southwestern Indian religious practice that utilized mind-altering substances. Having witnessed the destructive effects of alcohol on Indian people, she viewed peyote as another substance that seemed to have the same effect. Whether the Utes used the peyote only in religious ceremonies or as a secular drug for everyday use is unknown, but she opposed peyote under any circumstance or for any reason, even for sacred use. On some reservations whole families, she observed, "attend weekly meetings every Saturday night to eat peyote. It takes all day Sunday to recover somewhat from the drunk. Too often in their midnight debaucheries there is a total abandonment of virtue."

If this were not sufficiently disturbing, she offered yet another reason: "Children of school age are taken out of school in order that they may eat peyote" and are not only "permitted but encouraged and sometimes forced to eat it." Consequently, these children "are not in a responsive condition to justify the Government's paying salaries to teach them." Viewing peyote as a "substitute for liquor and drugs," she denounced it as an alarming threat to Indian advancement. Nor did she accept the idea that peyote use was a sacrament of Indian religion, since, in her view, "religion is the adoration of the Maker with a rational mind. No one in the state of drunkenness, by whatsoever cause, can be in his rational mind; and he cannot practice religion."[49] In these attitudes, she was like other reform-minded women of the Progressive Era and earlier "nineteenth-century feminists who," according to Davidson and Norris, "became strong temperance activists in response to what they perceived as a danger to both social and family welfare." And like these women, Zitkala-Ša was particularly outspoken when peyote was used by men.[50] That she willingly joined forces with her former critic, Richard Henry Pratt from Carlisle Indian School, shows the strength of her opposition to peyote and the lengths to which she would go to eradicate its use. Her appointment as secretary for the SAI lent credibility to her activist stance against peyote use.

The Society of American Indians was founded in 1911 through the impetus of a non-Native, Fayette A. McKenzie, a professor of economics and sociology at Ohio State University. The idea for the organization had actually originated some twelve years earlier among such prominent Native Americans as Charles Eastman, a Wahpeton Dakota physician, and his brother, John, among others. However, at that time they believed they could not gather enough support from Native Americans, non-Natives, and the Office of Indian Affairs to pursue it further. A number of educated and progressive, if not assimilationist, Indians attended the organizational meeting, including Dr. Eastman; Thomas Sloan, an Omaha lawyer; Charles E. Daganett, a Peoria employee of the Office of Indian Affairs; Laura M. Cornelius, an Oneida from Wisconsin; Henry Standing Bear, an Oglala Sioux from Pine Ridge Reservation; and Zitkala-Ša's former fiancé, Carlos Montezuma.[51] While Zitkala-Ša was absent, those present held up her work with the Utes as one way of advancing the social conditions of American Indians. The goals of the organization (which was first named the American Indian Association) were stated as follows: "The American Indian Association declares that the time has come when the American Indian race should contribute, in a more united way, its influence and exertion with the rest of the citizens of the United States in all lines of progress and reform, for the welfare of the Indian race in particular, and humanity in general."[52] Apparently their mutual interest in the goals of the SAI was one of the mechanisms that brought Bonnin and Montezuma together again as friends and activists for Indian causes.

Living and working in Washington DC, at the center of political power, enabled Zitkala-Ša to testify, along with Pratt, in congressional hearings about peyote use in Native religious ceremonies.[53] Her activism and testimony, however, brought her criticism from the opposite faction of the peyote argument, which included anthropologists and Native ethnographers who supported Native American religious freedom in all forms. James Mooney, an ethnologist employed by the Bureau of American Ethnology, had studied peyotism and advocated its use in Native religious ceremonies. Mooney had worked for years with Kiowas and documented the Ghost Dance and was an advocate of Indian religious freedom in all forms. He had lived through many attempts by the Indian Office to discredit him and knew that testimony was only credible if the witness was seen as a legitimate authority who understood ethnographic detail.[54] In response to the testimony of Zitkala-Ša, which she gave in her Native dress, Mooney attempted to discredit her Indian identity as inauthentic and incorrect. In his congressional testimony he not only disagreed with Zitkala-Ša's stance on peyote use but attacked her personally, thus distracting attention from her political message. He stated that her clothing was a mixture of pieces from several different tribes (thus demonstrating she was dressed inaccurately and was no longer culturally pure) and that she carried a fan used in peyote ceremonies (that she was herself a user of peyote in disguise).[55] He also impugned her identity by saying that she was someone who "claims to be a Sioux woman," or what is now termed a "wannabe."[56] This gendered, racial attack was continued by Mooney's colleagues, including some Native Americans. Cleaver Warden, an Arapaho ethnographer who supported peyote use, stated: "We only ask a fair and impartial trial by reasonable white people, not half breeds who do not know a bit of their ancestors or kindred. A true Indian is one who helps for a race and not that secretary of the Society of American Indians."[57] The debate over who has the authority to speak for Indians, who has the so-called racial and cultural purity, and whether women can be legitimate spokespeople continues today. The techniques used to undermine the authoritative positions of individuals who express different opinions, though common to American politics, must have been a shock to Zit-kala-Ša. Eventually, all of her ferocious work against peyote use came to naught. Congress decided against outlawing peyote and instead left its regulation to state and local jurisdictions.

"Yours for the Indian Cause"

Although these unfair and inaccurate accusations during the peyote controversy must have caused Bonnin personal anguish, the lessons she learned in political activism stood her in good stead in her future work with the SAI and with other Indian activist organizations. In that capacity she oversaw all correspondence between the organization and the Indian Office, presented lectures, and served as the official rep-resentative of the SAI. She also was a contributing editor to *American Indian Magazine*, a periodical that had begun its life as the *Quarterly Journal of the Society of American Indians*. *American Indian Magazine* served as a mouthpiece for SAI leaders and kept readers aware of the impact of legislation on American Indians.[58]

After a shakeup in the organization, Zitkala-Ša would assume an even more important role in the magazine's existence, but not until a faction led by Montezuma (who had turned increasingly against the Indian Office over the years) ousted Arthur C. Parker, a Seneca.[59] Parker's overly conciliatory attitudes toward non-Indians and his ad-monitions that Indians respond to the "Indian problem" by striving to "awaken" and "improve" themselves antagonized many members. Although Parker saw "the value of the organization as a pan-Indian community" and a means of Indian self-determination, his desire to avoid antagonizing non-Natives and divisions within the SAI over the question of how best to deal with the Office of Indian Affairs cost him the presidency of the organization and his position as editor in chief.[60] Montezuma, especially, held Indian Affairs responsible for the isolation Indians endured in American society and called for the bureau's termination, a demand that Parker resisted.[61] In 1918, Charles O. Eastman assumed the presidency of the SAI and Zitkala-Ša advanced to editor in chief of *American Indian Magazine*, a position she held until the SAI disintegrated in 1923.

Zitkala-Ša, who had begun contributing to the magazine in the October–December 1915 issue under Parker's editorship, had never espoused his point of view on how American Indians should define themselves and their roles in American society. Instead, she had limited her contributions to poetry and to an article in the form of a letter in which she described her community center work on the Ute reservations and detailed her opposition to peyote use. Contributions in other issues under Parker's editorship appear to have been carefully written so as not to directly oppose Parker's positions while simultaneously protesting the government policy of ineptitude, indifference, and outright abuse of Indian people. According to James Cox, her articles covered "an interesting mix of demands for sovereignty (water rights, land claims) and a request for colonial imposition (the prohibition of Native religious practices)."[62] Clarifying himself further, Cox notes, "Bonnin saw no contradiction in these requests. The American Indian future she envisioned included self determination in terms of ownership and control of the land, but no peyote use, which she believed militated against the ability to own and control the land 'wisely.'"[63] In other words, this complex and sometimes contradictory woman sometimes advocated sovereignty and at other times advocated government intervention and imposition. She believed that a judicious and well-considered use of both methods was necessary—at times one, at times the other.

Under Zitkala-Ša's editorship, the magazine focused less on toeing the SAI ideological line and more on the practical problems facing American Indians in the modern world. Zitkala-Ša still advocated the "improve yourself through work and education" policy that was a central theme of SAI rhetoric, but whereas Parker insisted on erasing tribal lines and working for a pan-Indian movement, she valued individual tribal cultures while also urging that Indian tribes unite under a pan-tribal umbrella to work for common causes.[64] Indeed, she took the pan-tribal ideal a step further.

World War I had just ended when her editorship began, and Zit-kala-Ša saw in the peace talks afterward a hope for American Indian participation in global society. After all, as she noted, American Indians had fought and died in the Great War, a fact that she used to demand that they receive citizenship rights, including the franchise in their own country at long last as a matter of justice.[65] From a practical standpoint, only as citizens could they become voting constituents, helping to elect or defeat men for a Congress that wielded such power over their lives. And only as citizens could they come under the Court of Claims that they were "by express statute excluded from," and which could not hear their grievances except with congressional consent. Zitkala-Ša also expressed her hopes for justice and settlement of U.S. abrogations of its treaties in the issues she edited and greater Indian freedom from bureaucrats and more Indian involvement in Indian Affairs policy making.[66]

She also called on Native peoples to learn English, acquire literacy skills, and practice "the virtues of our race, the honesty, clean living and intelligence" that exemplified Indians, and "to teach our children to be proud of their Indian blood and to stand the test [of meeting Euro-Americans] bravely."[67] In one editorial she called on Indian women to join the SAI, since as mothers they were the important teachers of Indian children, "our future hope."[68]

Zitkala-Ša's influential editorship and SAI activities were, nonethe-less, short-lived. By 1919 the pro-peyote members of SAI had become active participants in the organization, and a member of the pro-peyote faction, Thomas Sloan, was elected to the society's presidency. Zit-kala-Ša refused her own reelection as secretary-treasurer, and both she and her husband resigned. But it was not only the election of Sloan as president that caused them to withdraw from the organization. They were incurring what Leon Speroff terms "considerable financial ex-pense from their home" in maintaining and essentially underwriting the magazine through uncompensated labor, and they realized "that the Society was accomplishing little."[69]

After their resignation, the Bonnins remained in Washington DC, where Raymond, who had served as a U.S. Army captain during the recent war, began studying law in hopes of working for Indian land rights. For unknown reasons, after obtaining his law degree he was never admitted to the bar. The situation must have disappointed Zitkala-Ša. As editor of *American Indian Magazine* she had called for Indians to be given the right to choose their own competent lawyers. Obviously, representation by lawyers who were themselves Indian would advance their causes.[70] Nevertheless, whatever her dismay over her husband's thwarted ambitions, she was always in demand as a popular lecturer at various events and often gave musical recitals where she performed popular and classical works while wearing her Native dress.

Zitkala-Ša, as Gertrude Bonnin, also became actively involved with the Greater Federation of Women's Clubs, an organization that came out of the Progressive Era of reform. In 1923, she, Charles H. Fabens (lawyer for the American Indian Defense Organization), and Matthew K. Sniffen (secretary of the Indian Rights Organization) traveled to Oklahoma to investigate corruption in the allotment program as it was administered there following the passage of the Curtis Act. That 1898 act ended the autonomy of the republics of the Five Southern Tribes—Cherokees, Creeks, Choctaws, Chickasaws, and Seminoles—and forced tribal members to exchange their communally owned land for allotments. Within two decades, the full-bloods of these tribes had been plunged into abject poverty as they came under the jurisdiction of county courts and corrupt legislators. Subject to new taxes, they were now more easily victimized by real estate developers and corporate interests.

Working together, Bonnin, Fabens, and Sniffen published *Oklahoma's Poor Rich Indians: An Orgy of Graft and Exploitation of the Five Civilized Tribes—Legalized Robbery*, which appeared in 1924.[71] The pamphlet seemed to have little more than a firecracker effect that rapidly dissipated, but it lit a small fire that eventually led to other investigations into corruption in dealings with American Indians.[72] Moreover, the work later provided historian Angie Debo with important facts and insights for her pioneering work *And Still the Waters Run*, published in 1940, which not only described in searing detail and dispassionate analysis the dispossession and pauperization of the Five Tribes of Oklahoma but remains, even today, one of the single most important works in Indian history. It exposes the pernicious folly of the Curtis Act as economic policy and as cultural warfare against the Indian way of life.[73]

About this same time, Zitkala-Ša's friendship with John Collier put her in the midst of the Indian reform movement of the 1920s. After becoming a member of the National Advisory Board of the American Indian Defense Association, she formed the National Council of American Indians in 1926, an organization that moved away from the SAI's ideals of conciliation and persuasion. Her new all-Indian organization was overtly political and had as its goals bringing about change through gathering information, actively organizing the Indian vote granted by the Indian Citizenship Act of 1924, and lobbying for Indian issues before Congress. As president and secretary-treasurer, respectively, Zitkala-Ša and her husband visited reservations and Indian centers across the country, watchdogged the Office of Indian Affairs, and testified multiple times before Senate and House committees on legislation affecting American Indians. She used her well-honed writing skills to advocate for American Indians in her organization's newsletter as well as in letters to newspapers and legislators. Much of the time she worked in tandem with Collier and the American Indian Defense Association.

Zitkala-Ša's friendship with Collier ended bitterly after President Franklin Delano Roosevelt appointed Collier commissioner of Indian Affairs in 1933. Collier promoted the Indian Reorganization Act (IRA), which ended many of the abuses and corruption in the Bureau of Indian Affairs (BIA).[74] It ended individual allotment of Indian land, promoted day schools on reservations instead of the old boarding school system, revamped tribal government systems, and encouraged preferential hiring of Indians for BIA vacancies.[75] Despite Collier's generally good intentions, Zitkala-Ša opposed the IRA because Collier failed to consult the tribes when the act was conceived and written. She saw the IRA as just another interference and imposition of authority by the federal government on Indian people without their consent. Collier fired or ceased associating with anyone who did not agree with him on the IRA. The feud between Collier and Zitkala-Ša continued until her death in 1938 at age sixty-two. She was buried in Arlington Cemetery alongside her husband, who died four years later.

Very quickly Zitkala-Ša's literary work, her activism, and her writings in connection with that activism faded from the public view, with only occasional brief mentions and references in footnotes. That lasted until the recovery work, beginning in the 1960s, which brought the writings of minorities back into literary collections and national attention. Her work was not actually rediscovered until the early 1970s, when it became available to scholars of minority studies, women's studies, and American literature. With this resurgence has come long-overdue scholarly consideration. Some of the more recently published biographical information, however, offers conflicting information about Zitkala-Ša's religious convictions.

Born into traditional Yanktonai Dakota spiritual belief, she was, of course, indoctrinated into Christianity at White's Manual Labor Institute, a religion that she rejected when she returned home again after that first year of boarding school. This does not mean that she could not manipulate its symbols and metaphors for her own end. Her early literary writings used the language of Christianity and Christian concepts and ideals while simultaneously offering veiled and not-so-veiled criticism of Christians who do not practice what they preach, particularly those non-Native Christians involved in the boarding school system. On the one hand she supported traditional religious belief for the Sun Dance of her own Dakota people, but on the other she opposed the rights of other American Indians to follow their own religious practices that involved the use of peyote.

A determination of her exact religious beliefs and affiliations is impossible, but it would seem that she had a deep belief in a god and in living a life of decency and honesty while caring for all people. Various religious affiliations with individuals throughout her life (Hanson, for example) have led some scholars to maintain that she had converted to Mormonism. Other information suggests that she converted to Catholicism.[76] She may have been changing religious commitments due to her felt needs or the pragmatics of any given situation or time.

Zitkala-Ša's comments on Indian education, both those semi-disguised in literary work and critiques written and spoken openly, helped the movement to reform and eliminate the boarding school system. They also assisted in the ushering in of a system of Indian education that, although far from perfect, was reservation-based and allowed Indian children to maintain family and cultural ties. Zitkala-Ša took her own painful boarding school experiences and used them to help make the education process better for those who came after her. It is a strange contradiction that after her own boarding school experiences and her criticism of the system, she chose to place her own son, Ohiya, in a Catholic boarding school. Perhaps she felt boarding schools were better than the public school systems available to him at the time, or perhaps she thought that after all she had written about the system, no one in any boarding school would dare to treat her son as she had been treated. Further, Ohiya had spent his initial school years at home with his parents, and the Bonnins may have considered his educational level so superior to those of other boarding school contemporaries that he could not come under criticism. Or, her decision may have been another of her practical choices. With her busy life as SAI secretary before her and a constant round of public appearances as a lecturer and her lobbying efforts, she may have felt that the Catholic teachers at the boarding school could offer him more nurturing attention than she herself could give.

Zitkala-Ša's musical efforts, particularly *The Sun Dance Opera*, have been largely ignored since her death. At the time, however, the opera exposed a non-Native population to American Indian ideas and culture, thus offering proof that American Indian people were neither degraded and ignorant people nor romanticized noble savages. Rather, they were human beings who had a social and cultural history and values that could contribute to the building of a greater nation of diversified people.

Finally, Zitkala-Ša was a well-known and respected figure among Natives and non-Natives alike, even if she was not always liked by everyone, and even when her point of view on a given issue conflicted with those of others. It is notable that at her memorial service, her former friend who turned adversary, John Collier, memorialized her as the "last of the great Indian Orators."[77]

Zitkala-Ša, Gertrude Simmons Bonnin, was an orator; a writer of articles, poetry, and short stories; a transcriber of oral tradition stories from her own culture; and an activist who dedicated her life to the cause of bettering her own people. Her early essays, poetry, and short stories offer seldom-heard personal insights into the boarding school system for American Indian children and youth and provide sound reasoning for developing alternative educational venues that offered a more inclusive role for traditional Indian values and belief systems. Her efforts to portray American Indian religious practices positively through her writing and *The Sun Dance Opera* were among the earliest efforts to value American Indian spirituality. The work she began in this area was to result in the American Indian Religious Freedom Act of 1978, which decriminalized a range of American Indian sacred ceremonies ranging from the Sun Dance of the Northern Plains tribes to the potlatch ceremonies of the Pacific Northwest. Perhaps her most important accomplishment, however, is the model of personal commitment and activism she provided, not only for American Indian women but for American Indians of both genders and all Native nations, a model that is worth remembering and emulating nearly seventy years after her death.

Notes

1. Preface to Bonnin's excerpted works in the *Norton Anthology of American Literature*, Third Edition Shorter (New York: Norton, 1979), 1630–31.

2. Frederick Hoxie, *A Final Promise: The Campaign to Assimilate the Indian, 1880–1920* (Lincoln: University of Nebraska Press, 1984).

3. Blue Clark, *Lone Wolf v. Hitchcock: Treaty Rights and Indian Law at the End of the Nineteenth Century* (Lincoln: University of Nebraska Press, 1994).

4. William G. McLoughlin gives an excellent overview on this point in his introduction to *Cherokees and Missionaries, 1789–1839* (Norman: University of Oklahoma Press, 1994), 1–12.

5. This confrontation is more commonly known as the Battle of the Little Bighorn, where George Armstrong Custer, the still controversial soldier, met his end.

6. Zitkala-Ša, "My Mother," in *American Indian Stories, Legends, and Other Writings*, ed. Cathy N. Davidson and Ada Norris (New York: Penguin Books, 2003), 69.

7. See David L. Johnson and Raymond Wilson, "Gertrude Simmons Bon-

nin, 1876–1938: 'Americanize the First American,'" *American Indian Quarterly* 11 (Winter 1988): 27; Cathy N. Davidson and Ada Norris, introduction to Zitkala-Ša, *American Indian Stories*, xiv–xv.

8. P. Jane Hafen, introduction to *Dreams and Thunder: Stories, Poems, and The Sun Dance Opera* by Zitkala-Ša (Lincoln: University of Nebraska Press, 2001), xvii. See also Leon Speroff, *Carlos Montezuma, M.D.: A Yavapai American Hero* (Portland: Arnica, 2003), 206; and Dexter Fisher's foreword, "Zitkala-Ša: The Evolution of a Writer," for *American Indian Stories by Zitkala-Ša* (Lincoln: University of Nebraska Press, 1985), v–xx.

9. Zitkala-Ša to Montezuma, summer 1901, quoted in Hafen, introduction to Zitkala-Ša, *Dreams and Thunder*, xvii–xviii.

10. Zitkala-Ša, "My Mother," 68.

11. Zitkala-Ša, "The Big Red Apples," in *American Indian Stories*, 83.

12. Zitkala-Ša, "The Big Red Apples," 84.

13. Zitkala-Ša, "The Big Red Apples," 85.

14. Zitkala-Ša, "The Big Red Apples," 85

15. Zitkala-Ša, "The Big Red Apples," 87.

16. Zitkala-Ša, "The Big Red Apples," 91.

17. Johnson and Wilson, "Gertrude Simmons Bonnin," 28.

18. Zitkala-Ša, "My First Day," in *American Indian Stories*, 103.

19. Zitkala-Ša, "My First Day," 111.

20. Mary E. Young, "Gertrude Simmons Bonnin," in *Notable American Women, 1607–1950*, ed. Edward T. James, Janet Wilson James, and Paul S. Boyer, 3 vols. (Cambridge: Belknap Press, 1971), 1:198.

21. Quoted in Peter Iverson, *Carlos Montezuma and the Changing World of American Indians* (Albuquerque: University of New Mexico Press, 1982), 37.

22. Ruth Spack, "Dis/engagement: Zitkala-Ša's Letters to Carlos Montezuma," *Melus* 26 (Spring 2001): 178.

23. Zitkala-Ša, "Impressions of an Indian Childhood," *Atlantic Monthly*, January 1900, 33–47; Zitkala-Ša, "The School Days of an Indian Girl," *Atlantic Monthly*, February 1900, 185–94; Zitkala-Ša, "An Indian Teacher among Indians," *Atlantic Monthly*, March 1900, 381–87.

24. Zitkala-Ša, "Why I Am a Pagan," *Atlantic Monthly*, December 1902, 801–3.

25. Zitkala-Ša, "Why I Am a Pagan," 803.

26. J. S. Hohler, ed., *The Papers of Carlos Montezuma, 1892–1937*, microfilm

edition (Madison: State Historical Society of Wisconsin, 1985), reel 1, quoted in Speroff, *Carlos Montezuma*, 218.

27. Montezuma was not Zitkala-Ša's first fiancé. She had been previously engaged to Thomas Marshall, a Lakota from the Pine Ridge Agency. Both had graduated from White's school in Indiana. However, Marshall went to Carlisle from the White school, while Zitkala-Ša went to Earlham College. They were reunited when Zitkala-Ša taught at Carlisle. However, their engagement was broken off.

28. Iverson, *Carlos Montezuma*, 9.

29. Her first book, *Old Indian Legends*, appeared in 1901; the University of Nebraska Press reprinted it in 1985.

30. In several of her letters to Montezuma she comments upon the difficulties she encounters at the Yankton Agency, including coping with do-gooders who arrive unannounced on the reservation and with the "cranky" personality of her mother. See Spack, "Dis/engagement," 189–90.

31. Speroff, *Carlos Montezuma*, 219.

32. Speroff, *Carlos Montezuma*, 219.

33. Speroff, *Carlos Montezuma*, 190.

34. Zitkala-Ša, *Dreams and Thunder*.

35. Zitkala-Ša, *Dreams and Thunder*, 3.

36. Hanson taught music in the Vernal schools, so the two probably met while Zitkala-Ša was organizing the band for the Uinta Ouray Reservation.

37. Davidson and Norris, introduction, xx.

38. Davidson and Norris, introduction, xx.

39. Davidson and Norris, introduction, xxi.

40. For a thorough discussion and analysis of *The Sun Dance Opera* and the collaborative efforts of Bonnin and Hanson, see Catherine Parsons Smith, "An Operatic Skeleton on the Western Frontier: Zitkala-Ša, William F. Hanson, and *The Sun Dance Opera*," *Women and Music Annual*, 2001, http://www.questia.com/PM.qst?a+o&d=5001047768 (accessed February 5, 2006).

41. Review of *The Sun Dance Opera*, *Desert News* (Salt Lake City), March 1913, quoted in Davidson and Norris, introduction, xx–xxi.

42. This photo is included in P. Jane Hafen, "A Cultural Duet: Zitkala-Ša and *The Sun Dance Opera*," *Great Plains Quarterly* 18 (Spring 1998): 102. It also appears in Zitkala-Ša, *Dreams and Thunder*, 124.

43. Smith, "An Operatic Skeleton on the Western Frontier," 8.

44. Davidson and Norris, introduction, xxii.

45. Smith discusses Hanson's apparent change of heart in "An Operatic Skeleton on the Western Frontier."

46. Hafen, introduction to Zitkala-Ša, *Dreams and Thunder*, xix.

47. Bonnin to Montezuma, June 23, 1913, photocopy in box 2, folder 2, Collection 1704, Bonnin Papers, Brigham Young University. Originals in the University of Arizona Library Special Collections, Carlos Montezuma Papers, quoted in Smith, "An Operatic Skeleton on the Western Frontier," 11.

48. See http://www.Encyclopedia.com/htm/p1/peyote.asp (accessed August 3, 2005).

49. Zitkala-Ša, "The Menace of Peyote" (c. 1916), *American Indian Stories*, 239–41.

50. Davidson and Norris, introduction, xxii.

51. James S. Olson and Raymond Wilson, *Native Americans in the Twentieth Century* (Urbana: University of Illinois Press, 1986), 90–93.

52. Hazel W. Hertzberg, *The Search for an American Indian Identity: Modern Pan-Indian Movements* (Syracuse: Syracuse University Press, 1971), 36.

53. Most likely, Montezuma acted as a bridge between Pratt and Zitkala-Ša, enabling them to put aside old enmities and work together on the anti-peyotism legislation.

54. An excellent biography is L. G. Moses, *The Indian Man: A Biography of James Mooney* (Lincoln: University of Nebraska Press, 2002), esp. 179–205 for background and 197–203 for the conflict with Bonnin and Pratt.

55. This was a particularly nasty accusation and an inaccurate one as well, since many different tribes use fans in both secular and sacred performance, not just for peyote ceremonies.

56. Cari Carpenter, "Detecting Indianness: Gertrude Bonnin's Investigation of Native American Identity," *Wicazo Sa Review* 21 (Spring 2005): 150.

57. Carpenter, "Detecting Indianness," 150. As one of the first Native ethnographers, Warden had worked for many years with Mooney and George Dorsey of the Field Museum of Natural History. He firmly believed there should be no government interference with Native hegemony, especially in religion.

58. Young, "Gertrude Simmons Bonnin," 199; Marion Eleanor Gridley, *American Indian Women* (New York: Hawthorne, 1974), 199; Johnson and Wilson, "Gertrude Simmons Bonnin," 30.

59. Iverson calls "abolition of the Indian Bureau" Montezuma's "prevailing principle" in his last years. *Carlos Montezuma*, 147.

60. James Cox, "Yours for the Indian Cause: Gertrude Bonnin's Activist Editing at *The American Indian Magazine, 1915–1919*," in *Blue Pencils and Hidden Hands: Women Editing Periodicals, 1830–1910*, ed. Sharon M. Harris (Boston: Northeastern University Press, 2004), 179–81.

61. Olson and Wilson, *Native Americans in the Twentieth Century*, 94. Montezuma began publishing *Wassaja*, a periodical dedicated to ending the Bureau of Indian Affairs, in 1916. See Iverson, *Carlos Montezuma*, 106.

62. Cox, "Yours for the Indian Cause," 182.

63. Cox, "Yours for the Indian Cause," 182.

64. Bonnin, probably sensing that Parker was losing control over the organization and the magazine, had already begun such a move with her contributions to the last issue of the magazine published under Parker's editorship. In it she included so much material about her own Yanktonai Sioux tribe that the issue was referred to as the "Sioux Number."

65. Zitkala-Ša, "Editorial Comment," *American Indian Magazine*, Winter 1919; Zitkala-Ša, "America, Home of the Red Man," *American Indian Magazine*, Winter 1919; Zitkala-Ša, "The Black Hills Council," *American Indian Magazine*, Spring 1919; and Zitkala-Ša, "Hope in the Returned Indian Soldier," *American Indian Magazine*, Summer 1919, all are reprinted in *American Indian Stories*, 191–95, 199–211. Regarding the Black Hills, the United States had taken them from the Sioux in 1876 after declaring the "Sitting Bull bands" hostiles for failing to join the majority Sioux on the reservations by January 31, 1876, and despite the provision in the Treaty of Fort Laramie of 1868 that gave them the right to hunt in perpetuity in unceded territory (their location). The Supreme Court in 1980 declared the U.S. action a violation of the Fifth Amendment rights of the Sioux. See United States v. Sioux Nation, U.S. 371 (1980) and Edward Lazarus, *Black Hills, White Justice: The Sioux Nation Versus the United States, 1775 to the Present* (1991; reprint, Lincoln: University of Nebraska Press, 1999), 138–39.

66. See especially Zitkala-Ša, "The Black Hills Council," 201–6.

67. Zitkala-Ša, "Address by the Secretary-Treasurer, Society of American Indians Annual Convention," *American Indian Magazine*, Summer 1919, reprinted in *American Indian Stories*, 213–18, quote on 216. Zitkala-Ša also called on her people to learn English in "Letter to the Chiefs and Headmen of the Tribes," *American Indian Magazine*, Winter 1919, reprinted in *American Indian Stories*, 199–200.

68. Zitkala-Ša, "Address by the Secretary-Treasurer," 213.

69. Speroff, *Carlos Montezuma*, 242.

70. Zitkala-Ša, "The Black Hills Council," esp. 202–3.

71. Gertrude Bonnin, Charles H. Fabens, and Matthew K. Sniffen, *Oklahoma's Poor Rich Indians: An Orgy of Graft and Exploitation of the Five Civilized Tribes—Legalized Robbery* (Philadelphia: Office of the Indian Rights Association, 1924).

72. The Meriam Commission was one group charged with investigating corruption in the administration of Indian affairs. See Lewis Meriam, ed., *The Problem of Indian Administration* (Baltimore: Johns Hopkins University Press, 1928).

73. *And Still the Waters Run* was published by Princeton University Press in 1940; the University of Oklahoma Press, fearing legislative reprisals, canceled its contract with Debo, and the work's publication was delayed three years.

74. The Indian Reorganization Act went through Congress as the Wheeler-Howard Act of 1934.

75. For background information on Collier see Kenneth R. Philp, *John Collier's Crusade for Indian Reform, 1920–1934* (Tucson: University of Oklahoma Press, 1982). For information on the Indian New Deal and its administration, consult Graham D. Taylor, *The New Deal and American Indian Tribalism: The Administration of the Indian Reorganization Act, 1934–45* (Lincoln: University of Nebraska Press, 1980).

76. See Hafen, acknowledgements, Zitkala-Ša, *Dreams and Thunder*, ix–xi. Hafen notes that Zitkala-Ša had a Mormon funeral at Arlington, Virginia.

77. Quoted in Davidson and Norris, introduction, xxix.

9

DOROTHEA CROSS LEIGHTON

Anthropologist and Activist

Nancy J. Parezo

AMERICAN ANTHROPOLOGY, more than American history, began as an applied, as well as a theoretical, science designed to obtain concrete, useful information about North America's Native inhabitants, especially those living in the West and on the Great Plains. By *applied* I mean that research was intended to be put to some practical use, including that deemed necessary by the government. As anthropology professionalized between 1870 and 1900, it received financial support from the U.S. Congress and from federal agencies—the War Department and the Indian Service. These organizations (theoretically) required accurate information about American Indians' lives, cultures, and current conditions in order to set policies and distribute services based on treaty obligations. For example, before he became the first director of the government-sponsored Bureau of (American) Ethnology in 1879, John Wesley Powell was hired as a special commissioner of Indian Affairs to report on the problems facing the Numic-speaking peoples of the Great Basin after Mormon families moved into their territories and appropriated waterholes. While few of his recommendations were implemented—a problem with which all applied anthropologists have had to deal—Powell continued to maintain that government-sponsored anthropological research that involved firsthand, empirical data collection was the foundation the government needed to differentiate Indian groups and manage them on reservations.[1]

During the late nineteenth and early twentieth centuries, many women working in the West were involved in similar research initiatives, beginning with Alice Fletcher and her well-intentioned but ulti-

15. (*Opposite Top*) Dorothea Leighton at Ramah, New Mexico, ca. 1942, while she was conducting research on medical problems. *Given by Leighton to Nancy Parezo in 1985 for use in* Daughters of the Desert *interview project and others.*

16. (*Opposite Bottom*) Dorothea Leighton in a video still image from *Daughters of the Desert* interview project, directed by Barbara A. Babcock and Nancy J. Parezo, 1985. *Used by permission of the Wenner-Gren Foundation for Anthropological Research, Inc., New York* NY.

mately ill-advised attempts to implement the Dawes and Omaha Acts and facilitate Indian acculturation through Indian education. Such early efforts were individualistic rather than policy driven until 1934. Under John Collier's administration of the Indian Service (1933–45), this changed. Collier's goals of preserving Indian cultures and enhancing self-determinacy had been based on a wealth of studies in the 1920s and early 1930s that documented the lack of medical care on the Navajo reservation, the scandals surrounding the Bursum Bill, and the failure of the government's assimilationist policies. Collier sought to understand how social and cultural factors were affecting Indian administration and Indian lives. He turned to anthropologists and other social scientists for help, as historian Lawrence Kelly has described in his study of New Deal policy. Collier particularly desired advice on sociopolitical organization to devise tribal constitutions and stimulate economic development. He also called for studies on demography, culture and lifeways, and diet and health.[2]

The women involved in federal departments of Agriculture and Interior projects in Indian Country during the 1930s and 1940s reads like a who's who of anthropology: Frederica de Laguna, Margaret Welpley Fisher, Alice Marriott, Gladys Reichard, Rosamond Spicer, Emma Reh, Jane Chesky, Elizabeth Colson, Rosalie Wax, Laura Thompson, Ruth Underhill, and Ruth Unseem, to name but a few. Some studied contemporary social organization and reviewed tribes' prospects to develop self-governance organizations in response to the Indian Reorganization Act. Others studied settlement patterns, education policy, and prospects for social development, including projects of the Indian Arts and Crafts Board, for which Alice Marriott worked in Oklahoma. The division of education hired Ruth Underhill and Gladys Reichard to help train teachers and interpreters, develop grammars in Native languages, and revise boarding school policy. The Technical Cooperation unit worked with the Soil Conservation Service (Department of Agriculture) to improve the use of natural resources. Underhill conducted physical and human-dependency surveys to integrate plans for soil and water erosion control, focusing on land tenure, land use, and population distribution. Sophie Aberle, a physician who also had a doctorate in genetics, left her position at Yale University School of Medicine to become an Indian Service administrator, a scholar of Pueblo political organization, and an advocate of improved health care.

This alliance between social science researchers and government bureaucrats was not easy. Many agency superintendents complained bitterly and often that the anthropologists created friction between Indians and Indian Service personnel due to the nature of their questions, and probably simply because they asked Natives their opinions and views. In addition, the anthropologists quickly uncovered what was wrong and were vocal about the problems. As a result, Indian Service bureaucrats interpreted most recommendations—like the one to stop the Navajo sheep reduction program—as personal criticisms of their administration. In all cases, it took diplomatic as well as research skills for anthropologists to accomplish the research tasks assigned to them. But succeed many of them did.[3]

One area in which women researchers tried to make inroads was health. A concern for general welfare through support of medical services is one of the obligations the federal government agreed to assume in most treaties with Native Americans as part of the exchange for tribes' relinquishing title to their lands. These treaties often promised medical supplies and physician services in perpetuity as part of the government's trust responsibilities. The federal government, however, has never adequately funded health services to meet these moral and legal obligations. As legal historian Stephen Pevar has stated, "the federal government has failed to make a concerted effort to meet Indian health needs. What little the government has provided has been so substandard and inadequate that many Indians distrust government health services and refuse to use them even when they are available."[4]

As a result, Native Americans have had staggering health problems since the start of the reservation era. Government report after government report and private study after private study has shown that Indians have consistently had the lowest health levels and the highest disease rate of all major population groups in the United States. Even more disturbing has been the finding that Indians' rates of curable illness, such as tuberculosis, dysentery, and influenza, have often been over four hundred times the national averages. Many physical illnesses suffered by Indians have been directly related to malnutrition and substandard housing, due to the effects of living on reservations, where Indian Service personnel actively discouraged traditional life-styles, food, and health options. These tribulations have been reflected in high rates of alcoholism and psychological problems, including depression. These problems, combined with the fact that many Indians prior to World War II lived in small, isolated rural communities, far from medical centers, meant that Indians had shortened life expectancies and higher morbidity rates than the general population.

By the 1920s several reform groups were calling attention to health issues. They reported that the Medical Division of the Indian Service, which had been discontinued in 1887, then reestablished in 1909, consistently failed to receive adequate appropriations. The Snyder Act of 1921, Congress's first effort to improve general health care for Indians, authorized the expenditure of federal funds "for the relief of distress and conservation of health of Indians."[5] But these were inadequate, as authors of the 1928 Meriam Report later noted; the Indian Service, which administered the funds, "did a notoriously poor job of obtaining funds and recruiting doctors for reservation health services."[6] In addition, many of the doctors recruited were incompetent; salaries were extremely low; there was a lack of facilities and equipment; and the Indian Service policies focused only on curative rather than the preventive aspects of a good health program.

Health conditions on most reservations were abysmal in the late 1930s, even though Collier had secured increased funding, attempted to increase health education programs for Indians, find more doctors and nurses who would work in the remote rural areas, and modernized a few facilities. A few Native men and women were being recruited as health-care professionals, primarily as orderlies and nurses. Unfortunately, some of the health campaigns—for example, the Southwest Trachoma Campaign, to cure a major cause of blindness—had caused as much harm as good. One of the main difficulties was the antagonistic attitude toward traditional medical practices that combined healing with religion, evident in Indian Service official policy and in the attitudes of many Anglo-American health-care personnel to Indians. Historian Robert Trennert has described the Navajo situation in the late 1930s:

The scourge of trachoma had been controlled. Nonetheless, an over-whelming array of problems and failures remained. Turnover rates frequently left medical positions vacant, a fact largely attributed to inadequate salaries and bleak living conditions. Conditions at some small hospitals and sanatoriums continued to be unsatisfactory, if not appalling. Despite a clear recognition of need, Navajo medical facilities failed to keep up with demand. Most significantly, government doctors and nurses were still unable to effectively reach the suspicious and sometimes angry adult Indian population in remote areas. Nor had living conditions improved enough to eliminate the spread of contagious disease. Worst of all, the deadly scourge of tuberculosis continued to exact a fearful toll.[7]

It was not a good situation, and unfortunately, Collier thought that Indian Service personnel were making progress. It was in this setting that physicians Alexander and Dorothea Cross Leighton found themselves in 1940 and from which they developed the new field of medical anthropology, in the process changing Indian Service policy. In this chapter I will focus on this story, since it highlight's Dorothea's life and work as well as her work in the American West.

Dorothea Cross Leighton (1908–89) is best known for her work in the development of medical anthropology and public health, the use of life history and biography to understand culture and personality, and understanding how individuals lived in a sociocultural environment. She challenged existing government assimilationist policies by demonstrating the strength of individual cultures and showing that overgeneralizing assumptions that all Indians were alike and all Indians would become working-class Americans were erroneous. She was a psychiatrist trained at Johns Hopkins University during a period when few women were able to break into the field. With the addition of a cultural anthropology perspective she spent her professional life studying cognitive development; the relationship between sociocultural environment and psychiatric and somatic illness symptoms; child development; personality and culture; and psychobiology. She worked closely with the Navajos (Diné) over several decades but also conducted fieldwork with American medical personnel, Zunis, Inuit, and Aleutians as well as communities in

Nova Scotia, Nigeria, and Sweden. In addition to her husband, she collaborated with several well-known Americanist anthropologists, such as Clyde Kluckhohn and John Adair, to write what were and still are considered classic ethnographies of the Navajos and Zunis.

A dynamic, humble, down-to-earth humanist and scientist with a delightful sense of humor, Leighton said that she was simply a physician who became an anthropologist by accident. She believed in perseverance and seeing things through to the end: "I always liked to get in on something that was interesting and do as much of it as I could. If you have an idea that you want to carry out, you've got to stick with it until you finish it. Getting things finished has always been kind of a pleasure to me."[8] And that is just what she and her husband did.

Dorothea Leighton

Dorothea Cross was born on September 2, 1908, in Lunenburg, Massachusetts. Her family consisted of decisive, strong-willed, well-educated men and women of propertied Protestant heritage. Her maternal aunt was an early feminist who was "eager for women to get on with things." Her mother, Dorothea Farquhar Cross, was a graduate of Bryn Mawr and a high school teacher; her father, Frederick, graduated from M.I.T. and was a salesman before contracting tuberculosis, a malady that plagued him the rest of his life. After a series of short-term jobs alternating with stays in tuberculosis clinics, he became the treasurer of his family's wholesale grocery and the family returned to the family farm near Groton. To help make ends meet and to pursue her own educational reform interests, Dorothea Farquhar became an early proponent of the Montessori movement and started one of the first nursery schools in Massachusetts. Each of the Cross children attended Cross's Montessori school and, according to Dorothea, had immense fun.

Her parents expected that Dorothea, the valedictorian of her high school class, and her two sisters would attend Bryn Mawr and that her younger brother would attend M.I.T. Dorothea, however, set her career goals lower; she wanted to be a nurse, a field that at the time did not require an advanced degree. Her mother agreed that she could become a nurse but insisted that she obtain an education first to experience the joys of college. And enjoy college she did, although she was uncomfortable with maid service that was part of the room and board. One of the things she enjoyed most was making friends with women "from all corners of the earth."

Dorothea worked her way through Bryn Mawr, earning fifty dollars a semester. She also received several scholarships and twenty-five dollars a month from a wealthy cousin. Majoring in biology and chemistry, she obtained extensive laboratory experience. Upon graduating in 1930 she secured a position as a chemistry technician in the pediatric ward at Johns Hopkins Hospital in Baltimore through the recommendation of a friend. Soon, however, she found herself bored with the repetitive activity of hematology: "It occurred to me that nothing was going to happen to me except doing the same thing for the rest of my life if I didn't go further with my education." She decided to become a physician because she wanted to work with people rather than in an isolated lab as an underpaid assistant. Her intention was to be a general practitioner in New England, preferably her hometown.

Dorothea was accepted into Johns Hopkins School of Medicine and given a complete scholarship. In the 1930s Johns Hopkins was the only medical institution to admit women to its program on an equal basis with men. Mary Garrett, the wealthy daughter of the head of the Baltimore and Ohio Railroad, and Dr. M. Carey Thomas decided that Garrett would underwrite the new medical school, but only if equal numbers of men and women were admitted and their educations were not segregated. Thomas, president of Bryn Mawr for many years, had to obtain her doctorate in Europe due to lack of opportunities for women in the United States, and she wanted to ensure that American women fared better.[9] Dorothea was the lucky recipient of their dedication. Medical school was an exhilarating time, and she felt she experienced no discrimination. She was ready to gain the practical experience necessary to put her education to work when she graduated in 1936.

But Dorothea, who had been sheltered all her life and had come to believe that hard work and intelligence rather than gender influenced careers, experienced career-stopping discrimination when she applied for an internship in internal medicine. She sent out several letters to prestigious medical schools, but "by return mail I would get a letter back, 'Sorry you are a woman.'" She was rejected by all. Dorothea had never been turned down previously and had been encouraged to fulfill her career aspirations. Now, even though she was one of the top students in her medical graduating class, placing fourth, her only opportunity was the Hopkins-connected Baltimore City Hospital, where her faculty mentor gave her an internship. Luckily, this was an excellent public institution even if it did not have the prestige of Yale or Harvard. While it did not provide Dorothea with the research challenges she had envisioned, it turned out to be a valuable environment because she got to observe a great range of common diseases. She "got to see and do everything," including obstetrics, gaining clinical expertise that would be invaluable in her future undertakings in the West.

An important event occurred during her internship. On August 17, 1937, Dorothea married Alexander H. Leighton, who was also interning at Johns Hopkins. Alexander had been a fellow medical student at Hopkins who had previously earned a master's degree (1934) at Cambridge University, where he had studied under Bronislaw Malinowksi.[10] Alexander, a man of enormous curiosity and drive, had decided to specialize in psychiatry and neurology in order to conduct research on sanity and insanity, rather than pursue a clinical practice. Dorothea, who wanted a home and children in addition to a career, decided to alter her plans to match those of her ambitious husband. She had been moderately interested in psychiatry, but now she decided that for her and Alexander to be in different medical specialties "would be an awful mess." She set aside her plans and joined her husband as a resident in psychiatry at the Henry Phipps Psychiatric Clinic at Johns Hopkins.

The Leightons' residencies were memorable for their intellectual development. Dorothea spoke about it at length in interviews, discussing her admiration for their mentor, the clinic's director, neurologist, psychobiologist, and psychiatrist Adolf Meyer.[11] Meyer, an internationally known theorist with a deep concern for the care of mentally ill patients, had a holistic, culturally specific, and pragmatic approach embedded in evolutionary psychology. According to Meyer, mental and social problems represented maladjustments when an individual lacked the skills necessary to meet challenges in a specific social setting. This was a theory that could easily incorporate cultural diversity.

To understand patients' illnesses, Meyer urged his students to obtain their life histories and then focus on their problem-solving abilities rather than using Freudian psychoanalytic protocols. He also had each resident write his or her own life history, believing that self-reflection would increase their empathy for patients. Under Meyer's tutelage, Dorothea and Alexander learned important qualitative research methodologies: narrative construction, semi-structured and unstructured interviewing techniques, and the ability to listen to a person and then analyze his or her words in such a way as to uncover the interviewee's meaning in the context of his or her own life. They also began to realize how important culture was. For Dorothea there was one other important lesson: "He taught us a lot about getting along with people who were different than ourselves. He helped us see the individual in relation to society."

The Leightons also learned to respect other cultures. Meyer was interested in immigrants and the cultural construction of health and illness in different societies, for he felt this helped shape their personalities and influenced the types of illnesses they contracted. He encouraged the Leightons' desire to broaden their understanding by offering them release time to learn about anthropology, specifically how culture and personality correlated.

While completing their 1939 psychiatry residencies, the Leightons attended the monthly interdisciplinary seminars at Columbia University in which Ralph Linton, a cultural anthropologist, and Abram Kardiner, a psychoanalyst (assisted by Cora Du Bois), applied neo-Freudian analysis to ethnographic data. These classes were experiments to see if psychologists could deduce the modal and deviant personalities found in a particular group from an ethnographer's description of a culture. This ultimately led to the famous culture-at-a-distance studies of the 1940s and 1950s. More pragmatically, wanting to pursue studies that had some clinical applicability, the Leightons were interested in how different cultures viewed illness, how religion and medicine were culturally combined, and how biomedicine could be more useful to people. The Leightons were becoming activist cultural anthropologists; they decided to test their growing research skills in a Native culture.

At Ramah: Learning to Recognize Cultural Differences

The Leightons decided to take a "leave of absence from medicine in order to see what other people were like." Specifically, they wanted to learn how other cultures defined psychiatric conditions. Now it was time to learn about Native societies and ethnographic methods, to "find out what anthropologists talked about." While Alexander had traveled extensively in Europe, Egypt, and the Middle East, Dorothea had never been west of Detroit. To prepare themselves for a fieldwork situation, the neophytes returned to Columbia and audited as many courses as they could. Their goal was to learn to recognize critical social and cultural details. They decided to do a joint project rather than two separate projects. Dorothea firmly believed in the efficacy of a husband-wife team in field settings, because she had noted in her psychiatry rounds that male patients responded better to male doctors, and women patients to female doctors.

Now they needed to find a research community that would welcome them and an anthropologist to serve as a cultural broker. Alexander talked with Margaret Mead, who suggested Clyde Kluckhohn, a professor at Harvard University, who had worked with Navajos in New Mexico for many years.[12] Kluckhohn naturally steered them to the Navajos and to the individuals he had worked with and respected. Kluckhohn, a cultural theoretician trained at Harvard University, had received his doctorate in 1936 and was a proponent of interdisciplinary research that focused on social relations. While many anthropologists were territorial and tried to keep other researchers away from "their" Native communities, Kluckhohn regularly supported young researchers. "I can't tell you how important that really was," Dorothea recalled, "because Kluckhohn's manner of approach to the Navajo was so different from that of most other anthropologists." Kluckhohn gave them a crash course in Navajo society and culture without making them memorize abstract cultural classificatory schemes. While he gave practical advice, the Leightons were on their own to either sink or swim, like all neophyte anthropologists.

Having secured a grant from the Social Science Research Council, the Leightons headed west, for the first times in their lives, to visit

"Clyde's Indians" at Ramah in January 1940. It was an adventure of a lifetime, Dorothea recalled, full of hard work, new experiences, the unexpected, and a fair amount of culture shock. Simply driving in the West provided unexpected challenges.

> It was cold and snowy. You had to be careful if you wanted to go anywhere except stay on the main road, which went east and west. We wanted to go to Ramah, of course, and the road from Gallup to Zuni was just dirt. You had to get up early before the sun melted the mud and then you had to wait wherever you had gone until the mud hardened up late in the afternoon. We learned that. We got into the mud lots of times and out of the mud lots of other times. It was a technique you had to master.

They quickly learned that life in the Navajo world was different from life in the East. One of the most remarkable aspects was the infallibility of the Navajo grapevine.

> The Navajo knew we were coming down but I don't think they knew when because we had no way to get in touch with them before we got there. When we got down to the interpreter's house, there wasn't anybody in sight. There was a little smoke coming out of the hogan so we knew probably somebody was there. After we had sat in the car for a while, a little boy come out of the hogan, rushed out to the woodpile, and grabbed a piece of wood, and rushed back in again.
>
> Then we got out of the car, not knowing what Navajo etiquette was. After the little boy came out, we went over and knocked on the door. Somebody on the inside said, "Come in." It turned out it was the oldest daughter of our interpreter, David, who had had a little schooling and could speak English. Her father had coached her in what to say if we showed up. She said her parents had gone away but would soon be back. So we sat around and looked at each other for quite a while and sure enough they came.
>
> It turned out they had a guest hogan, just a little one, about fifteen feet from the big hogan. They were keeping it for us to use. It had up and down poles. They had a pet lamb that had been all around the hogan this whole time and used to go over and take out all the caulking between the poles. So it was a very airy place. We began sticking newspapers in it

after awhile but the lamb pulled that out, too. We set up housekeeping with our camping equipment. We had thought that maybe we would have to live in our car but this was much better to have the hogan—even with the lamb—because in the hogan you could sit up straight and keep warm. It was a lot of fun. Later on they built another one for their other guests who would come. So we had the chance to see how they made a hogan among other things.

The Leightons settled in and were soon being visited and assessed by the community to establish their sincerity and acceptability.

The Navajos in the general neighborhood had heard we were there. News moved fast. They were curious to see what we looked like, how we behaved, and what we were like. So a large company of them arrived one day. A small boy who didn't speak English came over and gave us a gentle idea that we should come to the big hogan. So we wondered what we should take. We decided on a couple packets of cigarettes. Then we went over to the big hogan. There was this huge crowd. They were all there in a big circle, all the way around the edges of the hogan. It was just full of people; women on one side, men on the other.

I don't know what we should have done. I guess we should have simply come in and just sat down. What we did do was to go around the entire circle and shake hands with everyone. The only person we knew was the interpreter. Having done that, we went around the circle again and gave everyone a cigarette. Hardly anyone started smoking. They just stuck them in their pockets. They didn't say a thing.

Then we sat down in a corner. I didn't go to sit with the women. No one said anything at all for quite a long time. Now that's hard for us. We expect people to do something or other, to fiddle around with a little unimportant conversation. But not a thing happened, not even our interpreter said anything. After a while—about fifteen minutes—they began to talk to each other. They never did talk to us. I don't think they ever asked David, our interpreter, about the things we had asked about. Our end of it was entirely silence. That was quite something. It taught us a great deal. I think our manners were better from then on because we didn't push ourselves on them.

The Navajos decided that the Leightons were acceptable, in part because they quickly learned to respect Navajo ways and were not pushy. They were also acceptable because they had skills that the community needed.

The Navajo already knew that we were doctors. Clyde Kluckhohn probably told David that we were doctors. David was very glad to hear this, for being a doctor was something that was very valuable to them to have around because it was a long way to the hospital. They wouldn't go to the Zuni hospital, which wasn't so far away, because it wasn't healthy to do anything with the Zuni. They had to go at least to Fort Defiance. That's a long way from where we were, about forty miles south of Gallup.

The Leightons quickly spent more time being doctors than psychological researchers. They served the community rather than simply studying it.

We would have people call on us for help by way of our interpreter. I remember going to a hogan late at night. Somebody's little girl was ill. The only light in that hogan was a fire in the middle of the place, which had one of those tin cans around it. It wasn't very helpful. That hogan was just full of people who had come to see what we were going to do. I don't know how many kids I stepped over trying to get to where that little girl was lying. Most of the kids were sleeping. I don't think they even noticed. It's interesting the things you get into if you have some desirable skill that the people would like to use.

In addition to becoming the community's personal physicians, the Leightons began interviewing men and women, obtaining eight life stories. In this they were guided by David, for like all good ethnographers they let their Navajo hosts guide them in their endeavors. They did this ethically, following Navajo rules of protocol—women talked about women's things, men about men's. They also worked through family and clan networks. "We let them just talk. All we did was to get things clarified sometimes. . . . We were doing the same thing we did in psychiatry. To see what kind of life they led and what they felt about it." The Navajos told them what they wanted the Leightons to know in return for twenty-five cents per hour, reciprocal compensation for their time and knowledge. In this way the Leightons learned about what was important to the Navajos, the range of variability in people's life experiences, and how the Navajos dealt with the joys and vagaries of life. Most important to Dorothea was that they learned that "Navajos are not all the same just because they are from the same tribe." They were able to talk about intercultural variability and avoid the trap of viewing Indians as homogeneous entities.[13]

I have included these brief interview excerpts in order to provide an idea of what Leighton, like other female anthropologists of her era, felt was critical. These elements included obtaining firsthand information from people only after the people had had time to assess the researcher's personality; presenting and interpreting this information in culturally specific terms as well as through theoretical lenses; avoiding the pitfalls of reductionist primitivism and evolutionary paradigms; respecting local customs, not rushing into a fieldwork situation and imposing outside rules of behavior on participants; and trying to understand people on their own terms in specific cultural, social, and historical contexts, as individuals rather than classificatory types. In short, Leighton advocated for respecting other ways of life and cultural diversity, a concept known as cultural relativism. She wanted to understand and help individuals, in part by understanding how they solved problems.[14] This was a very grounded and empirical approach rather than an abstract theoretical undertaking. She had no theories to prove or disprove; she simply wanted to know.

But the Leightons' work had theoretical and methodological implications. Dorothea and Alexander began to refine the life history technique to produce an unedited story about people's lives reflecting "how they saw life, what were their experiences, the good times and the bad troubles they had had." In this way they let the Navajos they interviewed decide what was important and what was not, rather than focusing on what Leighton called "anthropology's a priori taxonomies of supposedly important cultural traits." From this highly ethical and contemporary perspective they learned what had value to the Navajos: that the family is critical in the healing process and that Anglo-American medical doctors are considered to be on a par with herbalists, those who only treat symptoms using medicines. They also learned that biomedicine was considered to be flawed because it was not systemic or holistic. Doctors were conceptually distinct from Navajo religious curers (*hataɫi*), who searched for underlying causes to help restore balance and harmony to the patient as well as the community. Through the eight life histories they obtained, including one from a Navajo diagnostician (the specialist who identifies an illness and determines its ultimate cause and healing procedures), the Leightons realized that Anglo-American medical practitioners were approaching Navajos incorrectly and alienating patients rather than providing much-needed services as required by treaty obligations.

After six months the Leightons moved to their second field site. Anthropology is a comparative discipline, and they wanted to avail themselves of the opportunity to compare the Navajos with another group. They traveled to Alaska in May 1940 and spent the summer with the St. Lawrence Island Inuit, who turned out to be quite different from the Navajos. Here they had more adventures, saw more of the West, and perfected their life history and storytelling data-collection techniques, recording twenty-two verbatim accounts. As they had among the Navajos, they also observed behavioral patterns and honed their skills in participant observation. As before, they treated the sick, every day for three months.

Returning to Baltimore and a New Direction

Their time with the Navajos and Inuit had passed all too quickly for the Leightons. They returned to Johns Hopkins expecting to resume their residencies. While Alexander received an appointment, Dorothea did not, the victim of nepotism laws, gender prejudice, and paternalism. Hospital staff officials had decided, without consulting them, that the usual arrangement (two residents working alternative night duty) would put a strain on their marriage. "They didn't say it was really to give the job only to Alex since he was a man. They couldn't even think of what to do with me. It seemed to me that it was very poor judgment on the part of the psychiatrists." It was just an excuse; Dorothea had reached a glass ceiling and was without a job.

She spent her days "fooling around," putting their field notes in order and transcribing the stories and life histories. This led to their first two publications on the integration of psychology, medicine, and religion in Navajo concepts of health and illness.[15] As Dorothea remembered, "It was a busy time. Everyone knew the war was coming and nobody knew what to do about it. Alex joined the Navy as a reserve officer and lots of other people were doing that kind of thing, too. I think that it was kind of a time of change essentially." And it was soon a time of change for Dorothea.

In December 1940 the Leightons received a letter from John Collier asking them to come to Washington DC and tell him and his senior staff about the conditions they had seen on the Navajo reservation. They arranged a meeting and went the following February to discuss how to improve health-care services to Native communities. Using a case study approach, the Leightons talked about their specific experiences—what they had seen and what they had not seen—and provided suggestions to solve the problems. They discussed infrastructural problems and the failure of the current system to deliver adequate health care. Because the four available medical facilities were located on the edges of the reservation, most Navajos could not reach them in a timely manner. The doctors never bothered to go out into the community, something they could easily have done by setting up temporary clinics at trading posts. The Leightons also told Collier about the large number of medicine men scattered throughout the reservation, noting that "[t]hese highly intelligent, diligent and dedicated healers had been not only ignored but scorned and derided."[16]

They stressed the profound ignorance of agency employees concerning Navajo lifeways and concepts of illness and health. "None of them had the slightest idea that they were working with anybody different from the people they had always worked with. . . . As far as they were concerned it was just a sick body and that was all you had to think about." This, of course, was inappropriate, but it had not occurred to any of the Indian Service personnel to tell them any different. The Leightons said the doctors were second-rate, unaware of medical advances, isolated, prejudiced, and unhappy. "They were people who had run out of places to practice, more or less. They were not top notch at all. . . . I don't know that they were bad doctors but they were certainly lacking in any humanity interest." Most of them did not want to be there; "doing things that were good for Indians was not very popular." They also told of the deleterious effects such ignorance had on the physicians' treatment of Navajo patients:

> As soon as a patient arrived at the hospital the first thing the doctor would ask would be, "Have you had a sing [curing ceremony] for this?" If the man or woman made the mistake of saying yes, they had, then the doctor would say, "Go on back to your medicine man. We can't do anything. He's made you sick. Now he will have to fix you up again." You know that's idiotic. That's dumb, very dumb. . . . The doctors didn't seem to have the slightest interest in what kind of people the Navajos were, how they managed, or anything else. [They] would probably do quite a lot better if they knew a little more.

The doctors knew nothing of Navajo culture and showed no respect for the Navajos, and the patients never understood what was expected of them. Hospitals were seen as places of death, not places to restore health and balance. There was no place for a family, which had often walked sixty miles, to stay while their relatives were treated. The Indian Service medical system was a failure. The same ignorance was true of the majority of white people working on the Navajo reservation, the Leightons added. "They were just there for the money and few of them had sense enough to talk to the people with whom they worked and get to know them and find out that they weren't so different from ourselves. But the doctors needed it the most. They had never had a thought in that direction."

A stunned silence followed the recitation. Then Collier asked them what he should do. The Leightons recommended that he commission a series of monographs, one for each Indian tribe, designed to help Indian Service staff, physicians, and nurses understand the societies and cultures with whom they worked. People needed "a way to find out a little about the people they are working with." Each book should be concise, well written, interesting, and full of relevant facts, not unnecessary theory, biased assumptions, or evolutionary labels. There was to be special emphasis on each tribe's concepts of health, illness, and proper treatment for various conditions.

This was a revolutionary concept. Rather than asking Indians to change, to understand and unquestionably accept Anglo-American concepts and health care practices, the Leightons proposed that Anglo-Americans understand and accept the worldviews of each group of Indian people in order for the Indian Service to fulfill its treaty obligations. There was no Indian problem. There was an Anglo-American problem.

Collier turned back to them and said, "Would you please write this book?"

The Navaho Door

The Leightons thought about the offer and agreed to take on the project. Since Alexander was working full-time at the hospital as chief resident in psychiatry and as an instructor in the medical school, Dorothea did the bulk of the work, transcribing the lengthy interviews, arranging their data, and deciding what Anglo-Americans needed to know about Navajo culture. Collier had little money to pay her, but he did arrange ample funds for publication, editing, and an additional field trip for Dorothea. Her one condition on agreeing to the project had been that she return to the Navajo reservation to talk with doctors, nurses, schoolteachers, and agency personnel to "see if anyone would read" such a book.

This time Dorothea took her mother, since Alexander could not obtain leave from the hospital. They went in November and December 1941. "I went around the reservation and talked to a lot of people. There was uniform interest." The agency staff felt that the existing scholarly literature on the Navajo was of limited use because it was so theoretical and laden with jargon. People wanted useful, ethnographically correct information, written in an accessible style.

Back in Baltimore, Alexander had been called up in the navy reserves the day after the attack on Pearl Harbor to give physicals and psychological tests to new recruits. Still stationed in Baltimore, he helped Dorothea by looking over and "improving" the manuscript "a little here and there," but essentially he left the bulk of the writing to her. The outcome was *The Navaho Door*, published by Harvard University Press in 1944. Alexander was listed as first author because it was again assumed that Dorothea, as a wife, naturally should take second place, even if she had done the vast majority of the writing.[17]

The Navaho Door, a small, compact book designed for physicians, was written in a clear, distilled form, thanks to the efforts of their editor, Collier's assistant, Salish-Kottenai historian D'Arcy McNickle. Its purpose was "simply to try to understand the Navahos' way of looking at things, and to compare their point of view with our own and that of people brought up like ourselves in average American communities. Soon, as we observed and learned and some of our preconceived notions began to dissolve, we became fascinated with the problem of the mutual adjustment and cooperation between people who are separated by language, skin color, and a whole way of life. Inherent in this adjustment, it seemed to us, were some of the keys to the strife and wars of all the world."[18] The book outlined what Indian Service personnel needed to know about Navajo culture, values, philosophy, typical behavioral patterns, and society in order to more effectively work with the Navajos and provide better health service.

Dorothea described *The Navaho Door* as intentionally sketchy and episodic: "There was no use getting too fancy with all the fine details." Using short, fictionalized vignettes based on their life history materials, she painted pictures of the land and daily lives—of people herding, being well, being sick, going to school, fetching water, and losing their sons in the war. They included stories of how Navajos would react to biomedicine and what doctors and nurses might expect from their protocols and how they were delivered. The Leightons argued against the displacement and ridicule of traditional Navajo curing practices and argued that medical workers had to have a sound and thorough knowledge of Navajo culture in order to be effective. To help accomplish this desirable goal, they discussed Navajo concepts of health, illness, and balance so that physicians could interpret cultural belief and values. Their message was that by learning cultural respect the doctors would be able to influence Navajo acceptance of biomedicine.

For Dorothea the most important part of the book—and the part she liked the best—was the series of practical recommendations for agency personnel. The Leightons included suggestions for culturally appropriate treatment, ideas on how to introduce treatment protocols and ensure compliance, and tips on how to work with, not against, Native healers. Some of the suggestions were very specific: the language that should be used to introduce biomedical concepts to Navajo patients; how to work with families—not simply the ill patient; how to simplify medical concepts in ways that utilize Navajo concepts and vocabulary; how to be direct and personal; and finally, the value of patience and silence. This was an explicit plea for cross-cultural understanding and the complementarity of Navajo medicine and biomedicine.

Comparing *The Navaho Door* to her later books on the Navajos (*The Navaho, Children of the People, Gregorio, the Hand-Trembler*) and Zunis (*People of the Middle Place*), Dorothea modestly said that the book "isn't anything very powerful," except for "the recommendations on various things. They were my choices. They were just made up out of whole cloth by me. Just thinking of the situation, you know, and how I would do it in the practical circumstances." They are, in addition, a plea for sound, democratic policies toward Indians, for adequate funding, and for cross-cultural understanding. These recommendations were also Dorothea's explicit statement that the Indians of the American West were not going to be victims of Manifest Destiny.[19]

With *The Navaho Door* the Leightons unintentionally set the stage for a new field, medical anthropology, and influenced one other, community development, by establishing its theoretical and methodological standards. In this and her later work with the Indian Service, Dorothy had a profound impact on government policy. This was especially evident while Collier remained in office. In the introduction to *The Navaho Door* he wrote: "The discoveries and generalizations of the Leightons, in this Navajo area, have been found usable by the administration. Their implications are much wider than the area of health work alone. I believe that they would have instant and practical use to administrators faced with challenges and opportunities, which are at all similar, and I believe that this may mean nearly all administrators, at least in the 'colonial' and 'minorities' fields."[20]

Others were echoing this plea to add cultural relativism to health planning. In the first volume of *Applied Anthropology* (1942), neuro-psychiatrist and general practitioner Alice Joseph published an article titled "Physician and Patient" in which she discussed the relationship between Anglo-American physicians and their Indian patients and outlined barriers to mutual understanding. Joseph had worked on the health staff of the Indian Service and, like Dorothea (see below), as a member of the Indian Education Project at Hopi and in the Tohono O'odham villages. As had the Leightons, she spent a significant amount of her time practicing medicine. Based on her experiences, she concluded that when there was cooperation between white doctors and Native healers, there would be improvements in health:

> The health of Indians is threatened by unhygienic conditions, by climate, by insufficient clothing, by insufficient and deficient diet. All of these favor the spread of contagious diseases. To cure one sick person means here, more than anywhere else, to help a whole group, by giving a worker back to the fields of his village. It also means an improvement in the relationship between white men and Indians in general, because a sick man, cured in the right way and without neglect of his personal needs, is, against all other assumptions, essentially grateful and open-minded. . . . Our success, that is, the success of white medicine, will largely depend, not upon a passive surrender by the Indians of their old traditions and beliefs, but upon the white physicians' capacity for, let me say, moral perspective and for making practical application of that perspective in his relation with his Indian patients.[21]

Similar voices were being raised, and Collier changed Indian Services policies. But the war cut the movement short, as young doctors and nurses willing to listen to the reflexive message were transferred to the military. Change was further undermined as Congress moved from the policies of the Indian New Deal and some degree of self-determination to that of termination. It took many years before health-care practitioners' accommodation with traditional medicine became of interest to policy makers again. When this happened, *The Navaho Door* influenced a new generation of health workers, especially those who worked in the Indian Health Service during the Vietnam War era.

Indian Service Employee and Public Health Specialist

In 1942 Dorothea accepted a position of "Special Physician, Research" with the Office of Indian Affairs and became part of a large research group that applied psychological personality development tests to children from five Indian tribes (Lakotas, Navajos, Zunis, Tohono O'odhams, and Hopis). She worked with the Hopis and Zunis without Alexander, who was now a commander in the navy (1941–46). "This was a very good experience for me and I felt good about myself and the work we were doing." Called the Indian Education, Personality, and Administration Project under the direction of Laura Thompson, it was administered by the Committee on Human Development at the University of Chicago in conjunction with the Society for Applied Anthropology. Its purpose was to understand the role of culture in the formation of individual personalities and the range of psychological variation in culture by identifying modal personalities for a society in order to predict how individuals would react under different conditions. Along with other anthropologists and physicians, such as Rosamond Spicer, Jane Chesky, Alice Joseph, Clyde Kluckhohn, John Adair, Malcolm Collier, Florence Hawley Ellis, Sophie Aberle, Ruth Underhill, and Gordon Macgregor, Leighton studied how forced changes were affecting core Zuni and Navajo values. The result was three significant and theoretically important monographs: *The Navaho, Children of the People*, and *People of the Middle Place*.[22] *The Navaho* is considered a classic in anthropology and was required reading in most courses in introductory cultural anthropology and advanced ethnology, including the ones I took in graduate school in the 1970s. It is Dorothea's best-known work, an archetypal ethnography that discusses the basic elements of Navajo culture.

The Leightons lived in Washington DC after World War II while Dorothea worked on the Zuni material and had their first child, Dorothea. In 1947 they moved to Ithaca, New York, where Alexander was given a professorship at Cornell University to help develop the new field school in applied anthropology.[23] Again nepotism meant Dorothea was not offered a professional position even though she had more significant publications than young men recently hired for the innovative program. Instead of starting a clinical practice, she had another son, Frederick, and took over the care of a young cousin. With three children, she decided that care for the children, running the household, and serving as hostess for Alexander's many professional colleagues required her full concentration. "I was really interested in the kids and I think that the trouble with a lot of professional women is that they don't pay enough attention to their kids. It is very difficult to be a good mother and a good professional at the same time. I used to break my neck to be home when they came home from school." But she missed the research. As the children matured she began to work part-time again, eventually joining her husband in his ambitious seventeen-year study of Stirling County, Nova Scotia. Again the husband-and-wife team had a groundbreaking project, this time in psychiatric epidemiology. Their study uncovered the prevalence and character of psychiatric disorders in an apparently normal rural population. Their techniques were later incorporated into standard practices at the Centers for Disease Control. Dorothea developed a systematic approach to coding interview results; coauthored the final research report, *The Character of Danger* (1963); and penned several professional articles.[24]

In 1949 Dorothea was finally made an assistant professor in child development and family relations at Cornell University. She held this position until 1952, when she decided to work part-time in order to concentrate again on her family. Her new position was as a research associate in anthropology, an unpaid or grant-sponsored job without tenure. In 1958, with all her children in school, she accepted a tenured position as an associate professor in clinical psychology. She began to develop courses that introduced anthropological perspectives to psychology, and courses in medical anthropology, bringing her full circle from her training in the 1930s.

In 1965 the Leightons divorced and Dorothea embarked on her next career. She helped develop another interdisciplinary field, public health. At age fifty-seven she left Cornell to become a professor of mental health in the new School of Public Health at the University of North Carolina, a position she held until her retirement in 1974. During this time she functioned as a typical faculty member and department chair, concerned with curricular development, teaching, mentoring students, and university politics. She modestly states that she "got all kinds of things done," basically an "extension of what we had told Mr. Collier and his staff about the Navajo and sickness, their characteristics and habits." By "extension" Leighton meant that the theoretical, methodological, and practical goals of her original project with the

Navajos applied to her work in a department of public health. The assumption that biomedicine was automatically correct was as invalid in her new setting as it had been with Native peoples, and taking into account the cultural values and perspectives of the population to be served was equally essential for improving health care and extending it successfully to all segments of a population. While doing all this she also served as an instructor in the Forum for Educators in Community Psychiatry at Duke University and held a variety of positions in professional associations. An accomplished teacher after her retirement, she served as a visiting professor of anthropology at the University of California, Berkeley, in 1980 and 1981, helping to developed a medical anthropology program.

Conclusion

Dorothy Cross Leighton had a distinguished career. Unlike many of the other women in this volume, she spent her career primarily in academia, working in a variety of academic and clinical settings. It was a scientific life, devoted to policy development and making the world a healthier place for all peoples, regardless of their culture of origin. She considered herself an accidental anthropologist and southwesternist, learning from people rather than textbooks. "I really became an anthropologist through the teachings of people of other cultures," she wrote. "I believe that the process was greatly aided by my possession of knowledge and skill in an area that was of interest and use to those I visited. . . . Any kind of appropriate and applicable knowledge or skill has a similar effect in building bridges between peoples of disparate cultures."[25] Although she moved on to areas outside the American West, she returned periodically to the Navajo reservation to assess health care for the federal government and several nonprofit organizations. In 1982 she returned to her original work with the Navajos and wrote an article on Navajo women for a special issue of the *American Indian Quarterly*.[26] In this article she reflected on the women she had known in 1940 and their lives. Her work provided the foundation for work I and scholars of my generation were dealing with regarding Navajo women's lives in the 1970s and 1980s.

Leighton had never intended to influence Indian Service and later

Indian Health Service policies, nor did she foresee that she would be considered one of the foremost scholars of Navajo and Zuni life. But, unable to follow a traditional career in clinical medicine and psychiatry because of discrimination and nepotism, this is what she became. And others followed in her path.

In 1955 the medical unit of the Bureau of Indian Affairs was transferred to the U.S. Public Health Service and redesigned as the Indian Health Service (IHS). One of eight agencies in the Department of Health and Human Services, IHS is charged with attaining the highest level of health and welfare for eligible American Indians and Alaska Natives. Its broad goal is to ensure equity in health-care delivery, assist Native peoples in defining their health needs, establish local health-care priorities, and provide management for health programs through the direct administration of Indian health facilities and contract care. Since its inception, this has included the work of anthropologists to help develop culturally sensitive training programs for medical personnel, based on the model that the Leightons pioneered.

In 1956 the Leightons' program was implemented. The Cornell University Many Farms project, under the direction of anthropologist John Adair and physician Kurt Deuschle, worked with physicians to devise training for Navajo health workers as aides and interpreters.[27] Adair and Deuschle also instituted a record system adapted to the Navajo kinship system, clarified Navajo health beliefs, and collected epidemiological data on Navajo health conditions. Many other projects in the 1960s and 1970s focused on community health behavior. As a result of these changes, health care for Navajos has improved since 1940. Dorothea and Alexander made a difference. Their view that the delivery of effective health care must take culture into account is the only sound federal policy for an era of self-determination. It epitomizes an ethic of respect for individuals and cultures and demonstrates how scholars can and should apply their knowledge to solve contemporary problems.

Notes

1. John Wesley Powell, "Report of the Director, First Annual Report of the Bureau of Ethnology to the Secretary of the Smithsonian Institution for 1879–1880" (Washington DC: Government Printing Office, 1881), ix.

2. Robert E. Bieder, *Science Encounters the Indian, 1820–1880: The Early Years of American Ethnology* (Norman: University of Oklahoma Press, 1986); Frederick E. Hoxie, *A Final Promise: The Campaign to Assimilate the Indians, 1880–1920* (Lincoln: University of Nebraska Press, 1984); Lawrence C. Kelly, "Anthropology and Anthropologists in the Indian New Deal," *Journal of the History of Behavioral Sciences* 16, no. 1 (1980): 6–24; Louise Lamphere, "Unofficial Histories: A Vision of Anthropology from the Margins," *American Anthropologist* 106, no. 1 (2004): 126–39. For more on Fletcher see Joan Mark, *A Stranger in Her Native Land: Alice Fletcher and the American Indians* (Lincoln: University of Nebraska Press, 1988); and Alessandra Lorini, "Alice Fletcher and the Search for Women's Public Recognition in Professionalizing American Anthropology," *Cromohs* 8 (2003): 1–25.

3. See D'Arcy McNickle, "Anthropology and the Indian Reorganization Act," in *The Uses of Anthropology*, ed. Walter Goldschmidt, Special Publication no. 11 (Washington DC: American Anthropological Association, 1979), 51–60; Solon T. Kimball, "Land Use Management: The Navajo Reservation," in Goldschmidt, *The Uses of Anthropology*, 61–78; Katherine Spencer Halpern, "Women in Applied Anthropology in the Southwest: The Early Years," in *Hidden Scholars: Women Anthropologists and the Native American Southwest*, ed. Nancy J. Parezo (Albuquerque: University of New Mexico Press, 1993), 189–201; Lawrence C. Kelley, "Why Applied Anthropology Developed When It Did: A Commentary on People, Money, and Changing Times," in *Social Context of American Ethnology, 1840–1984*, ed. June Helm (Washington DC: American Ethnological Society, 1984), 122–38; Louise Lamphere, "Gladys Reichard among the Navajo," in Parezo, *Hidden Scholars*, 157–81.

4. Steven Pevar, *The Rights of Indians and Tribes*, ACLU guide, 2nd ed. (Carbondale: Southern Illinois University Press, 1992), 274–75.

5. Snyder Act (1921) 25 U.S.C. Sec. 13.

6. Pevar, *Rights of Indians*, 275; see also Lewis Meriam, ed., *The Problem of Indian Administration* (Baltimore: Johns Hopkins University Press, 1928), 229–34.

7. Robert A. Trennert, *White Man's Medicine: Government Doctors and the Navajo, 1863–1955* (Albuquerque: University of New Mexico Press, 1998), 199. See also Wade Davies, *Healing Ways: Navajo Health Care in the Twentieth Century* (Albuquerque: University of New Mexico Press, 2001); Lawrence Kelly, *The Navajo Indian and Federal Indian Policy, 1900–1935* (Tucson: University of

Arizona Press, 1968); Kenneth R. Philp, *John Collier's Crusade for Indian Reform, 1920–1954* (Tucson: University of Arizona Press, 1977); T. Kue Young, *The Health of Native Americans: Towards Biocultural Epidemiology* (New York: Oxford University Press, 1994).

8. Dorothea Leighton, interview with Jennifer Fox, November 21 and 22, 1985, for the Daughters of the Desert Project under the direction of Barbara A. Babcock and Nancy J. Parezo. Quotes from Leighton, unless otherwise attributed, are from these interviews. The tapes are housed at the Wenner-Gren Foundation for Anthropological Research in New York City. Additional information is from the Dorothea and Alexander Leighton Papers, Special Collection, Northern Arizona University. For an excellent summary of Leighton's career see Joyce Griffen, "Dorothea Cross Leighton," in *Women Anthropologists: A Biographical Dictionary*, ed. Ute Gacs, Aisha Khan, Jerrie McIntyre, and Ruth Weinberg (New York: Greenwood Press, 1988), 231–37.

9. Helen L. Horowitz, "M. Carey Thomas," *American National Biography* (Oxford University Press for the American Council of Learned Societies, 2000), http://www.anb.org/articles/15/15–00852.html.

10. "Alexander Hamilton Leighton, 1908-," *Contemporary Authors Online* (Gale Research Group, 2005), hppt://galenet.galegroup.com.ezproxy.library.arizona.edu/servlet/BioRC.

11. Hans Pols, "Adolf Meyer," *American National Biography Online* (2000), http://www.anb.org/articles/12/12–00614.html.

12. Alexander Leighton, "A Quest for Synthesis in a Splintering World," Margaret Mead Lecture, 1983, manuscript on file in Leighton Papers.

13. The transcriptions and field notes from this fieldwork are housed in the Leighton Papers. They are filed with health-care observations and evidence of the Leighton's reciprocity to the Navajos. They are also filled with descriptions of doctors and nurses and assessments of their character, knowledge, and sensitivity.

14. The Leightons made a movie about problem solving in 1940. This is one of the first color films depicting Navajos. They showed it to Collier and his staff.

15. Dorothea Cross Leighton and Alexander H. Leighton, "Elements of Psychotherapy in Navajo Religion," *Psychiatry* 4 (1941): 505–25; Dorothea Cross Leighton and Alexander H. Leighton, "Some Types of Uneasiness and Fear in a Navaho Indian Community," *American Anthropologist* 44, no. 1 (1942): 194–209.

16. Dorothea Leighton, "Anthropologist by Accident," paper presented at the American Anthropological Association meeting, Washington DC, December 4, 1982, manuscript, Leighton Papers.

17. Alexander H. Leighton and Dorothea Cross Leighton, *The Navaho Door: An Introduction to Navaho Life* (Cambridge: Harvard University Press, 1944). Later publishers treated Dorothea more fairly.

18. Leighton and Leighton, *The Navaho Door*, xviii.

19. Clyde Kluckhohn and Dorothea Leighton, *The Navaho* (Cambridge: Harvard University Press, 1946); Alexander Leighton and Dorothea Leighton, *Gregorio, the Hand Trembler: A Psychobiological Personality Study of a Navajo Indian*, Papers of the Peabody Museum of American Archaeology and Ethnology, vol. 40 (Cambridge: Harvard University Press, 1949); Alexander Leighton and Dorothea Leighton, *Lucky, the Navajo Singer*, ed. Joyce Griffen (Albuquerque: University of New Mexico Press, 1992); Dorothea Leighton, "Rorschach's of 87 Zuni Children," in *Primary Records in Culture and Personality*, ed. Bert Kaplan (Madison WI: Microcard Foundation, 1957), 1–274; Dorothea Leighton, "Rorschach's of 107 Navajo Children," in *Primary Records in Culture and Personality*, ed. Bert Kaplan (Madison WI: Microcard Foundation, 1957), 1–275; Dorothea Cross Leighton and John Adair, *People of the Middle Place: A Study of the Zuni Indians*, Behavioral Science Monographs (New Haven: Human Relations Area Files, 1966); Dorothea Cross Leighton and Clyde Kluckhohn, *Children of the People: The Navaho Individual and His Development* (Cambridge: Harvard University Press, 1948).

20. John Collier, foreword to Leighton and Leighton, *The Navaho Door*, xiv–xv.

21. Alice Joseph, "Physician and Patient: Some Aspects of Inter-Personal Relations between Physicians and Patients," *Applied Anthropology* 1, no. 4 (1942): 1. Trained in Germany, Joseph escaped to the United States with other Jewish refugees in the mid-1930s. Following her work in the Indian Service she worked for the Veterans Administration in New York as a psychiatrist and in private practice until her retirement in the 1960s. Like the Leightons, she was one of the founders of medical anthropology. Later she worked in Micronesia and taught at Harvard University.

22. Kluckhohn and Leighton, *The Navaho*; Leighton and Kluckhohn, *Children of the People*; Leighton and Adair, *People of the Middle Place*.

23. See Wade Davies, "Cornell's Field Seminar in Applied Anthropology:

Social Scientists and American Indians in the Postwar Southwest," *Journal of the Southwest* 43, no. 3 (2001): 317–41.

24. Dorothea Leighton et al., *The Character of Danger: Psychiatric Symptoms in Selected Communities* (New York: Basic Books, 1963); Dorothea C. Leighton, "A Contribution of Population Studies: Ameliorative Measure for the Disadvantaged," in *Commemorative Volume for Professor Eric Essen-Moller*, ed. Eberhard Nyman, Acta Psychiatrica Scandinavica (Lund, Sweden) 46, Suppl. 219 (1968): 103–8; Dorothea C. Leighton, "The Empirical Status of the Integration-Disintegration Hypothesis," in *Psychiatric Disorder and the Urban Environment*, ed. Bert Kaplan (New York: Behavioral Publications, 1971), 68–78; Dorothea C. Leighton, "Cultural Determinants of Behavior: A Neglected Areas," *American Journal of Psychiatry* 128 (1972): 1003–4; Dorothea C. Leighton, "Mental Health Problems," in *Community Medicine*, ed. Abdel R. Omran (New York: Springer, 1974), 175–296; Dorothea C. Leighton, "Sociocultural Factors in Physical and Mental Breakdown," *Man-Environment Systems* 8 (1978): 33–37; Dorothea C. Leighton, "Community Integration and Mental Health: The Use of Longitudinal Data in Documenting Changes," in *Social and Psychological Research in Community Settings*, ed. Ricardo F. Munoz et al. (New York: Jossey-Bass, 1979), 175–294.

25. D. Leighton, "Anthropologist by Accident."

26. Dorothea C. Leighton, "As I Knew Them: Navajo Women in 1940," *American Indian Quarterly* 6, nos. 1–2 (1982): 43–51. She also wrote up some of her unfinished Inuit materials in *Eskimo Recollections of Their Life Experiences*, Northwestern Anthropological Research Notes (Moscow: University of Idaho, 1984).

27. John Adair, Kurt W. Deuschle, and Clifford R. Barnett, *The People's Health: Anthropology and Medicine in a Navajo Community* (Albuquerque: University of New Mexico Press, 1988).

IO

RUTH MURRAY UNDERHILL

Ethnohistorian and Ethnographer for the Native Peoples

Catherine J. Lavender and Nancy J. Parezo

IN 1979, AT THE AGE NINETY-FIVE, anthropologist Ruth Murray Underhill rode through Sells, Arizona, the capital of the Tohono O'odham Nation, in a parade in her honor.[1] The Tohono O'odham (formerly called Papago) Nation celebrated her work recording their history. Throughout her long career Underhill published at least a dozen studies of the Tohono O'odhams as well as more than one hundred articles and twenty monographs on other American Indian communities. While she was not the only, or indeed the first, anthropologist to work with the Tohono O'odhams, by the 1980s her works carried the weight of sincerity, respect, and authority. The tribal council's testimonial for her read: "We, the People of the Crimson Evening, the O'odham, recognize your efforts and your talents in preserving and capturing the spirit of our people, for this generation and for future generations to come. For this service, we are deeply indebted. We, the People of the Crimson Evening, the O'odham, today wish to express our heartfelt appreciation." Chairman Max H. Norris, in a tribal resolution of August 21, 1979, stated: "it was through your works on the Papago People that many of our young Papagos, in search of themselves, their past, their spirit, have recaptured part of their identities. Your works will continue to reinforce the true identity of many more young people, as well as the old. It is with this in mind that we wish to express our deep sense of appreciation." Testimonials by 150 Tohono O'odhams echoed these views.[2]

Other Native groups felt the same way. In 1980 the Gila River Reservation O'odhams passed a tribal resolution thanking Underhill for her

17. (*Opposite Top*) Ruth Murray Underhill, photographed by Margaret G. Marbeck, no. F-27211. *Courtesy of the Denver Public Library, Western History Collection, Denver CO.*

18. (*Opposite Bottom*) Ruth Murray Underhill being honored by the Mojave tribal government for her work with the nation, in 1981. Seated: Chairman Anthony Drennan Sr., Underhill. Standing (*left to right*): Secretary Elliott Booth, Elder Edward Swick, Vice-Chairman Harry Laffonn Sr., and unidentified Mohave women. *Photographer unknown. Photo in possession of Nancy J. Parezo.*

efforts and giving her an inscribed tray. In 1981, more than fifty years after her first visit to Parker, Arizona, the chairman of the Colorado River Indian Tribes (CRIT) presented the "renowned" Underhill with a recognition plaque for her role in keeping alive "very treasured memories of the People of the River-Ahamakov." The tireless Underhill had also come to celebrate and inspire a new writing project on the history of Mohave culture by tribal members, under the direction of elder Edward Swick, her translator from the 1930s research sessions. She presented CRIT with her volumes of unpublished field notes and stories collected between 1930 and 1937 and gave the tribal government complete control over their publication, a groundbreaking precedent for historical and ethnographic work. "You write it this time," she told them. "White people have been doing this long enough. . . . This is an entirely new way of telling about Indian ways."[3]

A prolific writer and diligent researcher, Underhill was committed to literary excellence as well as scientific and historic precision. While today she is mostly remembered for her work with the Tohono O'odhams and the Navajos, she worked with men and women from many indigenous communities in the American West (Akimel O'odhams, Arapahos, Hopis, Mohaves, Northern Paiutes, Pomos, Tohono O'odhams, Rio Grande Pueblos, Zunis), writing individual ethnographies in a manner in which the people would recognize themselves, as well as summary ethnological works on several culture areas: California, the Southwest, the Plateau, and the Northwest Coast. Her résumé was immense and replete with textbooks; comparisons of religions, ceremonies, and lifeways; and ethnographic analyses of social organization, acculturation, perseverance, traditionalism, history, culture change, and art. She also wrote biographies, intensive personality studies, and novels, books that contributed to "the development of dialectical narratives of literary anthropology and the canon of American literature."[4] When she died in 1984, just days shy of her one hundredth birthday, Underhill had appeared on television and radio to educate the public about Native American history, served as a professor of anthropology at several colleges and universities, assisted her profession in various capacities, and worked with the Bureau of Indian Affairs (BIA) to preserve cultural knowledge for future generations of Indians. It was a rich, full life.[5]

Several intellectual, educational, and humanitarian agendas appear in this immense corpus of work. One is Underhill's long-term commitment to serve as an ethnographer for the Tohono O'odhams by trying to understand their social organization, gender roles, lifeways, art, religion, and personal narrative and life history using Boasian and Benedictian paradigms. Like all of Franz Boas's students, Underhill emphasized empirical cultural details learned from firsthand observation and conversations with knowledgeable and respected individuals. This meant that she tried to understand Tohono O'odham culture and history on their own terms, using emic worldviews, and to see the range of behavior exhibited by people. She also sought to record how people actually lived their lives. Like Ruth Benedict, she tried to identify the types of personalities found in Tohono O'odham culture and to understand the dynamic interaction between individuals and culture. These emphases resulted in such publications as *Social Organization of the Papago Indians*, *Singing for Power*, and *Papago Woman*.[6]

The second agenda is Underhill's quest to popularize and synthesize anthropological and historical information about western Native Americans, to eliminate stereotypes and eradicate misinformation and historical omissions. She particularly wanted to prove that Indians were not vanishing and that each group has a unique past, present, and future. She also wanted to show that Indians were not timeless or primitive. One work, *The Navajos*, was the first history of the Diné in which culture was embedded in historical situations; it documents change and continuity through time in a framework that inverts history and ethnography. In her popular works, Underhill tried to convey information to nonprofessionals in a form unencumbered by anthropological jargon, hoping these books would "help with the understanding of the Indian as a person and a citizen . . . and will assist the public to a little more constructive view of 'his problem.'"[7] Classic examples include *Indians of Southern California*, *Red Man's America*, *First Came the Family*, *Indians of the Southwest*, and *Red Man's Religion*. Other works, such as *Ceremonial Patterns in the Greater Southwest* and "A Classification of Religious Practices among North American Indians," are ethnological comparisons in the tradition of Alfred Kroeber and Robert Lowie, meant for a professional audience.[8]

A third agenda, related to the second, grew out of Underhill's position as a supervisor of education for the Indian Service. She wrote training materials for BIA personnel and educational materials for Native students on the cultures and histories of their peoples. All these works use narrative techniques devoid of anthropological jargon, and some strive for literary styles that reflect Native poetry. Many were designed as children's books to help Native children learn to read, since "It seemed silly to have the Indian child read about a subway or an electric train." Underhill felt that these readable works were her most important contribution. Others were designed as high school texts using the stories Indians told as the central themes. Each was illustrated by an Indian artist, such as Velino Herrera (Ma-pe-wi). These text books became widely read and were also used in off-reservation schools. Works in this genre include *Here Come the Navaho!*, *The Northern Paiutes of California and Nevada*, *Indians of the Pacific Northwest*, *Workaday Life of the Pueblos*, *Pueblo Crafts*, and the aforementioned *People of the Crimson Evening*.[9]

Underhill's fourth body of writing was creative literature, in what Kathleen M. Sands has called "ethnographic fiction."[10] Although not well recognized in the anthropological world, Underhill wrote several novels, both prior to and during her anthropological career. Her first, *White Moth*, explored gender roles in business environments through the eyes of an adventurous businesswoman. It focused on issues of modernity, such as management and labor relations. Her later novels, *Hawk over Whirlpools*, *Antelope Singer*, and *Beaverbird*, stemmed from her knowledge of Native American life and are notable for their ethnographic accuracy.[11] They are books aimed at young adults (age nine to sixteen), designed to fill a literary lacuna. Juvenile literature dealing with American Indian topics was highly oversimplified, according to Underhill, and there were few good adult novels about Indians' lives either.[12]

According to Sands, Underhill's novels are "well crafted, unsentimental, remarkably direct and explicit for [their] time, and stylistically sophisticated."[13] *Hawk over Whirlpools*, centered in the Tohono O'odham world, has as its protagonist a male child destined for tribal leadership who is sent away to boarding school, where he learns to distrust Anglos and their world. Underhill writes about the young man's attempts to fit into both worlds, his struggles as he develops character and strength, his mistakes, and his ultimate return to his village and acceptance of the desert and Tohono O'odham worldview. In the process, she provides ethnographic information for non-Tohono O'odham readers so they will understand motive and action in their proper cultural context. *Antelope Singer*, the story of an Indian boy and a white family that settles near his home, all of whom learn to respect each other through cross-cultural understanding, proved particularly popular. Reissued in England by Penguin Books, it won the Nancy Block International Award for promoting intercultural relations.

Connecting these four types of writing are a commitment to usefulness. Underhill wished to present firsthand ethnographic information in a readable form; to animate dry facts and theories; to enlighten professionals, Indians, and the lay audience alike; and to combine humanitarianism with scientific empiricism. In some cases there is also a commitment to feminism, an allegiance that stretched from her undergraduate days at Vassar through her serial incarnations as social worker, newspaper columnist, novelist, student, ethnographer, ethnologist, civil servant, and teacher.

Early Life

Ruth Murray Underhill was born in Ossining-on-Hudson on August 22, 1883, the daughter of Anna Murray Underhill and Abram Sutton Underhill, a New York City lawyer whose family first arrived in North America in 1636. Ruth was a descendant of Captain John Underhill, known as an "Indian fighter." She remembered her father as a farmer at heart who traveled to New York City three days a week, and her mother as a city dweller stuck in the country who yearned for a brownstone-fronted townhouse. Quietly religious and political pacifists, both learned to live together with the aid, as Underhill recalled, of much prayer.[14]

Ruth was the oldest of four children; she had two sisters (one of whom, Elizabeth, was a noted suffragist, lawyer, and one of the first female bank directors in the United States) and one brother, Robert, who became a doctor. They grew up in an upper-middle-class Quaker home where they had the run of their father's library in their Ossining farmhouse. Here Ruth's interests in Greek classics and the "new thought" of nineteenth-century authors like Charles Darwin were nurtured. Her father and her maternal uncle, Augustus Murray, tutored her, and at fourteen she read Greek. This language training—as well as yearly trips to Europe-presaged her later linguistic abilities. She learned several languages, including Greek, Latin, Spanish, French, German, Italian, and O'odham.[15]

Despite the large household, Underhill remembered her childhood as "very lonesome. . . . I was always quite a foreigner to the girls' gossip in our little circle."[16] Much of this was by choice. Underhill did not fit into girls' play worlds (and later women's worlds), nor was she interested in their concerns, such as playing with dolls or dressing to attract men. She liked the world of books and ideas, assumed to be the realm of men. Underhill always longed for peace, quiet, and tranquillity rather than boisterous, spontaneous fun. Her quiet, serious, studious demeanor and personality were ideal for ethnographic participation in southwestern American Indian cultures.

Underhill's parents enrolled her at the Ossining School for Girls, the preparatory school for Bryn Mawr College. Underhill decided, however, that she would rather attend Vassar College in Poughkeepsie, New York. She majored in English and won a prize for an essay on Shakespeare. An outstanding student, she was elected to Phi Beta Kappa and earned a bachelor's degree in 1905. Decades later, reflecting on her time at college, she noted that the institution was permeated with the thoughts of Vassar's president, "a nice portly gentleman [who] felt that his function was to prepare us for marriage." To Underhill, marriage and teaching seemed "tame."[17] The determined, strong-willed, and somewhat rebellious Underhill wanted independence. Uninterested in marriage, she wanted something worthwhile that did not involve teaching elementary school. With few options open to women during this period, she chose social work and became a caseworker for the Massachusetts Society for the Prevention of Cruelty to Children. This began her lifelong concern for child welfare and education. Underhill found social work more exciting than her other options, and it gave her a sense of relevancy.[18] It also provided her with the means to live independently in Boston. After a year, however, growing restless and deciding to see other parts of the world, she undertook the equivalent of the gentleman's grand tour. She began two years of travel in Europe but soon found she needed more focus. Thus she enrolled in courses at the London School of Economics and the University of Munich to hone her linguistic skills.[19]

When Underhill returned to the United States, she worked for the Charity Organization Society in New York City in 1913 and 1914. During World War I, employed by the American Red Cross, she began to experiment with popular writing. She penned a column for the *New York Sun* under the byline "Seraphine" and took a stab at magazine feature writing and advertising. She lived in Greenwich Village, a lively community of radicals and feminists. Underhill remembered that she "mingled with . . . 'charity cases,' Marxian enthusiasts, and psychoanalysts."[20] Despite the intellectual stimulation, she left to administer an orphanage in Italy from 1918 to 1920.

Now sophisticated and worldly, Underhill returned to New York City in 1920, resumed her social work, and began to experiment with writing fiction. As noted above, her first novel, *White Moth*, addressed the struggles confronted by young professional women in a male-dominated society, a concern that played a role in her later ethnographic writing. The novel focused on a young, extremely competent, ambitious, and hardworking woman who has risen against great odds to a managerial position in business, and the social problems she encountered as a result. Among her heroine's trials was the discomfiting experience of having to supervise her former high school sweetheart, who she discovers is cautious, unimaginative, and set in the old ways. *White Moth* illustrates Underhill's internalized rejection of conventional women's roles and reflects her ideas about women and their place in society—in short, her feminism. Underhill argued that patriarchy limited women's natural abilities to succeed in any arena—in this case the male-dominated world of business—and emphasized the negative effects women suffered when they betrayed their natural ambitions to please men. Favorably reviewed as both a romance novel and a critique of American society, *White Moth* reached multiple audiences. She was now a writer.[21]

To some extent, Underhill found it difficult to practice the independence explored in her novel. She still wanted a husband and a family, largely because her friends had married. In 1920 she married Charles Crawford, about whom we know little. We also know little of the childless marriage except that it ended in divorce in 1929, because Crawford had another woman. Underhill successfully shrouded most marital details in her life history and later interviews. When asked about marriage, she did not disparage the institution for women but simply said dismissively that she "just got the wrong man."[22] Shortly after the divorce became final, she celebrated with a "Crawford Unwedding Trip." She never remarried. One of her colleagues and friends, Richard Conn of the Denver Museum of Art, later felt that Underhill faced a daunting barrier with men: "She was just too smart for the boys. They couldn't keep up with her."[23]

Divorces, often emotionally messy, are sometimes emancipating and catalytic in terms of enabling people to change the direction of their lives. Underhill had three choices. She could return to the family farm in the Hudson River, continue social work, or strike out in a new direction. Determining that life on the farm would be boring and that social work had presented all its challenges, she decided to learn more about people and life. A firm believer in advanced education, she went directly from the courthouse steps to Columbia University. Here was the place to discover what happened in people's lives, but what should she study?

The forty-seven-year-old Underhill, "with half a life behind me," walked the halls of Columbia in search of a department that offered courses that would explain people, especially races, their motivations, and how they had developed. In economics, philosophy, and sociology she met with mundane, textbook answers that "sounded fine but didn't tell me anything of course." She also met with some disdain because of her age and sex. Luck and perseverance now entered the picture. In the anthropology department she met Ruth Benedict, who welcomed her and said, "So you want to know about people? That's what anthropology is. Come on in, then, this is the place."[24] Underhill immediately registered and moved back to Greenwich Village.

Underhill was lucky in encountering Benedict rather than some of the other Columbia professors, who stereotyped the middle-age woman as a frivolous divorcée, too old to begin graduate study. Benedict became her intellectual mentor, adviser, and friend, a close relationship that lasted until Benedict's death in 1948. Like Underhill, she had recently divorced. "We didn't talk about it," Underhill recalled, "but both of us felt drawn together."[25]

Ruth Benedict (1887–1948) is best remembered for her classic *Patterns of Culture*, which utilized an interdisciplinary approach to understand individual creativity and cultural constraints on personality in a configurational perspective. She was devoted to writing humanist anthropology like poetry; words were as important as concepts. It was this perspective that permeated Underhill's work. Benedict was also an ethnographer who collected myths and tales at both Zuni and Cochiti pueblos, despite her deafness.[26]

Importantly for Underhill, Benedict was also a devoted feminist, "a lady, a person of my sort," who wanted to help women become professionals who could succeed in academia. Like Underhill she had a passion for knowing, wanting more than simply credentials for a professional career, which is how Underhill saw her fellow male students. Benedict, not only Underhill's mentor but a kindred spirit in upbringing as well as intellect, had the patience to discuss concepts that Underhill found problematic.[27]

Underhill was lucky she found Columbia, because the anthropology department, under the direction of Franz Boas, was the discipline's leader, the site of cutting-edge theoretical developments. Boas (1858–1942) is best known for his studies concerning race, his developments in the concept of culture, and his quest to understand individual cultures before they disappeared in the onslaught of colonialism. He emphasized cultural and social particularism over abstract theory. Although Boas started out as an evolutionist and environmental determinist, he had changed his thinking by the time Underhill encountered him, in part because of his extensive work in the American Southwest. He now stressed the cultural biases that led to the formation of ideas about race, and he worked hard to counter commonly accepted ideas of scholars who called themselves "scientific racists" and eugenicists. In 1930 he had just published his influential *Anthropology and Modern Life* to fight scientific racism and was working on methodological issues, including the centrality of firsthand observational, long-term fieldwork as the basis for a rigorous anthropological science using an idiographic approach. Boas was also at the center of the emergence of cultural relativism in anthropology, and he advocated the use of cross-cultural ethnology and specific ethnographies to provide a broad critique of American society. Most of his female students were advocates and leaders of this movement. His constant debates with other scholars in public and professional forums about race, ethnicity, and cultural relativity had "a deep impact on the issues that women ethnographers addressed."[28]

Underhill found Boas earnest, very Germanic, difficult to understand, and determined to advance American anthropology using his paradigm, without debate from his students. She also found him dogmatic. To Boas, she said, "science is holy and should have precedence over everything. . . . Students would listen with bated breath and never criticize. Boas made no concessions to anybody. Boas did no catering." But he also felt that women, like Jews, were getting a raw deal in the academy, so he opened doors to those whom he found worthy, that is, those who had obtained a classical education and spoke foreign languages. Fortunately, Underhill spoke and read German flawlessly, which gained her Boas's attention as well as that of younger students struggling with his readings. Boas soon came to appreciate her intellect, inviting her for beers at the faculty club on Friday afternoons along with Reichard, Parsons, and Benedict.[29]

Boas had trained several of the most famous American anthropologists by 1930, including Ruth Benedict, Ruth Bunzel, Ella Deloria, Melville Herskovits, Zora Neale Hurston, Alfred Kroeber, Robert Lowie, Margaret Mead, Edward Sapir, Marian Smith, Leslie Spier, John Swanton, and Clark Wissler. His students had obtained jobs in universities and government agencies across North America. Most of them agreed with and followed his fieldwork procedures. One of the things Boas insisted on was that all cultural anthropologists conduct extensive research trips to Native communities and publish ethnographic descriptions and texts. One learned from firsthand interaction and participant observation, by speaking in the Native language. In this insistence he carried on the work of the first generation of ethnographers, which included Frank Hamilton Cushing, James Mooney, and Charles Newcombe, and condemned armchair theoreticians, especially those who espoused unilinear evolutionary paradigms. What was needed was in-depth information on individual cultures and Native voices. By 1930 Boas had turned away from sweeping theoretical pronouncements and toward ground-level theories based on painstakingly detailed studies of distinct cultures. If nineteenth-century evolutionary anthropology stressed biological determinism, Boas argued for cultural and environmental determinism. He differed from the earlier generation of anthropologists by insisting that anthropology was a rigorous scientific discipline, and that meant advanced doctorate degrees, not self-training. Columbia was definitely the place to study if one wanted to learn about ethnography.[30]

And it was especially the place for women to study. While women were being turned away from or greatly discouraged from attending other institutions of postgraduate training, Boas welcomed them—if they could meet his demanding criteria. During his tenure at Columbia more than twenty women received doctorates in anthropology, and others obtained bachelor's and master's degrees. Boas was instrumental in the educational and professional lives of a number of famous female ethnographers, including Ella Deloria, who is also honored in this volume. Unlike many other men in powerful gatekeeping positions in anthropology, he was willing to ignore popular assumptions about women's abilities and take women as his students, even though he lost several good secretaries (Ruth Bunzel and Esther Goldfrank are examples) to the allure of fieldwork. By 1920 Boas had so many female students who were ambitious and had independent and tenacious personalities that he wrote to archaeologist Berthold Laufer, "I have had a curious experience in graduate work during the last few years. All my best students are women."[31] For some, but not for the older Underhill, Boas became affectionately known as "Papa Franz." He was, according to Kroeber, "a true patriarch," a powerful and rather forbidding father figure who rewarded his "offspring" with nurturant support insofar as he felt that "they were genuinely identifying with him," though he was indifferent and even punitive on occasion.[32] Luckily for Underhill, there were strong female scholars to counter the negative effects of Boas's mentoring. She did not have to assume the role of daughter.

Although Underhill's feminism was well established before she entered Columbia University, she found there an established network of strong feminist scholars who influenced her thinking and ultimately came to encourage her. Benedict introduced her to one of the most important, Elsie Clews Parsons, who had also come to anthropology later in life after a successful career as a writer, social activist, and feminist. A sociologist by training and one of the first women in the United States to earn a doctorate, she was a founder of the New School for Social Research and had published several seminal works: *The Old Fashioned Woman: Primitive Fancies about the Sex, Fear and Conventionality*, and *Social Freedom: A Study of the Conflicts between Social Classification and Personality*. After meeting Benedict and Boas, she turned to anthropology and worked extensively in the American Southwest, writing classic ethnographies and fictionalized life history narratives such as *American Indian Life* that would enliven ethnographic statements.[33]

Underhill quickly became a great admirer of Parsons's ethnographic as well as her earlier feminist work. She found Parsons's crisp descriptions and her encyclopedic compendium—her grand comparative ethnology, *Pueblo Indian Religions*, published in 1939—especially useful later in life. From discussions with her, Underhill also began gaining a social scientist's focus on the structure and dynamics of a society, how roles and expectations influenced actual behavior, and how a range of behavioral variability existed around role expectations.[34]

Parsons was also extremely important in a practical way. Very wealthy, she underwrote anthropological associations, provided publication costs for dissertations and monographs, and funded Boas's fieldwork. She founded the Southwest Society as a small, single-person nonprofit organization to funnel monies to finance the education and careers of several budding anthropologists (including Leslie White, Ruth Benedict, Gladys Reichard, and Pliny Goddard) in the 1930s. She provided scholarships and tuition, money to Boas's and Benedict's students for their fieldwork (provided it was in the American Southwest), and funding to Columbia University to finance the salaries of several women graduates unable to find academic employment during the Great Depression. By paying for Underhill's fieldwork and publications, Parsons helped her establish her new career.

Underhill was four times lucky because she became Gladys Reichard's assistant at Barnard College. A student of Boas, Reichard was thirty years old when she conducted her first fieldwork on Navajo social structure, using Parsons's genealogical method. Deciding that religion served as the integrating force in Navajo culture, she devoted her career to that and understanding Navajo life from women's viewpoints. Reichard instilled in Underhill a love of the Southwest and provided insight into Navajo culture that Underhill called upon later in her career. Underhill remembered Reichard not as a theorist but rather as one who "liked to know exactly what people did and how and when and what color it was and where it happened." But she was also a woman "who went right for the goal, straight for it and got it. She was intimate with her Navajo friends. She knew what they thought and she thought the same."[35] Interested in writing for the general public as well as a professional audience, Reichard was one of the first people to tell Underhill that she could do this too.

There were also other young, strong female professionals, like Margaret Mead, who were potential colleagues but also rivals. Underhill was not enamored of Mead, thinking she required "fans and admirers."[36] All were experimenting with writing forms. The age difference loomed large here, however, and Underhill felt marginalized by her classmates. As she had at Vassar years before, she worked primarily by herself. The age issue also mattered to Boas. Reflecting years later, Underhill believed that he considered her marginal and a frivolous divorcée who was simply entertaining herself, supported by a small trust fund. He helped her in the end, she said, because she was a woman, and he believed that women and Jews were denied the professional opportunities they deserved. After seeing the quality of her ethnographic data, however, Boas changed his mind about her and arranged for more Arizona field trips. Still, she always felt that had she been young, Jewish, and male, funding support would have come earlier.

With the direction of Benedict, Reichard, Parsons, and Boas, Underhill had found the proper home for her quest to understand people and their motivations. In anthropology she could know everything about people.[37] The focus she now developed dealt with social structure and gender relationships, including inequalities. Now she needed a group to work with.

Underhill's work with the Tohono O'odhams began, she recalled, when Boas assigned them to her (even though she preferred the Pacific Islanders) because she had a car. He offered a fellowship of five hundred dollars from the Columbia Humanities Council and told her, "You go find out how those people live, and you come back and tell us." Unfortunately, Boas, Parsons, and Benedict never told her how to do it, although they used storytelling techniques of their own field experiences to convey "dos and don'ts." Methodology courses were then reserved for biological anthropology. One learned expectations and basic ethical standards from fellow graduate students. Like Bunzel, Underhill would invent her own methods by working intentionally with women and consciously evaluating her own role as an outsider descending on a Native group.[38]

Working with Tohono O'odhams

The Tohono O'odhams (Desert or Two Village People) live in the Sonoran desert region of Arizona and Sonora. Underhill knew nothing about them before traveling cross-country in her car. Nor did the University of Arizona professor she stayed with in Tucson, Clara Lee Tanner, know much about their lives, especially those who lived more isolated existences away from Anglo-American communities. Underhill was particularly curious about the old ways and how acculturative pressures affected lifeways.[39] Like many other scholars of this period, she believed it was imperative to collect baseline information about the old ways, because she assumed that, given the strength of American culture, acculturation and change were inevitable. Since anthropologists had scarcely studied the Tohono O'odhams, Underhill wanted to learn how their society was organized, how households were constructed and operated, what women's roles were in their society, and how worldview and religion permeated their lives. She also wanted to know their history, how they survived, and what their experiences had been since the beginning of time.

Underhill soon realized that the Tohono O'odhams are a patrilineal, clan-based society divided into five bands, facts she gathered over two years working with Tohono O'odham elders in eight communities who remembered the period from 1859 to 1890. She also learned the responsibilities of kinship, how farmland is inherited, gift-giving customs, how headmen are chosen, how people learn, how they practice medicine, their philosophy, and core Tohono O'odham values. She also quickly understood that cultural ideals and people's actual behaviors differ and that values and activities change over time. She ascertained this from talking with women, for Tohono O'odham men and women lived in somewhat different worlds at the time. Women were not allowed at tribal council meetings, as Underhill discovered when she first tried to attend. She decided to work with women as much as she could.[40]

By a fortuitous circumstance recounted in the first chapter of *The Autobiography of a Papago Woman*, one of the first people Underhill met was Maria Chona. Underhill's entry into the Tohono O'odham world was through Chona and her kinship network. Thereafter Underhill chose women respondents whenever possible. She found women easier to talk to, something she referred to later as a "fortunate accident" of her methodology.[41] "We were just feeling our way, all of us, at first," she later said. "Little by little, then, I came to see why this business of the women is the right thing. I'm getting a lot more than I would with the men and I shall keep right on with it. Then, it became my specialty."[42] Asked in 1980 whether she or her mentors understood how innovative her methods were, Underhill said, "I don't think they realized how different it was. One of the boys said to me once, 'Ruth, you look so harmless.' I said, 'Well, don't you understand that's technique? I'm not really that harmless, am I?' 'Oh, no,' he said, 'I just hadn't thought of that.' Because, the boys didn't think at all of technique and how they could get the stuff. They just went on and asked questions—why not?"[43]

Underhill, clearly conscious of her role as an outside investigator, a stranger who was asking people to trust her and provide traditional knowledge and stories, often felt that she was being intrusive. She was also conscious of the role that manipulation played in the gathering of ethnographic information. Like her professors, she had data-collection standards. She did not coerce information from people, as Matilda Coxe Stevenson had allegedly done. Underhill, trying to follow Tohono O'odham rules of etiquette, was quite concerned when she unintentionally asked inappropriate questions during her first days of interaction. She also appropriately offered gifts as reciprocity for the imparting of information and to acknowledge the value of the elder's time, as was customary in Tohono O'odham society and indeed in all American Indian societies of the Southwest. Upon receiving information, a learner should offer elders presents (generally trade goods, cash, or services) to show appreciation to the individual, the family, and the community. Underhill provided transportation to Chona and her family, driving her from her Tucson home to her family rancheria for interviewing sessions. She also gave her respondents' families culturally appropriate sacks of flour and beans. Finally, she assured all that she would not let BIA personnel use the information people gave her against them or the community, especially information on religion. People rightly feared that knowledge of their ceremonies, prayers, and beliefs would provide ammunition for the BIA to repress their religious freedom.[44]

Tohono O'odhams judged Underhill, testing her sincerity and sense of humor. They evaluated her partly by her willingness to learn O'odham (something unusual for Anglo-Americans, who considered English followed by Spanish the languages of choice) and partly by her willingness to live and dress as they did and to perform women's work without complaining. She won their respect by asking if she could work among them and requesting permission to return for a second summer of interviews. Her gray hair and forty-eight years earned her respect, as did her quiet demeanor and ability to be silent. She reflected later that her training and social skills gave her an advantage over young men: "I'd had some social training. . . . I brought conversations around. . . . Lots of men, you know, don't know how to do that. I'm amazed at the young, brash fellows that have no social ease at all. They just [say], 'Now let's see, what do you do when you want to choose a new chief?' Then they ask the questions one after the other. I would say, 'Oh, you had a new chief. How did you get him?' And [do it] slowly, slowly."[45]

This skill grew out of interviewing techniques Underhill had amassed during many years of social work. She had learned to listen to people and to gauge speech patterns in her language work; she had acquired the communication skills needed to talk to immigrant Italian families living in run-down tenements in New York, to orphaned children in war-ravaged Italy, and to New York City editors and publishers. A student of people, she had "people skills."

Underhill credited her Quaker upbringing for the success of her work with Tohono O'odham and later other Indian women. While "having been taught in my youth that women should always be rather quiet and not push themselves" helped somewhat in an interview session, Underhill maintained that it was really the Quakers' cultural values that gave her the ability to listen without being unafraid of silence.[46]

The differences between Tohono O'odham (and later Mohave) men and women soon became evident to Underhill. Ironically, her breakthrough in understanding came when she worked with Mohave men. She asked them why women did not sing the ceremonial songs that accompanied male activities and was told, "They sing to gain power. Women already have it." While superficially subservient in their roles to men, women saw their ability to bear children as a balancing factor. They had powers that men would never have.[47] Women had a quiet strength that had never been truly recognized in anthropological writings.

Parsons, Benedict, and Boas had struggled with Pueblo reticence and secretiveness about their cultures, in which informants refused to talk about things that were considered community knowledge—what Edward Spicer has called a survival strategy of persistent peoples.[48] Underhill, like Reichard, encountered less reticence, probably because of her personality. People would often think about how to make her understand, a common translation problem since words and concepts do not readily move from one language to another. What they worried more about was the possibility that Indian Service officials would use her research against them. She found it difficult to convince prospective interviewees that she would not get them into trouble. "I told many of them that I never told the superintendent anything, that he was not my friend," Underhill recalled. "They were glad to hear that, but they didn't really trust me." This was, of course, not unexpected.[49]

While Chona at first hesitated to discuss some information with Underhill, her concern over possible government retaliation for discussing the old ways or current problems was not an issue. "Chona wasn't afraid of the superintendent—what the heck if he wanted to tell her he didn't like smoking or whatever she did; well, that was her business and she'd tell him." In fact, Chona had little respect for either the federal government or its representatives. She stated her feelings at their first meeting by asking Underhill, "But did Vasindone [Washington] make our land? No! That was Earthmaker. In the Beginning. He make it for us—Papagos, Desert People!"[50] Not only was Chona unconcerned about the superintendent, she was never afraid of Underhill. She did not place the scholar on a pedestal or see her as more intelligent. Like other cultural mentors, Chona felt she was training Underhill, and like the best anthropologists, Underhill saw herself as a student.

Chona: Writing the Life of a Crimson Evening Person

Running through most of Underhill's work, but especially in *Autobiography of a Papago Woman*, is a strong vein of abstract intellectual feminism combined with grounded cultural relativity. In her examinations of women's roles among the Tohono O'odhams, Underhill emphasizes power inequities between men and women and applauds women's ability to negotiate power for themselves. In this pioneer work of feminist ethnography, Underhill set out to examine one woman's struggles against an overarching colonialist culture and the superficial paternalism of Native culture. She seems to draw comparisons between the aspirations of Anglo-American career women and those of Tohono O'odham women. Chona appealed to Underhill because she did not bend to male authority. She had divorced her first husband when he followed Tohono O'odham custom and brought home a second wife. Refusing to marry again after her second husband's death, she instead established herself as an independent woman in Tucson, living away from the social constraints of her family. Underhill's work subtly critiqued the patriarchal aspects of a patrilineal society, emphasizing the ways in which some of traditional Tohono O'odham society's conventions about women echoed those of Anglo-American women on the

East Coast. Underhill drew lessons to "take home" with her to New York from Chona's stories of resistance to inappropriate male attempts at authority and the inherent power women had in Tohono O'odham society, a theme of *Singing for Power*. As she learned, Tohono O'odham women "don't seem to feel the tremendous subjection that white women feel. They are not subjected! I have rarely seen one that was. They have their part; they have to do it. They know that it doesn't get any fame, that the men get the fame. But they're calm and gentle . . . not struggling for power at all. They just know they have it."[51]

Her text seems to imply that Underhill was the first Anglo-American in whom Chona confided. This was probably not the case in one sense, but it may have been true given the prevailing prejudices in southern Arizona at the time. Very likely Underhill was the first Anglo-American who wanted to learn from Chona and who treated Chona as an intellectual equal. Giving the reader a sense, however, that she was the first to win Chona's confidence was probably due to the anthropological writing styles of the period. Salvage ethnography and attempts to uncover and document pure cultural patterns meant the stripping away of acculturation. As a student of Boas, Underhill felt that "pristineness"—isolation from the cultural adulteration brought about by intense contact with outsiders—was an important element in legitimizing Native voices: the more culturally pure the interviewee, the more valuable his or her testimony.

Chona did possess a sense of herself as a real Tohono O'odham, despite her interactions (including marriage) with non-O'odham people. Nothing could take this away from her. She certainly considered her people's culture as the right way to live. She would have been a rare human indeed if she had not felt a sense of superiority about her culture. This included the essential relationship of the O'odham people and the land as well as how this differed in critical ways from Anglo-American and Mexican concepts of land. She conveyed this sense of interconnectedness to Underhill at their first meeting, and it became her first utterance in her autobiography. "I was born there," breathed Chona reverently, "on the Land." Truly seeing the land and comprehending what it meant to the Tohono O'odhams became the first test for Underhill in her quest to understand the world in Tohono O'odham terms. "Land, to me, was a possession to be claimed and fought over by farmers, builders, exploiters—yes—and patriots. From this old Papago woman I was to learn, it is the land that possesses the people. Its influence, in time, shapes their bodies, their language, even, a little, their religion."[52] As long as Tohono O'odhams stayed on their land, they would remain a people. Peaceful people, they chose "to be alone," according to Chona, when enemies and outsiders infiltrated their lands. Underhill saw this avoidance of conflict as Tohono O'odham activism rather than passivity. Perhaps this cultural pattern complemented her Quaker beliefs and her quiet, solitary personality.

The Autobiography of a Papago Woman is a truly collaborative piece of ethnographic writing, and this feature sets Underhill apart from her contemporaries. In this and many of her other works she strove to uncover commonalities with her Native American interviewees, especially the women. She looked for humanity's underlying sameness under the differentiation of cultural distinctions. She delighted in "translating" Indian civilizations using a cultural language that could be understood by the average non-Native lay person. Even her book titles—for example, *America's First Penthouse Dwellers*, a title with immediate iconic recognition for middle-class Americans—stress commonalities of experience and metaphors of prestige and desire. In the bio-autobiography, Underhill strove to establish a model of universal women's experience, despite Chona's convictions about the vast differences between herself and Underhill. To some extent this led Underhill to romanticize Tohono O'odham values, especially in contrast to Anglo-American culture, a technique that allowed her to critique American society. Comparing her childhood in a traditional upper-middle-class Anglo-American multi-room house to the openness of the one-room Tohono O'odham family dwelling, she wrote: "I remembered my own youth when, tiptoeing past my parents' door at night, I heard low voices. They were discussing us children, perhaps, our faults and what must be done about them. Or Father's financial situation. That was something about which we were never told. The result with us was a latent hotbed of curiosity and rebellion. Are my people so complex that they cannot afford to share their interests with their children?"[53]

Underhill learned that the key to Tohono O'odham society, and why

it would not fold under a supposed Manifest Destiny, was family to-
getherness. As she later told a reporter, the Tohono O'odham family
worked, ate, and slept together, and no secrets were kept from children. That model could serve American society.[54] By evaluating her
family—and by implication her culture—as dysfunctional by Tohono
O'odham standards, Underhill tried to connect her childhood to that
of Indian children. In her theory, all children have the same needs,
motivations, concerns, and anxieties. But Underhill also implied that
Tohono O'odham culture answered children's needs more humanely
and functioned better. This was a common view in 1930s and 1940s
anthropology: Indians had much to teach contemporary America about
how to live. Now Underhill wanted to ensure that the federal government, as it turned away from reprehensible paternalistic policies, took
the time to understand Native cultures. As she had in her social work
career, she would work from the inside.

BIA Employee and Public Scholar

Underhill received her doctorate in 1937 when her dissertation, *Social Organization of the Papago Indians*, was accepted for publication.
She had finished writing it in 1935 but had trouble finding a publisher
because of her "unscientific" writing style and grounded, qualitative
methodology. At this time, seventy-five copies of a dissertation had to
be published before the degree could be awarded. After some revisions
and the intervention of Parsons and Reichard and a subvention from
the Columbia Humanities Council (i.e., Parsons), the book came out in
1939 as a monograph of the American Anthropological Association.[55]

Underhill was without a job in the height of the Great Depression.
There were no academic openings in anthropology that year; according
to Fred Eggan, 85 percent of the new PhDs from 1930 to 1940 could
not find academic jobs.[56] Most turned to other institutions, like museums, or sought grants. But Underhill, older and needing something
more permanent, rejected the instability of living from grant to grant.

Boas was no help here because he only believed in academic service and thought he could place only so many women in academia and
museums. Underhill's entrée to a permanent job came from Gladys

Reichard, whom Underhill had assisted with the famous Navajo Ho-gan School in the summer of 1934. This landmark in linguistic an-thropology was funded by the BIA to teach Navajos to read and write in Diné.[57] The BIA then hired Underhill to teach in-service courses to agency personnel. During the 1934–35 academic year the U.S. Depart-ment of Agriculture employed her for the soil conservation economic surveys. Through Reichard's intervention Underhill was asked in the summer of 1935 to work at the Sherman Indian Institute in Riverside, California, again teaching basic ethnology courses on Indian tribes. During the fall she was hired temporarily to write up these lectures as a series of pamphlets, a project that took much longer than the intended few months.

From then until 1948 Underhill was employed by the U.S. Indian Service, first as an anthropological consultant to work on government policy and then in the education division with the title of associate su-pervisor and later supervisor in Indian education. The transfer came early because Underhill criticized as inadequate the new tribal con-stitutions that lawyers had drawn up for several tribes, especially the one for the Tohono O'odhams. She told Collier that it did not reflect the Tohono O'odham sociopolitical structure or economic realities of life in a desert. She urged Tohono O'odhams not to ratify it, which they did not. Wishing to present a united federal policy in the debate and strongly disliking any criticism from employees, Collier removed Underhill, whom he now viewed as something of an *agent provocateur*. In addition, he refused to allow her to work on BIA projects on the To-hono O'odham reservation and made sure that other federal agencies barred her as well. In 1935 he had her removed as head of the Papago survey team for the Soil Conservation Survey of the Department of Ag-riculture.[58] Collier also made certain that the strong-willed Underhill received no administrative or executive positions.

Prevented by Collier from taking an active role in the conceptual-ization and implementation of culturally appropriate policy, Underhill worked within the agency as a writer of educational ethnological and ethnographic manuals designed to train BIA employees and Public Health Service personnel and presented in-service workshops (see chapters on Marriott and Leighton in this volume). In 1938 she became part of the education division under Willard Beatty, housed in Santa Fe, New Mexico. She was pleased with this assignment, for she hoped she could influence some of the essentialism of BIA educational policy. If Indians were going to take advantage of contemporary education, she believed, it had to be on their terms and using their thought patterns. She used Tohono O'odham poetry as her model and advised the use of Native rather than European educational materials. Unfortunately, little was available.

During her government career, Underhill wrote nine books for the Indian Life and Customs and Indian Handicraft series.[59] Several of these, later republished for a wider audience, became required texts in classes during the 1950s through 1980s at both the undergraduate and the graduate level. Indian artists illustrated many of these books, which were widely read within the BIA system and by interested members of the public. More importantly, many Indian school districts adopted them for high school use. As a result, Underhill taught many American Indian readers her version of their history as well as what it meant to be "Indian."

During this period Underhill returned to the Tohono O'odham reservation for short "vacation" trips whenever her work allowed, visiting friends and clarifying and cross-checking her earlier research notes. During her years as a civil servant she brought out many of her best-known works, based on materials she had gathered during her dissertation research: *Autobiography of a Papago Woman* (1936), *Singing for Power* (1938), *The Social Organization of the Papago Indians* (1939), and *Papago Indian Religion* (1946). This body of literature solidified her professional reputation as an Americanist ethnographer. She was also active in professional organizations, but although she considered that work important, she gained the most joy from writing for the general public.

Underhill began being widely read with her 1938 publication, *First Penthouse Dwellers of America*, which received many good reviews. Oliver LaFarge praised her ability "to avoid the dry literalness which is the habitual scientific affectation . . . her work of equal merit has been put out in an unfrightening, attractive form."[60] The accolades continued over the years, although Underhill was not without her critics, especially individuals who called for a drier writing style. But in general the reviews abound with phrases that show how successfully she combined the craft of a good writer with the descriptive and analytical skills of the seasoned professional ethnographer, ethnologist, and ethnohistorian. Alice Marriott ended one review of Underhill's work tellingly: "The pity is that there is only one Ruth Underhill, and only a limited number of hours in a day for her to write."[61]

Underhill's emphasis on the lessons that non-Indians could learn from Native Americans and her ability to write poetically and engagingly made her work popular. Further, her career in social work had convinced her of the importance of public scholarship. As had happened to Ruth Benedict, the success of her publications caused some anthropologists to dismiss her work as overly personal and literary. Some have even tended to take her contributions to southwestern ethnography and the Tohono O'odhams less seriously than they have the work of highly analytical and stylistically dry writers like Elsie Clews Parsons or Leslie White.[62] It is ironic, then, that Underhill's work has been so embraced by American Indian tribal governments as authoritative and culturally appropriate, in part because of her reliance on Native forms of storytelling.

And Underhill specifically wrote for a Native audience as much as for professional or lay Euro-American audiences. She did this partly because her work required that she produce publicly accessible texts, that is, to spend federal monies in ways that would benefit all citizens, not only a small group of scholars. But she also did so because of her own literary aspirations. She longed to be respected not only for her research but also for eloquent writing. Her intellectual career began as a novelist, which indicated where her true passions lay. Further, the way she wrote indicates the value she placed on making texts beautiful and lyrical. *Papago Woman* illustrates most clearly this literary bent, as well as her quest to remain culturally appropriate. Throughout the text, Underhill strove to maintain the poetic cadences of Chona's tale, even as she fundamentally altered the narrative to fit the more European style of telling a life story in chronological order. In this groundbreaking episodic dual autobiography/biography, Underhill as narrator presents anthropological praxis as an interactive dialogue in which all participants are changed and valued—a stance of "new ethnography" years before young male anthropologists invented the term. She shows that for both herself and Chona, words and stories are ways of perceiving, analyzing, and understanding experience.

Underhill felt that she had to reorder Chona's story because Chona told it in a Tohono O'odham narrative style, in which themes, dramatic action, personality, and illustrative incidents rather than calendrical time are important. Relationships of places and people to each other carry the story.[63] From Underhill's Euro-American perspective, Chona "did not tell a straight story." Remembering later the process of writing down Chona's stories, Underhill said: "Wiggling her big horny feet in the sand and gazing off at the distant cliffs she might say, 'So when I was in the garden picking squash, this woman came out of the house.' 'This woman?' I would inquire. 'Yes, his second wife.' 'Oh, you didn't tell me he had a second wife.' 'Yes, the year after he married me.' 'Was this your first husband or your second?' 'It was the first and I think it was more than a year before he took that woman.'"[64] Like a detective, Underhill then attempted to place Chona's memories in an order more in keeping with the world of her readers, especially historians. Underhill remembered, "Chona did not trouble with the sequence of events but I tried to put them into my own scheme of time."[65] Underhill did so by trying to get Chona to key her experiences to external changes: the coming of the railroad, the birth or death of a tribal member, the moving of the community to new lands. Underhill found this process difficult because, as she wrote, Chona "had little sense of time," by which she meant that Chona found the necessity of remembering dates and ordering her world accordingly meaningless and irrelevant to her life.

As a result, Underhill wrote Chona's story not as Chona told it—as isolated incidents in response to Underhill's questions and her own remembrances over a three-year period—but as a reordered translation in a form Euro-Americans would find familiar. This, however, does not negate its importance as a document illuminating the lifeways of Tohono O'odhams. As Sands notes, "The polyphonic voices of Chona the dreamer, Chona the narrator, and Underhill the ethnographer and stylist are unified in a believable persona who perceives her world alive with a multiplicity of voices."[66] While the time sense of the personal narrative as it was spoken and told is lost, Underhill preserves Chona's words, syntax, and meaning as well as the flavor of her everyday life and how it had changed through time. She also strives through her rhetorical techniques to convey the essence of Tohono O'odham philosophy and survival skills; they were "a group who made a quiet adjustment to circumstances. They were people who worked hard and never complained."[67] She made certain that Chona's words and thoughts would be recognizable to Tohono O'odham readers. And they were. Tohono O'odham Joseph Enos said in 1981 that when he had read Chona's life and *People of the Crimson Evening* as a child, "here was my past. I was surprised. Those are my people."[68] Her use of Chona's words—in large sections where her stories are told verbatim—indicates how seriously Underhill took her responsibility to preserve Chona's life story and ensure that all Americans understood that Native peoples had much to say. Years before the new historians took up the cause, Underhill was clearly championing the value of oral history.

Conclusion

By 1947 Underhill was tired and realized that the BIA was changing in ways she found unacceptable. The agency, reorganized in 1945, had forced Underhill out, but Beatty had given her temporary assignments so that she could finish her writing assignments. Civil service age restrictions forced her to retire in 1948. But Underhill never retired. She immediately took a position in the Departments of Anthropology, Sociology and International Relations at the University of Denver, until 1952 when she retired again at age sixty-nine. But Underhill did not retire again. After a yearlong trip around the world, she taught sporadically at the University of Denver, New York State Teacher's College (now the State University of New York at New Platz), and Colorado Woman's College (now Temple Buell College). She also assisted in Denver's urban Indian initiatives, which loomed large due to federal termination and relocation efforts and the economic changes that were transforming Indian Country. She was especially concerned about how Native men and women would adjust to nonreservation life and retain their ancient cultural traditions. In addition to helping individuals, she decided to try influencing the average citizen through a new set of books that would demonstrate that "the amalgamation of white men and red, both racially and socially . . . is a responsibility, not for the government, but for the average citizen."[69]

Ruth Underhill has been described as a scholar, a witty humanist, and a scientist with poetical abilities who had "a deep interest in people and in social organizations . . . that carried her through many experiences, many countries and many university classrooms."[70] She was truly an ethnohistorian before the term was even conceptualized, and like all of the women discussed in this volume, she was innovative, eclectic, insightful, and ahead of her time in her research methodologies and her writing style.

And she was a lyrical writer. As archaeologist Cynthia Irwin-Williams says, Underhill had an "essentially peerless capacity for communicating to all of us that which she feels and sees and also the passions and visions of those she works with. In a literature today in anthropology characterized by a kind of desiccated technical verbiage and obscure jargon, Ruth's contributions stand absolutely alone in the beauty of their language and their lyric quality. Her own enchantment with the richness of their [Indians'] heritage emerges so clearly in her charming and graceful representations of patient, quiet, democratic ways of life."[71]

Underhill built a long-term relationship with Tohono O'odham men and women. They "were so good to me," she wrote. "They were always kind and willing and caring and helped me whenever I needed help so that I sort of remembered it as an ideal place to go."[72] It is fitting that Tohono O'odhams themselves summarize Underhill's career. One Tohono O'odham linguist, Penny Lopez, has referred to her works as critical references: "Sometimes we don't know the whole story and we can look at her books and see what it should be. We trust Underhill."[73] Community members agreed. At Underhill's 1980 honoring, Mary Grace Jones said, "I think her [books] are the most accurate of the books written. They give you a picture of how it was. You can pick them up and read again and again." Elder Joseph Enos stated, "We don't have to make Dr. Underhill an honorary O'odham. She is already O'odham in our eyes." There can be no higher tribute than the respect of the people with whom one works.[74]

Notes

1. Underhill Correspondence file, box 7, Ruth Underhill Papers, Denver Museum of Natural History and Science. See also "Papago Tribe Honors Ruth Murray Underhill," *Anthropology Newsletter* 21, no. 3 (1980): 3. Underhill was also made the grand marshal of the Forty-third Papago Rodeo and Fair.

2. Julie Pierson, "To Ruth Murray Underhill," poem in program for Tohono O'odham banquet honoring Underhill, December 9, 1979, Sells, Arizona; also published in "Papago Tribe Honors Ruth Murray Underhill." Max H. Norris, tribal resolution published in "Papago Tribe Honors Ruth Murray Underhill." The plaque presented by Vice-Chairman Enos Francisco read, "Our thanks to Ruth Murray Underhill who captured the spirit of our O'odham through her writings and made it possible for those of us today and tomorrow to appreciate the richness of our O'odham heritage."

3. Underhill quoted in "Underhill to Visit CRIT," *Manataba Messenger* (Parker, Arizona), October 9, 1981, 1, 7; "A Return to the 'People of the River,'" *Manataba Messenger*, October 20, 1981, 1. The events were filmed by ABC's *PM Magazine* and the Denver Museum of Natural History. Underhill did publish "The Battle of Spirit Mountain (Translated from the Mohave)," *The Masterkey* 19 (1936): 10–14.

4. Kathleen M. Sands, "Ruth M. Underhill: Setting the Standard in Literary Anthropology," p. 2, paper presented in the session "Ruth Murray Underhill: A Protean Anthropologist," organized by Joyce Herold, at the American Anthropological Association meeting, November 16, 1984, Denver, Colorado.

5. For extensive bibliographies of Underhill's work see Joyce Griffen, "Ruth Murray Underhill, (1883–1984)," in *Women Anthropologists: A Biographical Dictionary*, ed. Ute Gans, Aisha Khan, Jerrie McIntyre, and Ruth Weinberg (Westport CN: Greenwood Press, 1989), 355–60; Dorothea V. Kaschube, "Ruth Murray Underhill," *Southwestern Lore* 31, no. 4 (1966): 69–73; Catherine Lavender, *Scientists and Storytellers: Feminist Anthropologists and the Construction of the American Southwest* (Albuquerque: University of New Mexico Press, 2006); Barbara A. Babcock and Nancy J. Parezo, *Daughters of the Desert: Women Anthropologists and the Native American Southwest, 1880–1980* (Albuquerque: University of New Mexico Press, 1988). Underhill's papers and interviews with Joyce Herold are housed in the archives of the Denver Museum of Natural History and Science.

6. Ruth M. Underhill, "Vocabulary and Style in an Indian Language," *American Speech* 1 (1934): 4, reprinted in *Indians at Work* 3, no. 14 (1936): 17–19; "A Note on Easter Devils at Kavori'k on the Papago Reservation," *American Anthropologist* 36 (1936): 515–16; "Autobiography of a Papago Woman," *Memoirs of the American Anthropological Association*, no. 46 (1936), supplement to *American Anthropologist* 38, no. 3, part 2; reprinted as *The Autobiography of a Papago Woman*, Memoirs of the American Anthropological Association no. 46 (Menasha WI: American Anthropological Association, 1936); reprinted as *Chona, Papago Woman* (New York: Holt, Rinehart and Winston, 1979); "A Papago Calendar Record," *University of New Mexico Bulletin*, Anthropological Series 2, no. 5 (1938); *Singing for Power: The Song Magic of the Papago Indians of Southern Arizona* (1938; reprint, Berkeley: University of California Press, 1976); *The Social Organization of the Papago Indians*, Columbia University Contributions to Anthropology no. 30 (New York: Columbia University Press, 1939); *Papago Indian Religion*, Columbia University Contributions to Anthropology no. 33 (New York: Columbia University Press, 1946); *People of the Crimson Evening*, illustrated by Velino Herrera (Ma-pe-wi) (Lawrence KS: U.S. Government, Department of the Interior, BIA, Branch of Education, Haskell Press, 1951), also published as *People of the Crimson Evening: Papago Life before the Coming of the White Man*, Indian Life and Customs Pamphlet no. 7 (Phoenix: Education Division, BIA, 1951); Ruth M. Underhill and Edward Caster, "The Ethnobiology of the Papago Indians," *University of New Mexico Bulletin*, no. 275 (1935); Ruth Underhill with Donald Bahr, Jose Pancho, and D. Lopez, *Rainhouse and Ocean: Speeches for the Papago Year*, American Tribal Religion no. 4 (Flagstaff: Museum of Northern Arizona Press, 1979).

7. Ruth Murray Underhill, *The Navajos* (Norman: University of Oklahoma Press, 1956); "People and Projects: Ruth Underhill," *Human Organization* 8, no. 2 (1949): 25 (quote).

8. Ruth M. Underhill, *Indians of Southern California*, illustrated by Velino Herrera (Ma-pe-wi) (Lawrence KS: Education Division, U.S. Office of Indian Affairs, 1941); *Red Man's America: A History of Indians in the United States* (Chicago: University of Chicago Press, 1953; translated into Swedish, 1957); *First Came the Family* (New York: William Morrow, 1958); *Indians of the Southwest*, Know Your America Series (New York: Doubleday, 1961); *Red Man's Religion: Beliefs and Practices of the Indians North of Mexico* (Chicago: University of Chicago Press, 1965); *Ceremonial Patterns in the Greater Southwest*, American Ethnological Society Monograph no. 13 (Menasha WI: J. J. Augustin, 1948); "A

Classification of Religious Practices among North American Indians," *Report of the Fourth International Congress of Anthropological and Ethnological Sciences* 2 (1952): 320–24; see also "Some Basic Cultures of the Indians of the United States," in *The North American Indian Today,* ed. C. T. Loram and T. F. McIlwraith (Toronto: University of Toronto Press, 1943), 23–29.

9. Underhill quoted in Kaschube, "Ruth Murray Underhill," 70; Ruth M. Underhill, *Here Come the Navaho!,* ed. Willard W. Beatty (Lawrence KS: U.S. Government, Department of the Interior, BIA, Branch of Education, Haskell Indian Institute, 1953); *The Northern Paiute Indians of California and Nevada,* Educational Division, U.S. Office of Indian Affairs, Sherman Pamphlet No. 1 (Lawrence KS: Haskell Institute, 1941); *Indians of the Pacific Northwest,* Educational Division, U.S. Office of Indian Affairs, Indian Life and Customs No. 5 (Washington DC: BIA, 1944); *Workaday Life of the Pueblos,* ed. Willard W. Beatty (Phoenix: U.S. Government, Department of the Interior, BIA, Phoenix Indian School Print Shop, 1954); *Pueblo Crafts* (Phoenix: U.S. Government, Department of the Interior, BIA, Printing Department, Phoenix Indian School, 1944). Underhill also published numerous short articles in BIA service publications like *Smoke Signals* and *Indians at Work.*

10. Sands, "Ruth M. Underhill," 10.

11. Ruth M. Underhill, *The White Moth* (New York: Moffat, Yard, 1920); *Hawk over Whirlpools* (New York: J. J. Augustin, 1940); *Beaverbird* (New York: Coward-McCann, 1959); *Antelope Singer* (New York: Coward-McCann, 1961).

12. Other novels published at approximately the same time include Oliver LaFarge, *Laughing Boy* (New York: Houghton Mifflin, 1929); Francis Gillmor, *Wind Singer* (New York: Minton, Balch, 1930); Frank Water, *The Man Who Killed a Deer* (New York: Farrar, Rinehart, 1941); and Darcy McNickle, *The Surrounded* (New York: Dodd, Mead, 1936). The other major writer to specialize in children's books was Laura Adams Armer; see *Dark Circle of Branches* (New York: Longmans, Green, 1933).

13. Sands, "Ruth M. Underhill," 10.

14. "Underhill, Ruth Murray," *Current Biography,* 617; Ruth Underhill, interview with Joyce Herold, July 8, 1979, tape 1, transcription, pp. 1–5 [hereafter page numbers refer to transcription pages], Underhill Papers.

15. Griffen, "Ruth Murray Underhill," 355; "Obituary: Elizabeth Underhill, Suffragist," *New York Times,* November 10, 1982, 8. Underhill's other sister was Margaret.

16. Quoted in Griffen, "Ruth Murray Underhill," 355.

17. Quoted in Griffen, "Ruth Murray Underhill," 356, and in Diane Eicher, "She Bridged the Gap in Papago History," *Denver Post*, September 23, 1979, 6.

18. Underhill, *Autobiography of a Papago Woman*, ix.

19. "Underhill, Ruth Murray," *Current Biography*, 618.

20. Underhill, *Papago Woman*, ix. For more on this period of feminism see June Sochen, *The New Women: Feminism in Greenwich Village, 1910–1920* (New York: Quadrangle Books, 1972); and Judith Schwarz, *Radical Feminists of Heterodoxy, Greenwich Village, 1912–1940* (Lebanon PA: New Victoria Press, 1982).

21. Griffen, "Ruth Murray Underhill," 356; Lavender, *Scientists and Storytellers*, 191–216.

22. Quoted in Griffen, "Ruth Murray Underhill," 356. Photos from the trip are in box 17, Underhill Papers.

23. Richard Conn, Curator, Native American Art, Denver Art Museum, interview with Catherine Lavender, June 27, 1991. Conn noted, however, that Underhill had good relationships with men, including one while in her eighties and nineties with a professor of ancient history.

24. Underhill interview with Herold, May 12, 1980, tape 10, p. 26; Underhill quoted in Frances Melrose, "Study of Papagos Is Fondly Recalled," *Rocky Mountain News*, January 23, 1977, 8, and in Griffen, "Ruth Murray Underhill," 356.

25. Joyce Herold, "Elder Sister's Anthropology: Ruth Underhill and the Southwest," 13, paper presented at the Daughters of the Desert Conference, Oracle, Arizona, March 1985, on file at the Wenner-Gren Foundation for Anthropological Research, New York.

26. Ruth Benedict, *Patterns of Culture* (Boston: Houghton Mifflin, 1934); Babcock and Parezo, *Daughters of the Desert*, 27; see also Barbara A. Babcock, "'Not in the Absolute Singular': Rereading Ruth Benedict," in *Hidden Scholars: Women Anthropologists and the American Southwest*, ed. Nancy J. Parezo (Albuquerque: University of New Mexico Press, 1993), 107–28.

27. Underhill quoted in Herold, "Elder Sister's Anthropology," 11.

28. See also Lavender, *Scientists and Storytellers*, 20; Marshall Hyatt, *Franz Boas, Social Activist: The Dynamics of Ethnicity* (Westport CN: Greenwood Press, 1990).

29. Underhill quoted in Herold, "Elder Sister's Anthropology," 12; Franz Boas, *Anthropology and Modern Life* (New York: Norton, 1928); see essays in Franz Boas, *Race, Language, and Culture* (New York: Macmillan, 1948). See also

Regna Darnell, *And Along Came Boas: Continuity and Revolution in Americanist Anthropology* (Amsterdam: J. Benjamin, 1998); and Hyatt, *Franz Boas, Social Activist.*

30. Underhill's classmates included Ethel and Bert Aginsky, Jules Henry, and Edward Kinnard. For more on Boas and his teaching methods see Margaret Mead, "Apprenticeship under Boas," in *The Anthropology of Franz Boas: Essays on the Centennial of Birth,* ed. Walter Goldschmidt, Memoirs of the American Anthropological Association no. 89 (Washington DC: American Anthropological Association, 1959), 29–45.

31. Boas to Laufer, July 23, 1920, Franz Boas Papers, American Philosophical Society, Philadelphia. For a discussion on "fathers" of anthropology and mentoring, see also Parezo, "Conclusion," *Hidden Scholars,* 348.

32. George W. Stocking Jr., "Ideas and Institutions in American Anthropology: Thoughts toward a History of the Interwar Years," in *Selected Papers from the American Anthropologist, 1921–1945,* ed. Stocking (Washington DC: American Anthropological Association, 1976), 1–53, Kroeber quote on 7.

33. Elsie Clews Parsons, *The Old Fashioned Woman: Primitive Fancies about the Sex* (New York: Putnam, 1913); *Fear and Conventionality* (New York: Putnam, 1914); *Social Freedom: A Study of the Conflicts between Social Classification and Personality* (New York: Putnam, 1915); Elsie Clews Parsons, ed., *American Indian Life: Customs and Traditions of Twenty-three Tribes* (New York: Huebsch, 1922). Underhill later prepared an annotated bibliography of Parsons's writing. See folder 1, box 2, Underhill Collection, Penrose Library Special Collections, University of Denver.

34. Elsie Clews Parsons, *Pueblo Indian Religion,* 2 vols. (Chicago: University of Chicago, 1939). Parsons later returned the compliment and admitted to being "envious" of Underhill's literary skill, referring to *Singing for Power* as an "aperitif." Elsie Clews Parsons, review of *Singing for Power,* by Ruth M. Underhill, *American Anthropologist* 41, no. 4 (1939): 482–83.

35. Underhill interview with Herold, May 1, 1980, tape 9, p. 24. Reichard's popular works include *Spider Woman: A Story of Navaho Weavers and Chanters* (New York: Macmillan, 1934); *Navaho Shepherd and Weaver* (New York: J. J. Augustin, 1936); and *Dezba: Woman of the Desert* (New York: J. J. Augustin, 1939). The latter is similar in form and content to Underhill's *Chona.*

36. Underhill interview with Herold, May 1, 1980, tape 9, p. 24; Griffen, "Ruth Murray Underhill," 357.

37. Underhill, *Papago Woman*, ix.

38. For examples see Nancy J. Parezo, "Ruth Bunzel at Zuni: A Search for the Middle Place," introduction to Ruth Bunzel's *Zuni Ceremonialism: Three Studies*, ed. Parezo (Albuquerque: University of New Mexico Press, 1992); and Nancy J. Parezo and Don D. Fowler, "Taking Ethnological Training Outside the Classroom: The 1904 Louisiana Purchase Exposition as Field School," in *Annual of History of Anthropology*, vol. 2, ed. Regna Darnell and Fred Gleach (Lincoln: University of Nebraska Press, 2006), 69–102. Boas later criticized Underhill's personalistic and individual life focus, telling her that what she was doing was not ethnology. Luckily, Benedict and Reichard supported her focus on autobiographical work. Underhill stuck to her method because she felt it more accurately portrayed how individual lives were actually lived. Underhill interview with Herold, cited in "Elder Sister's Anthropology," 15.

39. Underhill's first report back to Benedict and Boas was an unpublished paper, "Acculturation at the Papago Village of Santa Rosa," copy on file in the Arizona State Museum library, Tucson.

40. See Donald M. Barr, "Pima and Papago Social Organization," *Handbook of North American Indians*, vol. 10, *Southwest*, ed. Alfonso Ortiz and William Sturtevant (Washington DC: Smithsonian Institution, 1983), 178–92, which relies extensively on Underhill's research. While some people have characterized the Tohono O'odhams as patriarchal, this is not a concept that the people would recognize or agree with. They do agree with the patrilineal emphasis and the fact that men and women have different spheres.

41. Underhill, *Papago Woman*, 91.

42. Underhill interview with Herold, February 21, 1980, tape 10, p. 25.

43. Underhill interview with Herold, February 21, 1980, tape 10, p. 24.

44. Nancy J. Parezo, "Matilda Coxe Stevenson: Pioneer Ethnologist," in Parezo, *Hidden Scholars*, 38–62. See Underhill, *Papago Woman*, chapter 1, for an example when Chona quietly teaches Underhill about not speaking names of the dead. It was also expected that an anthropologist living with a family should provide food for the family unit so as not to be a burden. Unfortunately, some scholars have called reciprocity gifts exploitation, seeing this practice as the illicit purchase of information. It is not. Gifts are culturally appropriate recognition of respect.

45. Underhill interview with Herold, February 21, 1980, tape 6, p. 44.

46. Underhill, *Papago Woman*, ix; Underhill quoted in Griffen, "Ruth Murray Underhill," 357.

47. Alan Cunningham, "Anthropologist Returns to Land of Mohaves," *Rocky Mountain News*, November 1, 1981, 1.

48. Edward H. Spicer, "Plural Society in the Southwest," in *Plural Society in the Southwest*, ed. Edward H. Spicer and Raymond H. Thompson (New York: Weatherhead Foundation, 1972), 21–73.

49. Underhill interview with Herold, February 21, 1980, tape 6, p. 42.

50. Underhill, *Papago Woman*, 3.

51. Underhill quoted in Herold, "Elder Sister's Anthropology," 17.

52. Underhill, *Papago Woman*, 3, 7.

53. Underhill, *Papago Woman*, 13.

54. Underhill and Enos quoted in Eicher, "She Bridged the Gap in Papago History," 6–7.

55. There is some confusion as to when Underhill actually received her degree. While 1939 is the official date, she completed her fieldwork in 1934 and wrote the dissertation in 1935.

56. Fred Eggan, Transcript of Discussion Comments, "Daughters of the Desert Conference," Globe, Arizona, on file at the Wenner-Gren Foundation for Anthropological Research, 1986.

57. Louise Lamphere, "Gladys Reichard among the Navajo," in Parezo, *Hidden Scholars*, 157–81; Louise Lamphere, "Unofficial Histories: A Vision of Anthropology from the Margins," *American Anthropologist* 106, no. 1 (2004): 126–39.

58. Griffen, "Ruth Murray Underhill," 358; Lawrence C. Kelly, "Ruth Murray Underhill: Applied Anthropologist," paper presented at the American Anthropological Association meeting, Denver, Colorado, November 16, 1984.

59. Ruth M. Underhill, *The Papago Indians of Arizona and Their Relatives the Pima*, illustrated by Velino Herrera (Ma-pe-wi) (Lawrence KS: U.S. Government, Department of the Interior, BIA, Branch of Education, Haskell Indian Institute, 1940). See also *The Northern Paiute Indians of California and Nevada* (1941); *Indians of Southern California* (1941); *Pueblo Crafts* (1944); *The Northern Paiute Indians*, Educational Division, U.S. Office of Indian Affairs, Sherman Pamphlet No. 1 (Lawrence KS: Haskell Institute, 1945); *People of the Crimson Evening: Papago Life Long Ago* (1951); *Here Come the Navaho!* (1953); *Indians of the Pacific Northwest* (1953); and *Workaday Life of the Pueblos* (1954). Underhill visited the reservations and communities of some of these peoples, but because of her work and teaching schedule she did not undertake as much exten-

sive fieldwork as she had done with the Tohono O'odhams. Some were cultural overviews designed to acquaint Anglo-Americans with the basics of cultures.

60. Oliver LaFarge, review of *First Penthouse Dwellers in America* and *Singing for Power*, by Ruth M. Underhill, *Saturday Review of Literature*, July 2, 1938, 18–19.

61. Alice Marriott, review of *The Navajos*, by Ruth M. Underhill, *Western Folklore* 16 (1957): 66.

62. Shelby J. Tisdale, "Women on the Periphery of the Ivory Tower," in Parezo, *Hidden Scholars*, 330–32.

63. Underhill examined this Tohono O'odham narrative style in several studies, especially *Singing for Power* (1938) and *The Social Organization of the Papago Indians* (1939). The style is evident as well in Dean Saxton and Lucille Saxton, *O'othham Hoho'ok A'agitha: Legends and Lore of the Papago and Pima Indians* (Tucson: University of Arizona Press, 1973).

64. Underhill, *Papago Woman*, 3.

65. Underhill interview with Herold, September 14, 1980, tape 17, p. 12.

66. Sands, "Ruth M. Underhill," 7.

67. Underhill interview with Herold, September 14, 1980, tape 17, p. 12.

68. Quoted in "Papago Tribe Honors Ruth Murray Underhill," 3.

69. Underhill quoted in "Underhill, Ruth Murray," *Current Biography*, 619.

70. "Underhill, Ruth Murray," *Current Biography*, 617.

71. Cynthia Irwin-Williams, comments on Ruth Underhill at a reception at the Foothills Art Center, Golden, Colorado, September 14, 1980.

72. Underhill quoted in "Papago Tribe Honors Ruth Murray Underhill," 3.

73. Quoted in "Papago Tribe Honors Ruth Murray Underhill, 3.

74. Mary Grace Jones and Elder Joseph Enos quoted in "Papago Tribe Honors Ruth Murray Underhill," 3.

Conclusion

Shirley A. Leckie and Nancy J. Parezo

As the contributors to this volume have shown us, the ten women chronicled here were pioneering scholars. Each helped to lay the foundation for later developments in history, anthropology, archaeology, and folklore that appear groundbreaking and contemporary today as they relate to current studies of the Native peoples of the trans-Mississippi West. Despite the advances women and minorities have made in history and anthropology, the contributions of these women were too often ignored in the past. This is especially true of the volumes dedicated to the important figures who have shaped these disciplines, especially in the regional specializations of the American West and its Native peoples.

Noted historian Anne Firor Scott, author of the first major book on southern women to appear in the second-wave feminist movement, *The Southern Lady: From Pedestal to Politics* (1970), characterizes Annie Heloise Abel in *Unheard Voices: The First Historians of Southern Women* (1993) as the founder of Native American history. We found no other historian who gives Abel that credit, but we agree with Scott's assessment.[1] The situation is similar for other women historians honored in this volume. Angie Debo and Mari Sandoz are too often overlooked as pioneers in ethnohistory and precursors for the development of the New Indian history. Finally, activist and writer Gertrude Bonnin, selected as a contributor to history and folklore and a chronicler of the harm wrought by assimilationist policies through her autobiographical works, is still discussed primarily as a literary figure, not as a public intellectual documenting her times.

Since potential and established female scholars were unwelcome in the professionalized disciplines of history and anthropology, the women whose lives we have examined here struggled hard to enter their fields, and even more fiercely to maintain their footholds. Male responses to women's professional careers ranged from outright hostility to effective mentoring that encouraged female scholars to complete their degrees or undertake independent research projects. Even the most supportive mentors, however, sent women not-so-subtle messages, cautioning them not to expect much in the way of full-time careers, advancement, or recognition within academia.

There were exceptions. Annie Abel seemed to escape this all-too-common fate as she rose to full professor at Smith College and established a strong reputation as a foremost scholar among her peers, both male and female. Beginning with her graduate-level studies, she was interested in American Indians and how they lost their lands. As scholars Theda Perdue and Michael Green inform their readers in their introduction to Abel's trilogy on the Five Southern Tribes as slaveholders during the Civil War and Reconstruction, she was the first scholar to perceive American Indians as agents on the historical stage.[2]

Despite her pathbreaking spirit in taking such a stance, Abel, like Dorothea Leighton, was more conventional when it came to her personal life. Her marriage at age fifty brought about her required resignation from the university. Although the union ended in divorce and she remained a productive scholar, she never regained her professorial status. Perhaps, as Suzanne Julin suggests, Abel welcomed her freedom from the responsibilities of full-time teaching. No male professor, however, would have resigned his position because of a change in his marital status. By contrast, Abel played out the seemingly predetermined, gendered script, resigning as a gainfully employed professional woman although she was past her childbearing years. The idea of the husband as the professional provider and the needs of the household came first.

Even when women pledged themselves to celibacy to pursue an academic career, they had no guarantee of obtaining a permanent position in higher education or one that recognized their potential and actual contributions to a discipline. Angie Debo, who built on Abel's works and pioneered in American Indian–centered history, discovered that gaining her doctorate led not to promotion but to dismissal. Although Debo received one of the most prestigious prizes—the Dunning Award from the American Historical Association—for transforming her dissertation into a book, her achievement never convinced her mentor,

Edward Everett Dale, to bring her into his department even as a part-time or adjunct instructor or lecturer, despite her embarrassed request. Even though Dale wrote letters of recommendation on her behalf when Debo sought positions at other institutions, he reserved his whole-hearted mentoring and professional favors for the careers of younger male colleagues such as Morris Wardell, who achieved little scholarly distinction.

Nonetheless, while living a hand-to-mouth existence supported by short-term grants that required constant renewal and new proposals, the ever-creative Debo incorporated anthropological findings into her works and created Indian history that placed Native peoples at the center of narratives, contextualized by their specific cultures and his-torical circumstances. This methodological approach and theoretical paradigm stance enabled her to tell the story of westward advancement partially from the perspectives of Native participants and their descen-dants, thereby raising serious questions about the "process" the Turner thesis had celebrated.

Always an activist, Debo hoped her writings would inform her compatriots about the injustices American Indians had experienced. Disappointed by the public's lack of response, she formed an ever-ex-panding network to lobby Congress against termination and later for a just settlement for the Native peoples of Alaska, one that gave them forty million acres of hunting land with all its resources rather than the ten million originally proposed. Well into her last years, she was still spurring her correspondents to contact Congress about protecting Tohono O'odham water rights and the homelands of the Havasupais, now threatened by the expanding Grand Canyon National Monument. She always cautioned her readers against the destruction of the en-vironment and the wasting of resources, dynamics that had marked America's expansion from Jamestown on.

A variety of historical stances and methodological modes that chal-lenged the often complacent disciplinary center was a hallmark of other women writing simultaneously with Debo. In some cases they developed strategies that defied society and the attempts of individuals to pull outstanding women back into a life of mediocrity. In examining the career of Mari Sandoz, John R. Wunder informs us that, lacking financial resources and writing in defiance of her father, she endured years of privation to attend the University of Nebraska–Lincoln and become a historian. At Nebraska she chose her courses and teachers so well that the skills they imparted, along with her experiences working for the Nebraska State Historical Society, allowed her to gain a strong foothold as a writer through the publication of *Old Jules*, without earning even a bachelor's degree. As was true for Debo, Sandoz's drive, resolve, and dedication to writing and publishing never flagged throughout her lifetime. As Wunder notes, Sandoz was so determined to keep publishing that she was still correcting page proofs as she was dying of cancer.

As did many of the other women in this volume, Sandoz died knowing that she had left a body of history behind that would remain a starting point for later scholars determined to tell an unflinchingly honest and ethnically diverse history of the American West. Contemporary historians chronicling the Sioux and Cheyennes cannot ignore her works or the extensive notes and maps she bequeathed posterity in Nebraska archives. Even more than Debo, Sandoz pioneered in the study of the social and cultural relationships between humans and their environments. Her work here is a body of integrated, regional history that is similar to many synthesizing anthropological studies. Finally, by recognizing Native peoples as situated fully in their cultures and by using their insights, she, like Debo, pioneered in ethnohistory.

Fiercely devoted to their fields of expertise and denied equal access to the supportive environment and full-time, tenured employment of the academy, women intellectuals often made their way as independent scholars, dependent for their livelihood on grants or "soft money." Isabel Kelly was truly prodigious in her pursuit of support and funding, and she literally, as Catherine Fowler and Robert Van Kemper so tellingly reveal, lived a life of "itinerancy" in the field. She bequeathed to her profession an extraordinary record of writing on archaeology in both the western United States and Mexico and about the Native peoples of both countries. Like those of Dorothea Leighton, Kelly's studies of community health helped lay the basis for medical anthropology and public health.

Successful female scholars, without access to the supposedly prestigious topics of a discipline, often pursued the intersection between disciplines (e.g., anthropology and health, history and cultural anthropology, history and environmental studies) and created and grew new purposely interdisciplinary foci of studies that have proven to be groundbreaking. Women in anthropology did the same by challenging the boundaries between increasingly autonomous subfields. Isabel Kelly began her career when most anthropologists, including her official adviser, Alfred Kroeber, believed that women entered archaeology only to meet men. He saw women's chances for having a successful career in the subfield as zero. Despite such prejudice, Kelly persisted in pursuing her greatest love, and she won Kroeber's respect and that of other major cultural anthropologists and archaeologists as well, in part by including local ethnographic perspectives in her studies.

As Kelly traveled muddy and ill-paved back roads in unreliable vehicles and overcame accidents and hospitalization, her interdisciplinary studies eventually took her beyond the western United States and Mexico to other Central and South America countries, the Caribbean, and even to Pakistan. Like Leighton and Marriott, she had to earn her living through research with practical applications, and this required alterations from standard methodologies and different types of writing. All three helped develop another of anthropology's important subfields—applied or developmental anthropology, a subdivision that cuts across all other branches of anthropology. Early on, Kelly challenged accepted methodology, including archaeological practices that focused on compiling overall outlines, and instead looked to the amassing of details as her method of attaining new insights. The tools she used to compile her works were intentionally interdisciplinary, flexible, and multifaceted. In addition to cultural and linguistic anthropology and archaeology, she used the strengths of geography, religious studies, and painstaking evaluation of material culture and art. Without ever holding a tenure-track position, she wrote a vast array of monographs, articles, and ethnographic works and compiled extensive collections of pottery and other evidence of material culture. She may have preferred her life in the field with its constantly changing challenges and hardships to a more sedate academic career. No one can know for sure, however, since she never had the chance to choose between the two.

All the women highlighted in this volume sought to uncover and document the negative effects of colonial expansion. They did so to challenge the widespread acceptance of the Turnerian dogma that the Euro-American expansion into the West had been both inevitable and beneficial for all peoples. Some of the women focused on ensuring that all players were recognized as part of what had always been and continued to be a multicultural setting not always singularly dominated by white, Euro-American men. Marjorie Lambert, a student of Edgar Lee Hewett at the University of New Mexico, was equally interested in learning about the American Indian, Hispanic, and Euro-American residents of northern New Mexico, especially in the Santa Fe region. She aspired to earn a doctorate in archaeology and have the standard academic career. After she gained her master's, Hewett sent her to the Museum of New Mexico, where Lambert moved beyond her charismatic mentor, who saw the Pueblo Indians as timeless and communally oriented peoples, to studying and teaching people about the Southwest as a continually changing multicultural region. In the process she helped develop the subfield of historic archaeology at a time when most southwestern archaeologists concentrated on the precontact period.

Rather than imposing preconceived ideas on the Native peoples of the Southwest, as others so often did in the 1920s and 1930s, Lambert worked differently. Employing Native and Hispanic men as part of her excavation teams, she found her "real instructor" in Jose Rey Toledo of Jemez Pueblo. As Shelby Tisdale explains, Lambert "consulted them [Native peoples] about her findings and incorporated their oral traditions and histories in her analyses and interpretations of the past." That practice, which remained uncommon among male archaeologists until the closing decades of the twentieth century, mirrored Frank Hamilton Cushing's ethnographic archaeology. It also foreshadowed the contemporary collaborations between archaeologists and indigenous peoples that provide the latter with more control over their intellectual histories and create partnerships. Lambert was doing this in the 1930s as standard practice. It took the rest of the archaeological world sixty years to catch up with her.

Lambert was years ahead of her time in other arenas as well, due to her respect for all peoples and their unique cultural knowledge. While serving as curator of archaeology at the Museum of New Mexico at Santa Fe, she conferred and collaborated with American Indian and Hispanic peoples, incorporating their viewpoints into displays and honoring their sensibilities. She successfully fought to keep materials from archaeological sites within the state and thus a part of the communities from which they came. Like all the women museologists of this volume, Lambert never incorporated in displays secret or sacred information or artifacts that would have violated the trust Native and Hispanic peoples had placed in her.

The other women discussed in this volume also abided by these ethical rules. In questioning the noted potter Maria Martinez, whose black-on-black vessels brought fame, tourists, and income to San Ildefonso Pueblo, Alice Marriott observed the restrictions established by the council of San Ildefonso. Her acquiescence exacted a price, for her research contained silences. Marriott's ethics and sensitivity to the values and wishes of Native peoples permitted no alternative.

Marriott's education had ended with the attainment of her second bachelor's degree, since the Great Depression prevented her from obtaining an out-of-state graduate education and the University of Oklahoma at that time offered no anthropology beyond the baccalaureate level. Undaunted, Marriott found other ways of expanding her knowledge and skills and developed an early form of experimental ethnology. While conducting intensive, long-term ethnographic fieldwork, she incorporated her own responses into her works. Now, rather than consisting solely of an authoritative monologue, her writing became a dialogue. She did this well before concerned scholars of the 1980s and 1990s began calling for such changes in ethnography. Her responses, based on close and trusted relationships with Kiowa families, earned their respect. Because the women in these families felt that Marriott's publications would transmit their traditions and critical aspects of their cultural values to their descendants, they became her collaborators as well as respondents. With them, and later with other Native women, Marriott had found her specialty.

Marriott is a prime example of another feature shared by many women in this volume. To reach a wider audience and make a difference in common American values, not only in academic spheres, she rejected stilted academic prose. Her books—especially *The Ten Grand-mothers* and *Maria, The Potter of San Ildefonso*—were lucidly and engagingly written, thereby attracting a far wider readership than most academic anthropologists ever acquired. Like the other women scholars honored in this work, Marriott bequeathed to Native peoples important information that has served them well in their struggle to persist as a people in the face of extreme poverty and often-virulent racism.

The same concern with writing for a wide audience and convincing the electorate to take a broader and less prejudicial view of Indians, particularly to eradicate the Turnerian and widespread assumption that all Indians were doomed to disappear in the face of Western expansion, appeared in the publications of Indian women who were scholar-activists.[3] Yankton Sioux Ella Cara Deloria is probably the best-known of these remarkable women warriors who learned from a wealth of life experiences what needed to be conveyed. Deloria taught school, was employed as a national health education secretary for the Young Women's Christian Association, and later became a physical education teacher as she struggled to support herself. After taking anthropology courses at Columbia University, she worked with Franz Boas each summer for more than a decade. From this collaboration she published important cultural and linguistic works, including *Dakota Texts* and *Dakota Grammar*, which remain foundational texts. Nonetheless, as Maria Cotera notes, neither Boas nor Deloria's other mentor, Ruth Benedict, ever broached the subject of helping Deloria obtain a doctorate, even though either of her seminal works would have counted as a dissertation for anyone in the doctoral program. Nevertheless, all Americanist anthropologists have benefited from her superb writing skills and ethnological abilities, and her texts are required reading in American Indian studies today.

More than a "Native informant" yet unable to become what Cotera calls "a fully accredited anthropologist," Deloria, as an "informed Native," found a way to capture the voice and complexity of her people without violating their trust or betraying their ethics and her kinship obligations and responsibilities. By becoming her people's "plain mouthpiece" in her still unpublished but, thankfully, archived, autoethnography, "The Dakota Way of Life," she developed a model of true collaboration for all Native scholars. In this work she used a culturally approved Yankton narrative style that included what the community wanted known about themselves. She also incorporated their frame of reference, not simply standard ethnographic categories of disassociated chapters on the environment, subsistence, and childbirth practices. And by weaving the "polyphonic voices," including those of both women and men, into her narrative, Deloria moved beyond "the conceptual and methodological norms that governed ethnographic practice in the 1920s and 1930s." In the process she provided more accurate historic and cultural information about her people and made it available to other scholars and the public. She saw—well ahead of today's critical theorists in an insight that was truly advanced in terms of the 1930s and 1940s—that the "othering," theoretically objective, and distanced authoritative stance adopted by her contemporary cultural anthropologists had its own unacknowledged biases and assumptions.

By adopting a stance as a Native "insider," Deloria transcended the standard anthropological orientation in which a male authority figure—the detached observer—wrote about Native peoples in a way that collectivized them and reduced them to monolithic categories. In such "masculinist" writing, the people became the men by default and the "objective" observer wrote in a seemingly detached male voice about other men, rendering women voiceless, invisible, and by implication, inconsequential. Women were not seen as the holders or activators of culture. Such ethnography—and by extension ethnological comparisons, on which governmental policy was made—painted an invalid picture of peoples and their cultures and allowed policy makers and implementers to assume that all American Indians were alike. This misuse of anthropological knowledge plagues the field to this day, in part because ethnographers have not yet listened to the truths Deloria knew.

Deloria was truly ahead of her time, for as Cotera informs us, she anticipated the methodology that Native scholars would bring to their anthropological fieldwork beginning in the 1960s. Non-Native scholars, however, often lagged behind. As late as the 1990s, Ella Deloria's nephew, the late Vine Deloria Jr., and the late Sihasapa Dakota Sioux Beatrice Medicine were still urging anthropologists to adopt methodologies closer to those Ella Deloria had used decades earlier.[4]

Yankton Sioux Gertrude Simmons Bonnin, who named herself Zit-kala-Ša, made her living by teaching and writing. Motivating both endeavors was, Franci Washburn maintains, her attempt to defend the right of Native peoples to receive full human dignity as American Indians with cultures equal to that of Euro-Americans. Overall, as a realist and cultural amalgamator, Zitkala-Ša wanted her people to adopt the best of the generalized American Indian and, in particular, Yankton Sioux way of life and the Euro-American worlds. An extraordinarily complicated woman, she sought to promote enough acculturation among her people to enable them to advance their interests while allowing them to resist assimilation and the disappearance of their traditions, values, and philosophies.

Zitkala-Ša assumed her task at a time when Indian intellectuals were deeply divided over acculturation and assimilation and when Native peoples were losing most of their land and much of its resources. American Indian cultures were, in addition, under direct assault from the Office of Indian Affairs, whose policies favored community termination and individual assimilation, often forced, without input from Native peoples themselves. In this context, Zitkala-Ša adopted a pragmatism that must not be mistaken for expediency. Her alliances shifted with her causes and her strategy for achieving her overall objective—the betterment of her people. In the process she antagonized both Native and non-Native leaders.

In addition to her involvement in various controversies, Zitkala-Ša left behind autobiographical writings, now often reprinted in anthologies and book series as remarkable firsthand accounts of the psychological pain assimilationist policies inflicted on American Indians. Such work countered the salvage ethnography approach of her contemporary anthropologists and historians by presenting timely and historically contextualized alternatives to the image of the timeless Indian who was both changeless and fading into extinction. She also compiled her people's stories into volumes that present vital insights into Yankton Sioux cosmology and by extension the philosophies of other American Indians of the Northern Plains. Thus they remain especially valuable sources for folklore and cultural studies as well as anthropology and American Indian studies.

Finally, by working with William J. Hanson on the opera *The Sun Dance*, Zitkala-Ša's skills as a musician helped produce a work of cultural synthesis that remains an artistic demonstration of what she manifested in her life—a synthesis of the best of Indian (i.e., Yankton) and white cultures. In this quest her work was similar to that of foundational ethnomusicologists Frances Densmore and Natalie Curtis Burlin, both of whom used music to successfully fight government regulations banning Indian sacred music. Like them and Deloria, Zitkala-Ša fought for the right of Indians to define themselves rather than have a definition imposed on them by powerful, authoritative Euro-Americans. Both Native scholars resisted intellectual imperialism in a way that foreshadowed the work of Native activist-scholars of today, such as Choctaw Devon Abbott Mihesuah and Wahpatonwan Dakota Angela Cavender Wilson. Indeed, Zitkala-Ša's work is considered one of the foundations of American Indian studies, which is dedicated to fighting colonialism, imperialism, and their negative effects and instead promoting self-determination and the civic rights of sovereignty.

While Zitkala-Ša was a very visible and highly vocal activist-scholar, other women quietly spent their lives making a difference by using behind-the-scenes influence on the Indian Service and changing the system from within. In their quests they also relied on the dynamics of interdisciplinarity—working from two disciplines, breaking down disciplinary barriers, and keeping the needs of the people with whom they worked always in central focus. Many did this from necessity when institutionalized gender asymmetries prevented them from reaching their original career goals. Physician Dorothea Cross Leighton, an internist and psychiatrist, found that her gender excluded her from obtaining critical institutional positions required to pursue her special medical goals. In addition, because her husband was pursuing psychiatry, the nepotism rules in place ensured that as the wife in a husband-and-wife research team she was the trailing spouse and the unpaid research assistant. But, as Nancy Parezo documents in her essay on Leighton, societal employment barriers did not stop this remarkable humanist-scientist. She essentially consciously carved out a career for herself on her own terms, first as part of a husband-and-wife team, then as a full-time mother and part-time researcher until her children were grown. Later she independently helped to promote the new field of public health. Along the way she talked herself into a groundbreaking job with the Bureau of Indian Affairs under John Collier. When the couple wrote *The Navaho*, one of Dorothea's most important works, she was the main author, even though her husband's name came first on the title page. It was assumed in 1940 that women deferred to men in such matters, but it never happened again. Leighton made sure that she and other women received due credit for their work.

The Leightons were a remarkable team. They developed a new approach to working with the Navajos that was significant for all Native peoples by combining ethnographic and psychological interviewing techniques that were modified to respect the values and protocols of each culture. By approaching health and healing with no a priori ideas during their fieldwork, they not only helped to lay the foundation for medical anthropology but also advanced ethnographic fieldwork methods to a new ethical level. And by using the life history technique, which revolved around a set of problems and responses, the Leightons enabled the Navajos to give them an "unedited story." In this way, the couple elicited what Navajos considered most important and accurate about their lives. Subsequently, the Leightons advised the Indian Service that in offering its services to Native peoples, the agency first had to understand its clientele and its needs, rather than demanding that Native peoples understand and accept the agency's offerings. That important idea has since become a bedrock element of modern Indian Service work with Native peoples.

Working within the governmental system but using a revolutionary educational strategy of multiple writing genres to convey her messages and combining ethnographic and ethnohistorical research methods that honored each culture and respected their knowledge was Ruth Underhill, the final woman met in this volume. She also worked for the Bureau of Indian Affairs as an education supervisor, researcher, and writer for most of her long and fruitful career. While Underhill is primarily remembered merely as the student or fictive daughter of Franz Boas who worked with the Tohono O'odhams, Catherine Lavender and Nancy Parezo document in their essay that she should be memorialized for a much greater legacy. One of the most prolific writers (and one of the longest lived), Underhill began her anthropological and historical career later than most other women, but she quickly demonstrated that age cannot stop a keen intellect and a determined scholar.

Underhill worked in a number of genres in addition to academic writing. She is probably best known for *Papago Woman*, one of the first biographies of an American Indian woman, and for her popular (rather than academic) books for the general public that synthesized cultural anthropology and ethnohistory for a number of Native American cultures in the American West. The most significant part of her legacy, however, is how highly she is regarded by the Native peoples with whom she worked.

That regard is well deserved. By helping to establish ethnohistory programs in several tribes, Underhill assisted with the transition to the New Indian history, in which the Native perspective takes center stage. Equally important, she gave each tribe her field notes, because she felt that she had recorded their history for them. She took this stance long before the question of who had the right to field notes became an ethical and intellectual property rights issue. Underhill's methods and her insistence on collaborating and giving back in the 1940s and 1950s are models for the twenty-first century. She did it right, and as a result she was honored by the peoples to whom she had dedicated her life.

While all the women of this volume faced the problem of making their way as professionals somewhat differently, they shared commonalities. All studied marginalized people. In part this arose because many women anthropologists received their assignments for reasons different from those governing the selection of men for ethnographic studies. As noted earlier, male anthropologists, and certainly Boas as well, welcomed women as scholars who could relate to Native women and thus obtain information unavailable to men.

Additionally, the historians in this volume probably had personal reasons for gravitating toward the study of those considered less important. In academe, where women were unwelcome, selecting lesser-known topics may have been a way of placating men who would otherwise find female scholars threatening. Annie Abel's almost overwhelming footnoting and checking of primary sources in writing book reviews to evaluate the scholarship of others suggest some insecurity.

Abel felt compelled to be extraordinarily painstaking and rigorous. Her later writing on the Five Tribes—a topic she described as "not important" but "interesting"—may have appeared a safer enterprise than other topics more securely in the male domain. Nevertheless, one must weigh such a possibility in the light of her unfailing interest in uncovering the wrongs American Indians had sustained.

Others, such as Angie Debo and Mari Sandoz, very likely because of the hardships and poverty they had experienced as children, affiliated themselves their entire lives with the less fortunate. Ruth Underhill, on the other hand, like other feminist anthropologists, was especially interested in gender relations among Native peoples because she wanted to understand as fully as possible the sexual hierarchy in her own society. If other cultures valued women's roles as much as men's, then the gender relations of her own culture were neither predetermined nor universal. Similarly, as Patricia Loughlin notes, Alice Marriott, in her study of American Indian women, not only saw a chance to carve out a specialty for herself but welcomed evidence that women's roles and functions in some societies were honored rather than denigrated.[5]

Whatever these women's reasons for devoting their careers to the study of marginalized groups and individuals, their research takes on a new significance today. The human rights of indigenous people are now both a national and international issue. In the United States, how Native land was taken and by what authority, and whether tribal governments were extinguished or still remain in place, and under what constitution or agreement, are problems that the federal government and its agencies confront in dealing with Native peoples. Also, the thorny issue of how to reconcile tribal rights with federal and state constitutions persists.

Ethnohistory, as a multidisciplinary way of researching and writing studies and monographs on American Indians, has flourished in part because the U.S. government, in the light of continuing controversies, needs the expertise of the anthropologist and archaeologist. Only through their insights can Native peoples be placed in broader cultural contexts. The government also requires the knowledge of the historian who can identify the documentary evidence in official statements, reports, treaties, and court decisions that shed light on the conflicting claims among Native peoples themselves and between them and non-Native peoples.

Ethnohistory, which combines all these perspectives, remains essential in such matters. In rendering, for example, the decision that the Creek Council was a fully coordinate branch of government and that Secretary of the Interior Thomas Kleppe had acted illegally by dispensing funds to the narrowly elected chief Claude Cox, Judge William Bryant relied heavily on Angie Debo's *The Road to Disappearance* as the most accurate secondary source available. Her work, with its painstaking documentation of tribal and governmental sources, indicated that the Creek Constitution of 1867 remained in force for the Creek Nation when Bryant rendered his *Harjo v. Kleppe* decision in 1976.[6]

Beyond national controversies, court cases, and the usefulness of ethnohistory there is yet another reason why these women, once marginalized, now assume larger importance. Today, as Western powers confront the understandable desire of emerging nations to obtain a more equitable share of the world's resources, wealth, and power, many historians are writing postcolonial works that focus on the marginalized peoples of the past or those who knew the harsh reality of imperialism in the not-so-distant past.

Had Annie Abel not undertaken to write her trilogy on the Five Southern Tribes during the Civil War, one can imagine a doctoral student early in the twenty-first century tackling the subject as a study in postcolonialism. That student would discover how the leaders of the Cherokees, Creeks, Choctaws, Chickasaws, and Seminoles strove to save the autonomy of their four republics (the Chickasaws were subsumed in the Choctaw republic) while making their way "between two fires"—the Confederate States at their borders and the United States from Washington DC. Rent by divisions from the removal period, now exacerbated by cleavages between the more acculturated mixed-blood elite and the more traditional full-blood Indians, they exemplified the fate of many peoples of today. Presently the peoples living in societies that until recently have been colonized find themselves, despite their independence, surviving in a world in which their internal divisions are similar to those of the Five Southern Tribes. While Abel's racial views, mirroring the impact of the Dunning school of historiography in the early decades of the twentieth century, are untenable today, Abel was, in her anticipation of postcolonialism, a truly pioneering scholar.[7]

Still, that was not the only way Abel was interested in topics that intrigue modern scholars. In the last decades of her life she was intent on compiling a comparative history of the treatment of indigenous peoples in Commonwealth Nations that had been or were part of the British Empire. Although she never completed that study, in her interest in that topic she anticipated Glenda Riley's pathbreaking *Taking Land/Breaking Land: Women Colonizing the American West and Kenya, 1840–1940* (2003).[8] More recently, Margaret D. Jacobs has begun examining the role gender ideology played in the colonizing of the American West, and calls on scholars to study the role that gender ideology played in other colonizing ventures throughout the globe.[9] Although Riley and Jacobs bring a far deeper sensibility and knowledge of women and gender history than Abel ever exhibited, Abel was, nonetheless, prescient in her understanding that the field of colonial relations toward indigenous peoples must be studied in a comparative framework.

Among historians, anthropologists, and archaeologists today, the study of marginalized peoples—marginalized as racial and ethnic minorities and marginalized as women because of prevailing gender roles—has become a mainstream interest. Thus, ironically, the women intellectuals in this volume were studying and writing about topics that have now moved into the academic mainstream.

In the ongoing conversations over time and generations that are history and anthropology, the insights of the figures in this volume were not taken as seriously or accorded the same respect as those of their male counterparts. None of them established schools as full professors as did Turner for historians. Now, however, the topics that interested these women in the early part of the twentieth century increasingly interest leading scholars today. Because of the passage of time, however, their contributions are often too easily overlooked and their insights are frequently attributed to newer scholars. Not only is this unfair, but today's scholars must know more about the history of ideas, just as archaeologists must understand how material culture developed and the ways that various cultures were influenced by other cultures and migrations.

Coming of age in the ethnocentric era so well described in Franci Washburn's essay on Zitkala-Ša, a time when leaders were determined to assimilate all races and ethnicities into the dominant Euro-American-based culture and Anglo-European system of law while denying women and people of color equal opportunities, these ten female scholars dared to write a narrative different from the prevailing master narrative. Courageous and intrepid, they devoted their lives to obtaining greater justice for the Native peoples who had inhabited the American trans-Mississippi West before Frederick Jackson Turner's "settlers" had conquered the entire region. Greater justice, in the minds of these ten women, began with setting the record straight. Committed to their disciplines, they persevered in researching and writing, although the eight never won the secure positions awarded men who made similar or lesser contributions. One exception, Annie Abel, retired frm academe after marriage; the other, Dorothea Leighton, began her academic career after raising children.

The new master narrative that all these women offered, despite their differences in age, background, discipline, and specialty, was this: American Indians had established and maintained, even as they constantly adapted to the ever-changing Euro-American society, alternative ways of life that had much to offer not only for themselves but also for others. These ten women understood from the beginning of their studies and careers that there are many ways to be human. Finding in Native peoples new and often more effective ways of expressing a fuller humanity, these women were eager to share their discoveries with their colleagues, their society, and posterity for the betterment of humankind.

Perhaps Angie Debo provides the best example of what these women were working toward. In three of her thirteen books she dealt with the Creek chief Pleasant Porter. In two of her works she referred to the affirmation Porter expressed as he sought to console his people after the U.S. Congress had passed the Curtis Act of 1898, which forced the Five Tribes of Indian Territory to terminate their protectorates and accept allotments instead of retaining their communal landholdings. As Porter affirmed, "The vitality of our race still persists. We have not lived for naught. We are the original discoverers of this continent, and the conquerors of it from the animal kingdom, and on it first taught the arts of peace and war, and first planted the institutions of virtue, truth and liberty." Native peoples had proved "that it was possible for men to exist and subsist here." He knew—as did the women of this volume—that Native peoples were "an indestructible element in [American] national history."[10]

In that light, the most important legacy these ten women bequeathed us was their narration of the stories of Native peoples, using the words of Native peoples as much as possible, and with as full an understanding of Native culture and the changes they had undergone over time as these ten women could possibly attain and communicate. In that way they assisted in laying the foundation for ethnohistory and developing it in its earliest years. In their capacity to keep working throughout their lifetimes, irrespective of material rewards or professional standing, these women were truly out on their own frontier. Out there they paved the way for the more humane, respectful, and accurate scholarship on the American West and its Native peoples that is emerging today.

This volume represents our expression of our deepest gratitude and appreciation for the works these intellectual foremothers bequeathed us. We hope that their stories and a deeper understanding of their significance will inspire today's scholars, and future ones as well, to keep their work alive by continuing the investigations they began and by developing new ways of adding the voices and views of Native peoples to the continuing scholarship of the American West.

Notes

1. Anne Firor Scott, *Unheard Voices: The First Historians of Southern Women* (Charlottesville: University of Virginia Press, 1993), 3. R. David Edmunds, in his centennial essay for the American Historical Association, never mentioned Annie H. Abel. See "Native Voices, New Voices: American Indian History, 1895–1995," *American Historical Review* 100, no. 3 (1995): 717–79.

2. Theda Perdue and Michael Green, introduction to Annie Heloise Abel, *The American Indian as Slaveholder and Secessionist* (Lincoln: University of Nebraska Press, 1992).

3. As late as 2001, a popular textbook coauthored by Ray Allen Billington and Martin Ridge contained a chapter titled "The Removal of the Indian Barrier." *Westward Expansion*, 5th ed. (Albuquerque: University of New Mexico Press, 2001).

4. Ironically, Beatrice Medicine experienced many of the same difficulties as Ella Deloria. She did not receive her doctorate until 1983, even though she had established herself earlier as an authoritative scholar on Native American studies, especially those related to American Indian women. Medicine characterized Ella Deloria as "the emic voice." For information on Medicine's career see Faye V. Harrison, foreword, *Learning to Be an Anthropologist and Remaining "Native": Selected Writings of Dr. Beatrice Medicine*, ed. with Sue-Ellen Jacobs (Urbana: University of Illinois Press, 2001), xiii–xvi. Medicine's excellent essay, "Ella C. Deloria: The Emic Voice," appears on pages 269–88.

5. Margaret Jacobs reminds readers that when Marriott was interviewing Martinez, gender roles were in flux. *Engendered Encounters: Feminism and Pueblo Cultures, 1879–1934* (Lincoln: University of Nebraska Press, 1999), 174.

6. Harjo v. Kleppe, 420 F.Supp. 1110 (D.D.C. 1976).

7. William A. Dunning, *Reconstruction, Political and Economic, 1865–1877* (New York: J. & J. Harper for Harper & Row, 1968, from 1907 edition). Dunning wrote when southern states had recently disfranchised the vast majority of black men in that region and had institutionalized Jim Crow segregation.

8. Glenda Riley, *Taking Land/Breaking Land: Women Colonizing the American West and Kenya, 1840–1940* (Albuquerque: University of New Mexico Press, 2003).

9. Margaret D. Jacobs, "Gender and Colonialism in the American West," presentation for the International Federation for Research in Women's History conference on Women's History Revisited: Historiographical Reflections on Women and Gender in a Global Context, Twentieth International Congress of Historical Sciences, University of New South Wales, July 8, 2005.

10. Angie Debo, *The Road to Disappearance* (Norman: University of Oklahoma Press, 1941). Debo repeated the quote in *A History of the Indians of the United States* (Norman: University of Oklahoma Press, 1970), ix. Regarding her history of the Creek Indians, she had chosen the title thinking that it would attract more readers than *The History of the Creek Nation*. Ironically, in her preface she identifies the Creeks as especially tenacious in maintaining their traditions.

Contributors

MARIA EUGENIA COTERA holds a holds a joint appointment as Assistant Professor in the Program in American Culture/Latino Studies and the Women's Studies Program at the University of Michigan, Ann Arbor. She has published numerous essays on Jovita González and Sioux ethnographer Ella Deloria, including "'All My Relatives Are Noble': Recovering the Feminine in *Waterlily*," in *American Indian Quarterly* (Fall 2004), and "Jovita González and the Legacy of Borderlands Feminism," in *Latina Legacies*, ed. Vicki Ruíz (Oxford University Press, 2004). Forthcoming is her edition of Jovita González's master's thesis, *Social Life in Cameron, Starr, and Zapata Counties* (Texas A&M Press). Currently she is working on a book on Ella Cara Deloria, Jovita González, and Zora Neale Hurston and "the Poetics of Culture."

CATHERINE S. FOWLER is Foundation Professor of Anthropology at the University of Nevada, Reno. She is an ethnologist and ethnohistorian specializing in the histories and cultures of Great Basin Native Americans (Southern Paiutes, Northern Paiutes, Western Shoshones), with additional interests in ethnobiology, material culture, museums, and the preservation of the anthropological record.

SUZANNE JULIN earned her doctorate in U.S. and public history from Washington State University. She lives in Missoula, Montana, where she works as an independent public historian on cultural resource and oral history projects in a multi-state area. Her most recent contracts are an assessment of the historic significance of eleven Veterans Administration properties across the country and a series of oral interviews with city officials and residents in Deadwood, South Dakota. Julin was introduced to Annie Heloise Abel's work as an undergraduate history student at the University of South Dakota when her advisor handed her *Tabeau's Narrative* and said, "Read the footnotes!"

ROBERT VAN KEMPER is Professor of Anthropology and Chair of the Department of Anthropology at Southern Methodist University, Dallas,

Texas. A cultural anthropologist, he specializes in Mexico, especially long-term community transformation and migration in Tzintzuntzan, Michoacán. His additional scholarly interests include the history of anthropology, tourism, urbanization, bilingual education, applied anthropology, and faith-based community development in Mexico and the United States.

CATHERINE F. LAVENDER is Associate Professor of History and Director of the American Studies Program at Staten Island College of the City University of New York. She has most recently published *Scientists and Storytellers: Feminists and Anthropologists and the Construction of the American Southwest of the Southwest* (University of New Mexico Press, 2006). She has also coedited, with Lillian Schlissel, *The Western Women's Reader* (HarperCollins, 2000). Currently she is writing a work about the murder of Henrietta Schmerler, an anthropology student, in Arizona in 1931.

SHIRLEY A. LECKIE is Professor Emerita from the University of Central Florida. She is the author of *Angie Debo: Pioneering Historian* (2000) and *Elizabeth Bacon Custer and the Making of a Myth* (1993). With William H. Leckie, she collaborated on works that combined western military history with social and family history. Throughout her research and writing she has been most interested in women's responses to the American West, their role in helping to construct a narrative justifying conquest, and the role of other women in challenging that narrative and their intellectual contribution to the re-visioning of the West.

PATRICIA LOUGHLIN is Assistant Professor of History at the University of Central Oklahoma, where she teaches women's history, history of the American West, twentieth-century U.S. history, and public history. Her first book, *Hidden Treasures of the American West* (University of New Mexico Press, 2005), examines the lives and texts of three women writers—historian Angie Debo, public historian Muriel Wright, and Alice Marriott—who created careers for themselves on the cusp of the academic world and sought a more popular audience for their writings. Currently, Loughlin is completing a book-length manuscript on the history of the University of Central Oklahoma for Oklahoma's centennial in 2007. She is also working on a collaborative project with artist Marvin Martinez, the great-grandson of Maria Martinez.

NANCY J. PAREZO is Professor of American Indian Studies and Anthropology at the University of Arizona. She is the author of *Daughters of the Desert* and editor of *Hidden Scholars: Women Anthropologists and the Native American Southwest*. Long interested in the history of anthropology and anthropologists' relations with American Indians, she recently finished *Anthropology Goes to the Fair: The 1904 Louisiana Purchase Exposition* with coauthor Don D. Fowler, published by the University of Nebraska Press.

SHELBY TISDALE is the Director of the Museum of Indian Arts and Culture/Laboratory of Anthropology in Santa Fe, New Mexico. She is the former Executive Director of the Millicent Rogers Museum in Taos. Tisdale is currently writing a biography on Marjorie Ferguson Lambert. She directed the publication of the Oklahoma Book Award–winning *Woven Worlds: Basketry from the Clark Field Collection*, which includes three chapters written by her, for the Philbrook Museum of Art in Tulsa, Oklahoma. Her latest book, *Fine Indian Jewelry of the Southwest: The Millicent Rogers Museum Collection* (Museum of New Mexico Press), came out in April 2006.

FRANCI WASHBURN received her PhD from the University of New Mexico and is currently an Assistant Professor at the University of Arizona with a joint appointment in English and the American Indian Studies program. Her novel *Elsie's Business* was published by the University of Nebraska Press in the fall of 2006.

JOHN R. WUNDER is Professor of History at the University of Nebraska–Lincoln and Docent in North American Studies at the Renvall Institute of the University of Helsinki. He is the author of numerous books and articles on the history of the American West and comparative history. His forthcoming works include *Nebraska Moments*, coauthored with Susan A. Wunder and Donald R. Hickey, and *Nebraska and the Kansas-Nebraska Act*, coedited with Joann Ross, both with the University of Nebraska Press. He is past president of the Mari Sandoz Heritage Society.

In the Women in the West series

Engendered Encounters: Feminism and Pueblo Cultures, 1879–1934
By Margaret D. Jacobs

Riding Pretty: Rodeo Royalty in the American West
By Renée Laegreid

The Colonel's Lady on the Western Frontier: The Correspondence of Alice Kirk Grierson
Edited by Shirley A. Leckie

Their Own Frontier: Women Intellectuals Re-Visioning the American West
Edited and with an introduction by Shirley A. Leckie
and Nancy J. Parezo

A Stranger in Her Native Land: Alice Fletcher and the American Indians
By Joan Mark

So Much to Be Done: Women Settlers on the Mining and Ranching Frontier, second edition
Edited by Ruth B. Moynihan, Susan Armitage, and
Christiane Fischer Dichamp

Women and Nature: Saving the "Wild" West
By Glenda Riley

The Life of Elaine Goodale Eastman
By Theodore D. Sargent

Give Me Eighty Men: Women and the Myth of the Fetterman Fight
By Shannon D. Smith

Bright Epoch: Women and Coeducation Institutions in the American West
By Andrea G. Radke-Moss

Moving Out: A Nebraska Woman's Life
By Polly Spence
Edited by Karl Spence Richardson

Eight Women, Two Model Ts, and the American West
By Joanne Wilke